CONVERSATIONS WITH TOM PETTY

EXPANDED EDITION

PAUL ZOLLO

OMNIBUS PRESS
London / New York / Paris / Sydney / Copenhagen / Berlin / Madrid / Tokyo

Dedicated to my son Joshua Zollo and my father Burt Zollo,
with all my love and music always.

Cover designed by Paul Tippett
Picture research by the author

HB ISBN: 978-1-787-60162-8
PB ISBN: 978-1-9158-4148-3

A catalogue record for this book is available from the British Library.

Printed in Turkey

www.omnibuspress.com

Contents

Part Three: Additional Interviews, Articles And Reviews

It always feels good to finish an album, because I've done it long enough to know these things are gonna be around longer than me... That's what's so great about music and composing: Something that wasn't there a few minutes ago is here. And it could be here longer than you.

Tom Petty

Acknowledgments

I'm deeply grateful to all those who helped me during the long creation of this expanded edition, as well as the original book.

It starts and ends with Tom, of course. Thank you forever: for your trust in me, for sharing so much for this book; for your good cheer, warmth, wisdom, honesty, candor, humor, reverence for rock and roll and songwriting; and for being one of the coolest people ever. Also for all the songs. A world without you is not one I wanted to be in. Your songs sure help. Every day.

Thank you, Dana, for your big, generous, loving heart, which transformed Tom's life forever. True love like you had is beautiful to see up close, and it's woven into every page of this book, and every song, from "Angel Dream" on. Thank you also for your ongoing trust in me, and embrace of this book. He was in such a happy place then, making *Highway Companion* in your home. That you enabled him to listen to his own music—and realize (as he said) it wasn't that bad!—is profound, and forever nourished his gentle spirit. Without you, none of this would have been the same.

Thank you, Mary Klauzer, forever. Even before I had a chance to earn your respect and trust, you gave me so much. Unlike so many who serve as gatekeepers and revel in their opportunities to say no, you were always happy to call with a yes. As you did many times. In my book of "World's Greatest People Ever," there's a whole chapter on you. Thanks Tony Dimitriades for your fine management of Tom and the band all those years, and your support.

Thanks to David Barraclough and Imogen Gordon Clark of Omnibus/UK for bringing this book back to life. Thanks also to Andrea Rotondo of G. Schirmer/Omnibus for your support of the original book.

Special thanks to my good friends: Jeff Gold and Holly Goldsmith, Tomas Ulrich, Darryl Purpose, Earl Grey (aka Urlie Gee), Docken Polk, Stephen Kalinich, Amy Linton, Karen Wing, Henry Diltz, Paula McMath, Louise Goffin, Lisa Dubell, Michelle Williams, Marvin Etzioni, Joe Henry, Michael and Cindy Hughes, James Coberly Smith, Else Blangsted, Jilly Freeman, Lee Hirsch and Sandy Ross, D. Whitney Quinn, Michael Wisniewski, Sean Heaney, Neil Rosengarden, Terry Paul Roland, Mark Humphreys and Melissa Morgan Humphreys, Malcolm Orrall, Susan Cox Downs, Lois Tedrow, Karen Graff, Mark Dubrow, Camille Bertagnolli, Marisa Damele, and Janet Heaney.

To my friends Aaron Wolfson, Manda Mosher, Melinda Newman, and Bob Keppler, all fervent Tom fans for as long as I've known you. Thank you for keeping his fire burning.

To my family—to Leslie, Zippy, and to my son Joshua, who loves Tom as much as I do—from seeing his last concert with me, to last night when you played your LP of *Damn The Torpedoes*.

To my mom Lois Zollo and to Peggy and David Miller, Peter and Debbie Zollo, Liza Miller and Shorty, Rob Miller, Jason & Katie Miller, Ben Zollo, Jimmy Zollo, Sarah and Jared Rabin and the youngest and cutest Tom fan I know, Leo Rabin.

To Caine O'Rear and *American Songwriter* magazine, Rob Seals and The Songwriting School of Los Angeles, Ben Schafer and Da Capo Press, to Dave Konjoyan and Nate Hertweck of The Recording Academy, and to Mark Felsot and Tom Petty Radio on Sirius.

And big thanks to Keith Eveland and all the great citizens of the ever-expanding Tom Petty Nation—thanks for being devoted Insiders always, for your love of Tom forever, for your great support of our book, and for your patience in getting through the hardest part: the waiting. This book is for you.

A Conversation with Dana Petty

When we started working on this book in 2004, you and Tom had been married for a few years, and he seemed happier than ever. I could tell he'd never known a love like this. He seemed blissful. Was that how it was?

DP: It was a wonderful time. But, honestly, our entire relationship was like that. Tommy would talk about it often, how for twenty-two years we were so ridiculously happy and content together. We didn't have to be doing anything out of the ordinary, just being together was enough. We didn't have any quirks or idiosyncrasies that got on each other's nerves. He'd often express how sad it was that most couples didn't have what that we had. Just being so happily in love, even after so many years. It was a love we never took for granted.

We were just as happy in the last months of our relationship, as we were when we first met and began to fall in love, maybe more. We had a fairytale relationship for sure. What gets me through each day is knowing how blessed I was to have found the love of my life in Tommy, and knowing that he felt the same about me. We created decades of wonderful memories together, and they're especially meaningful now that he's gone.

Now, in retrospect, I am so grateful to Tom for sharing so much of his thoughts, his truth and his history. Do you remember how he felt about doing the book and what led to it?

I had been after Tommy for years to write his autobiography. It was something he hummed and hawed about, but I thought it was important to put everything down in his own words so there would be a truly accurate record of his amazing life experiences. It's an understatement to say that he had an incredible life. It was a singular life in many ways, and lived by a truly good soul who brought so much to the world. He was such a gifted storyteller, and he had endless tales to tell that were almost always funny and often downright wild. He got great joy from telling them, and so did his listeners. His spirit was absolutely infectious and his joy in sharing his stories was palpable.

So, about fifteen years ago, we realized that Tommy wasn't going find the time or have the inclination to write it himself and that he should think about bringing in an author; we felt it was vital for him to tell his story to someone who was also an artist; not only a great writer, but someone with knowledge of songwriting, of rock and roll and its history. Hopefully, that person would even be a musician. You fit the bill, Paul.

Nobody knows this, but Tommy had just started writing his autobiography shortly before he passed. Sadly, he only got a few pages in, but it was something he was really looking forward to completing. So, I'm all the more thankful that you wrote this book with him and that there is this beautiful chronicle of his life experiences as told by him. This is beyond valuable now, and I'm sure his fans would agree.

It's funny; he'd often complain about doing promo interviews, but he enjoyed discussing his craft and taking about the work. So once he got going, an interview could go on for hours. As you well know, Paul. How many hours, days, weeks, and months did you spend with him? He really enjoyed those talks with you. He would always come back and give me the run down. It made him blissfully happy to recall these events of his incredible life.

There was only one session from among all of your interviews with him that caused him anxiety. It was the day you two discussed Howie Epstein. After you left, Tommy told me he felt like he didn't express just how much he loved Howie, and how valuable he was to the band. And, he felt guilty about going so deeply into those dark days of Howie's drug addiction, even though he was doing so to put those years in context. Tommy suffered a lot of loss in his life, but Howie's death impacted him like no other.

Breaking that gut-wrenching news to him that Howie was gone was so difficult. We were both shattered; the whole Tom Petty & The Heartbreakers tribe was shattered. Though, sadly, none of us were surprised. No one outside of the band's extended family could ever understand how hard Tommy, his bandmates, and crew tried to save dear Howie. Unfortunately, the only person who could have saved an addict that far gone is the addict himself. Like all addicts, Howie had experienced some severe trauma that changed the trajectory of his life.

Drugs were initially his way to cope and to escape the pain, but then his addiction became all-consuming. It was heartbreaking; he was the kindest, coolest cat I've ever known. We loved him dearly.

So, after that interview with you about Howie, Tommy was very anxious about what he said and what he should have said. He was worried, so I encouraged him to call you. I said, "Pick up the phone and call Paul and tell him how you feel, it's that simple."

And he said, "Yeah, no harm there, *right*?

I remember him calling you, and you were great. Whatever you said, it eased his mind. Thanks for that. It meant the world to him.

It said so much to me about Tom; that he cared that much about giving the wrong impression about Howie. The only other time he called me after a session was when we did a whole talk on being a celebrity and he told me a story of getting mobbed when going out for food with you. He called to ask if we could take that out of the book, because, as he said, "Nobody wants to read me complaining about being a rock star." But how hard was it for him to be an icon and deal with the public?

Like many public people, Tommy was a shy guy and didn't like the spotlight when he wasn't on stage. He understood that it came with the territory, but he really was just an all-around great guy, trying to live a reasonably normal life like anyone else.

But, yeah, things got scary a couple of times. I remember when we first got together, we used to go out a lot back then, and people would stare and whisper; I'd hear "Tom Petty, *Tom Petty*..." Often, while we were eating, or in the middle of a conversation, someone would come up and interrupt us. Even though they were mostly well-meaning, that stuff messed with my mind and made me acutely self-conscious, as it was all new to me. It barely bothered him but he would notice my discomfort. I became immune to it after a while, too, as I learned to realize that people loved Tommy and were approaching him out of love and admiration too. Tommy knew, and he taught me, that you can't let that stuff interfere with living as normal a life as possible.

And do you have any message for Tom's fans – and to future fans and readers of this book – about Tom and his music?

Tommy always said that he had the best fans in the world. He adored them and never took them for granted. He knew that each one of you played such an important role in making his dreams come true, and he was so grateful to all of you. You meant the world to him. He would often call touring "a near perfect existence," and he was referring to the community he and The Heartbreakers and the fans created *together*. Tommy knew he had the best gig in the world; making music and making people happy, and he loved doing it. He always said he would have done it with five people in a room, let alone 50,000. Music was in his soul, and his fans were responsible for making him feel as vital and charged-up at sixty-six as he was at twenty-six.

For new and future generations of fans just discovering Tom Petty & The Heartbreakers, I can honestly say that your life is about to become deeply enriched. Listen to the melodies, Mike's amazingly inventive and just-perfect guitar solos, Tommy's unique voice and rhythm guitar, Benmont's magical fingers on keys, and then the glue: Ron or Howie's bass and Stan or Steve's badass drums, Scott Thurston's added magic and backing vocals, along with Howie's sublime high harmony—all one-of-a-kind and simply, magically beautiful. Then listen carefully to Tommy's lyrics; everyone can find something in these songs that they can relate to in some way. The stories and characters might be from a singular, creative mind, but the emotions they evoke are truly universal. And the deeper you dig, the more gems you will find. It's also always joyful to listen to the artists that were huge influences on Tommy and who he loved throughout his life: the Rolling Stones, the Byrds, Bob Dylan, The Beatles, Chuck Berry, Buffalo Springfield, the Kinks, Little Richard, Elvis, to name just a few.

As longtime fans learned with the *An American Treasure* boxed set, Tommy left behind an absolute treasure trove of unreleased music. Everyone who played an important role in his creative process, especially Mike, Benmont and Ryan Ulyate, are curating these gems with love and an extremely high standard. The adventure will continue for a long time to come, and we can't wait to share it with you.

Love to you all,
Dana Petty
June 2019

Foreword To First Edition

When the idea of Paul Zollo conducting a series of interviews that would focus on my music came up, I thought it not a bad idea. For years fans have complained that there was no one source that covered our musical output in great depth and detail. I knew Paul from several interviews over the last decade. I found him good company and almost ridiculously prepared for each interview. He is a man whose writing has shown a great passion for songwriters and their methods. And these interviews would not be the exception. We met many times in 2004 to 2005 for talks that came to necessitate my re-listening to thirty-odd years of music as Paul would show up knowledgeable to the point of having learned to play the songs himself.

As the interviews progressed, it became clear that to understand the music one would also have to have knowledge of my life and how it has unfolded.

This, to be sure, is not an autobiography. That is for another book and another time. But to be certain, Paul has extracted what is certainly our most in-depth biography ever.

Mr. Zollo has knocked the dust off many a memory here. I hope you enjoy reading them half as much as I have living them. All the best.

Tom Petty, 2005

Introduction To First Edition

This book is divided into two essential parts: the life and the music of Tom Petty [the third section containing additional interviews, articles and reviews is new to the expanded edition]. I admit it's an arbitrary—and certainly fine and delicate—division, as Tom Petty's life is all about his music and his music is all about his life. So these parts overlap and even repeat at times, but they succeed in capturing what has been an extraordinary life in music, and an exceptional viewpoint on the music that reflects this life.

Tom was in a happy place and spirit as we conducted the many interviews that comprise this book. We conducted these discussions over many months in 2004 and 2005 at Tom's two Malibu homes. Sometimes we would sit in his home recording studio, surrounded by guitars, keyboards, mikes, and other abundant recording gear. We invariably used a conga drum as a table, and drank together—cold Coca-Cola out of the old-fashioned little bottles—which he had conveniently stashed nearby in the studio fridge. He wore a variety of hats, and occasionally purple-tinted sunglasses. His big, gentle dog, Chase, would sometimes join us and would obey Tom's tender commands to lie down on the floor as we spoke. On other occasions, Tom's beloved wife Dana would come in to say, "Hi," or to give Tom some homey news. One time she brought us fruit smoothies to drink, sensing we needed a break. Another time, after a lengthy and laborious session, she served us both some delicious bowls of chili in their big kitchen. Dana's presence always seemed to make Tom, who was already a genuinely happy guy, even happier.

It was an honor to conduct these interviews and compile this collection of remembrances. I had interviewed Tom on many other occasions, and always found him one of the warmest, most likeable, and open songwriters I've been fortunate enough to meet. He is an extraordinary songwriter and musician, in that his songs have transcended the decades, have appealed to many generations, and have persisted in sounding as powerful as when we first heard them. Starting in the early Seventies in his band Mudcrutch, and eventually forming one of the greatest American rock bands ever to play rock and roll, Tom Petty has succeeded in writing songs which speak to our hearts and our souls, and which have resounded timelessly over the many years. And, unlike so many of his peers who started at the same time he did and never surpassed their inaugural work, Tom has accomplished what few have accomplished in rock and roll: a steady stream of powerful music over thirty years. It's one of the reasons he has such an engaged and extensive fan base. As classic and consummate as his first albums were (such as the perpetually masterful *Damn The Torpedoes*), he has continued to grow as a musician, and has created successive masterpieces, both solo and with his band The Heartbreakers, such as the haunting *Southern Accents*, the magical *Full Moon Fever*, and the glorious *Wildflowers*. He never for a moment rested on his laurels, but continued to challenge himself and his band to create music that was as good and even better than what had come before.

And he was so prolific that each album had leftovers; songs that didn't fit for one reason or another and were relegated to the vaults. Fortunately for his fans, many of these rare leftovers were given new life by producer George Drakoulias, who compiled an exquisite six-disc boxed set called *Playback*, which goes a long way in proving that Petty's hits, as great as they are, are not his only great work. So many of the songs on *Playback*, many of which had never previously been released, could easily have been hits, so powerful are they, and so deserving of the attention that the hits received. "Our greatest hits are not necessarily our best songs," Tom said more than once, and it's true. There are countless songs that, if they had been released as singles with accompanying videos, could easily have been hit singles, as well. But Tom was always careful not to overextend himself or The Heartbreakers, and held a lot of classic songs back.

"I think I was at the top of my game," he said of the album *Wildflowers*, "in terms of craft and inspiration colliding at the same time." It's a truism that can be applied to much of his work—not only does the man know how to craft a song, he does it with the bountiful love he has for songs themselves, for that delicate but powerful amalgam of words and music, a love that perseveres for the great rock and roll songs of the

Fifties and beyond which have inspired him throughout his life, and were the initial impetus for his musical journey.

What follows is the story of his life and his music, and the music of his life. The two are really inseparable, though they've been divided here. Yet the spirit of rock and roll persists in holding the two parts together, as it has galvanized his work over the years and provided the world with an amazingly diverse and glorious compendium of astonishing, timeless songs.

"I don't want to be one of those people who are miserable even when they're successful," he said. "That's not the way I want my life to go." He's one of the rare ones who has succeeded in finding genuine happiness in the heart of huge commercial success, acknowledging that it's a challenge to match his previous works, which include countless classics, but he also admitted it's a fun and nurturing process, and one he has no inclination to cease. "Other people take vacations and go to Hawaii and play golf, or scuba dive. This is what I do. I write songs and I make records." He's prospered in his ability to be prolific over so many years, and has done so by staying connected to the thing he loves the most—the music.

He was born in Gainesville, Florida, on October 20, 1950. As a kid he met Elvis, saw The Beatles on TV, and recognized that rock and roll was the surest and most potent means of escaping his Florida existence and providing him with a life beyond his dreams. The rest is truly history—the history of his life and his art. And it's all here, in his own words.

Paul Zollo, 2005

Introduction To Expanded Edition

Ever since this book was published in 2005, it's been my dream to see a new edition of it in the world. It's a dream I saw clearly for years, as if it was already real, a vision of a new volume expanded with new photos, new cover and new chapters covering the twelve missing years of his work since we finished.

Tom knew a lot about dreams. It was seeing Elvis up close in nearby Ocala that set him on his singular path, a providential event so clearly articulated by the universe it seems like something a hack biographer would invent, yet it's true. The title of the movie which brought Elvis to Florida? *Follow That Dream.*

"Which," as Tom said, "I've always thought was a cosmic title."

He remembered it with stunning cinematic clarity. "I was eleven years old," he said, "sitting in a pile of pine straw, underneath a big pine tree in my yard. My aunt pulls in the drive and says, 'Tommy, would you like to go and see Elvis Presley?' Well, I thought, 'Yeah, sure.' I didn't know a lot about Elvis Presley... He was known to me as a fella who wiggled... I knew he was a rock and roll star. And I'd never thought much about rock and roll until that moment."

From then on, he never stopped thinking about it. For more than forty years, Tom faithfully followed that dream, and never let go. He was a realized man in that way. Unlike the multitudes who accumulate reasonable reasons to abandon their dreams, such as adulthood, marriage, and reality, Tom clung to his with ferocious fidelity, ultimately willing it into existence, as the little boy reveling in pine straw became one of America's most beloved and respected songwriters, and best pals with the royals of rock and roll, such as Bob Dylan and George Harrison.

Tom came to know that, though dreams can come true, they often do so in ways unforeseen. His dream of rock and roll stardom came true early on, and then surpassed all that he once imagined, as he never imagined doing it for long. He figured by the time he turned thirty, he'd be well beyond reasonable rocking age, and would ease into a profession more suitable for a man of advancing years, like being a producer.

As he said, laughing, "We *never* thought about growing *old* doing it!"

So, at the risk of starting this whole show in a minor key, I'll admit that, although this dream of a new edition is coming true, it doesn't match my original vision for one fundamental reason: Tom wasn't around to do it with me. Never had I even pondered the possibility that he could be gone from this world before this second, expanded edition would be in it. For years I harbored the happy hope of returning to those sunny days working on the book with him; meeting up again at his beautiful seaside home for a series of new conversations. I was ready to hang out again in his world of song and pick up where we left off, diving deeply into the joy of his music again.

Our original mission with this book was to create a complete record of his body of work, with his memories of writing and recording every song up till then. Since its publication, I've envisioned working with Tom to add all missing chapters since *Highway Companion*, where we left off.

Since that vision was not to be, I've done by best to fill in those gaps in other ways. Prior to this book, I had interviewed him on several occasions, and have included some of those conversations in this volume. The 2004 interview here is one we did for his relatively new website, and as a way of getting the ball rolling for this book, which I had recently proposed.

Those gaps are also filled in with reviews of his albums and concerts in those missing years, including one of his last show ever, at the Hollywood Bowl, on September 25, 2017. I wrote the review in the wake of that exultant show, before learning only a week later that he was gone.

I've also included some photos I've taken of Tom over the years during different appearances around LA. These include his 2008 appearance with Mudcrutch at the Troubadour in West Hollywood, and his beamish presence at Jeff Lynne's 2015 Hollywood Walk of Fame induction ceremony. There are also some of the photos from that final show, the third of a three-night stand at the Hollywood Bowl to wrap up his fortieth anniversary tour with The Heartbreakers.

I attended with my son, Joshua, who agreed with me the final night would be the most momentous one, given it was the end of this big tour. Because most of the press attended the first night, except for one other guy, I was alone in the big orchestra pit beneath the stage. Tom saw me right away and, in the midst of a Mike Campbell guitar solo, strode over in my direction, strumming his guitar. Suddenly he was directly in front of me, giving me the perfect smiling photo. The suddenness of that startled me, and I failed to focus. But, being Tom, and probably sensing this, he came back several times and gave me more—each poignantly exuberant—by which time I was calm enough to focus properly. When Dana saw those, she said she loved them, and confirmed my feeling that he gave me those as gifts, even sensing that I messed up my first shot.

Given all the joy he shared that night, which I did my best to capture, the darkest darkness of that sunny day one week later, the second day of October 2017, was impossibly awful to accept. But the brightest light shining through the ensuing shadowland was the great outpouring of love for him from people all over the world, and especially from his big burgeoning network of fans, who have been devoted for decades. They've steadily expanded into the great and loving Tom Petty Nation, many thousands of dedicated, devotional Tom lovers around America and beyond united by their singular love for this man and his music. I've met them all over this country, and it's been greatly heartening to bond over our boundless love for him. Always there is a deeply personal connection, a momentous part of their lives forever linked to one of his timeless songs. Or many of them! In their ongoing embrace of all he did, they mirror the purity which radiates through all his music.

Accepting Tom was truly gone was not easy for me, and I know how hard it was for all his fans. It was especially tough because to all of us he felt like a friend. And yet also an icon. Immediately we all were thrust into this surreal sorrow of experiencing the death of a beloved artist only to see and hear them alive again. Though we know his life is officially over, his music is as alive as ever, and his presence as palpable. His luminous spirit, beaming always with its fervent fusion of genuine humanity, tenderness, passion, whimsy, joy, sorrow, romance, and rock and roll, is not even slightly diminished by the man's official departure from our physical realm. It's alive in the tracks of his records, in the ingenious brilliance of his songwriting, in the playful whimsy of his music videos, in the rich musicianship, and in the profusion of his celebratory concerts, which exist on film forever.

Working on this new edition has not been free from tears, especially when watching videos of TV appearances he did on late night shows, such as those hosted by David Letterman and Jay Leno. Letterman loved Tom and had him on many times. Dave's still with us at this writing, though with a long white biblical beard, more an elder statesman of comedy, and not the quirky comic powerhouse he was back then. But seeing several performances by Tom and the band on Dave's show over the years brought back Tom's poignant words in this book about the surreal sorrow he felt seeing a *Saturday Night Live* rerun after the death of Howie Epstein. And there was Howie, in the pocket, as alive as ever, singing and playing with the band. It's cognitive dissonance at its most extreme, and it's the same for us. How bittersweet it is to watch Tom perform on *Letterman*, and there's Howie right behind him, forever locked into that solid Heartbreakers groove, playing bass and singing soulful harmony. And it sounds great.

Or the 1997 *Tonight Show With Jay Leno* show in which Tom & The Heartbreakers perform "Walls," after which Tom walks over to the couch to talk to Jay, where only one other guest is waiting. Robin Williams. More tears, as Robin is also gone now, ending that life of supercharged expansive comic genius in extreme sorrow. Back in the day—1982 or so—I'd go to The Comedy Store in Hollywood on late Monday nights, where Robin often showed up to do improv after working all day on *Mork And Mindy*. He was a force of nature, amazing to witness up close. Everyone—even the other performers—were simply in awe of his energy and genius.

On the show, Tom greets both, and easily slips into funny talk-show banter. Leno greets Tom with gratitude that he has brought his dog to the show.

"He's a real German Shepherd," quips Tom. "He speaks German." The crowd loves it. As they cut away to commercial, you see Tom and Robin embrace each other with big smiles, these two cherished insiders then on top of the world.

Seeing this brought home how deeply ingrained into the culture, the very fabric of America, Tom was, and remains. He was more than a great rock star and creator of a voluminous songbook of timeless splendor. He was also a treasured American entertainer—more in the realm of a Bob Hope than Buddy Holly by then. Because of his emergence during the MTV era, Tom and the band were much more than images on an album cover or rock magazine. They were on TV throughout the land. And not infrequently, as he said: "Talk about *famous*! That's when *everybody* knew who you were… *Grandmas* knew who you were! Because you're on TV every hour *all day long*! So we'd be in an airport, and *adults* knew who we were!"

He and I did this book together back in 2004 and 2005, meeting almost every Saturday at his home in Malibu (never before noon, as Tom kept rock star hours his entire life), during which I had the great privilege and true pleasure of delving into all his songs and records with him, and the life from which it all emerged.

Yet my memories of those times spent with Tom and Dana, seeing up close the tender bliss of their love, remain joyously vivid, as if it happened yesterday. I can still feel that electric rush of excitement I'd always feel as soon as he and I launched into our conversation. We both were into it. We didn't bother with small talk hardly at all. We wanted to talk about the music!

Back when we worked on the book through 2004 and into 2005, I'd always give myself ample time to drive from my North Hollywood home to Malibu, so as not to be late. Inevitably I'd be extremely early, which I didn't mind. I'd park outside his walls and listen to his music, call friends, and wait. And that waiting—there in the Pacific sun, outside of Tom's house—wasn't hard at all.

At noon I'd go in, and Tom, often with sleepy but smiling eyes, having recently awakened, would walk in, often with his coffee cup. He was always attired in cozy, often whimsical clothes—a funny hat, an old plaid suit, fur-lined boots, orange granny glasses, and more—which always lent a fun spirit to the proceedings. We'd start talking, and, as with your best friends, the conversation took off. We would have conversations that could go on forever, as he could tell my interest in his songs was genuine. I asked all these questions for the book, of course, but also because I genuinely wanted to know. Always he was warm, funny, focused, and extremely thoughtful, bringing insight and wisdom surprising in its depth.

Here you get only the words—and some laughter. What's not here is his spirited delivery, profuse laughter, and palpable joy when reliving great moments. Also not represented is my wide-eyed astonishment at so many of his stories—such as the one about his grandpa Pulpwood Petty's reason for moving to Florida, or ones about how wild his dad would be, such as him poking his fingers into an alligator's eyes.

Every now and then a story like that would emerge—completely unsummoned, unspoken till then—and it was thrilling to be the first to hear it, knowing it would be in our book forever.

Please know that, when Tom was speaking, most of the time he was smiling.

Paul Zollo, 2019

A Pure Heart

"The world doesn't need any more songs," Bob Dylan said when I interviewed him in 1992. Upon publication, that statement garnered a lot of attention and was widely quoted in the press. Yet that is not the full statement. They left out the most important part: "*Unless*," Dylan said, "someone's gonna come along with a *pure heart*, and has something to say. That's a different story."

A *pure heart.* And *something to say*. That is a different story.

In the history of popular music, has there ever been anyone with a heart purer than Tom Petty? It was a purity which radiated like sunshine through more than four decades of his career and shone in everything he did: all the songs, records, concerts, TV appearances. Never was he false. It was an understanding that grew more evident as his success blossomed and grew, and the magnitude of what he created became real.

"Yeah, I think that's what I've always been looking for," he agreed, "though I probably didn't realize it for a long time. But I'm looking for *purity*. I'm a *purist*."

He understood implicitly that this entire enterprise was built on a foundation of trust, without which it would crumble. That authenticity shone in the records of the great bluesmen he came to know and love, and early rockers like Buddy Holly, who baptized Tom in the river of rock and roll. It's that river that he rode through the decades, following in the expansively poetic wake and brilliance of Dylan, The Beatles, and others. Tom recognized that, by being both the writer and performer of the songs, he embraced the infinite promise of what is an existential art: these songs—the music, the words, the rhythms, the soul fire, the sorrow and joy, the hope instilled, the stories told—all flowed directly from this man's big heart.

His mission from the start was to keep it real. He was drinking from the well of the original rock and roll, and maintaining that authenticity was one of many hard promises he made to himself and his fans, and which he never broke. "When I hear Muddy Waters sing," he said, "or Slim Harpo, it's *very* pure. It's incredibly honest. It doesn't need a lot of instruments to make it so pure. There's a thing about music: If you believe the singer, then the song is going to work. It's all about believability. If you can believe the singer, it will work. So I think our quest was for purity."

It's that purity which drew him to the music, the knowledge that great songwriting, singing, artistry, and musicianship cannot be faked. It is real. Unlike the kind of magic that magicians perform, which are illusions designed to fool an audience, in music there is real magic, and that's where Tom lived.

"Music," he said, "is probably the only real magic I have encountered in my life. There's not some trick involved with it. It's pure and it's real. It moves, it heals, it communicates."

His faith in the redemptive power of real-time rock and roll never faded, and to the end he remained a true believer. Yet keeping that faith was never easy in an industry quick to exploit what they saw as a commodity, when to him it was more. Dylan reminded us that to Woody Guthrie the radio airwaves were sacred, and therefore not to be wasted on anything false. To Tom it was the same, as evidenced in his songs, thoughts, and words through the years.

"I *love* this music, this rock and roll," Tom said. "It changed my life. It *sustained* my life. It's absolutely the embodiment of the American dream. It made things possible for me that would have never been possible. And even if it hadn't, I loved it in such a way that I really respect it. And I care about it. I care *passionately* about it."

But at junctures when he saw that sacred river being intentionally polluted and worse, he responded with songs of deep sorrow and outrage, such as the title song of *The Last DJ* album, which laments the loss of "freedom of choice" and "human voice".

He wasn't phony. As his fans know, that pure spirit, which shone and laughed and rocked live with The Heartbreakers through four decades, was not faked. That passion which poured out of Tom and the band live emanated from his pure heart. It wasn't just show biz. It was real-time rock and roll, plugged directly into the source, and he felt it as powerfully as we did.

"Say I do a show at nine," he said. "It'll be *dawn* before I come down from it. It will be several hours after it before I really even make sense. I'll *pace*. I'll just be pacing around, and not really myself for a few hours. And then it will take me a *long* time to go to sleep, and then the process starts over again in the morning. You spend a day gearing to do it, and then a night getting over it."

He had an infectious spirit. I'll always remember being somewhat stunned, when working with him, just how strongly I could feel the intensity of his emotions. Songwriters generally are people who feel things deeply, as that is the well from which they draw their songs. Whether great joy, deep sorrow, vehement rage, or beyond—Tom felt it with the fullness of his soul. His big heart was legend. That, combined with his decided lack of phoniness, made him friends to everyone—from little kids to Beatles and beyond.

Whether relating the joyful chapters of his life—such as those featuring Dana, or working with the Wilburys, or his deep friendship with George Harrison—his exultation shone like golden sunlight. It radiated from him. In the same way, his sorrow was painfully palpable. His delivery turned somber; his voice pitched lower, his cadence slower and halting. And, though there were several seasons of sorrow woven through his years, none was harder for him to discuss than the death of his bassist Howie Epstein. Never was there more desolate darkness in our midst than the day he related Howie's story.

His big sensitive soul also meant he was never impervious to the emotional vagaries of human existence, as he says in these pages. At his level, he said, "people assume that you understand how great you're supposed to be. But the truth is, you're only a human. And you're still going to go through everything that humans go through."

In retrospect, it makes sense that a man who could entrance and inspire millions of people for decades would possess such an expansively stirring spirit. He was real, down-to-earth, humble, funny, and human. Yet there was also much miraculous about the guy, especially given that in real life he was such a tender soul.

In fact, Tom was often surprised too—and delighted—by songs that came through him. Always it was the result of hard, "lonely" work, as he called it. But sometimes a great one would simply come through, and those delighted and baffled him. It echoed his mother's response when she heard the first songs he started writing: pure astonishment.

"[My mother] was amazed," he said, "that I could do it. She'd say, 'I can't understand how you can do it if you didn't have any lessons, and you don't know how to write music. How do you do it?' And I said, 'I don't know, I just learned it from other kids.'"

That purity also made it tough for him to easily play the part of a rock star, as for him it was about music, and not stardom. Universal fame thing was tricky for him to navigate. It's one of the reasons he so respected friends like George Harrison and Bob Dylan, who had learned how to exist as global icons while remaining somehow earthbound. More than anything, he respected their ability to remain genuine and grounded in a perpetual hurricane. "To be a rock and roll star is an awkward position to put myself in," he said, "with my particular personality and temperament. I don't do it that well. As far as being in a room with a *lot* of people in it, I get kind of shy and scared."

Tom didn't scare easy, as he wrote, and would stand his ground even when few of his peers—or none—would join him. He never shied away from fighting the good fight. But always he came with genuine gratitude and humility, which, when combined with his natural sense of whimsy, kept him grounded, and allowed him to swiftly pierce any sense of show-biz self-indulgence.

When I suggested, for example, that it was the human element at the heart of The Heartbreakers which was key to their sound, he laughed and said, "Yeah. We're human to a *fault*! In fact, we're just a bunch of *lugheads making music*!"

It was the raw and pure promise of rock and roll which captured his soul early on, sparking the dream he kept running down his whole life. It wasn't about fortune, fame or folly. It was about capturing lightning in a bottle, connecting to that same electric spirit that poured right from the radio into his soul through timeless songs like "Wooly Bully," or "Little Runaway".

Though Tom Petty & The Heartbreakers were considered New Wave by some (primarily because of the DX7 synth Benmont used on "You Got Lucky"), and even punk by others, in fact they were rock and rollers from the start. Tom always made the distinction—it was not rock, it was rock and roll, with the roll being prominent.

And though popular music always was evolving during his lifetime, from rock and roll through rock, folk-rock, soft rock, fusion, punk, disco, New Wave, metal, techno, rap, hip-hop, house music, and more, he remained a rock and roll purist to the end.

In his music and in life, the guy wasn't phony. It was a lesson learned early on with the help of Leon Russell, after being signed to Leon's Shelter Records. He wasn't yet a rock star then, but on that very precipice, the reality of which was powerfully confirmed one night when not one, but two Beatles—George and Ringo—and one legendary drummer—Jim Keltner—showed up at Leon's house. Recognizing he was already in that very realm of rock royalty he'd dreamed of back in Gainesville, he found himself slipping on his dark shades at night to fit in.

Leon caught him and let him know right away it wasn't right. "Wearing sunglasses at night is an honor you *earn*," he said. "Lou Adler had Johnny Rivers and The Mamas & The Papas *before* he put them glasses on. Jack Nicholson made *really shitty Boris Karloff movies* before he put them glasses on!"

From that moment on, Tom dedicated himself to taking no false steps, and ascending to that summit in the truest way, with the real goods: great records, band, and songs. Nothing fake. He never expected anything to come to him—the artistry, the professionalism, the success—without serious effort. Like wearing dark glasses at night, all had to be earned and learned. A seriously self-educated student of songwriting, he was tireless in his pursuit of musical wisdom, spending endless hours in what Donald Fagen called "the college of musical knowledge," examining the architecture of great songs by reverse engineering these tuneful engines of chords and poetry. Denny Cordell, who signed Tom and the group to their record deal, sensed Tom's yearning to expand his musical knowledge and started schooling him with long listening sessions. Tom drank it all in with joy and gratitude, a process he never stopped.

(Decades later, when asked by Dana if there was any one thing he wanted most for his birthday, he said yes: to be able to go to the record store and stay as long as he wanted. "Usually, after only an hour or so," he said, "everyone wants to go!" Not Tom, as nothing else to him was more exciting. He stayed for hours, after which the store boxed up and shipped him the library of records he purchased.)

He was forever driven, dedicated, and diligent in his determination, not only to succeed, but to be great. He knew it all started with songs, and that becoming a great songwriter took more than talent. It took true artistry, that mastery of all aspects of songwriting which can only be gained from doing the work itself. Usually years of work. Because it isn't easy to learn to write songs well. Sure, some people simply have a knack for it, as did Tom. But to really do it well—at the level he soon reached and then surpassed—there's a lot to learn. He took it all in until it was in his blood, as he did over the years with the myriad challenges of rock and roll recording, the dance of sonics, silence, and space which lend dimension to a record.

Never did he feel he knew everything there was to know. His hunger for new wisdom about ways to make it work without wrecking the essential joy of the thing persisted till the end. "It's a constant education," he said. "The thing now is to keep refining, keep growing, keep finding things in us that we didn't know about ourselves. I think as long as we enjoy doing it, we'll keep doing it."

That joy came with the burden of maintaining, at any cost, the purity. Always his aim was high, and he had little tolerance for any perceived sense of falling short, perhaps most famously when he smashed his hand against the wall "to powder" because of an inability to get "Rebels" to sound right in the studio. That joyful, easy-going Tom we know and love was a state to which he aspired but often couldn't reach. As his life went on, he learned more and more about how to surmount the challenges, especially that of transforming the songs into records, a process which grew much more fun for him and less tortured. Also, the presence of his angel dream, Dana, profoundly transformed his spirit, and allowed him to dump a lot of his baggage and start to appreciate all he'd done. But it was a gradual metamorphosis, as he recalled with much laughter after spending time with his daughters:

"My kids," he said, "were laughing about my image. They said, 'The world pictures you as this laid-back, laconic kind of person, and actually you're the *most intense, neurotic person we've ever met*!'"

Pausing for laughter, he added, "And that's kind of true. You're not always what people picture you as. I'm *not* a laid-back person."

And, though he'd seek the wisdom of others, he was wise enough to reject it if it didn't address his process. When Roy Orbison told him that if an idea is good, he won't forget it, Tom knew for him it wasn't true. Tunes that came through him were always shaped by his emotions at that moment—whether deep sadness or pure joy. Too many times he'd lost a melody forever by assuming he'd remember it and been wrong, a problem rectified by making a little recording—just a cassette, at first—as a safeguard.

That dynamic is forever preserved in the purity of his spirit in song. When he was happy and celebrating the splendor of life—as in "Wildflowers"—or the journey of wisdom itself in "Learning to Fly"—that joy lives in the song. At the same time, when he was feeling broken, that also was instilled into visceral songs of deep, heartfelt sorrow, such as "Insider," "Room At The Top," or "Echo." Even when depressed, he never stopped working for long, and transformed that sorrow into some of his most beautiful melodies ever, and always with words from his heart. He never abandoned that purity, and when he saw it being diluted, he spoke out, both in words and song. Music mattered deeply to him, and he had no forgiveness for those who exploited it. Throughout the years, as he related often, it was that joy of writing a new song and bringing it to The Heartbreakers that made him want to do it again.

Sure, he was diligent. Extremely. And his standards were high. Though some masterpieces, like "Refugee" and "Wildflowers," came through in moments, others took months to perfect. He'd work as long as necessary. He took his job seriously, and realized, early on, that he needed to write an album's worth of songs each year. Though he knew he could be out on the town every night, living the rock star life to the hilt, he understood he needed to stay home and write.

"So Stan [Lynch] would be out every night," Tom complained, "and I'd be home working."

While writing, Tom was a tough self-critic, quick to eject nascent songs if they seemed weak. This left him with what he considered his best work—the "A songs"—and the ones almost as good but not quite—the "B songs." And he'd toil over those B songs to fix what was keeping them down, and do his best to turn them into As.

But, as he explained, he did it because he loved it. Nothing brought him more joy or satisfaction. "I write them for *me*," he said about his songs. "And I figure if I like them, someone else will."

Because, much more than any chart success, or any amount of monetary reward, his true motivation, and the secret of his remarkable creative consistency, was his love of writing a great new song, and then inhabiting it. Always he danced on the edge of mystery, not even knowing where songs came from, and learning not to question it too much so as not to wreck the reception. When recording "Even The Losers," he had the whole song written except the chorus. Emboldened by the deep groove of The Heartbreakers and trusting the universe, he started recording it with them. When he came to the chorus it all emerged, as if it was already written. And there was the message of the song, and its title, arriving on its own accord: that even losers sometimes get lucky.

As he says in this book about the writing of many songs, including "Refugee," "Down South," and "Southern Accents," he was both surprised and enervated by their power when they emerged. "It's the kind of thing," he said, "that really makes me want to keep doing this."

That self-generating joy, even during the dark times, drove him through the decades. He was a guy in love with rock and roll, and it's a love he injected into every song. It was his heart, his passion, his soul, his essence.

Though he was a dreamer, he was a realistic one. He was an artist, but one existing within an immense profit-based industry. Though some record execs shared his reverence for rock and roll, as time went on their numbers diminished as they were gradually replaced by the marketing guys. This business of music, as he knew from the start, was never about ethics or art, it was about business. The business of making money.

> And I said to myself, this is the business we've chosen; I didn't ask who gave the order, because it had nothing to do with business!
>
> Hyman Roth, from *The Godfather Part II*

Although that quote is from *The Godfather Part II*, spoken by mob boss Hyman Roth (played by Lee Strasberg), it applies to the music business as well. Tom knew this was the business he'd chosen, and wasn't naïve about its methods. Yet neither was he impervious to anguish any time they obstructed the purity of his mission. Sure, it was about having hits and selling out shows and being successful. But never at the expense of the fans. From the first moment The Heartbreakers landed in London to a mob of frenzied fans, he knew the dream was no longer becoming true; it had already done that. He was a veritable rock star now. But he knew it was only because of them—the ones who loved his music, danced and romanced to his songs, bought his singles and albums, and came to his concerts—that he was there.

So anytime he saw the business flourishing at the expense of the fans, he stood his ground and fought. When he discovered his label was going to hike up the price of his LPs, he protested publicly, wrongly presuming many of his peers would join him.

It's the same reason he kept his concert ticket prices as low as possible, substantially lower than bands such as The Eagles or the Rolling Stones. Which meant that even when his tours sold more tickets than others, they were never among the top-grossing ones, as heralded by the press. It frustrated him that people didn't know this, but not enough to charge his fans more. They came first.

The most overtly egregious example of his this is when he brought in his first solo album, *Full Moon Fever*, to the record company, and something happened he'd never before experienced. They rejected it. They didn't hear a single, they said, in this album which had not only "Free Fallin'," but four other hits.

Looking back now with astonished wonder, it's hard to fathom how no one could hear the obvious greatness of this beautiful song cycle Tom created with Jeff Lynne. But it's because of this very shift in the industry towards marketing more than music that such extreme errors in judgment not only occurred. They were unanimous.

This sorry shift in thinking was crystallized for Tom soon after this rejection, when he and Jeff Lynne were at a party with the legendary producer Lenny Waronker. After telling him what happened, he said he wanted to hear the music. With no tape to play, Tom and Jeff got out their acoustic guitars and performed "Free Fallin'" for him. He loved it. "Sounds like a hit," he said.

That gave Tom some hope. "He never even heard the record," Tom said. "Just the two of us strumming guitars and singing it. And *he* could tell what it was."

That season of discontent with the industry came to an end, but it was never gone. After the release of *The Last DJ*, which resounds as a biting indictment of both radio and record companies for cheapening their most valuable resource, critics called him bitter.

"I'm not bitter," he said. "I'm just *sad*." To him, there was no excuse for what he saw as a corporate vulgarization of what to him was sacred.

"It's cheaper for the record companies to manufacture artists who aren't going to make any waves than to deal with somebody with a point of view and some integrity," he said. "But integrity in music and art should be *respected*."

There's that purity again. Even in the Eighties when America's new president was a former movie star named Reagan and the culture was in flux, he stayed true. In those days, who else even included the words "integrity," "music," and "art" in the same sentence? Integrity always mattered to him, at a time when the concept was becoming extinct, and the pathway to pop stardom became more akin to winning a game show than developing artistry.

"Marketing has become more important than product," he said. Pop stars no longer were self-created, but pre-packaged for full marketing potential, a complete betrayal of that purity at the heart of his life. He endured it, but with open disdain. "They're presented as pop stars," he said. "That's *fine*. But I wish they weren't presented as *musicians*. They're not. And I think the public is short-changed by that."

Now that's what I call music.

From "Joe."

"I think I was at the top of my game," he said the first time I interviewed him about the blossoming of the rich bounty of songs which became *Wildflowers*. It's a phrase I used when I wrote about his final concert (included in this book). Having just completed a long, triumphant, fortieth anniversary tour—some fifty-three shows—he ended with one last celebration at the beloved Hollywood Bowl. It was more than a show; it was an exultant celebration of rock and roll hosted by one of America's last great rock and roll heroes.

Exactly a week to that night, he was gone. Though the shock and sorrow of his abrupt departure hasn't diminished much, the truth resounds. In the very center of an immense traveling rock and roll circus for just over four decades (four times as long as The Beatles were a band), Tom Petty & The Heartbreakers were great always. Not once did he let those reins slip.

Back when we started this book, it was already quite evident that the guy was a genius songwriter, and one with a joyfully grounded, somewhat zen attitude towards songwriting, He was the very antithesis of the troubled, neurotic songwriter for whom the creative process was forever tortured. Tom, alone with guitar, words, tune and groove, was in his element. Unlike other famous songwriters whose connection with the muse became diminished by the pressures of success, Tom's connection intensified, and the scope of his songwriting expanded in every direction. Sure, he'd been through dark times—problems with the business, with drugs, divorce—but he emerged ultimately unbroken. He held onto the thing that always gave his life the most meaning: his music. And, unlike almost all pop stars and songwriters who do their greatest work in their twenties and never surpass it, Tom started strong and got better. And then even better. He kept expanding, but never let go of the reins. Always his music was about authenticity, and he maintained that truth while being remarkably dedicated, resulting in a voluminous songbook of splendor and soul.

Asked how he did it, he'd be the first to explain it was because he loved writing songs more than anything, a tendency illustrated perfectly when we discussed the creation of *Highway Companion*, then under way.

He'd been working non-stop for months, writing and recording his new songs with Jeff Lynne in his home studio. He'd been happily working on the new Southern song, "Down South," somewhat of a sequel to "Southern Accents." It was almost complete, and he was especially excited about it. But he'd promised Dana he'd take a break from work for a little romantic getaway in Mexico. He purposely did not take a guitar, intending to relax with Dana and suspend work for a few days. But that's not really who he was. He quickly started Jonesing for a guitar, and asked the hotel to get him one. He told them he just needed a cheap guitar, nothing expensive. But, because of the source of this request—one of the planet's most beloved and iconic musicians—they purchased him a beautiful Spanish classical guitar with gut strings. Not cheap.

He loved that guitar, and brought it home with him. While there, ostensibly vacationing, he diligently improved and completed "Down South," and wrote an entire new song as well—the beautiful "Around The Roses," which he also recorded for the album.

Always he invested the fullness of his soul into all his songs. Even his story songs, written in character, reflect Tom's truth always, his choices, his world-view. From the American girl raised on promises to the fool betting on happiness in "American Dream Plan B." always he revealed the kind of yearning and hope that lived in his heart and those of most humans.

Such is the nature of the songwriter's mind: every passage of life, even dark, painful parts, evoke vividly visceral emotion to songs. The old songwriter joke is the usual response to any romantic breakup. "Yeah, it's been *devastating*. I did get a great song out of it, though!"

Tom used heartbreak—which he refers to here as the greatest ailment known to man—as the nucleus of countless songs, all of which resonate with genuine sorrow. Something we all know. With a great knack for collecting resonant thoughts and images for songs, he discovered symbolic shorthand for the complexities of the human journey.

Evidence of this abounds through these pages, such as when he had first moved to Los Angeles, and was living in a tiny Encino apartment so close to the freeway that its sound roared incessantly, day and night. But, rather than be rattled by this, instead he found a window into a character.

"I remember thinking that [the freeway] sounded like the ocean to me… That was my ocean. My Malibu."

Tom's purity shone even in his unabashed love for Los Angeles. Though he honored his Gainesville roots, he was an instant Angeleno. Though Scott Fitzgerald said years earlier that few men can contain all of Hollywood's equations at once, Tom embraced it all with an open heart.

Unlike so many who are disheartened upon arrival in Hollywood to find squalor where they expected stardust, he saw only the sunny side of this place, even in its darkest corners.

"We fell in love with LA within an hour of being there," he said. "We just thought, 'This is *heaven*'. We said, 'Look—everywhere there's people making a living playing music. This is the *place*.'"

Never did he hesitate to scale the castle walls; he saw his ascent as inevitable. "Everywhere you looked, there was a record company!" he said. "I just thought, 'Well, all we've got to do is go in to every one, and we'll get a deal.'"

He and his gang first lived at the Hollywood Premiere, a "hooker's motel" on Hollywood Boulevard. It was east of Western, a designation he even mentions, as it's simply beyond the point one wants to pass. Yet, even there, he was happy.

Most people have dreams, but few stay true to them. Tom did. Often dreams are discarded because of the mandate of adulthood, that time to put away childish things—like guitars. But Tom never did let go, and never did he allow his dream to get grow ragged. First sparked by his providential Elvis encounter, that dream fully combusted into a rampant wildfire of the soul when he saw The Beatles on *The Ed Sullivan Show*. From that moment on, he was transformed. Already a serious music fan, because of The Beatles he became positively reverential. On that black and white TV in his childhood home, he saw all the dimensions of a life he would soon inhabit. Never was it about a solo star trip like Elvis. It was about a band. A band of friends who, like The Beatles, all happened to be phenomenal musicians.

What he ultimately realized, of course, was distinct from The Beatles. What Tom did, essentially, was to be both Lennon and McCartney in his band. He was the source of the songs. He did collaborate on many classic songs with Mike Campbell, of course, but not like John and Paul, who each did everything. Mike gave Tom great tracks of rocking guitar progressions, over and into which Tom wrote all the words and melodies. He also sang lead on each song, so that it all emanated ultimately from his singular soul. It was his band.

That hope and fire instilled in him by The Beatles stayed with him forever. Never did he lose sight of how deeply music can enrich a life. When I asked him once if he was able to fathom how profoundly his songs mattered in the lives of millions, he paused reflectively for a moment, and then said, softly, "I *hope* so. I remember how much it meant to me."

That redemptive promise of music is something he never abandoned. Never was he very far from that kid back in Gainesville. Even decades into iconic rock stardom, his world was forever framed by that Gainesville window. What abounded in his songs were the thoughts and visions of his mother heroically enduring what he knew he needed to escape—from the haunting prayer vision of her in "Southern Accents," to the persistence of human hope, even through hopeless times, in "Something Good Coming" from *Mojo*.

It was a dream of liberation, of being delivered from Florida into the world itself, electrified by the original current of rock and roll. Tom's genuine joy, graced by purity and passion, never diminished. From his last album, *Hurricane Eye*, to the very final night of his final tour, he never faltered. He went out at the height of his powers. Which is the way, I think, he wanted it. He never wanted to do anything that wasn't great. Though it wasn't evident during the final shows—to me, anyway—that Tom was in severe pain with a bad hip. He knew that doing what he was doing at The Heartbreakers' level of genuine passion—creating euphoric rock and roll revival celebrations every night to crowds as big as the populations of little towns—would become impossible, eventually.

It brings to mind his funny answer to the question of why he worked out so much: "Because nobody wants a fat Tom Petty." No doubt he also felt nobody wanted a lesser Tom Petty in any way. The last thing he'd want would be for fans to attend a concert and say, "Yeah, it's always great to see Tom. I mean, it's wasn't *amazing* like it used to be, but still it was great to see him."

That never happened. His decades of unbroken passion remain a testament to his spirit of purity. Even at this most momentous juncture, he wasn't going to leave any of his fans feeling cheated.

While assembling the new pieces for this collection, I looked at some of the original reviews of this book, as well as a multitude of readers' reviews, posted online. Most were quite positive, loving this rare opportunity to spend time with Tom. But one recurrent criticism, though understandable, was ironic: people perceived me as "gushing," and felt that I was too unrestrained, and perhaps false, in my sustained, unrestrained expressions of awe throughout the book at the greatness of his songs.

The thing is, that isn't phony. Had I restrained myself, and not referred to his multitude of miracle songs *as* miracle songs, that would have been false. As a songwriter myself, I am genuinely astonished by the sheer brilliance of his songs, and by his tireless diligence, remarkable consistency, and productivity. It was precisely because I was a songwriter and musician myself that he and I bonded, as he liked that I could play his songs, and understood the fullness of his genius—not only the words, but the music itself. In that way, I came to know intimately the full breadth of his accomplishment. Because, for decades, he consistently discovered gold. Had he written only a handful of those songs, he would deserve such unmitigated awe. But he did it for more than four decades.

So, sure, while that might be considered gushing, it wasn't calculated for effect. I was talking to Tom Petty, after all! Are those not miracle songs? To this day I hear him singing on my spiritual radio, and those songs are as powerful as ever, if not more. Late last night, when these Angeleno streets on which I drive in moonlight times are mostly empty, I listened to one song of his, "Hungry No More," over and over. It was all I needed. Tom left us a vast songbook which is forever expansive with poignancy, power, and purity. It's a source that is never depleted, which we can all return to for sustenance through the rest of our days, because it can take rhino skin (as he wrote) to get through this world unhurt. However, having his soul, spirit, and love injected into these songs sure helps a lot. His songbook now lives in the unbound mystic, like an entire America, coast to coast, of wildflowers.

"I *never* thought our trip was going to go on so long," he said with wonder. "I thought, if it went on for five years, in those days, that was *really* successful. We never thought about growing *old* doing it. That those songs have *survived*, and that I still hear them, is *amazing*." He then paused for a moment, and took a drag on his cigarette while looking out towards the sea and sky. Slowly exhaling, as the smoke curled around, he laughed, and said, "I *never* would have dreamed that. *That* was beyond my control."

Connecting with so many Tom lovers in a way I couldn't do back in 2005 has been heartening, and has bolstered a spirit darkened by his absence. I know so many people all over who felt the same thing. This loss was especially tough, so all these years since this book's season of creation, gratitude abounds in my heart that it continues to have a place in the lives on his fans.

Many times, though, people say, "*Dude!* I am *so* jealous that you got to know Tom Petty! I wish I could have."

I know what you mean, but I've got a feeling Tom would want you to know something: that if you loved him and his songs, you did know him. You knew him well. Because that was really him. It was not a pose, nor was it a way of concealing his real self. It was truly Tom, on record and in concert. He poured the full measure of who he was into his songs. All of it—the full rainbow of the human journey, from refugee to hero and beyond, the love, romance, fear, humor, anguish, worry, sorrow, faith, rage, gratitude, redemption, and always hope—was there in his songs, every aspect of who he was.

So, any time your heart and soul are uplifted by his music, remember that he's singing to you. And he's smiling.

PART ONE

Life

Chapter One

Dreamville

There's a rumor that your grandfather killed a guy in Georgia, which forced the family to move to Florida. Any truth to that?
TP: This is what my father told me. Very late in his life. We were out on a tour bus. I asked how did the family end up in Florida if they were from Georgia. So then the story unfolded. My father's mother was a full-blooded Cherokee Indian. "Native Americans," as they call them now, but my family always called them "Indians." We never referred to it [Laughs] as "Native American."

What happened is that my grandfather was a white guy. My grandmother was a cook in a logging camp. He worked in the logging camp. They made it into pulpwood. He married my grandmother, which was not popular, to mix the races. They didn't dig it at all. So they were going to make it out of there. And they were on a horse and wagon. I don't know if he stole the wagon.

He was stopped on a road by several guys. Some kind of violent situation came down about him being with an Indian. And somebody got insulted, and my grandfather ended up killing a guy. That's what my father told me. Though I had *never* heard that in my life till then. They killed a guy and fled to Florida. Which makes me wonder if he didn't change his name when he went into Florida. I don't know. I asked my dad if he changed his name, and my dad said, "I don't know. He always had this name." So I have no idea.

This is the story as told to me by my father. So I take it to be true, I guess.

You didn't hear that story till you were an adult?
Yeah, it was in the Nineties, actually. I remember one night we were in the bedroom of a tour bus, and we were talking, and I said, "Hey—how did the family wind up in Florida?" It had never come up. Because I knew that we had relatives in Georgia. And there was always this talk about Georgia. But no one ever explained how we came to be in Florida. They came down to Florida, and they both got jobs as migrant fruit pickers. And then they'd move on to the next place. And then my grandfather eventually got back into the pulpwood business. And actually was called Pulpwood. That was the name he went by: Pulpwood Petty. I know that was true because I met another guy, this older guy named Beck. Probably in his sixties, or almost seventy. And he met me and he goes, "Hey—are you related to Pulpwood Petty?" It turned out he really did know my grandfather somewhat. He said, "All I know about him is that he used to actually *hitch* down the road to work. He was a hitchhiker, and I'd pick him up sometimes and give him a ride."

I only met my grandfather a few times. He wasn't around much. He wore a big hat. He was a very mysterious guy. [Laughs] That's what I remember as a kid, the guy that wore a brown hat. Didn't say a hell of a lot.

Did you know your grandmother?
Yeah, I knew her for quite a while. They lived in the country. They were country people. Had a corn crop, probably an acre. And chickens. [She] was in complete denial about being Indian. Didn't want that out too much. Didn't want to talk about that. Now I can see why. It was sad, really. The Indian thing was not a popular subject. They wanted to be white. Meaning my grandmother and her other two sons.

Did it mean much to you as a kid, being descended from an Indian?
It didn't mean much because I didn't know about it. I *kind* of knew about it. It was sad. And you couldn't help but know it when you saw [my grandmother]. That she was an Indian, or that she was *something* different than what I was used to. And we all ended up with this really straight hair, Indian hair, and Indian noses. I'm the only blond, blue-eyed guy in the family. Everyone else is dark-skinned Indian. My

mother, who was of English and French descent, was fair-haired. So I came out this way. My brother didn't. He's dark-skinned.

But it wasn't something that was brought up a lot, and my mother didn't like the whole idea at all. That we were Indian. So it wasn't like today when I see Indian families, and they're quite proud of it, and they stay on the reservations. [My grandparents] didn't want to do that. My grandmother was a real small-time farmer. They lived near poverty level. I remember the house had newspaper patches, where they'd patch up a wall with a lot of newspaper and varnish it. And I thought that was really bizarre, because we came from the suburbs. [Laughs] So I did know her a bit, but not really *that* well. We'd only go see her two, three times a year. We'd go see her Christmas Day and maybe Easter Sunday. But we never saw them much.

Were they far away?
No. They were probably about a hundred miles away, back in the sticks. A place called Reddick. That was the nearest little village, little town, to where they lived. They kind of lived back in the woods from there.

You have one brother.
Yes. Bruce. He doesn't play music. He's seven years younger. He lives in Tallahassee, Florida, and works for a company. He's a sales rep, he's got a real straight job. He really loves music and he knows it pretty well. But he never wanted to play it, because he saw all the strife I was going through, so he kind of backed away from it. I think sometimes he wishes he had. Because I tried to encourage him to do it. I told him, "It's the best job around." [Laughs] But he didn't go for it.

Was there a piano in your house?
No. I wish there had been.

Did you start singing early on?
Yes. Somehow I learned so many songs from listening, from the age of about eleven to fourteen, which has served me well later. I just *absorbed* all these rockabilly records. *Tons* of stuff I was interested in. I really had this knack for learning all the words. I don't know why. My dad says I could memorize nursery rhymes when I was three. He would read me this book, and when he came back to it, he was amazed that I had memorized some of it. So I never had trouble memorizing songs.

I think the first song I sang on a microphone was probably "High Heel Sneakers" [written by Tommy Tucker]. I remember doing that and I remember doing "Love Potion #9" [written by Jerry Leiber and Mike Stoller, performed by The Searchers]. That was a big hit at the time. I just got up on the mike and did it. But I had no idea of singing in pitch. I didn't even know about that stuff. I just sang. I didn't even know what harmony was, really. I thought everybody sang and it came out that way. [Laughs] It would be a good year or so before I figured out, oh, there's different lines to make harmony. I was that uneducated.

Did you learn those songs from records or from radio?
From both. Usually somebody had the records.

45s?
Yeah, 45s. We didn't have a lot of money. You couldn't get all the records you wanted. Sometimes you'd go around town and find somebody who had the record. The word would be out that so-and-so's got "Love Potion #9." You'd go and borrow it. A lot of parties. You'd see these girls who had tons of records playing them at the party, and you'd try to hustle them, you know. "Hey, let me borrow this. I'll bring it back Monday." [Laughs]

Did you already want to be a musician then?
Oh yeah. That's all I ever wanted to be. I never thought of being anything else.

What did your dad do for a living?
He was an insurance salesman. He kind of jumped from job to job. There was a while there, when I was really young, when he owned the only grocery store in the black part of Gainesville. It was all black clientele. Back then they had everybody segregated into neighborhoods. And so, in the black neighborhood, he had the only grocery store.

When I was quite young, like three and four, my memories of it are being taken down there, and I'd play out back of the grocery store with the young black kids of the neighborhood. It was kind of bizarre, because I'd spend most of the day with black kids. And then I'd come home to this white suburban vibe. [Laughs]

And that went on for a while, and then I guess that went bust, and he got a panel truck that sold what he called "wholesale dry goods," like handkerchiefs and cigarette lighters, and all that crap you see behind the counter in convenience stores. He had a whole panel truck of that stuff, and he had a route that he invented [Laughs] and he drove around North Central Florida, and he drove around selling this stuff off his truck to stores. And that didn't pan out. That went on for a few years. And then he got into selling insurance. That's what he did for the rest of his life. Those were the three jobs I remember him doing.

Did your mom work?

Yeah. My mom worked in the tax collector's office in Gainesville selling car registrations and license plates. She worked there quite a long time. So they both did eight-hour days at least. And my dad really never came home much when we were awake. He usually came home after we were asleep.

My dad was pretty wild. He used to always be going to get his car out of a ditch somewhere. [Laughs] I thought it was *completely* normal to run your car into a ditch. [Laughs] Because there were so many times he hit a ditch with his car. Now I realize, *wow*. And he was quite a gambler, he loved to gamble, and my mother hated it. It was quite a turbulent household, really. Very turbulent.

Why was he hitting ditches? Was he drinking?

Yeah, he was quite a drinker. He was just as wild as the wind, really. So my childhood wasn't really all that bad, but it had elements of being bad because of the household—there was a lot of fighting. My mom and dad fought a lot. It wasn't always good.

So you and your brother were on your own when you came home from school?

We were on our own till about 6:00, when my mom would come home. My grandmother looked after us quite a bit. My mom's mom. I was quite close to her. And she was a really big influence in my life. She really favored me quite a bit and really tried to build up my confidence all the time. She was really sweet to me. She lived not too far away, and she'd come over and watch us when we were really young. But when we started to be, say ten or eleven, then we were on our own.

When you were on your own, what would you do?
We'd just bum around the neighborhood. Back in those days, people just let their kids out till dark. We'd just bum around with other kids. We lived near a big city park called the Northeast Park, in Gainesville. It bordered a small, wooded forest. We ran around, my brother and I, and we played a lot of cowboys and Indians. That was the big game back then. We had a lot of cowboy stuff. A lot of cap pistols. We did that when we were really young, and then when I got the guitar, that pretty much occupied all my free time. I'd come home and play the guitar.

Did you know your mom's father, too?
Never met him in my life. My grandmother *hated* him. A very interesting thing: My dad's name was Earl. My grandmother on my mother's side's ex-husband's name was Earl. My mother's sister married two guys named Earl. [Laughs] First husband named Earl, no good; then she married another guy named Earl. And my middle name is Earl. My grandmother would not say the name "Earl." She thought it was some kind of jinx. She called my dad "Petty." And my uncle, they called him Jernigan, 'cause his name was Earl Jernigan. And she referred to him as Jernigan and my dad as Petty, because her ex had been named Earl. She didn't like my father at all, because he was a wild, gambling drinker guy. And her other daughter had two husbands named Earl. [Much laughter.]

It was a *trip*. Earl Jernigan was a very interesting guy. He wasn't a Southerner. He was the only Northerner in the family. And his whole love was film, motion pictures. And he had the only business in town that was a film business. He had the only place where you could develop film or buy it.

And anytime there was a movie shoot, probably within a hundred miles, he would go. And they did quite a bit in this place called Silver Springs in Ocala, because it had the underwater tanks, because the water is crystal clear, and the glass-bottom boat originated there. You could ride and look at the fish through the glass bottom of the boat. And they had these big windows that you could film through. He worked on several big-time movie shoots. They would contract him to do whatever he did. He was a trip. He didn't like my family much, and I see why, because they had nothing in common. He was actually far too hip to hang around with the Pettys; it really bugged him. At the time I didn't understand why he never wanted to be around, but I understand it clearly now. But I remember, he had done *Return Of The Creature From The Black Lagoon*, and he actually had one of the rubber suits of the creature in his house, and we thought that was *so* cool. [Laughs]

I was eleven years old. I remember this *vividly*. I was sitting in a pile of pine straw, underneath a big pine tree in my yard. And I was thinking, "What am I going to do today?" Just kind of sitting there. Just old enough at eleven to kind of wonder what might lie ahead. And my Aunt Evelyn pulled into the driveway—her husband was Earl Jernigan.

My aunt pulls in the drive and says, "Tommy, would you like to go and see Elvis Presley?"

Well, I thought, "Yeah, sure." I didn't know a lot about Elvis Presley. I remember when I was a kid of five or six there was some controversy in the household, and he was known to me as a fella who wiggled. And I did a little impression with a broom of wiggling like Elvis.

But I couldn't really put together in my head who Elvis was *exactly*. I knew he was a rock and roll star. And I'd never thought much about rock and roll until that moment. So it was gonna be in about a week's time we were gonna go see Elvis. Because my uncle had been hired onto his film that he was shooting, which was called *Follow That Dream*. Which I've always thought was a cosmic title.

My aunt picked me up with my two cousins and drove us to Ocala, which was about thirty miles away. And there was a huge crowd when we got there. The biggest crowd I've ever seen in the streets of Ocala. And we were driven through the crowd and around the back and into the film set. They were filming on the street, in a scene where Elvis pulled up in a car and walked into a bank. A simple scene. So they had set up a bunch of trailers with a chain-link fence around it for a dressing room. And we were taken back to the dressing room area. And then, I swear to God, a line of white Cadillacs pulled in. All white. And I'd never seen anything like that. It wasn't a funeral. They were all white. Cadillacs. And I was standing up on a box to see over everyone's head. Because a big roar started up when the cars pulled in. And then guys in mohair suits and pompadours started jumping out of every car. And I said, to my aunt, "Is that Elvis?"

She said, "No, that's not Elvis."

Then the next one came out, and I said, "Is that Elvis?"

"No, that's not Elvis."

And then suddenly I go, "That's Elvis." He stepped out radiant as an angel. He seemed to glow and walk above the ground. It was like *nothing* I'd ever seen in my life. At fifty yards, we were stunned by what this guy looked like. And he came walking right towards us. And his hair was so black, I remember that it shined blue when the sunlight hit it.

And he walked over and we were speechless. My uncle said, "These are my nieces and nephews, Elvis." And [Elvis] smiled and nodded at us. I don't know what he said, because I was just too dumbfounded. And he went into his trailer. And then we got really excited. Like that first brush with fame will do to you. And now *hundreds* of girls were against this chain-link fence. And there were just photos of Elvis and albums everywhere you looked in their hands, and they were trying to get Elvis to sign this stuff. And one of his Memphis mafia guys was there. They were handing the record jackets over the fence, and he would take them into the trailer and come back with them signed, and give them to the kids. So, being young, the way I put this together in my head, was, "*Damn*, if I had a record jacket, I could get an autograph." It hadn't occurred to me that he could have just signed any piece of paper. I wanted a proper thing.

So we stayed around the rest of the day, and we watched him shoot this scene. Which was really funny, because every time he pulled up in the car, the crowd would break through the barricades and just charge him. So it took them hours just to shoot this little scene of him getting out of the car and walking in the door. Because they couldn't control the crowd; they were just *insane*. And I thought at that time, "That is one hell of a job to have. That's a great gig—Elvis Presley."

And then my aunt said she would bring us back again. And so I made up my mind that if I was going back again, I'm gonna have an Elvis record for him to sign. And I caught the fever that day and I never got rid of it. I began collecting anything I could find on Elvis. There was a guy down the street who had a sister who had gone to college and was older than us. Because Elvis' heyday had kind of passed. This was 1961, 1962. I traded my Wham-O slingshot to this kid for a box of 45s, and in this box there were *so* many Elvis records, and they were all the greatest ones. And there were a few others, like Ricky Nelson and Jerry Lee Lewis. And some stuff in there that was great, too. But it was the Elvis stuff I was really interested in.

There were no books of any kind on Elvis, no information anywhere. The only place you could get information on him were teen magazines. Where you'd see photos of him. But there was very little information in those. Then I found one that had an ad in the back, where you could send away for something called *The Elvis Presley Handbook*. You've got to dig—I'm eleven years old, fifth grade, I'm *completely* enthralled with Elvis Presley. None of my friends could relate at all to Elvis Presley. But I thought it was cool, and I thought rock and roll was cool, and I just *loved* the music. I played it *endlessly*. My dad was concerned that I didn't go outside, that I just played these records all day. I wasn't thinking of being a musician. I was just a fan.

And so I sent a buck to England for this book, *The Elvis Presley Handbook*, much to the ridicule of my family for wasting a dollar. And it took months to come, but the day it came was like *Christmas*. The book came, and it had every fact and it had a review of every song he'd done, and the chronology of when the records had been released. And I could see what I had and what I didn't have. And that's what kicked off my love of music. That was the dream I followed, strangely enough.

It would be some years later, two to three years later, when The Beatles came, that I would catch the fever and want to play guitar. But learning all of those Elvis songs, and having that kind of background in rock and roll of where it had come from, has served me to this day. It became an invaluable thing to have. So, for that, I thank him.

And you never were taken back to see Elvis again?
No, we were never taken back.

Would your dad be home on weekends?
Sometimes. He loved to fish and hunt.

Would you go with him?
It was kind of mandatory for a while that I went with him. But I never liked it. My dad was a *hard* man, hard to be around. He was really hard on me. He wanted me to be a lot more macho than I was. I was this real sort of tender, emotional kid. More inclined to the arts than shooting something. I didn't want to be trapped in a boat with him all day. He was sort of a legendary fisherman around town. He was *so* good at it. That's what he did all the time. Fish and hunt. If he wasn't working.

Did you eat the fish?
Yeah, we ate a *lot* of fish. We learned how to clean fish. We ate it so much I couldn't stand it, really.

What kind of fish?
He would catch everything from perch to bass to trout. If he got bass or trout, that was pretty good eating. Perch wasn't that great.

Did you like the time on the boat with him?
No, I didn't like him that much. I was kind of afraid of him the whole time. He didn't mind just *popping* you. He'd really just kick your ass. [Laughs] So I was always kind of afraid of him, to tell you the truth. I didn't want to be stuck in a boat with him. He carried pistols, and he was this really kind of wild character.

What would he hunt?
He hunted quail, dove, and deer. In deer season, they would get out the heavy artillery.

How did you feel about that?
It was *awful*. I only went a little bit and then he realized I was completely useless in that situation. It was sitting in fields, just fucking cold, to shoot a bird. It always seemed stupid to me. I didn't like it. But I remember it well. I remember birds stuffed in bags, and cleaning the birds, picking all the feathers off. It was *gross*. I hated it. Then you had to eat them. I ate dove and quail.

How was that?
Quail was okay, but eating a dove? It sucked. It tasted like shit. But he grew up in the swamps of Florida.

One day this small alligator came up by the boat—and I actually saw my dad take his forefinger and his thumb, and punch the eyes in on the alligator. To show me that he could knock the alligator out. Took his *thumb and his forefinger, pushed* the alligator's eyes in, and the gator rolled over in the water. It was like he was *nuts*. He was just nuts. But he wasn't afraid of anything. I once saw my dad grab a rattlesnake by the tail, swing it round his head, and pop his neck. That's pretty wild shit, you know? So I was kind of scared of him.

When I got older, when I was *grown*, then we kind of bonded in some way where we could talk and hang out. But when I was younger, I was really kind of scared of him. I didn't really want to cross him. I just kind of wanted to stay out of his way if he was home. But we didn't really like him a lot. He just caused a lot of turbulence.

Did he and your mom fight a lot?
Yeah. Think about it: He was drunk every day. [Laughs] He'd get drunk every night, he'd disappear for days, he was just *crazy*.

Was your mom there for you?
She was always there for us. She was a great mom. But we felt really sorry for her, having to put up with him all the time. She should have left him; I don't know why she wouldn't leave him. It was a weird way to grow up, in some respects.

But then my dad could turn around and be really kind and sweet. He had this duality to him. He'd give me so much shit about being in a band, you know, and then you'd turn around, and one day he's bought you a Fender amplifier. [Laughs] "My God, thanks." So I think he kind of had this duality, where maybe he had a really rough life. But he did have a kind side where he could be really nice to you.

When did you start guitar?
My mom and dad got me a guitar for Christmas when I was twelve. But it wasn't really a great guitar. It was just a cheap acoustic guitar called a Stella. Metal strings. I didn't know how to tune it up. I had a Mel Bay guitar book. But it was so much work to even press the strings down on that guitar. So it sat around the house for years. And I think, when I was about thirteen, The Beatles came. And after The Beatles everyone wanted to get a little group going in the neighborhood, and my dad bought me a Kay electric guitar. And that's when I started to really take it seriously.

My mom got me guitar lessons. I only went to two, because I went to one, and the guy taught me a couple of chords, and how to tune up. I went back, and it was like going into this other land that I didn't really want to go into. He was more of a classical teacher, and he didn't really want to deal with pop music. I think what did it was that he told me that you always keep your [left] thumb on the back of the neck, and then instantly I saw someone on television that I admired and his thumb was over the neck. And I went, "I'm not going back."

I met a kid in the neighborhood, who actually knew how to play, and he started showing me stuff, and I learned at a much quicker rate from my friend. He showed me chords, and we sat and played guitar. And you know, you learn really quickly that way. The first key I learned was *C*, so you had to have *F*, and *F* is a tough one. I remember playing "Wooly Bully." It was the first one I mastered, and I could play "Wooly Bully" on guitar, and I was on my way. And from there it just went on.

Who was the kid?
There were actually two kids in the neighborhood. One guy was named Richie Henson and the other guy was named Robert Crawford. They lived not far away, and we'd get together and compare notes. I remember Richie teaching me the barre chord, and things like that.

And you picked it up pretty easily?
Yeah. I had to practice. But you do pick it up quicker if you're sitting in a bedroom with friends and you all really want to play along. We'd have a lot of fun getting together. It was always like somebody showed somebody something, and then they show it to somebody else. "Here's the solo to 'I Saw Her Standing There'." This kid down the street figured it out. So he showed somebody else. And you learned that way.

Were you playing acoustic?
No, we had these little Kay and Harmony electrics. And Robert Crawford actually had a Gibson SG, a really nice guitar. Richie had a Harmony solid body guitar. So the instruments weren't too bad, really. And we practiced a lot. We *loved* playing.

Did you have an amp?
Yeah, I had a little Gibson amp. I've still got it. A Skylark. A very small amp.

Did you start writing your own songs then?
Yeah. I started writing songs because I didn't really know how many songs went, and so in my idle hours I would sit and try to invent my own songs with the chords I knew. And that came *surprisingly* easy.

I think I was probably writing songs as soon as I could play, as soon as I knew enough chords, I was trying to put together my own song.

The words were coming easily, too?
Yeah. I didn't have a lot of trouble with it. Though I wasn't taking it real seriously. It was just a hobby. The bands didn't really play original songs, they were all playing the hits of the day. But it was something I did love.

What was your first song called?
I think it was called "Baby, I'm Leaving." It was a 12-bar blues kind of thing. It was in *C*. My first chords were *C*, *F*, *G*, and *A* minor.

Nice to have that A minor in there.
Yeah. *A* minor was really good.

When you started learning new chords, would you put those in your songs?
Oh yeah. Right away. [Laughs]

Would you write down your songs?
Yeah, I'd write down the words. Though I could usually remember how they went.

Was your father proud that you could play?
Yes. He was really proud of it. When he would have a friend over, he'd say, "Bring your guitar out, and play a song for this guy." He was very proud of it.

Would you play your songs for your mother?
Sometimes I would. She was amazed that I could do it. Just *amazed*. She'd say, "I can't understand how you can do it if you didn't have any lessons, and you don't know how to write music. How do you do it?"

And I said, "I don't know, I just learned it from other kids."

Were your parents musical at all?
No. My dad wasn't musical in any way, and I don't think he was a huge music fan. He did like some country music. My mother, though, she liked records. She liked musicals and show tunes. I remember her buying

the *West Side Story* soundtrack, and I really loved all those songs. I still really do. I think it's an incredibly well-written piece of music, that whole show. It was incredible. She bought things like that, and Nat King Cole. Which I thought was really square at the time, but now I look back on it, and it was very good music. She played the phonograph. She liked gospel and stuff like that. But nobody really played any instruments.

When you started playing, did your parents encourage you?
Yeah, they thought music was a good thing. They didn't like the length of my hair. They were really shocked by that. That me and my buddies were letting our hair grow long. They were *really* shocked by that. Because it was unusual in '64. We wanted to look like The Beatles. We thought it would be hip for our band. And then you could let it grow through the summer, and then school would start and they'd make you cut it again. There was a dress code in school where they wouldn't let you have long hair. But me and my dad fought many a battle about hair. For years, there, it was just like he didn't understand it. He didn't understand it at all, [Laughs] why we were doing that. But eventually they gave up.

Do you remember the first time you heard The Beatles?
No, I don't remember exactly the first time. But I remember that period. I think I heard "I Saw Her Standing There" before "I Want To Hold Your Hand." That was the B-side, and they were playing both sides. I'm not sure, but I think I heard that one first. And I bought the single. That great single with the picture sleeve on the front of them in their collarless gray jackets. And I just loved it. I just played it to death.

I think that I probably had two singles by the time we saw them on television. I had "She Loves You" as well, with "I'll Get You" on the back. It was on the Swan record label. This black label that said "Swan Records." And once we saw them, we were never the same.

There was nobody else with a self-contained band like them. There were singers. The only bands I had seen were at the teen rec center, and they played surf music, mostly instrumental music. Maybe the sax player took a vocal every now and then. But pop stars weren't self-contained units then. I'd never even dreamed of that. To me, I would have loved to have been a rock and roll star. But I just didn't understand how you got to be a rock and roll star. How did you suddenly have a mohair suit and an orchestra? But the minute I saw The Beatles on *The Ed Sullivan Show*—and it's true of thousands of guys—*there* was the way out. *There* was the way to do it. You get your friends and you're a self-contained unit. And you make the music. And it looked like so much fun.

It was something I identified with. I had never been hugely into sports. Sports never really spoke to me. I liked sandlot baseball. But I didn't like it once it got really organized. I didn't really watch sports on TV. I was more into the arts. Which I think weirded my dad out for a while. But I didn't really have a huge interest in knowing what baseball players were or anything. But *this* really spoke to me. I had been a big fan of Elvis. But I really saw in The Beatles that here's something I could do. I knew I could do it. It wasn't long before there were groups springing up in garages all over the place.

When you would write songs, would you tape them?
No, I didn't have a tape recorder until *years* later. My mother bought me an Ampex reel-to-reel tape recorder for Christmas when I was eighteen. It was really cool. You could overdub on it. It had this thing called "sound on sound." In mono you could just keep tracking and tracking. It had terrible hiss, [Laughs] as you could tell. But it was a *lot* of fun. That was the first tape recorder I had.

Would you do harmonies?
Oh yeah, I'd do everything. Just stack and stack and stack. And it'd all come back like "Hissssssssssssssss." [Laughs] And it was all in mono, because you had to use one channel to overdub on the other. But that was a great help. I really did learn a lot about recording. I'd plug my bass direct into the tape recorder, and play the bass direct. It was fun. It was great fun.

Were The Continentals the popular band in Gainesville around this time?
Yes. They were the big band in town. Don Felder was in The Continentals, who went on to The Eagles. The first band I got in was called The Sundowners. We were all really young, and our moms had to drive us to the gigs. But we worked. We actually worked.

How did The Sundowners form?
I knew this kid named Dennis Lee. I met him at a dance because he had long hair, and I had long hair, and there were only maybe four or five kids in all of Gainesville who had hair over their ears. So we kind of found each other. And he mentioned, "I'm a drummer, I have a set of drums." So I went over to his house one day with my guitar, and we kind of played and fooled around. But we didn't have a band, we just kind of fooled around.

Then there was this chick I was hot on. She was a really good-looking girl. Her name was Cindy Crawford. [Laughs] Go figure. And she was very beautiful.

And I talked to her one night at a dance. And she said something like, "So you have a band?"

I said, "Sure, I got a band." [Laughs]

She said, "I'm in charge of this dance in the school. We have a DJ, but we were going to have a band in the intermission. I thought maybe your band would like to do it."

So, seizing the opportunity, I said, "Sure, my band can do it." And so I really quickly went and got Richie Henson, who was the guy I sat around playing guitar with. And I told him, "We're forming a band." And he went and got Robert Crawford, who was a little older than us and quite good on the guitar. And Dennis Lee on the drums. And we got together one afternoon in my front room and played. And it was the biggest rush in my life, the minute it all happened.

You played guitar, too.
Yeah, we didn't have a bass. We just had three guitars, and one big Silvertone amplifier that Robert had. And we all plugged into that. It had six inputs. [Laughs]

So three guitars and drums.
And we had a guy who played sax. He only played one gig with us and then kind of bowed out. 'Cause there wasn't much for him to do.

We learned four songs. All instrumental. "House Of The Rising Sun." "Walk Don't Run." We all wore blue shirts and jeans, so we looked like a band. And it went over great. We wound up playing the next intermission, we played the same songs again. And then at the end of the night, we were packing up our gear, and this older kid came up, and said, "Do you guys ever play fraternity parties?" We said, "No, we've never played anywhere but here." He said, "Well, I can get you some bookings. If you learn more songs." And we thought, "*Wow.*" So, literally, that was on a Friday and on that Saturday we were in Dennis Lee's garage, trying to learn more songs. And it never stopped from that moment.

That guy did come through with some gigs. And then there was the Moose Club dance. It was the big teenage dance. They had a battle of the bands. And whoever won got a contract for the whole summer, to play every Friday night. And we won. And we got paid one hundred bucks a gig. Every Friday. Then we started picking up Saturday gigs, too. This was heavy shit—we were fourteen years old. Can't even drive a car. And we're getting high-school gigs. And Dennis's mom would drive us. Put our gear in her station wagon, and wait till it was over, and drive us home. And I was just a little kid—fourteen years old. And it's never stopped since. [Laughs]

My mom was like, "Where did you get this money?" And I told her I got it for the show. But she didn't believe me.

She said, "*Really*, where did you get this money? If you took this money, you're gonna have to own up to it."

I said, "I swear to God, Mom, they paid me this for playing." She didn't believe me. So she called the Moose Club, and the guy said, "Yeah, they get the door, and that's what they made."

So, by the end of the summer, I'd made a couple hundred bucks. And, to be fourteen, that's a *lot* of money. Or it was then. I put it all back into my equipment. I got a better amplifier. And my dad, who was really sweet, got me a really nice Gibson bass. So I guess [my parents] were supportive if they were doing that, buying me a nice bass.

When did you switch to bass?

Very early on. Probably that next week [after we put the band together]. I think there had to be a bass. So I tuned my guitar down. But that didn't work very well, because the strings were all floppy. And my dad bought me a bass. I got out the Sears catalogue and found a Silvertone bass. And I went to him with the catalogue and I said, "Will you loan me the money?" I think it was fifty-five bucks for a bass. And he said, "That's got to be a crummy instrument for that money." Though they were actually nice instruments. Though it looked crummy. [Laughs]

And he said, "No, I'm not loaning you money for something that cruddy." And then I came home a few days later, and he'd bought me a Gibson bass. And a Fender amplifier. And I was *stunned*. I'd never felt that kind of love from my dad in my life. And he bought it on a payment plan, where I had to make the payments on it. But, you know, *God*, it blew my mind. So I became a bass player.

He somehow knew Gibson was a good bass?
Yeah, he asked around, and he bought the whole rig off of someone who was selling it. It was a Gibson EB-2 bass. I still have it. Even then, it was a *really* nice instrument. And a Fender piggyback amp called a Tremolux. Which was a little smaller than the Fender Bassman. It wasn't really made for bass, so I couldn't play it real loud because it distorted. But I was in *hog heaven*. I couldn't believe it. [My dad] really supported me. It wasn't hard to make the payments, because we were working. But it took all of what I had. It was probably thirty to forty bucks a month payment.

So then [my friends] started to show me the names of the notes. "This fret makes *A*," and "this fret makes *B*." And that was how I started [on bass], just thumbing the note that the chord was. And then I learned a run and a bass pattern. And I was quite good. I got pretty good at the bass, and singing and playing bass at the same time.

Singing lead?
Yeah, most of the time.

Isn't that tough, to sing and play bass at the same time?
Well, I didn't know it was hard. [Laughs] So it wasn't, really. I didn't know it was supposed to be hard. So I could do it. I can still do it, to some degree.

I was really determined to play bass well. The guitarist in the band showed me basic scales. So once I knew where the notes were, it wasn't that hard. I learned all the notes on the neck, and where they were, and then I think I always had a pretty good rhythm. And though I didn't really realize it, I think I did have a pretty good sense of where the bass should be.

Were you aware that McCartney was the bass player for The Beatles?

Oh hell, yeah. Everybody knew that. And everybody knew that they wrote their own songs. And really, most bands were exactly that lineup. Maybe in a few years you'd see somebody who had a keyboard. There weren't many portable organs made at that time, until the Vox portable organ came out.

Did you have a favorite Beatle?

No, I liked them all. They all carried that same weight. [Laughs] Ringo was just as important as John. It was kind of like that in those days. So we liked everything.

Did you play Beatles' songs in your shows?

Somewhat. The Beatles' songs were really hard to sing. We weren't good harmony singers, so we drifted more to the Stones and The Animals. And The Kinks and The Zombies. But to do The Beatles was tricky because there was a lot of harmony, and we didn't know anything about singing harmony, really, so it took a while to do that.

Were you a Stones fan?

Oh yeah. We loved the Stones. Everything they did, we just loved it. People weren't cynical about music then. You were really rooting for everything then. You wanted to like everything. So the only challenge then was having enough money to have the records. I didn't have a huge record collection, because I couldn't afford it. Every record I got, I really played to death, and I really treasured it. 45s or LPs, anything I could get. I used to go around and collect Coke bottles to cash them in and get three bucks to get a record.

What was the first LP you got?

The first LP I got was Elvis. *G.I. Blues*, it was called. And that's when I was probably eleven or twelve, before I was playing music. But I remember when we got that *Meet The Beatles* album. Me and my brother talked my dad into buying it one night. *That* just blew my head off. So from that moment on I was trying to get a hold of any Beatles or Stones record that was out.

Did you remain a big Elvis fan?
I was until '64, and then Elvis was getting so shitty by then. [Pause] It had never been the music of my generation. I was an odd kid for even being interested in Elvis. So, when The Beatles came, I lost interest in Elvis, because [The Beatles] were the music of my generation, and I was a huge record buff. So I lost interest in Elvis, though I kind of felt an allegiance to him. I still went and saw those shitty movies for a while. But I knew the difference by then. It didn't have the vital that these new records did.

You said you encouraged your brother Bruce to play music, but he saw all the strife you were going through, and didn't want any part of it. What strife?
My dad and I fought *all* the time. About having long hair, and dressing the way I did. It looked really bizarre. It looked really freaky, in that time period. This was before the hippies. It was *so* weird. I can see why it weirded him out. To see somebody like me, or the guys I was running around with—people wouldn't serve us in restaurants. They didn't like it. Especially in the Deep South. And you could get your ass kicked if you were in the wrong spot.

So he was embarrassed by it. He didn't want to go anywhere with me. I guess it would be sort of like today, if your kid had fifty piercings and a green mohawk. It was kind of like that, to have Beatle-style hair, and boots, and the kind of clothes we were wearing. We thought it was super-hip and we were into it, but older people, they didn't dig it at all, which made us like it more.

They hated it at school. I'd keep getting kicked out of school for my hair. The school would make you cut your hair. So we would kind of grease it down. We'd go through the whole day with all this Vaseline in our hair. We'd really grease it down behind our ears to try to hide it. And then, when the weekend came, you'd wash it all out.

But my dad and I just had constant physical fights. I'd get the shit kicked out of me. And my brother didn't think it was worth all that. I'm sure it had some kind of traumatic impact on him. He wanted to take the easy road around that. He had short hair. And he was more athletic. Which my dad loved. Because I wasn't athletic and didn't have any interest in sports *at all*. I knew the name of no baseball player; I didn't give a shit. Never watched sports. I liked to play with my friends, but I didn't like the idea of organized sports. It just wasn't for me. There was nothing wrong with it. It just wasn't for me. And I was this skinny little kid, and I didn't fit into that whole football mentality of the South. But my brother could play football.

So my dad, I think he liked Bruce better for a long time. 'Cause Bruce kind of fit the mold of what [my father] wanted in a kid, and I was just this pale, little, skinny kid with long hair.

And yet you did impress him by playing music.

Yeah, he had to give that up, [Laughs] you know? And then the more and more money that started to come in, I guess he started to understand it. But I think he thought we would make more money if we cleaned up our image. And I'd say, "No, it doesn't work that way."

The Sixties were very turbulent with me and my dad. He hated long hair. He just *hated* it. He hated me growing my hair out, and it was a *constant* war. And I remember, early Seventies, when I was in [the band] Mudcrutch, we were playing five nights a week at this place called Dub's, the big college bar, and one day I was sitting in the front room writing out a set list. And we played five sets a night; we did a lot of songs. And he said, "What are you doing? What are you writing?"

I said, "It's the set list for the gig."

And he said, "You know that many songs?" I said, "Yeah."

And he said, "That stands to reason to me because when you were really young, I used to read you this series of books that were full of nursery rhymes and fairy tales. And you memorized them all when you were two and three years old." So he said, "I'm sure that's where you got the ability to know all these songs." And he was blown away that I knew all these songs. And damn if I didn't see him that night at Dub's. I'd see him in the back of the room. He watched from way back for a while. And then he'd disappear. And then a day or two later he told me he thought we were really good. He said, "This is a really good group you've got." This was like the early Seventies. So he appreciated it on some level.

Did The Sundowners have matching uniforms?

Yeah. We went to the self-service shoe store and bought Beatle boots. It was the only place you could buy Beatle boots. With Cuban heels. We all wore Beatle boots everyday. [Laughs]

To school?
All the time. And we had the peg trousers, the real tight pants. And Dennis Lee's mom made us our first set of uniforms, and they were collarless jackets, like The Beatles wore. But they were pink, with black trousers. We looked pretty sharp. Then we got ruffled shirts, because we saw The Kinks, and they had the ruffled shirts. She made us all ruffled shirts. So in those days a band had to dress alike, or you weren't really a band. It was in those days that bands dressed alike. Around 1965. And then the Stones were the first people that I remember who didn't wear uniforms. And that was kind of a uniform in itself. That was kind of their thing. But it took a while for everybody to go that way.

Was "The Sundowners" a name you invented?
It may have been. But it may have been one of the other guys. But we all liked it, and it stuck.

They were great days. It was 1965, and The Beatles were huge, and music was exploding, and we just couldn't wait to rehearse and to play.

So your lineup for The Sundowners became bass, two guitars, and drums?
Yes. And I was the lead singer. We rehearsed in my house in this little tiny room that had been a storeroom out back that my dad had built onto the house. It was really tiny. The drummer's house had just been re-carpeted, so we took all the old carpet and literally nailed it to the walls and the ceiling. We just had enough room to cram our gear in there, and then we'd stand in there and play for hours. And the cops would come daily. From complaints. They were really nice. They'd say, "You can play another hour, and then you're gonna have to knock it off." This would go on every day. [Laughs]

Now it's funny to me how many neighbors take pride in it, and say, "Oh yeah, they used to play just down the street from us." But, in truth, they'd call the cops on us.

Did you have your own mikes?
We had one. We had the Electro-Voice 664. [Laughs] That was the popular mike at the time. My first microphone [Laughs] was a speaker wired backwards, taped to a music stand. And we'd sing through this speaker. And we knew that wasn't going to work very long. And I actually mowed lawns around the neighborhood, for two dollars a lawn,

until I had enough to buy a Shure microphone on an installment plan at the music store. And that was really the first microphone we had. And we all got together and bought a little PA system. It wasn't very big or very powerful. And that became a constant thing for bands, to have a PA loud enough to get over the amps.

Then we got another mike, so we had two 664s. And, when we'd sing harmonies, two guys would sing on one mike and I'd usually sing the lead on the other.

So you learned how to sing harmonies?
Slowly. It was a little tricky because I didn't even know what harmony was. We'd just all start to sing. [Laughs] Sometimes it just sounded like shouting. So slowly we figured out that this guy sings this part, and this guy sings this. And you could never hear yourself. There were no monitors. I guess they heard it out front, but we never heard it.

Was there another singer besides you?
The other guys would try to sing the backgrounds and the harmonies. Like in "Twist And Shout"—"Shake it up baby..." Two on a mike, like The Beatles did.

We worked constantly. Every weekend. And, in the summer, more than that. Fraternity gigs and high-school dances. We would always have at least one gig per weekend, and sometimes two. Sometimes three. Gainesville had so many opportunities to play. And really a lot of bands.

There was a fraternity row where they had parties every Friday and Saturday. And they had money, and you could play there. And they had socials that you could play in the afternoon. It would be only an hour gig. So, if we were really lucky, we'd have a social in the afternoon and then we'd do the show that night and maybe a dance. You'd usually play four or five hours. We were working guys. We were either practicing or playing all the time. We were obsessed with it. *Completely*

I have never been to a prom in my life. It cost me a girlfriend at one point. Her name was Jackie Taylor. I couldn't go to the prom because I was playing another prom. So the only prom I ever saw was from the stage. I never had that kind of life. I wasn't taking part in high-school activities. I was in a band. I was never in the in-crowd at school. I always saw it as irrelevant after I started to become a professional musician at the age of fifteen. The whole social circle seemed *completely* irrelevant to me.

By the time I was sixteen, I was playing with guys that were several years older than me, and to give a shit about who was in the in-crowd at school just seemed completely useless to me. I still suffer that today, because, like my wife and her friends, they'll get out their school albums, and they'll talk about school, and I have nothing to relate to. I didn't have much of a school experience. [Laughs]

Didn't it make you somewhat of a star in school, being in these bands?
It did and it didn't. There was a certain kind of girl who went for that. And then there was a certain kind who didn't. And the ones who went for it—well, the word "groupie" wasn't around yet—but they were the more fast, heavy-mascaraed girls. [Laughs] A lot of eyeliner.

I heard you once sold corsages out in front of a prom to make money.
Once or twice I sold corsages at University of Florida football games. I'd stand outside of the stadium and sell them to guys who wanted to buy them for their girls. I also sold Cokes a few times. I went around with racks of Coca-Colas, selling them in the stands. But I only did that a few times. I never did that regularly. It wasn't something I wanted to do. And there was a lot more money in the music. [Laughs] But there was never enough money. There never seemed to be enough.

Enough for what?
For everything. For records, and things you do as a teenager.

Did you ever write songs for girls? Did you write one for Jackie?
No. I wasn't thinking that way. I was just trying to write songs, but I didn't have any kind of crush on anybody where I wanted to write something for them.

Did you hear Dylan back then?
Yeah, we heard him. But not until "Like A Rolling Stone." That's when I first heard him, when that came out as a single. And we loved that right away. We learned that, did it in the show. We learned all his singles. But I didn't have Dylan albums until *Blonde On Blonde* [1966]. I heard *Highway 61 Revisited* [1965]. A friend of mine had that. But I

actually bought *Blonde On Blonde*. That's where I really got into Bob. And I started to really dig his thing.

Did you perform songs from *Blonde On Blonde*?
Quite a few of them.

Did you hear the Byrds then?
Oh yeah. The Byrds was where you first heard of Dylan. When they had "Mr. Tambourine Man." And they did quite a few Dylan songs. So there was that awareness, and it seemed like almost at the same time that he came out with "Like A Rolling Stone." And then he was having hit singles. "I Want You" and "Rainy Day Women." "Positively 4th Street," that was another one. So it was kind of odd later on to play them with Bob. [Laughs] And we sort of played them exactly the same as we played them back in '65.

Did he influence your songwriting?
He influenced everybody's songwriting. There's no way around it.

Did it change the way you wrote? He wrote expansive songs—did you start writing long songs?
Not really long songs, but no one had ever really left the love song before. No one had lyrically left that. So, in that respect, I think he influenced *everybody*, because you suddenly realized that you could write about other things.

From The Sundowners, you joined The Epics. Did you audition to get into The Epics?
I filled in a few nights. On bass. Their bass player couldn't make a few gigs, and I filled in. Then they started campaigning to get me to join their band. And I kind of felt this loyalty to The Sundowners. And then me and The Sundowners' drummer really had a huge disagreement, didn't like each other. I left and went into The Epics. On my sixteenth birthday, I remember it. October 20, 1965. I remember because I got my first driver's license that day, and I joined The Epics.

As bass player and also lead singer?
The Epics had another guy who sang too, the rhythm guitarist. So we shared lead vocals.

At Mudcrutch Farm, 1970. *Red Slater*

Mudcrutch L-R: Tom Leadon, me, Randall Marsh, and Mike, 1970. *Red Slater*

Poster for the first Mudcrutch Farm Festival, 1970.
Red Slater

The night I met Mike Campbell, 1970.
Red Slater

Chewing my pick in Gainesville, 1970. *Red Slater*

Tired and apparently confused. Somewhere in 1977. *Richard E. Aaron/Getty*

Outside Cherokee Studios. Hollywood, 1979. *Joel Bernstein*

Mixing *Damn The Torpedoes* at Cherokee Studios, 1979. *Joel Bernstein*

Very early Heartbreakers at the Shelter Picnic. Malibu, 1975. *Steve Wilson*

Our first day in England, 1977. *Adrian Boot*

Me and Ron with our new leather pants. New York, 1977.
Steve Wilson

My first top hat. Given to me by an audience member at Knebworth, England, 1978.

My Gibson Dove guitar on which I wrote all my songs from '70 to '91. *Joel Bernstein*

Santa Monica Civic Center, 1978. *Steve Wilson*

Outside my Encino studio, 1984. *Dennis Callahan*

The Heartbreakers at Britannia Row Studios, 1979. *Joel Bernstein*

Waiting on a video set, 1981. *Dennis Callahan*

Producing Del Shannon's LP, 1981. *Dennis Callahan*

And I just kind of walked around as the kid in all this, as the kind of junior guy in the band and stared at it wide-eyed. Then they added on another guitar player, after I was in it for a year, Tom Leadon, who was Bernie's brother and he was actually a year younger than me. We got very tight, because we were the youngest guys in the band. And Tom was a good musician. Still is.

We played in that band until it became Mudcrutch. And when it became Mudcrutch, Tom and I stayed, and I think a couple of The Epics stayed, but then they quit. They decided they didn't want to take this so seriously, so they quit; they wanted to party and have a teenage life. They quit, so we put an ad down in the music store. The center for all activity in Gainesville was a place called Lipham's Music.

Did you work there?
I did work there briefly.

Don Felder, who later went on to be a member of The Eagles, worked there too?
Don Felder worked there, and so did Bernie Leadon [who went on to be a member of the Flying Burrito Brothers and The Eagles].

Did Felder show you how to play piano there?
Yeah. He would sit down with me when business was slow and show me the chords on the piano, and that's *exactly* how I learned to play it. I didn't have a piano at home, but I bought a cheap organ. I took the organ home and I would practice.

That store was kind of the hub of everything. That was where all the musicians went and hung out, and they had this great inventory of instruments and amplifiers. People would come from all over North Central Florida to go to Lipham's. You'd see the Allman Brothers in there. You'd see everybody. And their gear.

So we put an ad there for a drummer, and this guy named Randall Marsh responded to the ad, and we went out to his place. And that's where I met Mike Campbell. Mike was his roommate. And we went out there to jam.

We said to Randall, "It's a shame we don't have a rhythm guitar," and he said, "My roommate plays guitar." And Mike came in with this Japanese guitar and I said, "I have my Rickenbacker guitar with me, and you can play my Rickenbacker." And he said, "I think I'll just play this."

He kicked off "Johnny B. Goode" [written by Chuck Berry in 1958], and when the song ended, we said, "You're in the band, man." He had to be in the band. And he didn't necessarily even want to be in the band. He hadn't asked. Somehow we convinced him to stay in the band. And that became the Mudcrutch that people know. I still meet people all the time from Florida who were around there in those days. And they knew Mudcrutch. Mudcrutch got to be *very* popular in Gainesville. That band really worked.

What was the lineup of Mudcrutch then?
There were four of us, and sometimes five when Benmont [Tench] was in it. Benmont came later. He played a summer with us, but he was in school in New Orleans and had to go back to school. And we'd become a four-piece again. Until we just really talked Benmont into leaving school. And he stayed in the band a long time.

Where did the name "Mudcrutch" come from?
I don't actually remember. I just think it was the era of psychedelic names, like Chocolate Watchband and Strawberry Alarm Clock. Things that didn't make any sense. So somebody came up with it one night, and we all thought it was a funny word, and we stuck with it.

Benmont was playing organ in the band?
At first, he just had a Farfisa organ. Then he got an electric Wurlitzer piano.

Do you remember when you first met him?
Yeah. I remember when he was very young, when he was about twelve or thirteen years old. He came into Lipham's one day and sat down at an organ and played an entire Beatles album. I think it was *Sgt. Pepper*. He played the whole thing. I remember, because he did all the organ stops, and I remember him getting the harpsichord sound for "Lucy In The Sky." And it kind of drew a small crowd who just drifted over to watch him. It was *amazing*.

Did he sing too?
No, he just played it all instrumentally. He could do things like that. He can play *anything*. When we'd be really bored, we'd play "Stump Ben." Like you'd name a song and see if you could stump him if he couldn't

play it. And it was *very* rare that you could stump him and he couldn't play it. At least most of it. He's an *incredible* musician. I've never ever encountered a musician any better, and *very* few on his level. He's really an extremely good musician.

We were all on the other side of the store, and we said, "Can you believe this kid?" I remember meeting him then and being aware that there was this little kid who could play like you just can't beat. But I never saw him again until, God, about 1970, and my roommate came in the door one night with this guy, and he was all bearded and had really long hair, and a stack of records under his arm. In those days you'd bring records over to turn people on to them.

Slowly I realized it was Benmont. It was like, "You're the kid!"

And he said, "Yeah, I have a band in New Orleans and we play..."

I said, "We have a gig tomorrow night, do you want to play with us?"

He said, "All I have is my Farfisa organ."

I said, "Okay, you're in."

And he went down, and he played five sets with us with no rehearsal. And he played incredibly great. Then our mind was made up that he would be in the band. We just had to wait it out for him to finish going to school. Until we had a record contract. And once we had the record deal, I had to go to his dad, and talk his dad into letting him drop out of school and go with us.

His dad was a judge?

A judge, yeah. It was a scary moment, going into his office and sitting there talking to him about letting Benmont go with us to California. But he did. I think he was wise enough to know that he needed to let Benmont get it out of his system. He gave in. Ben wasn't even old enough to sign the record contract; they had to sign for him. So that's how Benmont came in.

You mentioned you mowed lawns in Gainesville. Did you have any other odd jobs? I heard that you were a gravedigger.

For a short spell I did it. Yeah, it came back to hair again. You couldn't get a job with long hair. Digging graves, you could. It was a city job. They were governed by rules where they couldn't tell you to cut your hair. There was very little actual gravedigging. There was mostly just mowing the grounds and that stuff. I didn't do it too long, but I did it for a while, because money was tight, and I needed to do it. I would do that, and play that night. We had a club gig at the time, I remember. I'd do my graveyard thing, and then go to the gig and play that and have to get up at seven in the morning, so I was really wasted all the time. But it didn't last long. I think I only did it long enough to get a little grub stake, a little nest egg.

I got fired, actually. I got fired. And then, when I was seventeen and out of school, I thought I would go to a bigger town and try to get into a bigger group. Got on a Greyhound bus, went to Tampa, Florida, checked into this really weird hotel, [Laughs] this really scary place. And got myself a room in this hotel, and got a job working in a barbecue restaurant. And it was such a gross job, washing these terrible trays of greasy shit. And I would sweep the floor. They fired me pretty fast from that. I couldn't handle it. So, when I got fired from that, I drifted back to Gainesville, because I never did get anything going in Tampa. I couldn't link up with anybody.

Was Jim Lenahan in Mudcrutch?

Yeah. He was the lead singer for a while. I met him in high school, and he was actually a drummer in another band called The Agents. And he had long hair, and he was one of the five or six guys in town with long hair, so you would kind of group together so that you wouldn't get your ass kicked. Because there was the real danger of rednecks beating the shit out of you. He wore an eye-patch, too, which was kind of exotic, I thought.

For effect, or did he need one?

Just for effect. [Laughs] We met in an art class in high school. He was a couple years ahead of me, but we were in the same art class together. I remember we got thrown out and had to take our desks to the sidewalk. [Laughs] And I really liked him. And he was old enough to drive, so he was my transportation for a long time. He drove me around.

And then he quit playing, and I kind of lost touch with him for a while. So when The Epics guys quit Mudcrutch and we were trying to put it back together, we thought we needed a singer. So we got Jim to join the band. And he now is our lighting guy. He's been with us ever since. He quit singing. We actually fired him at some point over some silly issue. We fired Lenahan, and that's when I really had to start singing a lot.

Were you okay with being the singer?
I always thought I wasn't that good. I always thought we should have a proper singer. My voice is such a specialized, stylized thing. Though I'm actually a much better singer now than I was then, in terms of tone and things like that. But I always felt we needed a real singer. It took years to kind of realize that I *was* the singer. I always felt like I'm the singer till we get one. [Laughs]

Did you start doing your own songs at this time?
Oh yeah. Definitely. And I have to thank Jim Lenahan. He was the first person to really encourage me to do it. Because we met up over a lonely Christmas holiday. I was living in a shack with no heat. [Laughs]

You left your parents' home?
Yeah. At seventeen. I couldn't wait to get out of there. I just lived in abject poverty.

Did you all live together in the shack, or was that your place?
No, we didn't all live together. I lived in the shack, which was really kind of a run-down duplex apartment. Randall and Mike lived in a place we called the Mudcrutch Farm, which was kind of a run-down tin-roofed house. And it sat on maybe five or six acres of land. It had once been a ranch or a farm, and had become very run-down. I lived in the apartment for a while, and then I moved back home, probably a year later. And I slept there, but I was never there. It was one of those things where I stayed at the Mudcrutch Farm, but there was no place for me to sleep there. So at night I'd usually go back to my parents' house and sleep there. But I was never really seen. I came in the night, and I'd sleep there, and there'd be nobody there when I woke up.

Were your folks okay with this lifestyle?
I guess so. I think by then I had broken the bronco. They were accepting of whatever went on. They felt that they just had to let me go my own course now. And I was paying my bills. And so I think they respected that. That I worked really hard and made some money. My

mom kept telling me that I'd better learn to do something for when this burns out. I said, "It ain't gonna." "Something to fall back on"—that was the phrase she always used. And I used to say, "We ain't gonna fall back. There ain't gonna be no falling back, you know?" [Laughs]

Did you have a car?
No. I didn't have a car, but Jim did. He had a van. And he'd come over, and we'd sit up and drink wine and talk. I'd play him songs I'd written, and he was *really* enthusiastic about it. He encouraged me to write. And I'd sort of write one just to show it to Jim. And that's when we decided he should be in the band. Because we'd sing them.

Would you show your songs to Mike?
By the time he was in the band, every rehearsal was usually original songs. We worked really hard at originals. Because we knew that there wasn't any way out unless we did. There wasn't any way to get a record contract if you were just covering the Stones.

Would you write out lead sheets [the chords and lyrics of a song notated on music paper]?
No. [Laughs] It would be like, "Here's how it goes, here are the chords." It's *still* like that. [Laughs] It's still like, "Here's how the chords go, you take it from here."

Were you still playing bass at that point?
Yeah, I still played the bass, but I bought an acoustic guitar somewhere around '69 or '70. I traded in my 6-string Rickenbacker for an acoustic Gibson Dove. Which I still have, and on which I wrote almost all my music on until about 1990. I actually wore it out.

You recorded your song "Up In Mississippi." Which is a really great-sounding track, and a good song.
We were pretty good. I mean, for the time. For really being novices. I hadn't written a *lot* of songs at that time. And, yeah, we made a little record and brought it out on a 45. It got played in Gainesville quite a bit. 'Cause we bribed our friends into calling the request line. So it actually got into the Top Ten in Gainesville. And it really helped us as far as our gigs. We started to draw more, and could charge a little more, because we had a record.

There are two solos on it. Did Mike play both of them?
No, one is Tom Leadon and one is Mike.

Did you record that live?
We overdubbed the vocal. And I think there's an acoustic guitar. So that was probably overdubbed too. That was on 8-track.

Was that fun for you to record?
Oh *God*, yes. We fell in love with it. Totally. We just fell in love with the whole idea of being in the studio and hearing it come back on those great big speakers. And it sounded so *good*. But it was all the dough we had to pay for one session. And we had a friend of ours—he owned a pepper farm. And he had a big year and made some money, so we talked him into investing it into a record. So it came out on the Pepper Records label. [Laughs] And the odd thing is, to this day, someone will come up to me with that record and want me to sign it. They're *very* rare, I guess, but there are people who have them. How they got them, I don't know. We used to take them to the stores, and say, "Hey, would you put this in your racks? And then we'll come back by, and if you sold any, you can keep the money. But just put them in your racks."

And they'd do it. They'd put it right up on the counter in a rack, with a sign that said, "Here's Gainesville's Mudcrutch." And we never sold very many, but the airplay helped us a lot.

What was that like, hearing yourself on the radio the first time?
Oh man, it was such a *gas*. *Such* a gas. They had this thing every day at 5:00, they would take requests. People would call in and vote on what the Top Ten was for that day. And then at 6:00 they would play the Top Ten. So we'd go around, and get *all* our friends, and *everybody* we knew to call the radio station at 5:00 and vote for us. So we were frequently in the Top Ten every day, because we had so many people calling. To get votes to be in the Top Ten.

Did Mudcrutch play with Lynyrd Skynyrd?
Several times. Groups were really good back then. You had to be pretty good to get a gig. There was a lot of competition. Somewhere I had a poster of that, of Lynyrd Skynyrd and Mudcrutch. Actually, Mudcrutch was on the top of the bill. Lynyrd Skynyrd were from Jacksonville. They would come to gigs when we played. People came from everywhere,

they came from Daytona Beach, and from Miami. Literally, everyone in Florida came to Gainesville to play. There were just *so* many gigs and so much opportunity to play. And then, as the Sixties started to boom, and the hippie thing happened, there were a lot of outdoor gigs, and what they called love-ins, in those days. So *everybody* came through there.

So Gainesville was a good place for you to be?

Incredibly good place. So many musicians came out of there. Two guys from Gainesville started a band out here [in LA] called The Motels. And then there were the two guys in The Eagles, Bernie and Don. Really good musicians. You *had* to be a good musician to compete. There was intense competition for shows. So we worked really hard at it. It was all we did.

Is it true that you would put on rock festivals called the Mudcrutch Farm Festivals?

Yes, that was our ace in the hole. It was one of those things you just blundered into. There was a huge field behind the shack. And someone got the idea that we could set up in the back field and put posters around, and have people come, and play. So we got this other group we knew, an R&B band called The Weston Prim Revue. And we got them to play, and we played. And *so* many people came. And there wasn't even a Porta-John. There was nothing. This shows how innocent it was.

After that happened, some cats from the college that were real promoters came out and said, "Hey, let's do another one and we'll help you with it." And then, for the next one, we had a *lot* of bands. I can't remember who they were, exactly. But I remember some came from Atlanta. And just a *massive* amount of people came. *Thousands* of people. It really upset the neighborhood. You wouldn't think of trying to do something like that with no organization today. [Laughs]

And so the cops came in, and they said, "We can't shut it down because there are thousands of people here, and there will be a lot of trouble if we shut it down." Then the people who owned the property evicted Randall and Mike. They said, "You're out of here, you can't do this." So then we figured, well, if they're throwing us out of here, we'll do one more. What can they do?

So, by the time we did three, and it really mushroomed into a big deal, that was the key to our success. We became really famous around town, and when we played a lot of people came. Before that, we used to play at Dub's. We would play there six nights a week. Five sets a night. Got a hundred bucks a piece a week.

That's where we really learned to be a band. Playing that much is really going to get you tight. But we didn't really want to do that. We wanted to get into more concert gigs where we could play original music. They didn't like original music in the clubs. So we used to say, "Here's one by Santana," and we'd play our own song. [Laughs] When that happened, I remember we could play an auditorium and draw a thousand people. Not a lot, but we did it. And we would go on around the state, and get a name for ourselves.

Then they'd have these huge things in this place called the Plaza of the Americas, an outdoor thing at the college [University of Florida], and they'd have shows there with a few thousand people out there. Though they weren't paying. So Mudcrutch developed quite a big rep, and we got to the point where we'd been around every post there was. We played everywhere you could play ten times. And we realized we were just on a merry-go-round, that we would just keep playing the same bars and the same thing and not really get anywhere.

So that's when California came into the picture. Because Bernie [Leadon] had gone to California and had a lot of success, and started The Eagles, and he would come home now and then. We'd talk to him. And then Tom Leadon, when he left the group, he got a job with Linda Ronstadt playing bass. And that was before she was really happening. But he was going on tour with Linda Ronstadt. We were really impressed, like, "Wow, you got a gig."

Then he got in some group that actually had a hit single, in some band named Silver. A completely forgettable single, but it was a *hit*. That did it. "Okay, we're going to California. That's the way it is. We're going to LA. Where the Byrds are." Because the South had become completely inundated with the Allman Brothers. The Allman Brothers had gotten big, and every group had become an imitation of that. Literally everybody but us was an imitation of the Allman Brothers. And they were playing really long songs, and jamming. And we hated it. We liked the Allman Brothers, but we hated all the imitations. We thought it was stupid. We were kind of like a three-minute kind of band. And we didn't fit in anymore. And we didn't want to be there any longer. We wanted to go to LA, where we always felt like we belonged.

Gainesville was great for you, yet you felt you had to leave. Even though you were playing for thousands of people?
We weren't always playing for thousands of people. We might play a gig for a thousand people. And then, on Monday night we might be playing for two hundred people in some beer bar somewhere. The circuit was wearing out. We had to play anywhere to make enough money to eat and pay our rent. So we were doing all kinds of gigs, like playing in country bars with Wyatt Earp ties on. [Laughs]

Then maybe the next night or the next week we were at a pop festival somewhere. And we were back to that. So we were constantly just trying to keep enough gigs to pay the rent, and keep working. But we could see it wasn't going anywhere. How big can you get in Gainesville? We had certainly hit the top of the ladder there. We were probably even then the most famous band in Gainesville. I *imagine* we were. Even then. I *still* meet people who tell me they saw Mudcrutch. That they were fans, and would regularly go out to see us. But we knew we had to break out of there.

Did you ever consider going to New York?
New York seemed really cold to us. We knew we weren't Manhattan kind of guys. And we weren't. We could kind of picture ourselves in LA. But we would have never survived being in New York.

We loved the Byrds and we loved the Beach Boys, and Buffalo Springfield and the Burrito Brothers. And we kind of felt we belonged here [in LA]. And we always have, though we're still never referred to as an "LA band." We're always referred to as a Southern band. But the truth is, every bit of music we've ever made was in LA. We've been in LA for over thirty years. We're a Los Angeles band.

But at the start, we went all around. We would play in Atlanta. Anywhere we could play.

Booking your own gigs?
Yeah. There was probably a string of manager guys that came through, that weren't really very good, but they were willing to take on the job of trying to book us. We went through all that.

Did you go to Macon, Georgia, first to try to get a record deal?
Yeah, that's where the Allman Brothers were. Capricorn Records was there. That was the closest place to go. We were told we were "too

English" for them. They were into this Southern sound. We were definitely turned down. And we didn't like the scene in Macon anyway. We hung out and got a gig there. And it was just this down-home barbecue thing. We didn't want to do that. We wanted to go in a whole different direction. So it was a good experience, because it taught us right away that this wasn't what we wanted to get caught up in. And it's probably a blessing that we didn't get signed in Macon.

Did you graduate high school?
Eventually I did. I had to go three summers extra [Laughs] for six weeks a summer. And then they graduated me. But I didn't graduate with my class. Because I missed huge amounts of school. There was one year I missed forty-two days.

Because you were playing?
Yeah. And my parents were really upset about it. There was this constant tug of war.

Benmont used to come to some of your gigs, when he wasn't in the band. And he heard a song you wrote called "Unheard Of Kind Of Hero" and was impressed that it was something you wrote.
Yeah, I remember Benmont coming and seeing us. I think we were playing in a real redneck country bar in Lake City, Florida, where we had to wear those Wyatt Earp ties. [Laughs] But we had to make a living, so we went there, and we knew enough country songs that we could play it. But they were always kind of weirded out by us because we had long hair, playing country music. And that was *completely* unheard of in those days.

I remember Ben coming there, and him sitting in a booth watching us.

He was impressed by Mike Campbell's playing. He said how it wasn't about flash, it was about fun.
Mike was really good. I'm sure he was about as good as he is now. Just really, really good. He lived to play the guitar. He played it night and day. I was talking to Bugs [Alan Weidel], our roadie, who has always been there since the early days, and I told him how I remember Mike sitting there in a field, a big yard outside of the house where he lived,

and I'd see him sitting in the grass by himself with an acoustic guitar, [Laughs] playing away to no one.

But he's still like that. He still plays all the time. He can play anything with strings. Just the other day he came into the studio with this *huge* load of instruments. He brought in a koto. And some kind of crazy Indian instrument he had. And he can actually play them. He can play anything with strings on it except a fiddle. He tried to for a while, and it was really painful hearing it. He couldn't get the bow thing down.

Did you record a demo in Benmont's father's living room?

Yes. There was a guy in town named Rick Reid who had the first mobile recording van. It had a 2-track Ampex recorder in it. He worked in a stereo store, and you could rent him for a day, and he would come over and record you. You know, he made a really good recording. It was all live to the 2-track. If you listen on the boxed set [*Playback*], there's a track called "On The Street" that Benmont wrote and I sang. And that's the actual 2-track recording. Recorded in Benmont's living room.

If you listen to it, it's *amazing* how good it sounds, and how tight we were. We were all singing background harmonies. It's completely worked out. It's really one of my favorite tracks we ever did, and it was done right there in his living room. We recorded about seven or eight original songs. And we had reel-to-reel copies made up. And that's what we took to LA when we made our first trip. We had a box of reel-to-reel tapes. The cassette hadn't come in yet.

How about your 45 of "Up In Mississippi" that you recorded in 1973?

We thought we were way ahead of that. So we didn't really present that. We thought we were much better than that. And we probably were.

Chapter Two

California

So you went to California with the intention of getting a deal?

TP: Yeah. We sent tapes out to LA from Florida. And most just got rejection after rejection. And all we knew about record companies was that, in *Rolling Stone* magazine, there were addresses of companies, so we would just send a tape to that address. And *Playboy* had a record label in those days, called Playboy Records. And we got a response from a guy named Pete Welding, who was actually a really respected writer, I found out later. He was really respected in the jazz field, and he was A&R for Playboy. He rejected us, but he was nice enough to send us a song-by-song analysis of why he was rejecting us, and what could be better, and what we should work on. So I took this to be really encouraging. And we drove out to see Pete Welding in LA.

We drove there. Me and our roadie, Keith McAllister. And Danny Roberts had a van, so we drove. Tom Leadon was already out here. He had left our group. The idea was to come out here and see him, and try to hook up with something. It was the greatest trip of my life, really. It was this incredible journey through the country. I had never been west of the Mississippi. To suddenly see cactuses, we would pull the car over and get out and say, "Shit—look at this!" We were so naïve.

We got here, and we had to sleep on the floor of a friend of a friend. And I could see that we really weren't welcome. [Laughs] And it was kind of really uncomfortable. I don't think they thought we would really come, but we did. So they let us sleep on their floor for a couple of days. In their living room.

We drove in to Hollywood. And then it seemed really easy to me, because we went down Sunset Boulevard, and in those days there were record companies *everywhere*! Everywhere you looked, there was a record company. There was MGM Records, and of course there was Capitol. I just thought, "Well, all we've got to do is go in to every one, and we'll get a deal."

And we fell in love with LA within an hour of being there. We just thought "This is *heaven*." We said, "Look—everywhere there's people making a living playing music. This is the place."

A lot of people who arrive in Hollywood expecting glamor are disappointed or confused by the reality of the place. Was it that way for you?

No. To me it seemed like everything I wanted it to be. There were literally record companies all down Sunset Boulevard. You could see them, with their names on them. There'd be A&M, MGM, RCA. You just *saw* them down the road. So we would just go in the front door of every one with a tape and say, "Hi, we just got here from Florida, can we play you this tape?" We didn't know that that just wasn't done. So I think just having the balls to do that got a lot of people to listen to us.

The only addresses we had, we'd written down from record ads in *Rolling Stone*. And I was trying to find some more, so I went into this diner, I think it was Ben Frank's on Sunset, and I went to a phone booth to look up record companies. And on the floor of the phone booth there was a piece of paper. And I picked up the paper and it's a list of twenty record companies, with their phone numbers and addresses. And at the same time, I kind of went, "Shit—there's a lot of people doing this." But I swear to God it was there. And that's how I got the number of Shelter Records. Which was out on east Hollywood Boulevard. And we drove out there with a tape.

Did that hurt your enthusiasm at all, the thought of so many others vying for a record contract?

No. We were young and the world was at our feet. At that age, anything seems possible. We'd get turned down, but I just kept thinking that there are so many of them, we're bound to hit one that's gonna take us. And that's what happened. We hit paydirt at MGM, where they wanted to do a single. The first day out. And the next day London Records. Which was a big label then. And they wanted to sign us right away.

Then Capitol Records had a great interest in us. And wanted to book demo time in their studio. We were so silly and indignant that we didn't want to do a demo, and we didn't know there was a difference between record companies. We were really green. We just felt that if they put out records, that was fine with us. We didn't know there'd be any difference between Shelter Records or Capitol Records. They all put out records nationally, or internationally. That's all we were interested in.

Yet Capitol had their big building on Vine, and was the label for The Beatles. Didn't that impress you?

Yeah, that impressed us. London Records impressed us. They had the Rolling Stones. "Any of them will do." That was how we thought then. We turned down Capitol because we didn't want to do a demo. I think we had, in the back of our mind, this idea that if we *had* to, we would come back and do a demo. But the truth is that we've got another label and they're willing to sign us, so why would we go back to Capitol and do a demo? We didn't know the difference. We didn't even know what music publishing was. We had no idea what it was. We thought it was songbooks. We didn't have any idea.

Were all of you bringing in tapes, or were you the main guy doing that?

Yeah, I was the messenger. [Laughs] We went to Playboy Records to see Pete Welding, but he no longer worked there. We walked in, and we said we'd come all this way, and they put the tape on, and the guy turned it off in thirty seconds, didn't even hear the whole song, and said, "No, we pass." I thought, "Shit. This is going to be a little trickier than I thought." He didn't even hear the song. So we just kept going to record companies and walked in. This is how different it was then. We'd just walk in and say, "Hey, we just drove here from Florida. Would you just listen to this?" And some of them did. They would say, "Oh okay. Let's hear it."

That first day MGM liked the record. And the guy said, "Well, you know, we'd like to make you a singles deal for your first single." And we went crazy.

He said, "Who is your manager?"

And we said, "We don't have no manager."

"Well, who is your lawyer?"

"Lawyer? We don't have no lawyer."

And he said, "Okay, we can fix you up with all that. Come back, and we'd really like to make a single." And I told him a single wasn't really what we wanted to do. We wanted to make an album. He said he'd be interested in cutting this one song, but he didn't know about an album.

And then we went to London Records. And there they showed some real interest. The guy said, "Yeah, I'm really interested in signing you." That was the *first* day we were here. I remember calling Mike that night and saying, "Hey, we got a record deal, you ain't going to believe it." And I don't think he could believe it. He said, "Are you kidding?"

We stayed for a few more days, and on the last day we were here, we went by Shelter Records, and gave the tape to this girl named Andrea Starr, who became a lifelong friend of mine. She opened the door, and she thought we were cute, she told me later. She took the tape to Simon Miller Mundy, who was their A&R guy. We went home [to Florida] and sold everything we owned, and got ready to come to California. And literally, in a rehearsal, the phone rang and I answered it, and it was Denny Cordell. I thought he was calling about a car we had for sale. And it was him, and he said, "I really want to sign your group. I think you guys are really great. I think you guys are like the next Rolling Stones." I was like, "What is this?"

But we knew who Denny Cordell was. We knew he had done "A Whiter Shade Of Pale" and the Joe Cocker stuff. We knew that he was a real guy we were talking to on the phone. But I had to say, "Well, I'm really sorry, but we already promised London Records we would sign with them." And he said, "I'll tell you what. If you're going to drive out here, I've got a studio in Tulsa, Oklahoma. And that's going to be not far out of your way. Why don't you stop in Tulsa and meet with me, and then you can see if you like us."

Leon Russell had a place in Tulsa, and Shelter was built around Leon. And there was a whole scene of Tulsa musicians there—there was J.J. Cale and Carl Radle. Jim Keltner. Lots of really great musicians. So we stopped in Tulsa, and we met Cordell in the middle of this windstorm on the street. He took us to a little café and talked to us, and then he took us over to the studio they built in a church. It was called the Church Studio. It was a really nice studio. He said, "So spend the night, and tomorrow we'll go in and do a session. And we'll see how you like it." And we were like, "Wow, we get to do a session in a studio! Hell, yeah, we'll spend the night."

We spent the night, and we spent the next day recording, and he went, "That's it. I'm sold. I want to sign your band." And we liked him a lot, much better than the guy at London, who was an executive type. We liked Denny a lot, so we said, "Okay, we'll go with you."

What songs did you cut?

There was one he particularly liked called "Making Some Noise." Not the one that came out later on *Into The Great Wide Open*, but a different song with the same title that was about going to a rooster fight. And he really liked the idea of a rooster fight.

And he signed us. And we were really short of dough. So he said, "Okay," and gave us a wad of cash, and told us to drive to his office in LA, to the Shelter office. We literally drove off the freeway to the Shelter office and walked in. And said, "We're here." [Laughs] But we were broke. They gave us some money and put us in this place called the Hollywood Premiere Motel, that was really a hooker place on Hollywood Boulevard, east of Western Avenue, *way* down there. Their offices were also down there.

We went to Shelter the next day, and that became our hangout, the Shelter Records office. It was in a house on Hollywood Boulevard. They had this big office there. We would just hang out there every day.

This is how different it was then: They got us two houses in the Valley. And moved us in. Nice houses with swimming pools. In Canoga Park. We didn't know. We thought this was normal. We didn't even know what the Valley *was*. We just went where we were told. There were two houses, because there was quite a few of us. We brought all the girls and dogs and everything. This was heavy shit, man. A house with a swimming pool. *Wow*, you know? No furniture. No beds, nothing. We had lawn chairs for furniture. [Laughs] And we found some mattresses to sleep on. But this was heavy shit. I remember thinking, "I'm living in a house with a swimming pool."

Did you mind being so far away from Hollywood?

Well, I didn't know it was far away! [Laughs] I didn't know. I did think it was a quite a long drive to Hollywood. But I was really just finding my way around LA. I didn't really understand it, that you only use a certain part of it. We were still driving all over it for anything.

In those years we quit playing live. There were a couple of years there when live playing stopped altogether. Because there was nowhere to play. There was the Whisky and the Starwood. But if you didn't have a record out, you couldn't play there. So we didn't play live. There weren't all these little clubs like there are now. That didn't happen until the middle Seventies. And I think we had a lot to do with that, and people like Elvis Costello, and when the New Wave thing broke, then a lot of clubs started happening. But there was only a handful when we got here in '74. And the ones that were worth playing, you had to have an album or record of some sort. So our focus went completely to making a record. So that just stopped till we had made records.

How long did you live in the Valley?
For a while. I moved to a little guesthouse in Burbank. Literally a two-room guesthouse with a bathroom. It was me and my first wife. We moved there, and then I went from there to Leon Russell's house in Encino. I was put there to watch the house when he was on the road. So I went from this two-room place into this big mansion. That's how I met Leon. I would just look after the house when he was on tour. Not a bad gig, really.

Did you meet your former wife, Jane, in LA or Florida?
I met Jane in Florida. I think I first met her when she was dating Tom Leadon, and came to a gig. And we got married the year I came out here. It was '74. We got married about a week before we came out here [to California].

Soon after we moved to Los Angeles, I was told she was pregnant. So my first kid was born nine months later, Adria. I think some people think we got married because Jane was pregnant, but that wasn't the case. We didn't know she was pregnant. And we were married for a long time, and had another kid in '82, Kim. And it was a tough thing to hold together, really, because I was gone so much of the time. I toured all the time. In those days, I was a really, really busy guy.

Being on the road all the time, was it tough being away from your daughters?
I was so young, I didn't know really how to do that. I just improvised as I went along. And I'm lucky, because I came out with these fabulous kids. They were just the best kids, always upbeat and really good, and bright, and just the best kids. So that was a help. I was gone quite a bit of the time, but I tried to be the best dad I could be. But it's tough, man. Pulling off a marriage and being in a rock and roll band, especially one that is successful, is tough. I think I had come from a really dysfunctional family, and deep down, I really wanted a family. I think Mike was the same way. We both never really had that as kids. Mike came from a broken home. He also married that same year, I think, and has been with the same girl to this day. I think that was what I was looking for—some stability, somebody who was home.

After staying at Leon's house, I went from that back almost to the street. I went to the Travelodge Hotel, living in one room. And by then I'd had a kid, a baby. I actually used to put Adria in a drawer. I'd pull out a drawer and she slept in it. And then I was so busted that Adria and Jane went back to Florida, for a while, and I was out here on my own. And moved into the Winona, which was really just a hooker stop on Hollywood Boulevard. It was across the street from Shelter, so I lived there for a while.

How come they left and went back to Florida?
There was no dough. I couldn't afford a family. Now I had a kid. And I didn't have the money. I didn't want to live in that situation. In a motel. You didn't even know if you were going to eat. So they went back and stayed with Jane's family for a while. Not for really long, and I just kind of worked on my own out here. And then I got a little more money, so I rented an apartment that was not far from Leon's house. In Encino. So I got to know Encino pretty well, because Leon lived there. And so I just based myself there so I could go to Leon's to work. I rented a small apartment, and didn't have much money or anything. But life seemed good. I wasn't complaining.

Did Leon hire you to write lyrics?
Yeah. I was signed to his publishing company. He had heard a song of mine, and wanted me to just be on call to write with him whenever he

wanted to write. He was living this kind of life where he recorded a lot every day at his own studio. And I'm really grateful to him, because he did give me a shot at *seeing* a lot. A lot of people working. I met a lot of people. Some of them very famous people. And I got to see them all work. I don't think I ever *wrote* much there. I don't think we sat down very often to work. We did sometimes. But it never really came out. It never really came to fruition. I might sit and write lyrics for an hour, but it never really seemed to happen.

I always felt more like I was watching the house. [Laughs]

How long did that period last?
A year. Or close to a year.

Did you like Leon?
Yeah. He actually came and picked me up from this little motel in Hollywood where I was staying.

The Winona?
Yeah. Another whorehouse motel. He picked me up in a Rolls-Royce. I had never been in a Rolls-Royce. And that went on for a while. Leon was making a record with all different producers for every track. And I met all these guys. I met Brian Wilson, and went to his house. And Terry Melcher. And George Harrison and Ringo.

You met George and Ringo? How did that strike you?
Oh man, I'm just this shit-kicker from Gainesville and I'm sitting in a room with The Beatles, you know? George was really nice to me, as he would be. He gave me a *Dark Horse* T-shirt. So there was a lot of mind-blowing shit going on at that time.

You must have eventually bought a car?
Yeah, I got a car when I got a record deal. We all got cars. We got $10,000 between us. I got two grand, and I spent about $1,800 on an Opal GT, that was really old, but it got me around. Mike bought a Karmann Ghia. It was the first cars we ever had, so we were really quite pleased with ourselves. [Laughs]

So Shelter eventually took Mudcrutch over to Village Recorder, and we started to try to make a record. That's when we realized we didn't know anything about recording. We knew how to play live, but we didn't know anything about recording. It didn't come back the way we thought it would. And [Cordell] was very patient with us. He'd have us practice, and then he'd bring us back. All that we cut which was very good was the single that came out. "Depot Street" and "Wild Eyes." And those were pretty good tracks.

But before they even came out, he sent us back to Tulsa. He said, "I'm gonna send you to Tulsa, and just leave you in the studio for two weeks with the engineer there and let you figure out the process that you need to learn about." So we went to Tulsa. We stayed there for weeks with an engineer. And there we started to learn how to make a record.

Did you like that idea of going back to Tulsa?
Not really. I didn't want to go to Tulsa much, but I was into the idea of being in a studio every day. Which we were. And he would come check on us. Look in on us. See what kind of progress we were making. And he liked the progress we were making.

When you went to Tulsa, did you teach yourself how to record?
There was an engineer. The house engineer. He taught us a lot about how to mike things up. How to make this sound or that one. We got to overdub a lot. And there's an *art* to overdubbing your voice. It's a bit like being an actor. You have to keep yourself in that moment. And re-create it.

So it was just trial and error, doing it a lot, learning about it. I'm really grateful to Cordell for giving us that time. Because most groups don't have it. They're just dumped in the studio. They get six weeks and that's what happened. But we were kind of trained; [Laughs] we got the chance to learn and spend a lot of time recording with no bill, no recording costs. It was really nice.

So being sent back to Tulsa was a good thing for you?
Yeah, it was great. The record company owned the studio, so they weren't billing us. And it was another adventure, going to another town and living there.

After your two-week stint in Tulsa, did you master the art of recording?
"Master" is a little heavy. We got *better* at it. It was a long process. You're always learning more about recording. I wish in those days we knew everything we know now. Because now we're pretty proficient at it. Recording is not difficult at all. We know our way around the studio really well.

But in the beginning it was tough?
Yeah. You had to learn how to get this sound, from this side of the glass to that one. [Laughs] People don't understand that they are different arts, playing live or making a record. It was a little bit of a challenge. Actually, it was a *big* challenge. But we loved it. I was just completely mesmerized by it; how it went down. And when you did pull something off, it was such a rush, that it would inspire you to go through a lot more shit to get another one. But there have been times when it was really *hard* to get a track, and get it to sound right.

How did the sound come back? What was the problem?
You learn that when you're recording you have to kind of trick the microphones into making the noise you want them to make. And if you're playing through a big amplifier, like you would play live, it sometimes tends to shut the microphone down. A lot of the art of recording is learning how to use the space in the arrangement, where you *don't* play. Where live, you tend to play more than you would on a record. You need to leave space for the music to breathe and find its dynamic.

It was things like that, like learning that you don't *necessarily* have to play as much here. Or how do we arrange this to make this really *pop* and present itself? Because playing live is a different art form. It's a different kind of thing. And we were really good at that, but we knew very little about how to make it come back over the speakers like we wanted it to.

How long did you stay in Tulsa?
Probably two weeks. It wasn't a long time. We were still Mudcrutch at this time. The Heartbreakers didn't happen till the next year, after Mudcrutch had broken up. Mudcrutch became disillusioned; we made an album, but it never came out.

A whole album of your songs?
Some were Benmont's. We made a record, but we weren't completely happy about it. And the idea back then is that you put out a single first. And if the single got some action, they brought the album out. And the single didn't do anything.

The single was "Depot Street" [released in 1975 with "Wild Eyes" as the B-side]?
Yeah. And we became very disillusioned. And then I could see it wasn't going anywhere. And I was frustrated. And I just went, "I'm quitting," you know? I went to Mike, and said, "If I quit, will you stick with me?" And he said, "Yeah," and I quit. [Laughs]

With the intention of forming a new band with Mike?
Yeah. I didn't really know. But I knew that Cordell wanted me to make records. And I wanted Mike to stay with me. And I think that was the idea: I was going to be a solo artist.

Did you like that idea?
No, because I'd always been in a band. I'd always been part of a group. We had supported each other. I'm still like that. I still think of everything we've done as a band. I didn't want to be alone with hired hands. I wanted to be part of an outfit that stayed together. So I was never comfortable with the idea [of being a solo artist]. It didn't last long. A few sessions were done, but I didn't like the idea. Even though they were great musicians. Jim Gordon on drums, Al Kooper playing the organ. And Mike was playing guitar. That was kind of cool. But I wanted a band more like the Rolling Stones or the Byrds. I wanted to have a set lineup that we worked with all the time. And I'd never been in a solo situation; I'd always been in a band. So I didn't understand the other way. And I'm *glad* I didn't. I'm glad I didn't go through all of this alone. I'm glad I had my friends with me.

Was that a tough decision to make? Did you give serious thought to being a solo artist?
I did, yeah. When that started, and when Mudcrutch broke up, I felt like, "Damn, I put all this energy and all those years into Mudcrutch and the band broke up and I had nothing to show for it. Nobody knows who I am." [Laughs] I think Denny Cordell urged me to be a solo act.

And it was okay—I mean, I only did a few sessions, and I did them with really great musicians and it was okay, but it didn't feel like what I was used to.

And then I walked in the Village Recorder one day and The Heartbreakers were playing. Benmont had put them all together. [The lineup was Benmont Tench on keys, Ron Blair on bass, Stan Lynch on drums, Randall Marsh also on drums, and Jeff Jourard on guitar.]

And it *instantly* hit me that, *man*, you know this is home. "This is where I should be." And I quickly did my pitch about talking them into going in with me. [Laughs] Well, my pitch was, "I've got a record deal, and so you know you could go all the way around the search for record labels, just come with me." And they all knew me and I think that they quickly decided to go in with me.

Benmont had stayed on playing in some soul band. He'd hustled his way into some time at the Village Recorder, and he was going to make a demo of his own stuff. He put The Heartbreakers together—all Gainesville guys. Stan had come out from Gainesville, and Ron Blair and Randall Marsh. I can't remember all of them, but The Heartbreakers were there. The ones I was interested in were the four: Ben, Mike, Stan, and Ron. And Ben invited me to play harmonica. [Laughs] I was out here [in Malibu], right across the street in Denny's house. Strangely enough. And he called me, and said they were in Santa Monica, and would I like to stop by and play harmonica? Yeah.

So I drove over there and I went in to do my harmonica track, and I went in and heard The Heartbreakers playing. And I thought, "Shit—this is amazing."

So I went to Denny, and told him I had this really good band of guys from Gainesville. And he said, "Okay, well, bring them in. We'll see what goes."

We kind of creeped them in. On the first session we did, Stan [Lynch] didn't play. Jim Gordon played drums. We did "Strangered In The Night," which is on the first album. And then we kind of moved Stanley in. [Laughs] And when Cordell heard the band, he kind of liked the whole idea, and we were all pretty good-looking kids, and they knew they could market us that way. And that's what happened. And we've been together ever since.

You were recording your solo album with great musicians; it must have sounded good.

Yep. There's a bit of it on the boxed set, which gives you an idea. "Louisiana Rain" was done back then with a slightly different lyric. It sounded great, but I was really band-oriented. I'd always been in a group and I was more interested in the idea of putting five people together and *keeping* them together and seeing what that would create. That seemed more interesting to me than just calling the best musicians in and doing the track, and then having a pickup band that you put together for each project. Which a lot of people do, but it seemed to me a much more creative endeavor to have five distinct personalities and work within that kind of framework. Good or bad.

You are always going to have weak links or things that you can't do as well as if you called Jim Keltner to play the drums. But you get another kind of magic that way, when the people are really close and you are working as a unit.

Cordell didn't think it was solid enough?

We just weren't mature, we were just kids [Laughs] and he was used to working with these incredible guys. We were just kids, and we played like kids. There would be the odd times like "Hometown Blues" where we had Duck Dunn play the bass. So [Cordell] was always trying to get us to really listen to those great rhythm sections like Duck Dunn and Al Jackson, Charlie Watts and Bill Wyman, you know, these *really* great rhythm sections.

We would do listening sessions a lot with Cordell. The session might start with an hour of listening to records. He'd say, "Listen to his, listen to that, listen how they're playing and listen how they're accenting this." So in that way we kind of learned. Hopefully. [Laughs]

You had Ron Blair on bass. Did you like him as a bass player?

Yeah, I did, for a long time. He was quite good on the bass. Even today he is still like that. He practices and really learns the song well. Ron was great until he got sort of disenchanted with what was going on and just withdrew, really. I mean it got *much* too big for Ron at that time. [Laughs] It was really more of a life commitment than he wanted to make.

And you had Stan Lynch on drums.
Oh yeah. [Laughs]

What were your first impressions of Stan?
Stan. Now there's a book in itself.

He came from another group that was sort of a second tier, a little younger than us, called Road Turkey, which had Jeff Jourard's brother Marty Jourard, who would later join The Motels. It was Marty Jourard and Stan who were in a band together called Road Turkey, and they were on the bill with Mudcrutch a lot, a lot of gigs. I remember doing a whole summer off and on at this one place called the Keg [in Gainesville], where we were both on the bill and we both did two sets a night. And that's where I got to know Stan.

Stan was a little bit younger than us. But he was a very good drummer and he was really conscientious, and he worked *really* hard. But he had a really explosive personality and he could get *really* pissed off. I always thought that Stan was passionate in all directions. [Laughs] He could be really sweet and really loving and then the *biggest* sort of *asshole*. But he did it all one hundred percent passionately.

You liked his drumming.
Yeah, I loved his drumming onstage more than I did in the studio. He was really a *powerhouse* onstage. Sometimes I still miss him onstage. He was *so* powerful. I used to say he had this fifth gear that he could go into and just really make everything explode. He was really good at that, and he always knew the songs really well. And he really wanted to be good. He was a big cheerleader. His personality was a *huge* part of The Heartbreakers. There was *me* and there was *Stan*. And those were the two main personalities. The other guys kind of just tried to manage both of us. But he had a huge thrust in what was going on.

In the studio it could be quite difficult with Stan, because he wasn't really a studio drummer, and he didn't like the idea of sometimes being cut back to just playing time and so, just like kids do, we had our arguments in the studio and we'd work really hard and sometimes I think we worked harder than we *had* to to get a rhythm track because Stan would just be really difficult. But like I say, we were *kids*. We weren't these super-professional guys like we are now. [Laughs] We were going through growing up at the same time.

Was Stan's playing too busy in the studio?
Sometimes it was too busy.

But was he solid in terms of keeping the beat?
Yeah, it's really hard to be a studio drummer. It's *really*, really hard. Recording is the hardest on the drummer. It's different than playing live, because it's so microscopic. If there's a squeak on your bass pedal, it comes through really loud. It's very intricate, and so it's really hard on them. And they've gotta keep the time and the feel, and if they drop that at all, *boom*, the whole thing goes.

But we made a *sound* that was quite unique to us. When I look back at it, I don't think I'd have changed anything, because it made a sound that was us. You know, like "The Waiting," no one could have played that but Stan. No one could have played a lot of those things. They wouldn't have been like that. So he had his own style of playing, and we butted heads a lot for twenty years. [Laughs] But I think we sort of loved each other too, like brothers. But we fought a lot. *Everyone* fought with Stan, really.

Over the material?
Over *anything*. Over what we were eating. [Laughs] Stan was as big as life and very confused about a lot of things. He could be really passionate in two directions. You just didn't know really where you were with Stan. His personality was *huge* and he has to be responsible for a *lot* of what happened because he was such a cheerleader. Nobody wanted to do anything bad because you'd be judged by Stan. You wanted to pull off every gig.

He and I had *incredibly* good communication onstage; he could read the movement of my shoulder. He could go *anywhere* I wanted to go. He never took his eyes off me. This is something I still go through with [Steve] Ferrone [current drummer in The Heartbreakers]. Stan *never* took his eyes off me. *Anything* I did was accented on the drums. Any movement I made. We had a great eye communication where I could turn around and look at him, and he knew just exactly what I wanted to do.

So Ferrone, who is a whole different kind of drummer, he's learning now that in a show you never take your eyes off me because things might change. So, yeah, Stan was really good. It was a lot of work making the records, but then again I don't think any of us were as good at making records as we are now. The craft side of things is not very hard now. We know how to make a record. It's still hard to come up with the material, but making the record isn't very difficult now.

So Stan was much better onstage as a live drummer?
Oh, *absolutely*. Absolutely. He's very powerful. He reminded me sort of like Keith Moon in a way. He had that kind of power on the stage. He was *very* powerful. *Very* powerful. And he sang, as well. He sang harmony. He was like our main harmony singer in those days before Howie. Yeah, before Howie came along Stan was really the only other person that sang much, and he sang a lot of the harmony.

I've said a lot about Stan. But I want to make it clear that I wasn't always an easy person to deal with. I could be very, very demanding of people. Onstage, offstage, in the studio with people. I was pretty turbulent, looking back at it. I was a pretty turbulent person. I don't think I was an asshole. But I think I was intense. *Very* intense. So I don't think it was always somebody else's fault. I'll take the blame as much as anyone else [Laughs] for what went on. But I was very intense, very serious about this. We were going to do it. We were going to make something *great*. And sometimes that requires a lot of intensity. I think it was just born into me. I'm *incredibly* changed. I think I'm a much changed person from those days. I think I'm a lot mellower.

Was that a gradual process?
Well, I think it comes with age. You get a little wiser. Maybe I've gotten a little better at my craft. I know I'm not nearly as turbulent as I used to be. [Laughs]

My kids have this huge laugh about me. I just spent some time with them, and they were laughing about my image. They said, "The world pictures you as this laid-back, laconic kind of person, and actually you're the most intense, neurotic person we've ever met." [Laughs] And that's kind of true. You're not always what people picture you as. Like "laid-back." I'm not a laid-back person.

Did Stan bring in Ron Blair?
We all knew each other from Gainesville, but I think Benmont was the catalyst that put everybody in that place at once.

Jeff Jourard was on guitar?
Very briefly. He was also from Gainesville. But we decided really early on that we had too many guitars. [Laughs]

So The Heartbreakers came together while you lived at Leon's house? Probably.
I *think* I had a leg in both camps for a little while. But once The Heartbreakers got going, I was with them. The thing at Leon's just kind of burned itself out. It got to where there was really nothing for me to do anymore. His album was done, and he was going back on the road. Once that project was done, there was nothing for me to do anymore. So I was gone.

Back to the motel?
[Laughs] Back to the motel, literally. [Laughs]

Did they have the name "The Heartbreakers" already?
No. I think Cordell had the name. But I'm not sure. I don't think it came from me. Things like that just didn't seem significant at the time. [Laughs] I wanted the name to be "the King Bees." And they didn't like "the King Bees." I thought it sounded good. And I always liked that Slim Harpo song. I'm not sure where "The Heartbreakers" came from. Mike thinks it came from Cordell. I think when "The Heartbreakers" came in, we liked it much more than "King Bees," or some of us did, and that's what flew.

Was it always Tom Petty & The Heartbreakers?
It was going to be "Tom Petty," because I didn't want to go through the Mudcrutch thing again. Did all this work, and no one even knows who I am. But at least I want to get my name in the billing so people would know who I am. I was right upfront with them about it. I said, "Look, I'm not doing this unless my name is in the billing. This is the way it goes. It's my record deal." And they thought that was fair.

Roger McGuinn told me that was a really smart thing. He said, "I should have done that with the Byrds." He said, "It would have made a big difference in my career if I would have been 'Roger McGuinn & the Byrds'." Though I think it was cooler just being "the Byrds." But it was for those reasons. And they all knew that, too. And that was kind of understood that I was the singer and the writer.

I understand that Cordell taught you a lot about music.
Yeah. Every day at 6:00 I went to the Shelter offices. Work ended there at 6:00. And there he would get out his records, and teach me musical history. We would play records way into the night. Every night. All kinds of music. Everything from Lloyd Price to Bo Diddley. Because I didn't have a lot of records. I couldn't afford them. I didn't even have a record player; he got me one. And he turned me on to a lot of records and lent me his records. That went on for a couple of years. We would meet at 6:00 every day. And, a lot of time on Sunday, I would come out here to [his house in] Malibu and spend Sunday with him as well. And we would do the same thing—play records all day.

Quite an education for you.
It really was. He was quite a man. He was really something else. An English gentleman, but with sort of a pirate side to him. [Laughs] And he *really* knew his music. He *really* knew it well. He did a lot to shape my whole personality, I think.

It's true that he took you to art shows, and told you to think about art in relation to music?
Yeah. Pretty far out. I remember taking a break from the studio to go to an art show. I couldn't put it together. I wanted to go back and record. And he said, "No, there's a connection here. Just take this in." He was a very cryptic guy. He spoke very cryptically. Made you work a little bit to understand what he was saying. [Laughs] I think he really shaped the whole personality of the group. He had to have a huge influence on us. So we owe him a great deal.

Chapter Three

Anything That's Rock And Roll

For the first albums, *Tom Petty And The Heartbreakers* [1976] and *You're Gonna Get It!* [1978], were you writing with Mike Campbell or did that happen later?

TP: That happened later. Mike was always making his backing tracks and playing with tape recorders. I think it was Cordell who suggested [Mike and I] try to do something together. And that took off sort of slow. There was one track on the first album that we wrote together, called "Rockin' Around (With You)." That came from a little riff that Mike had, and then I wrote the rest of the song myself. But he was the inspiration for it. And then maybe he had one or two on the next album. But where he really blossomed was *Damn The Torpedoes*, when he came in with those incredible songs. "Refugee." "Here Comes My Girl." That was when it really blossomed.

Did Benmont want to continue writing?

Yeah, he did. He just couldn't come up with anything that seemed to fit. He's a good writer. He's come up with a lot of songs for other people. But we haven't ever really written much together.

Was the first album difficult to create?

It was, in that it took a long time to find the right ten songs to make the record. There was a lot of trial and error. But that record didn't seem as difficult to make as *Damn The Torpedoes*, which was a *really, really* hard record to make. I think the first two we made, we didn't think that much.

And those first two were produced by Denny.
Those were more about feel, and they were made in the Shelter studio, which was a real funky studio. Then we moved to Sound City, when we started to work with Jimmy Iovine. And that was a whole different world. There we set out to do something *big*. We wanted to do something nobody else had ever done. [Laughs]

The first album had some great songs on it—it has "American Girl" and "Breakdown."
It's funny, isn't it, how those songs have endured all these years. It's the last thing I would have ever dreamed.

In those days, when we did that record, there weren't that many rock and roll stars over thirty. You didn't think it was going to go on that long. My dream was that maybe I could learn to be a record producer. And, when this burns out, I could produce records. That is really what I thought I would end up doing: Being a record producer, or a songwriter.

I never thought our trip was going to go on so long. I thought if it went on five years, in those days, that was really successful. We never thought about growing old doing it. That those songs have survived, and that I still hear them, is *amazing*. I *never* would have dreamed that. That was beyond my control. [Laughs]

On your first album you have "Hometown Blues."
Yeah, that was recorded at Leon's place in Encino, as I was housesitting for him. I wrote that song, and I started recording it on my own there. I think I got Randall Marsh, Mudcrutch's drummer, to give me a backbeat to start the track, and I might have played a cymbal or two on it. You can imagine how that was: We were in this huge mansion in Encino with this big recording studio in it. And we were kind of using used tape and just trying to create something.

Did you know how to engineer?
Not very well. [Laughs] But somehow I got that track going, and I got the drums down. And then the track laid around until The Heartbreakers arrived. Mike and I played guitars on it. And one night we were at Sound City Studios working, and Denny ran into Duck Dunn and Steve Cropper. And he said to them, "Hey, come in here and listen to this." And he put that track on. And they *loved* the track. So Duck sat down,

and got his bass out to do the bass part, and Cropper kind of guided him through it with these weird code things, like, "Turn! Walk!" And Duck put the bass part in and kind of made the whole thing come together. And we became friends forever right then. Yeah, [Dunn] is one of my great idols. He's one of the best musicians I've ever met. And I loved Booker T. and all that stuff. So that's how that one was done.

After the first album was released, you started to tour?
Yeah. We went to England. Because the first album became a hit right away in England. It took a year here for it to catch on. Which seemed like a long time for us, but now it's not that unusual.

But then we thought we were a failure. We thought we had failed in America because it's not catching on. It caught on in a few cities. San Francisco and Boston. And it took a long time for it to seep out. But immediately it hit in England big. So we went to England, where we were actually met off the plane by the press, and we were rock and roll stars. It was a *huge* rush. We were just overwhelmed. We were on tour, and the girls were going crazy, and we were in England, the home of our heroes.

And then suddenly we're back in America, and we weren't on that level at all.

In England, you had a hit with the song "Anything That's Rock'N'Roll"?
Yeah. We did *Top Of The Pops*. It was great. We actually went over there as a support group for Nils Lofgren. And wound up staying through that tour, and then we did a headline tour before we came back. So we stayed for quite a while in England. And then when we came back here, because we were getting on the cover of *Melody Maker* and the weekly music things there. I think in some way that probably drifted back here, that we had that buzz in England. And then we had San Francisco and Boston, which were really hot for us.

Before England, Al Kooper had a solo record, and he gave us the gig of opening up for him on a tour of clubs. So we went to Florida, and played a couple of bars there on our own. And then we went to South Carolina, and opened for Kiss—and that was weird. And then we picked up the Al Kooper tour and went to six or seven cities. In the middle of winter. It was really kind of a not well-attended tour.

Our fourth gig was in Boston, at a place called Paul's Mall, and there was only about nine or ten people at the bar. WBCN, the radio station, *recorded* it. They broadcast it live. So a bootleg record was made. And it's really good. I hear it now, and it's really good. And the funny thing is that it's just this really burning track, and when it's finished you just hear [Claps hands slowly] a few hands clapping. [Laughs] But when I heard it not long ago, I thought, "*Shit,* we were good. It's no wonder people started to notice, because we were really good."

Before we did that tour, because it was so expensive here to rehearse, we all moved to Florida. And we got two apartments in Florida, and we all lived in those apartments. And we rented a warehouse. We'd go out there and practice every night. We did that for about a month before we started the Al Kooper tour. So we were tight by the time we went on the tour.

But that was before England. And then we went over to England, and that happened. And then our record started playing [in LA] on KROQ. We were an alternative band. The New Wave was being invented. So they started to play "American Girl" on KROQ. And we got this gig at the Whisky-A-Go-Go. We used to play the Whisky-A-Go-Go fairly regularly. And that's where things really went bang. Robert Hilburn [author, former music critic for the *Los Angeles Times*] was coming down, reviewing the shows at the Whisky and giving us great reviews. And then things really started to go. We got some more tours. Roger McGuinn gave us a tour. He recorded "American Girl" right away. And he put us on the road with him, and we went out and did a college tour. And we played the Bottom Line in New York. So things started to roll then. And they never slowed down again.

It was the time of the New Wave, but you didn't conform to the style of the New Wave in any way.

I think we kind of invented the New Wave. [Laughs] Punk had caught on right when we were in England. In '77. That's really right when it happened. The Sex Pistols and all that stuff. I remember meeting the Sex Pistols and them coming to the shows. And Elvis Costello. But we weren't that. There was a lot of confusion. We were labeled a "punk group" for some time. It was a little bit of a problem, because they'd seen me with the Pistols. It's funny how tame that stuff sounds now when you hear it. Because at the time it seemed so radical.

We liked old music. We were into Carl Perkins. [Laughs]

And when you came back to LA, there were bands that started to imitate you.
Yeah. That was a real eye-opener. Seeing people do an imitation of you was really strange. But that was going on.

It took a full year here for your first album to catch on?
Yeah. It came out in late '76, and then in '77 "Breakdown" was the first one to hit the Top Forty. And the record started to sell. It was amazing. We were so busy in those days. God, we were busy. Touring. We did a lot of photo sessions in those days. 'Cause there was no MTV or anything, so it was all about being in the music magazines. So we were incredibly busy. Always on the run, is how I remember it, anyway. Just keeping an amazingly full schedule. [Laughs]

Did you enjoy that?
Yeah, I loved it. I ate it up. You get tired, but when you're that young, you bounce back pretty fast. So it was great. We were always up all night.

When it came time to record your second album, *You're Gonna Get It!*, in '78, you wanted to do something different. You didn't want to repeat the feel of your first album?
We certainly wanted the success. But we wanted to branch out a little. We didn't like groups who did things over and over. So we wanted to try to do something a little different. But that record was made *so* fast, that second record. And the truth was we didn't really need to bring out a record. I don't know why we felt this urge. I think we were just bored with playing the same songs, because the first record was still doing real well when the second one came out. But we felt this urge to get another record out, and we went in and did that record really fast, and wrote it really fast. And *probably* should have taken more time with it, looking back.

It came out really well.
Yeah, it did, for what it was. I think it's only twenty-eight minutes long. [Laughs] It was just the first ten things written. And we did it at lightning speed.

And you could do that with Denny?
By that time, Denny was pretty much leaving us on our own with this guy named Noah Shark, who was kind of the co-producer/engineer guy. [Denny] brought him in and would leave us with him, and maybe two times a week we would get Cordell there, and he would sit down and say, "Okay, here's what we've got to do with this; here's what we've got to do with that." And then he would leave us on our own to work. It wasn't that he wasn't there. He was. But I kind of remember that record being more on our own. With Cordell taking kind of a supervisor position. 'Cause he also ran a record company. He was really busy. And that's how Jimmy Iovine came in for the third record. Denny just didn't have the time.

Did you write the songs for it fast?
I had written "Listen To Her Heart" and "I Need To Know" before we went in to do the album. So I had those two, which we had been playing in the show, so we knew them really well. The rest of it was written pretty quickly, because we didn't really take a long time. I think by the time we had ten songs, we quit. There were no outtakes. There wasn't anything left over. Oh yeah, there was one song left over. It was called "Parade Of Loons." But it was so distorted, it wasn't recorded well, so I didn't want to put that out.

Intriguing title.
It wasn't a bad song. It was kind of about all the loons that were appearing. We suddenly had all sorts of people around us from all different backgrounds with all different motives.

A lot of loons.
Lot of loons, yeah. But it didn't make the cut.

How did you choose the song "You're Gonna Get It" as the title song?
Noah Shark, the producer, sat me down one night and almost beat me into it. [Laughs]

Did you resist?
I did. Cordell wanted to call the album "Terminal Romance," which I thought was a better title. We also had a better cover. A much better

cover taken by Annie Leibowitz. And Noah Shark, who, for some reason, had some power over us at that time, hated the cover and hated the title. And he sat me down one night and just finally convinced me that he was right. So we wound up using that really gloomy cover. But Annie's cover was much better. And probably "Terminal Romance" was a better title. But Annie was kind of all over the map at the time, too. I wish we would have gone the other way with it.

Your song "Restless" has a hip drum-bass groove to it.
That's about all it has. [Laughs] I think that's about it for that song. I think at that point we were driving our way through to finish the album. Bugs said he never wanted to hear it again. It was one of those that I sang all night. It wasn't a great song. I'm sure if we would have waited another day, we could have come up with something better.

Is your roadie/guitar tech, Bugs, in on all the sessions?
Yeah. Every one we've ever done. He's got to get the gear there. He's got to get the amps and the guitars. He started on the first album, and he's been on everything I've ever done, including the Wilburys. He's always been there to get the gear together and to look after me, and to get us dinner, or whatever goes on. So he has a kind of keen perspective on things.

And he lets you know what he feels about your songs.
Oh yeah. And he's also driven me everywhere I've ever gone. He still drives me wherever I go. So we spend a lot of time in the car talking, just him and I. So he's a roadie, but he's also very keen. *All* our crew guys are really big music fans. We like to have people around us who really like music. And they're all very honest. They don't go for jive stuff. They're very pure. [Laughs] Maybe more than me. And that was one song ["Restless"] I remember him saying, "If I never hear that one again, that would be okay with me." [Laughs]

I love him very much. He's very much one of our brothers. He's looked after us for thirty years now. He won't ever give an interview. He's never spoken two words to the press. That would be beneath him. It would be against his code. He knows where all the bodies are buried, though. He probably knows the whole story better than anybody. Including me. [Laughs] Because he's heard everybody's perspective on it.

Chapter Four

Tangles And Torpedoes

You stopped working with Denny Cordell. Was part of your impetus for the switch the fact that Denny wanted a big cut of everything you were earning, and you didn't feel it was fair?
TP: It was his one flaw. Business. He was from that old school from the Sixties in which the artist didn't really get a lot of money. [Laughs] I got fed up with it when I started realizing we had been ripped off. That our publishing has been ripped off, and we were still on the royalty rate from Mudcrutch. Which was about a penny a record. It was nothing.

By then there were businesspeople—managers—coming around and telling me, "Hey, you've got a bad deal here. You've got a hit record and you should be renegotiating the deal." And he wouldn't renegotiate the deal. It was too much by *Damn The Torpedoes*. The second album had gone gold, and we knew that we were perched to have a big record. We were right there where if we made the right record, it was going to be a big record. And this caused a huge court battle. Which is a whole other book. [Laughs] But that was when we decided that it was worth fighting Denny in court and getting onto another record label that could do more for us.

Was it tough fighting this guy who helped launch your career?
It was really tough. But the weird thing is that we remained friends. He remained very friendly to me, but in the court, when it came down to that, he was just a *tiger*. [Laughs] I had to fight like hell to get free.

When did you connect with your current manager, Tony Dimitriades of East End Management?
Tony was there at the release of the first album.

How did you meet him?

We could not a find a person in all of LA that wanted to manage us. And we had made our first record, and we had no manager and nobody that wanted to do it. But there was a guy, an Englishman, a friend of Cordell's, who managed Joe Cocker. And his name was Reggie Locke. Who we owe a great deal to, because Reggie, bless his heart, was just a terrible businessman, but a *really* passionate kind of manager. He *loved* the group and he *loved* the music and he had a *lot* of enthusiasm. And Reggie came and said, "*I'll* manage these guys." And Reggie *really* was a great cheerleader. "Everyone's a winner," he used to say.

So Reggie owned up and said, "Listen, I'm no good with business and money. I'm not good at it, but I have a friend from England who is a former lawyer"—solicitor they call it—"Tony Dimitriades. And I think that I should be partners with him because he is quite good at tour financing and he understands the money end of it better than I do and I'm not responsible enough to watch the money."

So enter Tony Dimitriades. The first album had just been made and Tony showed up and Tony really liked the group. Tony had managed a group called Ace that had this single, [Sings] "How long has this been going on?" Paul Carrack sang it. And Tony, that was his sole music business experience, he had been the manager of Ace and that was falling apart. And so he came into our camp, and it wasn't very long until we realized Reggie's great and he got us there. We were breaking in England and everything. But he's really shaky on the money. I can't remember if he left before we went to England or after. I think it was before. I think we went on this kind of really *dire* tour, that's right. Yeah, we went on tour with Al Kooper. It was the first tour we did and we wound up in Baltimore or somewhere like that in a motel with no money. And we didn't even have enough money to get to the next gig. We were *out* of money. And we phoned Tony, and he said, "Well, Reggie spent the money." [Laughs] "And I've got to say, I've got to bow out because I don't want to be party to this, because Reggie's just too loose with the money." Reggie spent all the money and so Tony pulled some sort of deal where he got some money off the record company and we had enough money to just finish the tour. But that was the end of Reggie as far as being a manager. But we still like him. And whenever we see him we're real glad to see him and he understood. He had a lot to do with getting us off the ground and he really built up our confidence a lot. He was really a passionate Englishman, loved his rock and roll, and he really believed in us.

And Tony has been with you ever since.
Yeah.

Did Tony's associate Mary Klauzer come on the scene yet?
No. She came along in 1978. Tony had a couple assistants that we'd hated. And he was still doing business out of his bedroom in his apartment building. We didn't have an office. We just worked out of Tony's bedroom.

Where did he live?
Hollywood. In this apartment complex. Mary came along, and she told me this later, that her first job was to give me a ride home from somewhere. And [Tony] said, "Listen, if he doesn't say anything, or he's mean to you, don't let it get to you because he doesn't like anybody." [Laughs] And that was her first instruction. And I liked her a lot instantly. We got along great on the ride home. And she's been there ever since. And she's taken care of every single one of us. Everything in our lives, she takes care of and always has. She probably doesn't get enough credit but she is the home fire. She takes care of our lives, right down to any time we leave the house or go out or do *anything*, Mary is right there setting up the whole thing making sure everything runs smooth. Dealing with everybody. She's a wonderful person. And really gets along with people and has probably smoothed over a lot of things for me because I was quite a turbulent person in those days, [Laughs] in the early days.

Were you?
Yeah. I had a huge temper and I'd get really pissed off, and I was really passionate, too. And I think she was kind of a balance to that. She could bring me back to earth, or explain to whoever I'd offended that I didn't really mean it. And she's just remarkable. I mean, even to this day, if we're leaving the house to go somewhere a fax will appear with a map and who's going to be there and where you go. She's really meticulous that way.

And then Jimmy Iovine came in [as producer], and the rest is history. He had done some work with John Lennon, engineering. There was an album out by John called *Walls And Bridges*, and Jimmy played a role in that, and I liked that record. And then Cordell really found Jimmy. He suggested him. Jimmy hadn't really produced anything except that Patti Smith track ["Because The Night" written by Bruce Springsteen]. And he had engineered Bruce's *Born To Run*. So I thought, really, I was hiring him as an engineer. And he showed up with his own engineer, Shelly Yakus. Which I hadn't planned on.

Were you intending to produce the next record yourself?
I thought Denny was going to produce it. And Jimmy would be kind of the liaison between Denny and us. But it turned out that Jimmy and I produced it together, and we became fast friends. We got very close, doing that. We were two ambitious kids trying to pull it off. And we did. But it was a lot of blood, sweat, and tears.

Was it Jimmy who initiated the practice of doing countless takes and spending hours to get a drum sound?
Oh yeah. We had never thought about that before. He wanted to do a much more sophisticated kind of recording. On that album we came up with that big drum sound. That I think, after that, was really imitated everywhere. I think that record changed drum sounds for a long time.

They got bigger in the mix.
Yeah, bigger and bigger and bigger. And it's not my favorite sound, those huge drums. 'Cause when you have the drums that big, it's really hard to fit things around them. To fit the guitars and stuff around them was really tricky. But that was Jimmy's vision, to create this drum sound. He'd be changing the drumheads dozens of times. [Laughs] I remember taking a *day* to get a snare drum sound. That, to us, was just *outrageous*. Took a whole day to get a drum sound. It was really boring and hard to understand. But we got there.

You said that both you and Stan were turbulent. On the recording of *Damn The Torpedoes* [1979], was there a lot of turbulence?
I remember that when Jimmy Iovine came into the picture around 1978, when we started to make *Damn The Torpedoes*, he was *really* tough on Stan. *Really* tough. They did *not* get along. And Stan was one of those people that would kick up a lot of smoke to keep you from looking at

him. [Laughs] Like, if he was the problem, he would just kick up a big fuss where you'd get confused and look all around, but you wouldn't really zero in on him.

I don't really want to *knock* Stanley. Because it all went great. We all wound up in great positions in life. And I don't think it would have happened exactly the same way without him. I really liked him, for some reason [Laughs] or another. We were good friends. So I don't want to knock him. But he was certainly the most difficult Heartbreaker and I think he would admit that, too.

I think he had a lot of insecurity in a lot of ways. It probably goes back to Gainesville. When Stanley and I first met, he was still in high school. And I think we were a few years older than him so he kind of looked up to us in some ways. And to him it was quite a big deal to be playing with us, even back in Gainesville. He saw us as the top band and so I think he had a little bit of insecurity, which is true of most people that are difficult [Laughs] or hard to deal with. You usually find that they are a little insecure about something.

So I think that might have been his problem, but like I say, we were *boys.* [Laughs] We weren't men. We were boys and we were going through a really *wild* life experience.

The result, after all that work, was *Damn The Torpedoes*, which was an immense hit. It had so many great songs—"Refugee," "Don't Do Me Like That," "Even The Losers," "Here Comes My Girl." Did you write some of these in the studio?

Oddly enough, the songs were all written. I think I only wrote one song during the recording. And that was "You Tell Me" on the second side. There are only nine songs on the record. I had written "Refugee," "Here Comes My Girl," and most of "Even The Losers." "Don't Do Me Like That" was the first hit off that record. That was a Mudcrutch song that we worked on way back when he sent us to Tulsa. We cut it down. "Louisiana Rain" was another one that was cut for my solo project. Jimmy went back to the tapes at Shelter, and went through everything I had ever done, and he found those songs. And wanted to recut those. So they were written.

"Century City" was written during the record, certainly. Because that was where I went for the lawyers and the lawsuits. So that was written then. So, with that record, things were never the same. Things became very mega at that point. [Laughs] Very large.

In a good way? Was it positive?
Yeah, it was positive. As usual we were just running like wild men day and night. The big difference now is that a lot of money was coming in. We started being affluent young men. [Laughs] But even that didn't really dawn on me. It didn't seem that real or that significant, for some reason. It was great to have all the attention and the huge crowds coming in. *That* we really loved. I remember, in those days, not really knowing the difference between, say, $8,000 and $80,000. Eight thousand dollars sounded like so much to me that I'd forget a zero. And I could see accountants being a little shocked, and saying, "No, man, no, we mean $80,000." So money was coming in, and was just being put in the bank. One day I looked up and I had a lot of money. But my life didn't change on a day-to-day basis because we were just living in hotel rooms and touring all the time. As a matter of fact, as the story goes, we were doubling up in hotel rooms. We stayed two to a room. There'd be me and Ron, Mike and Stan, and Ben and the road manager. We'd all double up in three different rooms.

Then we got a new road manager around late '78. And this guy got his own room. And so that left Ben with a single room. So we devised a rotating thing where every few days somebody got the single room. Then one night we were in Miami, and we were going down the hall, and the road manager put the key in his door, and was going in his room. And I said, "How come you get your own room?"

He said, "Because I demand it."

And I said, "Hell, what if *I* demanded a single room?"

He said, "You want a single room?"

"Yeah. We all do."

He said, "Okay, let's all have single rooms." And from that point on, we all got our own rooms. It was just that nobody from the office or anywhere had bothered to tell us we could afford them. They were just waiting for us to discover that. And so that's kind of the way we started to learn that we had a little more money than we *used* to have, things like that. But nobody was gonna tell us. We just had to stumble onto it.

How did your father respond to your success?
He had this real left-handed way of complimenting you. [Laughs] Right before he died he said to me, "You know, you've done really well. You've done really well with your life. Because I've got to say, I never would have dreamed you could have made a dollar doing what you're doing. [Laughs] I never dreamed that you could do it. But you did it, and I'm really proud of you."

That must have been great to hear, after all those years.
My father really liked the idea of us getting wealthy when we were young. And then he became a *huge* Heartbreakers fan. Wore a Heartbreakers jacket, and went to every gig in Florida. And had an endless amount of people—fans who would turn up at the door—he'd bring anybody in the house. And some of them just stayed for weeks. I thought it was kind of creepy.

But he *really* stepped into the role of Tom Petty's dad in a big way. And he gave interviews. It pissed me off. Because I'd see him, and instead of, "Hey, how've you been, how are you?" it'd be like, "Hey, can you sign these things for me?" and "Will you do this?" and "Will you do that?" and "Will you speak to this fan for me?"

But he'd never say, "Oh, by the way, how are you?" It took him *years* to kind of come back around to "How are you?" 'Cause that became his identity. Tom Petty's dad. So it was funny to me to see him embrace that in such a big way when he'd been such an asshole about it. [Laughs] So he was quite an interesting guy. [Laughs] Very unusual.

When did he die?
Nineteen nineteen-seven.

So he saw the fullness of your success.
Yeah. I bought him Cadillacs and [Laughs] he really dug that.

And a truck?
Yeah, I gave him a truck. I would have bought him a house. But he wanted to stay there where he knew all his neighbors. So I had the house remodeled for him. Updated. And virtually anything he wanted, I took care of him. Though some people around me, they said, "Why do you do this?"

How did your mom respond to your success?

She wasn't like [my father]. She was always concerned about me. And, in the late Seventies, she worried that the girls were going to hurt me. [Laughs] There were girls diving on me and stuff. She saw a gig and I guess chicks were coming over the stage everywhere we went. Especially in Gainesville, we were just followed by crowds of kids, and even their house was completely covered in kids. And film crews. And people from the TV station. It was *impossible* to go to the house, really, in Gainesville. I usually set up another place to meet with my parents. They lived in a little four-room house. And the media and the kids, when they knew I was coming, they would descend on the house. So we'd usually meet somewhere else. It was kind of cute—she'd be worried they were going to hurt me. [Laughs]

One night I got really torn up onstage. I got pulled into the crowd in Winterland [Ballroom], up in San Francisco [December 1978]. And I guess they put it into one of the music magazines, a picture of me being mobbed by the crowd, and being torn up. That's one of my memories. What happened that night is that the crowd was very close to the stage, all on their feet. And I was walking the edge of the stage. As I leaned forward, somebody got me around the legs. And I fell into the crowd. It was really like falling into a lake of people. I went down, down, down, toward the floor. But I never hit the floor, I just landed on people. And then people were coming over the top of me. And they were literally grabbing me everywhere. There was a bandana around my neck, and they somehow stretched that almost to my belly. When I came out I noticed that. My shirt was ripped open. The vest I had on was ripped off from the back. And I really thought I was gonna die, because there was no air. And I couldn't even see; everything went dark. And then suddenly I see a little hole above me. And in that hole I could see Bugs, looking down from the stage. And he literally did a dive, like you were diving into a pool, a hands-first dive, and came down the hole of people, and landed on top of me. And kind of grabbed me around the shoulders. And then there were a few seconds there where we looked at each other, and both of us thought we were goners. Like we're gonna die right here in the middle of this mob. And what happened is that more and more security people started jumping in, and they made kind of a human chain, and pulled us up. And we made it to the top. And when I got to the top, I was really stunned. My lips were broken and bleeding.

I was really bruised up and pretty shaken. Ever since then, I've been a little nervous about getting near the edge of the stage. I've seen these bands that dive onto the people and get passed around. Well, my crowd just tears you to bits. It's a funny thing; it still stays in my mind. There were bodies stacked on top of us maybe six feet deep. And it's a hard thing to get any air and to get up through that. Bugs and I looked into each other's eyes. And he was looking at me like, "I'm gonna take care of you." But I did see that flash between both of us that we might die here. And it's like one minute you're doing a rock and roll show, and the next minute you're in fear for your life. I think that's the only time that's ever happened to me. But it really did something in my head and has always stuck in the back of my mind.

There was a picture of it somebody took from the stage down. It was printed in a magazine, and my mom saw the photo and was really disturbed about it. That what I was doing wasn't safe and that I wasn't being protected. So that was probably one of the things that made her nervous that I wasn't safe.

But she was also very proud of my success. I sent her gold records and stuff with her name on them. She put them all on the wall.

She and your dad stayed together?

Yeah, but she died in '81. She had seen us have this huge success and everything, and I always felt that she knew that I was okay. She just cared about me. She didn't really care about the "Tom Petty." She stayed the same. She cared about me. And it's one of my great regrets, and it's really sad, that I could have done so much for her. And she died. It was devastating. But, had she lived, I think I could have given her a really great life.

You once said that nothing is sweeter than having a hit record.

[Laughs] It was really rewarding. It felt great. All that work wasn't in vain. Things were just happening at such a pace. And everywhere you looked, there was a huge payoff for doing the work and for working so hard. And it really was a payoff for those first three years. Of everything we had done. It was *all* this building and momentum. Then, when it got to that point, it all paid off at once. But I'll tell you, the years before that, I remember them very fondly. Like being a cult group and being not quite so big. I remember that very fondly. It was a real comfortable time, although we were driven to be more successful. We didn't have the weight of being a big business. We were just young and happy to be doing what we were doing. I remember that as being a really nice time.

With *Damn The Torpedoes*, by the time we got to the next record, things were a lot more serious, and then there was this huge pressure to do it again. That was something we had never faced. Things changed then.

How was it to hear your songs on the radio?

It was *killer*. In those days, in LA, there were three or four rock and roll stations. Playing *new* rock and roll music. Imagine that. [Laughs] I remember sitting in my den, and I had this big dial on my tuner, and I could really just spin that dial and go across the stations, and hear us *all* over the place. Sometimes I could hear the same song playing at the same time on different stations. And being a radio nut like I was, it was like, "*God, this is amazing!*" I remember Mike calling and saying, "Hey, turn on your radio," and "Now go to this station!" Because we were being played all at once on every station. It was ridiculously saturated. I don't know if it was everywhere, but it was here. [Laughs]

A lot of songwriters, when they have that kind of immense success, aren't able to deal with the pressure to follow it up.

I can see why. It's really intimidating. Because you never thought about it until then, and then it's like, "Oh shit, I have to do it again. What if I can't do it?"

How did you deal with that?

It was a lot of pressure. I worked really hard, is what I did. We got to a point where I said, "Okay, we're not going to tour now. I'm going to bear down really hard and try to write some songs." I think a lot of people don't do that. The lure of the money is so big. But I was at least smart enough to know that wasn't going to go away. That's going to be there. So what we have to do is stop the touring, and work really hard on the songs. And we'll get the songs good enough. And everything else will fall into place.

Did your management and record company agree with that?

The funny thing is, when that kind of success comes, *everybody* agrees with *whatever* you want to do, all the time. [Laughs] Suddenly people treated us differently.

It's like the old saying goes: You don't change, but *everything* around you does. Everybody does. But you don't. You're still the same person. But everybody treats you differently. And they've changed. Their perception of you has changed. So there's not much that you want to do that everybody doesn't go along with.

But at least Tony [Dimitriades] remained objective, and he never became a yes man. He knew that would be to no one's best interest. The trick to living your life from this point is being able to tell yourself how much is too much. 'Cause, from now on, you're on your own, brother.

Chapter Five
Changing Horses

You were on Shelter Records and then you switched over to MCA/Backstreet. Why did that switch occur?
TP: That switch occurred because, when our first two albums came out, Shelter was distributed by ABC Records. And then suddenly, with no word to us, our contract was sold to MCA Records, when they changed distributors back to MCA. So this stunned us a little bit, and frightened us, that we were just gonna be handed around to people we didn't know, and didn't have any relationship to. Plus we really had a bad record deal. We were on the same deal that Mudcrutch had. It was really a terrible deal. And we felt that we'd had a little bit of good luck with the first two records, and we deserved a better deal. They didn't see it that way, of course, so I had to dig my heels in and refuse to work if they wouldn't make me a better deal.

They also owned all my publishing, which I didn't think was fair either because when the deal was made, I didn't even know what publishing was. So a fast one had been pulled on me, and I wanted it made right. But it turned into a standoff there, and it was only solved when a guy named Danny Bramson came on the scene. He was involved with MCA. He had been working the Universal Amphitheater, which they owned. And he had turned it into quite a profitable venture. He had the ear of the top guys at MCA. And Danny's solution was to ask them if he could form his own label there at MCA. They made me a new deal. And I would stay at MCA, but under the banner of Backstreet Records, where I would have complete creative control. My publishing would be returned to me. And I could pretty much operate without having to report to anyone besides Danny Bramson. So this pretty much solved the problem; even though I remained at MCA, I felt better about it because I was with a guy I knew and trusted, and he gave me complete creative freedom. That probably took five or six months of digging my heels in, kind of a Mexican standoff. We even did a tour that we called "Why MCA." [Laughs] Because they *sued* me, and it went on for a while. But in the end it worked out. It's nothing I don't think that most groups go through. When they start to sell a few records, they usually go in and try to get a better deal.

And so *Damn The Torpedoes*, our next album, was released on Backstreet Records.

Even with the new deal, in 1981 MCA wanted to raise the price of your fourth album, *Hard Promises*, to $9.98 and you wanted to keep it at $8.98. Was that a struggle for you?

That was quite a struggle. That caused me quite a lot of pain. Because I didn't have a line of artists backing me up. It seems to me today that, maybe if they listened to me then, things wouldn't have been as bad as they became. I could see then that you can't price this music out of the reach of the common person. That's who your audience is. I really didn't want it hung on me.

How it started is that I knew this was going to happen, that [MCA] was going to raise their prices across the board. But the way they were going to do it was with me first. Because they knew that I had a really anticipated record and they were going to lay it on *me* to be the first $9.98 album. And I said, "Oh, no you don't. You're not laying that on me." So that's when I stood up and said, publicly, "I'm not going to do it. I'm not going to allow it to be done."

And the strange thing is, I not only got away with it somehow, but it really did hold prices down for years. Which I was really proud of. It was years before they could really do it, before they could get away with it.

Mick Jagger told me, at the time, that it held down the price of *their* record. They were going to do it to them, and then I came out on the cover of the *Rolling Stone* [March 19, 1981] tearing a dollar in half. And he said they actually threw that down on the table in a meeting. And they said, "No way we can do it. No way we can bring the price up."

I was proud that I pulled it off, but what I was not happy with was that I had just been through all that legal trouble with *Damn The*

Torpedoes, and I found myself right back in a record company conflict. I think it wore on me pretty bad that time.

At that same time, autumn of 1981, you suffered from tonsillitis, and had to have your tonsils taken out.

That was no fun, either. I was on the road with tonsillitis, and I had to cancel gigs and sit in the hotel room, trying to get better. Because nobody understood that it was a *chronic* tonsillitis. They kept thinking I'd get better. I'd go onstage and not be able to really sing very well. And that really affected me mentally for *years*. It just *terrified* me, the idea of going onstage and not being able to sing. I still deal with it, to some degree. It traumatized me. And so, yeah, I was actually put in the hospital and had my tonsils removed in the midst of a tour.

And that, with the price thing, is when I *really* realized that being famous can be hard. It's one thing to read about something somebody's doing in the press, or something they're going through, but when it's you, it's like "*Shit*," you know, [Laughs] "it's really *me*, and I'm going through this. It's not some newspaper story, it's my *life*. It's becoming sensationalized and being used to sell magazines." So it wore on me quite a bit. I think I came out of that not wanting much controversy in my life at all. I just didn't want it. I was really tired. All I wanted was to put out my record.

Yet the songwriter in you was never stifled. Despite the legal problems and the health problems, you continued to write great songs.

It's always been my sanctuary. I could always withdraw into that music. I think that goes back to my childhood. I withdrew into music. I went into that world. And it was this nice, safe, wonderful world. And so, I think it shaped my personality for life, that I can always go into that. It's like slipping on a suit of clothes. You can go into that world of writing, and it's soothing and rewarding at the same time.

I think *Hard Promises* is when this became a job, as well. It became a job, it had to be done. [Laughs] Which is the first time that it really hit me that way. That this *has* to be done, and it *has* to be good, and it *has* to be successful. Which really ain't the way to go about it. So it wasn't as much fun, that record, as the one before it.

Which was *Damn The Torpedoes*, which wasn't much fun itself.
Well, it was *hard*, but we were still having fun. But, by *Hard Promises*, it had become *real* serious. And we were taking it very seriously. But I just withdrew into the writing. And I spent a long time alone. It's a lonely job, you know? [Laughs] And I kind of made myself work on a schedule. Get up every day, have some lunch, go into the music room, and stay there sometimes till midnight. Just working and working and working. But it worked, and it paid off.

You wrote great songs.
I was lucky.

You got lucky.
I got lucky.

In July 1981, your duet with Stevie Nicks on "Stop Draggin' My Heart Around" was released. Which a lot of people assumed you crafted to be a hit single for the two of you.
The song *wasn't* crafted for Stevie. If you hear the original on the boxed set, all they did was take that track and overdub Stevie onto it.

Which is surprising because it seems like she is singing the melody, but she is really singing harmony and you are singing the melody, right?
Yes, on the choruses I am. They put her in singing the verses. But in the choruses I'm really singing the melody and she is singing harmony.

Stevie came to me around '78. And she was this absolutely stoned-gone *huge* fan. And it was her mission in life that I should write her a song. And we were a little wary of Stevie. We didn't quite know whether to like Stevie or not, because we kind of saw this big corporate rock band, Fleetwood Mac, which was wrong—they were actually artistic people. But in those days, nobody trusted that sort of thing and we just kept thinking, "What does she want from us?" And then, of course, she turned into one of my great, great friends forever. But Stevie was really adamant about me writing her a song.

And so I think that, around late '78, she approached me about producing her first solo record. Now Stevie, there's a Cecil B. DeMille movie. This is a person that's larger than life in a hundred ways. And I *loved* her voice. I thought she sang great. And I said okay and I went down to the session to produce a record for her. I went down and I did one track and it was a completely different world from anything I had seen. Dealing with girls was a *whole* different thing and Stevie was in a whole different place than we were.

Emotionally?
[Laughs] Every kind of way. She was very sweet and we *liked* her. But she had just a whole different kind of work ethic than we had, and there were a *lot* of people, a lot of hangers-on. The whole Elvis kind of theme of a *big* entourage. We'd never been a very big fan of that. And so after a track I went, "Look I can't do this. I don't have the time. I'm too busy and I don't think that I'm going to be a big help to you. But I know a guy who might be good for you named Jimmy Iovine." And so, as time went by, and we hung out a bit, we got to know her more and more, she would come over to my house and just hang out and play records or whatever. And we'd sing a bit. We used to sit around and play the guitar and sing.

Sing harmony?
Yeah, just anything.

She's a great harmony singer.
She's *incredible*. We could make a pretty good sound, singing with the acoustic guitar. And so finally I wrote her this song called "Insider" and I brought it down and Jimmy just flipped over the song. He thought it was *incredible*. Really great, and I really liked it. I was really proud of it.

Had you ever written a song for someone else?
No.

Did you write it with her voice in mind?
Yeah. And I *loved* it. I thought it was one of my best songs to that point and I cut it there, just me and my guitar. And then Stevie sang it with me. And then we put the band on after. And by the time the track was coming to fruition with the band and everything, I was getting a little depressed about giving away this song. [Laughs]

And I understand that you felt your single of "A Woman In Love" would have done better if not for the duet with Stevie?
I'm sure of it. 'Cause they came out roughly the same time, and Stevie's record was huge. And so it was an awkward position for us because it was billed as "Stevie Nicks with Tom Petty & The Heartbreakers" and a lot of the radio programmers didn't want to have two Tom Petty & The Heartbreakers songs around the same period. Especially while one was getting this *extreme* amount of airplay. So it was a little awkward for us.

When exactly did Ron Blair leave the band?
It was between *Hard Promises* [1981] and *Long After Dark* [1982]. After the tour of *Hard Promises*. It was quite a long tour. I think that's when he started to drift. I remember him saying, "This is bigger than I wanted to get into. This is more than I signed on for." [Laughs] And now he's right back in it.

He was very sincere. He quit the music business *completely*. Something had popped, and he didn't play music at all. Maybe it was the traveling. Or maybe he wasn't happy in the band, I don't know. He got married, and he bought a bikini store on Ventura Boulevard, and he just sat in the store and watched girls try on bikinis. [Laughs] And I don't know how well that went, because he later divorced. And I don't know what he really did. But I'd see him from time to time, because he stayed friendly with Mike. And he'd drop by rehearsals occasionally.

Howie Epstein, who replaced Ron, was playing bass with Del Shannon of "Runaway" fame. How did you first hear Howie?
Del Shannon told me about him. When I was producing Del's album [*Drop Down And Get Me*, on which The Heartbreakers played] after *Hard Promises*, we didn't have a bass player. That we could count on, anyway. And Del Shannon told me, "I've got this kid who is really good on the bass. He's a good singer, too. I think we should have him down."

I said, "Fine."

And then in walked Howie. And I really remember vividly him coming into the room. Because he had a kind of striking appearance. He had Cuban-heel boots and a big pompadour, and a big gold earring. And he played the bass really well on the track. And then what *really* caught my interest was when he sang. He did some backgrounds with Del. And I went, "This is it." The guy had a really good high harmony voice. And that was my dream for The Heartbreakers. I felt if anything was needed, we needed somebody who could sing those tenor parts.

So I basically just stole him. I went to a rehearsal of Del's, where they were playing live. They were playing in Phoenix, Arizona. And [Del] wanted me to sit in with the band. So I went down and saw the rehearsal. And then I was really knocked out with [Howie] because I saw him go through the whole set. And it was stunning, the way he sang. So I tried to get to know him a little bit. He was not an easy person to get to know. 'Cause he was kind of quiet and shy. So I hung out with him, and then went to Phoenix and played with him there. And it was in Phoenix where I cornered him in this hotel.

And I said, "How would you like to join The Heartbreakers?"

He said, "I'd really like that, because I'm really a fan of The Heartbreakers. I've actually bought your records, and I really like the group. And I wasn't intending to do this forever—to play with Del Shannon. Yeah, I would really like to join."

So I had to go back and tell the band about him. And I think they weren't sure of him at first, because he was more of a guitarist who had picked up the bass for a gig. But he was a really good bass player. But I was more interested in his singing. I knew that he could cover the bass. But he had this voice that was really great, and it really blended with mine in a particular way.

These little movies come into your mind. I remember somewhere we were changing planes, and we were walking through an airport, and here comes the Del Shannon band walking the other way. And Howie was there. And we all started to talk. And I said to him, "You're coming in, right?"

And he said, "Yeah, I'm coming in."

Del called me one night really angry. And he said, "Listen, you can't take Howie." And I felt bad. He said, "Listen, you can't take Howie. He's my right-hand guy. I've got a tour lined up, and you can get anybody that you want, and you just can't take Howie."

And I said, "Del, I love you. I'm taking Howie." And that's the way that went.

Did Del ever forgive you?

Eventually. Yeah, he forgave me, and we were friends the rest of his life. But I don't think he was too happy with me there for a while.

Actually, I saw quite a bit of him in the last year of his life. One night, George [Harrison] and Jeff [Lynne] and I went down and sang on a track he was doing. And he would come around from time to time. Jeff and I wrote a song for him, and Jeff was producing it. We made a deal—I started a little label called Gone Gator Records and the first release was gonna be Del Shannon's record. And Mike was producing the rest of the album—Jeff was doing the single and Mike was doing the rest of the album.

And I remember we were on the road. We were going through the night on buses. I had been sleeping, and we pulled into some town like Akron, Ohio, or Toledo, and we got off the bus and I remember standing in the cold out there, and Mike came up to me and said, "I've been trying to radio your bus. Del's dead. Del shot himself. He's dead. I heard it on the radio."

I said, "No, that's a rumor, it can't be true." And I went into my room and put on CNN, and sure enough he had shot himself and he was dead. And that really took the shimmer off of making a record. I did put the record out, but I didn't feel good about it anymore. And I still don't understand why he would kill himself at that point, but I guess there was a lot more to his life than I was seeing. He was a very talented man, and I knew him for many years, and I still miss him. [Shannon passed away on February 8, 1990.]

But, as far as taking Howie, I think he forgave that.

The Heartbreakers have always been such a close-knit group. When Howie came into the band, did the band accept him?

The band embraced him. He was very cool. One thing that really impressed me about him was that he had no interest *at all* in fame. *None.* He gave very few interviews in his life. The press were always in his face then. He didn't want to talk. He didn't want any part of that. He wanted to be a musician. And I really liked that about him. And God he could sing. He had that *beautiful* voice. I still miss it to this day. And it really expanded our harmony singing. We could do *so* much more, having Stan and Howie. And then later on we had Scott Thurston and Howie. Man, it was great. We could really sing. We could do a lot of singing. That's what I always hoped we could do. Howie was a real natural. He sang right on pitch, and he sang with a lot of tone. And could really stay with me; he could really capture my phrasing. He was just great. He really covered the bases well. I miss him to this day. I miss his voice so much. He was my singing partner. He was my guy I sang with. I miss his voice so much. He was *so* reliable. And his blend was always going to be perfect, and his pitch was always great. He could sound just like me. Exactly like me. There's a track called "Something In The Air" in which we are singing double lead; we're singing unison together.

And you really can't tell that it's not me double-tracked. But we actually just sang it at the same time.

And the great thing was his tastes were very similar to ours, and his background. He had started as a teenager in bands. And he liked the Byrds and The Beatles and all that. He knew it all really well. So it was really cool, because something we *hadn't* counted on is he really had the same tastes as us.

But he fit in very well. Howie was never on anybody's side in the politics of the band. He never took Stan's side or my side. He was neutral. And that's kind of the way he was. *Very, very* sweet. Just a big-hearted guy. Very nice guy.

I understand that he didn't have much ego in the studio, that if somebody else came up with a good bass part, it didn't bother him.

He didn't say it. I think he could understand it. Nobody likes it much, being left off. But I don't think it bothered him, because he was usually on the record. Even if he didn't play the bass, he was going to sing. The Heartbreakers are pretty good about that: If I've got a good guitar solo, Michael will say, "Yeah, you play it." Or if one of us has a good keyboard part, Ben will say, "Yeah, well, you're doing it good. You go ahead and do it."

When you made *Hard Promises* in 1981, you said you wanted to make something new, and move ahead in your music. Did Jimmy agree with this approach?

I think Jimmy thought we were playing it a little loose, that we should be sticking more to what we *had* done. But he also had the sense to go, "Well, I'm here to get the best of what they have to offer. And I'm just gonna let them lead and I'm just gonna try to get it down on tape the best that I can." I think there might have been a conversation or two, in which he said that "It's not really a rock and roll album as much as

Torpedoes was. Maybe you ought to stick to your guns more." But I think he went along with it. But I always had the feeling, I don't know if it was ever voiced, but I always had the feeling he thought we were being a little bit frivolous. But I was trying to get somewhere else. He understood it. It wasn't a big conflict. He was on board.

Smoking pot had a big influence on The Beatles; it changed their songwriting and their recording. Did it have an influence on you and The Heartbreakers?
[Laughs] Probably not. There was certainly plenty of pot around. I don't think all The Heartbreakers were pot smokers. I've never been a drinker; it just never worked for me. So pot kind of appealed to me, because I could get into another space, and it was kind of groovy. But today I don't like it, because the pot is much too strong. They've evolved pot to where it's almost like acid. [Laughs] Whereas in the studio we used to smoke a joint, now we wouldn't dream of it because it would just stop the session dead. But there were times when we could smoke pot and be inspired. Or get into that space where it was fun to write.

Did it affect your writing?
I don't think drugs really make anything any better. They're *probably* more detrimental than helpful. But I'm sure there were times when it helped me kind of focus, or get in the mood to write something. But it was nothing we ever took that seriously. We weren't religious about it. And in The Heartbreakers there was very little drugs. None of us were boozers. I think Benmont drank quite a bit for a while. It's hard to imagine, but he did drink pretty heavily for a long time. And then he completely cleaned up his act and doesn't touch it anymore. So I don't think it influenced our songwriting.

You mentioned that Howie would stay neutral in band politics. Did Benmont also stay neutral?
Ben always had something to say. Still today. He has plenty to say, and I respect it. He *really* is a purist. Doesn't like us using a sample, or anything like that. He'll knock that down instantly. We'll tell him, "The whole world uses a sample to get a sound." "No. No, we don't," he'll say. "We make our own." He's always had a lot to say. He's very knowledgeable, not only about being a musician, but he knows a lot about the music and the history and the evolution of it. And he's a lot of

fun to talk to on that level. And he's very passionate. And he would go back and sometimes he'd side with me and sometimes he'd side with Stan. So I think, yeah, he was pretty opinionated.

People always say how influenced you were by the Byrds, but you once said that people don't understand how influenced you were by The Beatles. And The Beatles certainly evolved from album to album. Was that part of your inspiration to move to a new place with each album?

Yeah. I think they had that effect on a lot of people. You know, before The Beatles, you didn't really see rock stars trying to evolve. They were *quite* happy to have a hit, and often the follow-up was almost exactly the same. That's what I've always really been amazed at—The Beatles had that incredible success and really could have put *anything* out, and it would have been a hit. But they *kept* their head and weren't affected by all that going on around them and focused on *music*. And I think that was our model. We're going to keep our heads, and we're going to try to make better and better music. And so, in that sense, yeah, we wanted to be like that.

We thought the Stones had done kind of the same thing. I think the Stones were watching The Beatles, [Laughs] to be honest. But I think their thing built and evolved. I sort of like the idea—even to this day—of refining our craft. We're trying to take what we do and refine it, and get it a little more pure with each release.

More pure?

Yeah. I think that's what I've always been looking for, though I probably didn't realize it for a long time. But I'm looking for purity. I'm a purist. [Laughs] I want a kind of purity in the music. When I hear Muddy Waters sing, or Slim Harpo, it's very pure. It's incredibly honest. It doesn't need a lot of instruments to make it so pure. There's a thing about music: If you believe the singer, then the song is going to work. It's all about believability. If you can believe the singer, it will work. So I think our quest was for purity. [Laughs]

Chapter Six

Who Got Lucky

Howie said that *Long After Dark*, which came out in 1982, was one of his favorite records. He said, "It sounds the way we sounded then." But I understand you have problems with that record.

TP: It wasn't that I didn't like it. I just had this feeling that we were treading water. I would say it's a *good* record, and when I hear it now, it's much better than I thought it was. But the only complaint I had with *Long After Dark* was that I'm not sure that we're really moving forward here. It's a good little rock and roll record with good songs and good playing. But I don't know that we advanced a lot on that record. So I think that was my only complaint with it.

You said at the time, "I thought we were making wrong decisions all the time. That we had gone too far afield and wanted to get back to a good rocking record. It was a tough record for me."

It was a tough record because I never knew what it was. [Laughs] I *didn't* know if we were making the right decisions about songs. And there were songs being left off that record that were really good.

"Keeping Me Alive." "Turning Point."

Yeah. Really good songs. Jimmy and I were butting heads at that point. Jimmy didn't like the contrast mix of those songs. He thought they were *country* songs. I didn't see them as country songs. I saw them as something a little more organic, more acoustic-oriented than we had done. I think I would have really liked to go in that direction. He didn't like the idea of it. So I think I finally gave in to the way he was thinking. But I think it would have helped that record to have those songs on it.

Those songs are on the boxed set. And when you hear them now, they don't sound like country records. But I think that's a guy growing up in Hell's Kitchen—Jimmy, a New Yorker—he saw that as country music. And that was one thing about Iovine. I don't think he knew music like we did. I don't think he knew every Chuck Berry song. All of us were huge record fans. We know our roots. We know where the music comes from, and we know all about it. And to this day we're still studying very, *very* much. And we're enthusiastically exploring the history of the music all the time. And he didn't have that. I think he was starting from a different place than we were. I really think Iovine wanted to be a businessman by that point. Maybe I'm wrong, but by '82 I think Jimmy was on the phone more than he was in the studio.

Is that right?

Well, the truth hurts. I think he'd agree. And it was good for us, in a way, because he was constantly *promoting* us. After *Damn The Torpedoes*, Jimmy became really fascinated with the music business. Which the rest of us had no interest in it at *all*. And you could see that was his true calling. Because now he owns the record industry. [Laughs] I really think that he would have to agree that he was going in that direction. He was on the phone. I remember taking razor blades and cutting the receiver wire all the time on the phone. [Laughs] Or I'd walk over with a big pair of shears and just cut the cord off the phone. So that was the end of that. [Jimmy Iovine is founder and chairman of Interscope Records. The label started in 1989 and now shepherds artists such as Eminem, No Doubt, and the Wallflowers. In the past, Iovine has produced Stevie Nicks, U2, and The Pretenders, among others.]

Would he laugh or would he get pissed off?

Well, both. [Laughs] He'd laugh and sometimes he'd get pissed off. That's how we were. I didn't think Jimmy was experimental enough. I think he was playing it too safe. When I started *Southern Accents*, I started it without him.

But on *Long After Dark*, you cut those songs and then he rejected them?

Yeah.

But I thought you were pretty much calling the shots. Was he able to get his way, or did you give in and agree to keep them off the album?

I was calling the shots. But he had a lot of influence on me. We were very tight. We had been tight for a number of years. I respected his opinion. He never said you *can't* have it on the record. But he's really good at talking me into things. [Laughs]

You did a video for "You Got Lucky" in 1982. Was that your first?

No. We made videos before we knew they were videos. We made them back in '78. We made a video for "The Waiting." For "A Woman In Love." "Insider." "Stop Draggin' My Heart Around." "Letting You Go." And before that we did "Refugee" and "Here Comes My Girl." And what we would do is make a film of the song, and wherever you couldn't be you'd send the film. We'd send it around. Europe.

We never really wanted to play on *The Merv Griffin Show*, or *Don Kirshner's Rock Concert*. We didn't want to appear on those shows. So what we'd do is send the film, and they would play the film. And when MTV did come along, they were so hungry for product that they began to play all those old films. We just called them promo films, they weren't called videos. And we actually thought the term "video" was weird, because they were on film. They weren't serious *big* huge projects. You'd show up, and they'd say, "Stand over here, and sing 'Refugee'." [Laughs]

Was it fun?

Yeah, we thought they were kind of fun. And we were well ahead of the game on videos. By the time we got to "You Got Lucky," we were *well* ahead of the game, because we'd done a lot of videos. And "You Got Lucky" was really a groundbreaking video. It really changed everything. No one had ever—even Michael Jackson—done a prelude to the video. A bit of business before the song started. And we never lip-sync or anything in that video. That was the idea. We were sick of lip-syncing. And we were going to make a film and not sing in it. But, boy, did it explode. It really did change the way the videos went. There were a *lot* of imitations after that. A lot of bands out in the desert. And

I noticed that Michael Jackson started doing the little thing in the beginning of the video; he'd have a little bit of business before the song started.

And talk about famous. [Laughs] That's when *everybody* knew who you were. Like, you know, *grandmas* knew who you were. 'Cause you're on TV *all day long*, you know? [Laughs] It was not like you just made an appearance. You're on every hour all day long. So we'd be in an airport, and *adults* knew who we were and were coming up to us.

MTV was this *incredible* promotional device. It was *really* great for promoting your songs. It was really exciting. There was this whole new thing happening, and we were right in the front of it. And we made really good videos. We tried to be inventive there, too. It was a *lot* of fun. I always liked films, and I liked being on the set. I liked learning and seeing what the directors did. We got really involved in it. I wanted to be there through the edit and through the whole thing.

Were they your concepts for the videos?
Yeah, pretty often. I think more than not. Actually, I think they were always my concept in some degree. That's the way we are. [Laughs] We wouldn't want to be put in a situation that we had no control over. 'Cause that's just dangerous.

It changed music, in that people were now watching music, as well as listening to it. Did you embrace that change?
It was a double-edged sword. The greatest thing about it was that if you got a hit on TV, you had a hit record. It was a really great promotional tool. The other side of it was that I felt if you hear a song, you make your own movies, in your head. But it really nailed down, visually, those songs in people's heads. I don't think you can hear "Don't Come Around Here No More" and not think of that video. And not think of *Alice In Wonderland*. It's impossible. You know, you just don't do it. And so that wasn't so good. I think it would have been better to be a little more ambiguous with that end of it. Let the songs kind of create their own movies. But the other side of the coin was that it was like a new kind of art form, and it was exciting to be involved in it. I thought it was. Though we complained about it.

Did you?

It got to where we'd really complain about having to make a video for every release. Sometimes it was a nuisance. It was really more fun when you made a little film on a low-budget kind of guerrilla filmmaking process. But, as it got more popular, the industry grew, and it became its own industry. And the films got much more expensive to make.

And the record companies, to this day, have this really shitty deal, where they make you pay for the video. And you get no royalty for the video. MTV doesn't pay you. Or VH1. They don't pay anybody. They get the product for nothing. And then the cost of making the film is deducted from your record royalties. So it got to where we would be spending a million bucks on videos for an album, and that would be deducted from our royalties. That end of it really made us angry. We thought the record companies should be paying for the films, because it was their kind of promotional device. But that just wasn't the way it went. And now a video can easily cost a million bucks. So we've pulled out of that game. We became disenchanted with it, so we just quit doing it.

The liner notes of *Long After Dark* list vocals by Benmont. Did he sing harmonies on that album?

Benmont often sang in the background. He sang on "Refugee." [Sings] "Don't have to live like a refugee..." That's Ben and Stan. I can clearly hear Benmont sing on that. He sings somewhat in the shows, too. He does the third voice sometimes. And often if there's a call-and-response kind of thing, he would be involved in that. So I wouldn't be surprised if he sang on *Long After Dark*. But we're pretty hard on singers. Mike never sings. You've got to sing in tune. And you've got to really hit your note. If you haven't done it a lot, that's a hard thing to do. In an arena, where the sound is swimming around. It's kind of a trick. Mike's really got his hands full with what he's doing with the guitars and stuff. It was usually me and Stan and Howie. And now it's me and Scott [Thurston] and Ben. And occasionally Ron might do a response line, but it's a small part. But we're pretty hard on singers. If you can't hit your note right every time, you're gonna get a lot of shit.

Chapter Seven

Don't Come Around Here As Much

You started *Southern Accents* in 1984. And I understand you drove around the South and would write down words that could be potential song titles.
TP: That was when we were touring the Deep South. And I just would write one-word titles. "Apartment." "Rebels." "Trailers." Things like that. So when I came home, I had kind of a sketch of what I wanted to do. And then I just started sketching them out. What a *really* crazy album that was.

You intended to make it a double album?
Yeah, it was intentionally going to be a double album. And it got cut down to one. We never even finished. That was a weird period because I don't think we'd ever been off the road that long. That was the first time we'd really *stopped*. It was like, "Go, go, go, go, go, go!" The whole time. And then suddenly, *boom*. We stopped. We came off the road. This was in '83. We toured *Long After Dark* all around Europe and America. And then we just stopped.

So this is the first time that the evils of success started to creep in. Because we had all this time on our hands. And we were living in Los Angeles. And we started doing cocaine and pot. And drinking started to show up. Cocaine was really popular in the Eighties, around that time. And we had never really done cocaine much. Because we just had never been around that kind of scene. So I think that when that comes into the studio, everything gets confused. But I remember there was cocaine around then and a lot of drinking. We were the wildest we ever were then. In our personal lives. We were just wild and crazy.

We had too much time on our hands. I didn't know how to live in the world. I just didn't know how to do it. We'd always been in this really uniform schedule: There's going to be a sound check at 4:00, and then a meal at 6:00, and you're going to play, and then you're going to travel here. And if you're home, there's a session Monday through Friday. It was really organized. Suddenly we were just home. Eight years have gone by, and we don't know what to do. To me, it just seemed like one big fast thing that never stopped until then.

And then *I* realized, "Hell, I'm not very good at living life." And also, it was the first time we were recording at home. I built a studio in my house. And it got very loose. Sort of like a party. There were a *lot* of people showing up. And The Heartbreakers had always been a very closed set, you know? [Laughs] Really tight. There was nobody in the sessions much. Not many visitors. Suddenly there's a lot of people coming around. Work was very slow. We weren't coming up with track after track. It was moving *very*, very slow.

How was your songwriting during this period?
Well, I wrote "Rebels." I think that was the first thing I wrote. And that kind of set the stage for what I was doing. And "Rebels," I couldn't get it right. It drove me *mad*. I couldn't get it right. I had done a demo. Just me and an electric 12-string. It sounded great. I *couldn't* get the track cut.

You were producing?
Yeah. Then Dave Stewart [of Eurythmics] showed up. [Laughs] He's one of the biggest characters I've ever met. I met him in the Eighties. When music really turned to shit. People were *trying* to do something, but it was all these fakey keyboard sounds. A lot of prancing and posing. So Jimmy Iovine was looking for songs for Stevie Nicks. And he came to me. I said, "I don't really have anything left over. I don't have anything I can give away."

And he said, "Well, you know I'm frustrated, I'm trying to find writers. Who do you think would be a good writer?" And Dave had just come out with that "Sweet Dreams (Are Made Of This)," which I thought was a really good song. And then I heard one or two more that I thought were really good. I said, "You should try this guy Dave

Stewart. He's in England. I don't know him, but he seems consistent as a writer. He seems really good." So the next thing I know, not many weeks later the phone rings, and it's Dave Stewart. And he says, "Hey, I'm here, and Jimmy told me I got the gig from you. I've come over to write some stuff for Stevie and other people. And why don't you come down? Let's get together. I'd like to see you."

We hooked up at a studio in Hollywood. Sunset Sound. I went down there and we hung out, and we got along really well. Quickly. And it was his first trip into LA and he was going to stay a while. So we really hit the town. We started hanging out. He came to my place in Encino. And we were hanging in my studio, and we were working. We wrote the song "Don't Come Around Here No More." And Dave was helping me produce it. And that became kind of a month-long job doing that track.

It is entirely unique.
It's so unusual; it's not like anything I've ever heard before.

That drum beat and that sitar sound.
Just the whole arrangement. And it's such a weird song.

How did you write it? On acoustic guitars?
Somewhat. Dave had the basic idea for it. He had the chord pattern. And I think I added some chords in, and tagged on that thing at the end, where it goes double time. We kind of edited Stanley onto that.

Does Stan play that whole track?
[Dave] had that beat on his drum machine. So we took that, and then there are some real drums, as well, through there. And then it goes to full-on Heartbreakers. So it was quite a production.

There's a little bass lick in the beginning of the song that's a real quick, spacey lick. And that was David sending the tape to England, because he knew this great bass player he'd been working with, and he wanted him to play the bass. And he sent the tape to England, and the tape came back, and it was just this really weird jazzy bass playing [Laughs] that was useless, but I did keep one lick that starts the song. [Sings lick]

But it was kind of a wild trip. There's even one point where, going into the middle bit, we recorded a piano note, and actually had Bugs pull the tape across the capstan really fast with his hands. [Laughs] And it made this *brrrrrr* kind of really weird sound. So we were kind of nuts.

We were getting into that and going all over town. And *lots* of people were coming around. And Dave liked it so much that he bought a house just a block or two away. In Encino. Which is still going to this day. He bought the house and started adding onto it immediately. With no permits [Laughs] or anything. And he built a pretty nice studio there. Later on, the house was sold to Michael Kamen [the late, gifted arranger and composer who created the great orchestrations for *Wildflowers* and Pink Floyd's *The Wall*], bless his heart. And he did a lot of work there, and the Wilburys did their first album there, or part of it, anyway.

So we were just having a ball. We went to Nudie's and bought cowboy hats and had the tailor, Glen Palmer, make us rhinestone cowboy suits with embroidered skulls. And we were going around wearing these. That's some indication of where we were at at the time. [Laughs] We were having a ball. He would have these parties that I still think about sometimes. These really wild parties that always seemed to have midgets. Timothy Leary would be there. And McGuinn. It seemed everybody in LA would be at these parties. And we were just hanging around and having a good time. I remember that year '84 as being really creative, though we were overdoing it a little bit. But there was a lot of creativity going on. I think the rest of The Heartbreakers were a little wary of Dave. They didn't embrace Dave the way I did. It was the first time somebody from the outside had come into The Heartbreakers' circle, which was a really tight little circle.

You had producers come into this circle, right?

Well, they did, but not in the way Dave did. He was writing with me, which they were really suspicious of. [Laughs] And Dave's a really vibrant character. So I think they were a little wary of him. Though they got to know him, and I think they got to like him.

We had a ball. I mean, we were going everywhere, going to all kinds of clubs and this and that. Staying up all night. Just having fun. So Dave kind of remained in the picture for years and years, one way or the other. I still see him. And we're still friends. And then he convinced Annie Lennox to move out to Encino as well. So she was there part of the time. And I kind of remember the period fondly.

That was Dave. Dave would go away to England. And then sometimes my gate would ring. And it'd be Dave, completely unannounced. Maybe if I hadn't seen him in months. The gate would ring, and it'd be Dave, and he'd be in a safari outfit, where it looked like he'd been in the jungles of Borneo or something. [Laughs] I remember that once. And he was just, "Whoa—let me in." And he walked in the house, and my kid was eating some cereal, and he said, "Give me some of that. Have you got some of that?" [Laughs]

And he'd just be sitting down eating with the kids, and immediately plugged right back in. But you'd never know when to expect him. He may show up on a big Harley-Davidson. And he had a big, long '60s Cadillac with the big fins on it. He was very flamboyant. Dave was one of those people who really liked being famous. He really enjoyed it. He thrived on it. Where I was a little more withdrawn from it. But he *really* enjoyed it. He was just a ball. We had *so* much fun.

On "Don't Come Around Here No More," was that a real sitar? No, it's a Coral Sitar. They were made in the Sixties. They're pretty cool instruments. It's like a guitar, but there's an autoharp thing built onto it, under Plexiglas on the top. So you tune this, with lots and lots of strings, like an autoharp, so it will ring on the note that you want. And then it actually sounds like a sitar. Each note on the guitar makes a sitar sound. So they were used a lot in the Sixties. Like the Boxtops. "Cry Like A Baby." There's one on that. I bought one, and we had it there, so it became the main lick.

Then, of course, there was the video. That was an idea Dave and I had. Dave was right away saying, "Well, you've got to make a great video of this." And he said, "Well, I see myself with a sitar on top of a giant mushroom." Okay. [Laughs] And that's how we started on the idea.

But it was a crazy time. That record, "Don't Come Around Here No More," there's a cello on it. I said, "Cello would be good," and Dave said, "Don't worry, I'll get a cello player." And he comes to the session and he says, "Yeah, I've got a guy coming from the LA Philharmonic with a cello."

So this guy shows up. Dave and I were in our rhinestone cowboy suits, sequined up. And I think [the cello player] was a little frightened by us, maybe. He came in, and we said, "Hey, come on in, and plug into this vibe. We've got this really good thing for you to play." And he said, "Well, I need to see the music." So, of course, Dave hadn't gotten the music written out. I said, "The idea is that we'll just play the tape, and you jam along and play what you want, and we'll find the best bits that way." And [Laughs] I remember the guy saying, "Well, I've never played anything that wasn't written down." And that to me just sounded *so* strange. He'd never played *anything* that wasn't written down. And Dave said, "What's your name?" And it was Larry or something. And Dave said, "Larry, you're going to have a lot of fun tonight." [Laughs]

And so we got the guy just to start to jam. And he was really elated by it. He was *amazed* by it. That he could just start to *play* something and it would sound good. And we showed him how he could find a bit, and we would edit it in, and use this bit or that.

And that was kind of the epitome of Dave. That's the way Dave was. He was a madman, but a really sweet one. Really a sweetheart. But loony as they come.

And there are other strings on that track, aren't there?
The other strings are Benmont on a string machine, on sampled strings. That's all Ben; Ben came up with that arrangement about midway through.

It was a long record to make. We were making it to be a single. I wanted it to be a single. It was intended to be a single. And we worked probably two or three weeks on it. To get it all done. Trial and error, this and that.

Did you write the melody?
Yeah. Dave had some of the melody in his head.

I like the stops in it, where you sing the word "Stop!"
That was his idea. To go, "Stop!" And we used girls, which was kind of an accident. Because, when we started it, we were working at Sunset Sound, and Stevie [Nicks] had booked the time. And the girls that sing with her had turned up for the session, but Stevie had canceled the session. So the girls were still there. Dave said, "Let's get them out here and see what they can do." And then they did that great bit. [Sings "Ah ah ah ooh ooh."] And then there's a girl named Stephanie who we brought in to sing that really high, wailing thing at the end. [Laughs] She was having a little trouble finding her thing. And Dave actually ran into

the room in his underpants as she was singing that bit. And that actually worked, and she went up into that register and did that note, and then burst out laughing. But he was that kind of guy. He figured, well, this will get her jazzed up. So we were really happy with it. I think when we brought it to the record company, they were very mystified by it. Because it wasn't like anything I had ever done. I think they were a little concerned that it was a little too far off the map. But I thought, at the time, Prince had come out with "When Doves Cry." And I saw it as kind of going for the same kind of thing in a different way. And I remember saying, "Listen to this Prince record. That's really far out, too, but it's really popular." So I think they got behind it. Especially when we made the video, they thought it was really going to go, and it did.

Did The Heartbreakers like it?
[Pause] I don't know. I think Mike didn't like it at first. I remember him coming over one day and saying, "I played this at home and everybody hated it." And I thought, "Well, I don't hate it. I think it's really good." I believed in it. I really liked it. I still like it when I hear it. You know, it wasn't something we were going to do a *lot*. But it was just *anything* to get out of what we'd been doing. I desperately wanted to find a new page. [Laughs] To get somewhere we hadn't been. And that helped, in that sense. I'm really proud of that record. It really came out good.

Are you going to work with Dave again?
I don't know. I haven't seen him in a while. He lives in England. He drops in now and then. But he always drops in out of the blue. You never know when he's going to appear. I used to see him when I'd go to England. He knew George [Harrison], as well. When I'd go to George's house, he'd show up there sometimes. We were very close. My kids always thought Dave was kind of strange. But they liked him a lot. He was really weird. He videoed everything. Once I went over to his house, and he'd been in the hospital for something, he videoed the whole thing. I went over there with my kids one time, and he said, "Whoa, wow, you've got to see this—I videoed this nurse giving me an enema in the hospital." And I'm like, "No... I've got my kids here." And he said, "You don't see anything, it's just my face." And I said, "Dave, I don't want to see you get an enema."

But we did one thing that was really, really great. He had a TV show [*Beyond The Groove*] briefly going in England that was just film vignettes that he did with different people. And he did one with me that was really good. I've only seen it once. I actually saw it when I was staying at George's in England, and it came on TV that night by chance, and we watched it there. And it was filmed out in Griffith Park [in Hollywood], where they have that cave that's been used in a lot of films.

Yeah, the Bronson Caves.
Yeah, it was filmed there. And I did this sort of ad-lib thing, where I was there by this campfire. It was supposed to be this apocalyptic thing, after the third war. And that's all he gave me, and I had to ad-lib from there. And I did it pretty well. And the *greatest* thing about it—and only in Hollywood could this happen—in the middle of the scene, an entire regiment of western cavalry came riding up. They were on the wrong set. They'd gone the wrong way, and they're riding into our set. So, without dropping a beat, I kept the improv going. And we got the cavalry for free.

And then we did another one that is really good. You know how they pull cars on a trailer in films, the cars not really rolling, it's usually on a trailer and there are cameras mounted all around it? He put me on this Cadillac and drove me *all* over town. All over Mulholland and the Valley. And I just did this improv the whole time. And it's hard to find. It's on one of our video collections. It's about a twenty-minute clip. I don't know if it ever got used or not, but it's really fun. For weeks after that I'd see the trailer go by, with lights all over it, with Dave standing in the back. I mean, he was *crazy*. [Laughs]

He wasn't always *right*. Because he tried so many things, he could be *terribly* wrong sometimes.

About music?
About anything. He spread himself thin, I thought, at times. But when he got something good, it was really good. He's a very underrated guitar player. But I don't think he's ever had that kind of light on him as a guitar player because he does so many things. I think a lot of people thought he was a keyboard player, which he really isn't.

Yeah, we really had a good time. The only thing he did that I didn't like is that he talked me into taking horns and girl singers on the road right after that.

You weren't into that?

I wasn't. But for some reason, I listened to Dave, who kept telling me it'd be a great idea. And I never even talked to the horn players. I showed up at the first rehearsal with *no* idea of what they were going to do, or what the girls would sing. The band *hated* it. And we quickly dispensed with it. But we did make a live record in that period, so there are horns all over the record. Which I'm not all that crazy about. So you live and you learn. But that was all Dave's fault. [Laughs]

There are horns on *Southern Accents*, on a few songs.

I think that was the idea, that we were going to be doing that album, and we could reproduce it more faithfully if we brought the horns and the girls. But we're just not that kind of band to have a lot of side people. For the first time then, people who weren't in The Heartbreakers started to appear on Heartbreakers albums. I think only a *few* people, maybe Stevie [Nicks], had ever been on a Heartbreakers record.

So we started to use girl singers on that. And horns. Dave said, "Horns. You've got to bring horns in. You've never done anything with horns, and it will be a different vibe." So we did that. We did a few tracks with horns. But the trouble was, I think it flawed the album. I think we made a great single with "Don't Come Around Here No More." But I think it flawed the album. Because it left the concept. I thought it was a Southern phrase: "Don't come around here no more." But it didn't really have much to do with the album. And important songs—"Trailer"—were relegated to B-sides. The album suffered that way. And I think it didn't get finished, because I was just *exhausted* and couldn't finish it. There was a lot of partying going on. And my house had just become crazy. There were all kinds of people there. We were recording in the middle of the night. It was just a little bit nuts.

I needed guidance and help. So I brought Jimmy back. And he was wise enough to say, "I'm pulling you out of your house, first thing." And we went down to Village Recorder and finished the record there. But we still hadn't finished "Rebels." [Laughs]

You wanted horns on it?
Well, I wound up with horns on it. I did this whole production. I did it so many times. And we were mixing it. And I was in the other room. And I played the demo. It was so much better than what we were doing. And I was *so* pissed off that I couldn't get the track as good as the demo that I slugged the wall. And completely shattered my hand. I *shattered* it. To powder.

Which hand?
My left hand. You can still see the scars where they sewed it up. I powdered it.

Did you break the wall?
No. [Laughs] The wall was fine. And I suddenly had a hand as big as Mickey Mouse. It was *really* scary. I went to the hospital. And they said, "You're going to have to go to a specialist." And I went to the specialist, and by that point my hand was *so* big, it had swollen up *so* bad. The guy said, right away, with me and Tony there, "Well, I'll tell ya—if you were a carpenter, or a plumber, I wouldn't be concerned. But I'm not sure we'll be able to get your mobility back in your fingers." People said, "He's broken his hand and he'll never play again." And I didn't buy that. I thought, "I will play again."

So I had a big-time operation on my hand, and it's filled with metal studs where there's no bone. And then they wrapped wire around. It was really an *amazing* operation. And the guy *completely* rebuilt my hand. I was in the hospital for a bit. And I just stopped recording and then I had therapy for almost eight months on my hand. And exercising it. Even electro-shock therapy—it hurt so bad to move your fingers that the brain won't let you do it. So they'd run an electric shock through there that moves the fingers.

It was quite an experience. I went through a long time of not having a hand to use. I finished the album that way. That was the end of the double album. And it was just, "Okay, we have to finish what we have." I couldn't play anymore.

That sobered me up. That was the end of the partying, and the end of any vices. I nearly took myself out of the *game* here. So that was the end of that. I got Jimmy Iovine to return and complete *Southern Accents*.

It's a great album.
Yeah. It came out good, I think. But in my mind I'm always missing the next disc. [Laughs] I was always thinking there was going to be more to it that I didn't cover. I don't think it's really a good *concept* record, because it doesn't cover enough. But it's a good record to hear.

Were you ever happy with how "Rebels" turned out?
No.

It became a hit.
Yeah. I still think it could have been better. I don't think the vocal's that good on it. I could have sang it better. I think it's kind of blurry and garbled. I think I could have enunciated it better.

Did you sing it after your accident?
I can't remember. Now what I would have done is taken that vocal from the demo, and just built the record around that. But I didn't have that kind of craft then. I wasn't smart enough to do that. I kept thinking I had to do it again, because it wasn't *recorded* that well. Now I think I would have either just put it out like that, or built it around the vocal. I don't think I ever sang it as good as I did on that demo.

You know my roadie, Bugs, we'd be driving along. And he said, "I still can't listen to that record. [Laughs] I still can't listen to 'Rebels' because it reminds me of night after night after night. And how frustrating it was."

After you hurt your hand, was it a long time before you could play a chord again on a guitar?
It was almost eight months. I don't know if I could have made a chord or not at some point, but before I had any dexterity in my hand, it was about eight months. But I always thought in my mind that I would do it.

You had no fear of losing your ability to use that hand?
Of course I had a little fear. But I always thought I could do it. Though my hand is a little more limited than it was then. I don't quite have the same range of motion in my hand. I've got this thing where the front fingers kind of pull [Laughs] the little finger a little bit. So I think it hampered me a little.

Did it affect your guitar playing?
A little bit. I had to learn a new way of playing. I had to practice a lot, and just find ways around the limitations. So it was a bad idea to break my hand. [Laughs]

You said you were doing a lot of cocaine. Did that affect your songwriting?
No. I think it affected my breaking my hand.

Did you cut a song with Denny Cordell for *Southern Accents*?
Yeah, but it wasn't used. And it was a really great track. It's on the boxed set. It's called "The Image Of Me." A Conway Twitty song. And we did a really different arrangement of it. It's one of my favorite things that we ever recorded. It's really good. That was when the album was going to be a double album. We hadn't seen Denny in quite a while, and he showed up. And we did that at my house. And he brought the song, and turned me on to that song. And he was funny, because he wouldn't let us punch in. There was no dropping in. You had to do everything live right from the go. We were used to, if you made a mistake in the vocal, to come back and punch in halfway through or something. But he wouldn't allow that. He wanted an absolutely live performance.

That got cut when you decided to make a single album instead of a double?
Yeah, there were a few things that got left over. We've always had this enormous vault of left-over things. There was always more, at least in those days—past *Torpedoes*. On *Torpedoes* there was nothing left over; we used literally everything we did. But from *Hard Promises* on out, there's always been a lot of stuff left over.

I understand at this time Mike gave you the track which became Don Henley's "Boys Of Summer" and you turned it down. True?
Yeah. He brought that track in, which became the Don Henley record. But he had done everything on that track. I remember telling him the chorus was wrong. [Laughs] The chorus was wrong. It went to minor instead of major. I remember sitting at the piano and showing him that if it went major there when the chorus comes, it would be much more

effective. Then he made me a tape of it that I had, where the chorus just drops out. There was nothing but a backbeat. For me to write a chorus for it. But I never could, or I was just too distracted to get around to it.

So you did work on it?
Briefly. It sounded *so* different to me than anything on *Southern Accents* that, when he came to me and said, "Well, Don Henley really wants this track. Would you mind if I gave it away, because I really want to do something with it?" I said, "Yeah, go ahead," because we were going to bring out "Don't Come Around Here No More" as a single. I think [Mike] played everything on that track ["Boys Of Summer"]. And Don sang over it. So he was having a big hit at the same time that *Southern Accents* came out. I was happy for him. I'm glad it worked out for him.

Do you like how the song came out?
Yeah. It's a classic song. It really came out good.

Did they end up going to the major on the chorus?
Yeah, they did. [Laughs]

When Mike gives you a track, does he sing on it, or is it totally instrumental?
It's totally instrumental.

So you write the melodies and words to his tracks.
Yeah, sometimes I even write a bridge, or change a chord here or there.

Do you work to the tape?
He'll give me a tape, but what I like to do is learn it on piano or guitar. Then I work on it that way. Because that gives me the luxury of going somewhere else. If you work just with the tape, it can get a little monotonous. Though I did do that on "Refugee." I worked right to his tape. Which was really different than the way we recorded it. Different arrangement.

Do you have lyrics in mind when you're writing to one of Mike's tracks, or do you allow the music itself to dictate what the words should be?
I start cold. I just start cold. If something's there that I get a feel for, it starts to happen. And if I don't, I just don't pursue it.

So there's lots of his tracks you pass on?
Oh, he writes *hundreds* of tracks. I mean, *God*, he writes so many. He'll give me a tape with twenty things on it. Of which maybe I'll find one or two [Laughs] that I can work with. But he writes in *bulk*. Track after track.

I remember writing ["Refugee"] really quickly to his tape. The words came really quick. And that bridge was on the tape. I just had to come up with a melody, really. I don't think he saw it the same way as me, where the chorus would go. But it worked out great.

That's how we write together. We never sit down face to face. He usually gives me a tape and, if I find something on the tape I think I can work with, I'll take that and learn it myself and then work that way. And then when we go into the studio, we may or may not refer to the demo tape. Sometimes we'll just play it *completely* different. And then sometimes we will refer to the tape, and say, "Oh, this is good, let's try to make it like that."

Chapter Eight

Runaway Trains

Soon after making the album in 1985, you toured on *Southern Accents*, released a live album [*Pack Up The Plantation*], and you met Bob Dylan. You played with him at Farm Aid?
TP: I suppose it was right after that. Benmont had been doing some sessions with Bob Dylan. So *he* knew Bob. I didn't know Bob, though I had met him before.

Where did you meet him?
Strangely enough, I met him in '77 or '78. We went to see him [in concert]. Me and Bugs got two comps to see Bob Dylan. We left the Shelter studio, and we went to drive to the Universal Amphitheater, had a flat tire, and both of us got out on the road trying to change the tire. So we were just covered with grease and dirt. And we got to the Universal Amphitheater and we found our seats, and the show had just begun. And then, midway through the show, Bob introduced the celebrities in the audience, which was kind of unusual for Bob.

It was like, "Joni Mitchell's here," and there'd be applause. And then suddenly he said, "Tom Petty's here." And there was applause. And that was the first time it really hit me that people knew who we were. Because I'd only made two records then. Then a guy came up to us while we were sitting in our seats, and said, "Bob would like you to come backstage." So we went backstage, and had a brief conversation. Nothing of any substance, because we didn't know each other. But I met Bob. So I had been introduced to him. A few years later, Ben and Mike had been playing with Bob on some of his sessions.

Bob had not been touring much at the time. And a little bit to my surprise, Elliot Roberts [one of the band's former managers] said to me, "I was talking to Bob today, and he wanted to know if you guys would back him up at Farm Aid." Live Aid had recently happened, which we played. And that was a big spectacle. [Live Aid took place on July 13, 1985, at Wembley Stadium in London and JFK Stadium in Philadelphia. These simultaneous benefit concerts drew dozens of performers who raised money for the victims of famine in Ethiopia. The event was organized by Bob Geldof of the Boomtown Rats.] I remember being backstage and there seemed like miles of dressing rooms, of trailers. We were put in an area where it was Bob Dylan and Keith Richards and Ronnie Wood and Led Zeppelin and us. And we were all out there around a picnic table watching the show on television backstage.

And then Bob went on just before the finale with only acoustic guitars, and there were people tuning up behind the curtain, and it was a pretty disastrous set. And he said something during the concert about that it wouldn't be a bad idea to raise some money for farmers. So Willie Nelson, hearing that, went to Bob and said, "Hey, why don't we throw one of these for farmers?"

So Bob, this time, didn't want to play acoustic, he wanted to have a band. He wanted to have an electric band behind him. So we went down and we rehearsed. We rehearsed a *lot.* And played a lot of songs. And he *loved* The Heartbreakers. It was quick and easy. You could throw something out, and The Heartbreakers were pretty good at just grabbing it and going with it. We rehearsed and learned more songs than we needed for the show.

Would he lead the rehearsals?

Oh yeah. He would lead the rehearsals. He would just play us a little bit of what he wanted to do, and he would play it on guitar so we could see what the changes were. And then we'd just start to play. And he kind of got it to where he wanted it to be.

So we went to Champaign, Illinois. It was in a big football field [Memorial Stadium at the University of Illinois]. That was a lot of fun, because it was much better than Live Aid to me, because I didn't like a single act that I saw in Live Aid. It was so crappy. Maybe I'm wrong, but *I* didn't like it. I liked Led Zeppelin. [Laughs] Jimmy Page actually took me by the arm and walked us to the side of the stage to watch them, so we enjoyed that. But it didn't seem like *our* kind of show, the people that we really liked. Farm Aid really was [our type of show]. There were all these really cool people. Roy Orbison was on it, Johnny Cash, the Beach Boys, Randy Newman. You name it, they were all there. It was an incredible show.

So we came on at Farm Aid, and we played a short set. And then Dylan came on, and we backed him up, and it went really well. And then afterwards in the trailer, Bob came back, and said, "Hey, what would you think of doing a tour? I've got a tour of Australia [1986] I want to do and what would you guys think of doing that?" And we'd all been *huge* Dylan fans, and we were very intrigued by the idea of playing with Bob. So off we went. And that went on for two years. We'd do part of it, and then more would get added on, and then more would get added on. We really did the *world* with Bob.

You were interweaving your songs with his songs?
At first we didn't play many songs of ours. We'd only do four or five in the show. And it'd be like when Bob felt like it. He'd say, "Hey, I'm going to let The Heartbreakers do a number now." And we'd do a couple of numbers. That'd be it. Maybe again later in the set we'd do a couple more.

That went on about a year. And then, later in the tour, he thought people were going to want to hear more from us. Then we got to do a forty-five-minute set.

Then Roger McGuinn was added to the show. He would open the show up acoustic, and then we would do our bit, and then Bob would come on after an intermission, and we'd back Bob up. But, you know, we were *huge* McGuinn fans, too, so this was like kids in a candy store. And we had known Roger for a while. He got added to the show, and then we all felt like "We just can't sit here and watch him do these Byrds songs alone with an acoustic." So we quickly became Roger's band as well [Laughs] and we did the Byrds' stuff. Which was a great thrill, to do that. And so we did the Byrds' stuff, and then we'd do *our* show, and then there'd be an intermission and we'd do Bob's show. Which sometimes could be a two-hour show. So by the end of the night, *man,* we had played a *lot.* We were onstage the entire show, just about, except for a period where we'd leave the stage and Bob would do four or five alone. And he was great, he was really great.

When you backed up Dylan, you did his original arrangements of his songs?
If you're going to play with Bob, it's a little like playing with a jazz artist. They may improvise a little. I don't know if he does that anymore, but in those days he would improvise. Or maybe do a song with Benmont suddenly that we didn't really know. But he trusted Benmont, I know. I remember he did an Inkspots number one night with Ben that was *really* good. But we didn't know it, and we knew not to play.

Would he sing his songs the same way each time?
I think he'd sing them the way we'd been rehearsing them at that time. And we rehearsed a lot.

It's surprising, because one doesn't think of Dylan as liking to rehearse very much. But he didn't mind rehearsal?
No. We would rehearse a lot. A lot of songs we rehearsed we didn't play. But we were a good unit. We had a real backlog of songs. He has a lot of material, and we knew a lot of material. And some nights we'd do a different show. Every night we'd usually do something we hadn't done. It wasn't like I've heard people say that you can't play with Bob because he's so erratic. But he wasn't. He was professional. He knew what the show was going to be, and we usually knew what the show was going to be.

You said that after shows you like to get out of the venue immediately, and not glad-hand backstage. Was Dylan the same way?
Yeah. I think so. Bob highly values his privacy, and has to go through a little bit of struggle to have it. So he was the same way. We were always like that. Maybe in the very earliest years we didn't take off, but at least by the *Damn The Torpedoes* period I got right out of the building. I've never wanted to do that hang around after the show thing.

I know some people, they'll hang around until the last person is gone. Just to hear how wonderful they were. But I can't really have a conversation with somebody about what's going on here or there as soon as the show's over. I'm *miles* above the crowd with my adrenaline. So you find yourself smiling and nodding. But it's all false. You're not really even hearing them. Record companies hate it, because I don't greet people. I've even heard that I'm aloof or arrogant. But I'm not. My brain won't deal with that. It can't. It's too fragile. [Laughs] I can't deal with people before the show or after.

And it's a great effort to sometimes go out and meet sick children, or the odd person who has to be met, or celebrities that have come. They all feel that you should say hello to them. And, on a normal night, I'd be more than happy to hang out and talk. But when I've got that job to do, I've got to get myself into a certain place mentally, which takes a little time. And then afterwards, it takes a long time to come down from it.

We learned really early on, too, not to get into a huddle after the show and talk about everything that went wrong. Because everybody is going to see the show differently. We can fight all night about it, but it's not going to make any difference to what's gone down. It's already gone down. [Laughs] And there was never a night when the audiences weren't just incredibly ecstatic at the whole thing. We always had really good audiences. And we always went over great. So we figured out that there's not much point in arguing if the audience is going crazy. So we would really give each other our notes on the show the next day, usually at the sound check. We'd say, "This could be done better," or "Maybe we should change this." That would all go on the next day. We didn't stay in the room and argue about it like I've seen a lot of groups do.

Dylan is such a mysterious guy. Did he remain mysterious when you worked with him, or did you get to know him?

He's not the kind of person who is going to tell you everything about himself. But I found him to be a good guy. I like him. Liked him then, like him now. He's a really good musician, and a great songwriter.

One of the nicest things about Bob is that he's an honest guy. Really, really honest. Not someone that would ever lie. Not someone who would blow his own horn. And I enjoyed all those years working with him, and I think we had a genuine friendship. Still do. We had a lot of long talks. He knows a lot about music.

What kind of music?

Well, he could go back with songs to sea chanties. Folk music. He really knew a lot of folk songs, a lot of early R&B, a lot of early rock and roll songs, fairly obscure songs that I didn't know. Some of the times I remember the fondest are the rehearsals where Bob might start playing some songs that we didn't know, and you'd discover something new.

When you have that kind of success, and you're the best songwriter who ever lived, a lot of myth is built up around you. And it's quite a lot to carry around every day. But I admire him for remaining a good guy, an honest guy.

I'll tell you this about him: I saw a lot of people running circles around Bob, being afraid of him, or afraid to say what was on their mind. Trying to anticipate what he was trying to say or do. I always found that if I asked Bob a direct question, I would get a direct answer. So maybe our friendship wasn't that difficult, because I made up my mind that I would treat him like anybody else. Though I certainly was in awe of his talent. But people are just people. [Laughs] And I don't remember ever asking him a question when he didn't give me a direct answer.

He can enunciate his view of the world really well. And he can enunciate it in a way that's poetic. That's a gift. That's not something you learn, or get out of a manual. It's just a gift. So I was lucky to be around him. I never took it for granted that I was getting to work with someone that was a master of what he was doing. But I never found him to take himself too seriously. He was a professional. Never showed up late, made every show. [Laughs]

I found Bob to really put his family first, and to have a great concern about his children. The man himself is a professional musician and a family man. A troubadour of the truest sense.

During one span of the tour, you were interspersing your songs with Dylan. How did that feel to do that?

Scary. You know, because you're there with the *greatest* writer who ever lived. [Laughs] But you try to just not think about that. And people were really happy to hear us play, too, thank *God*. So I think it really intimidated me at first, but once you've done the show a few times, you get used to it.

It was great playing with Bob. I even got to play the bass on some songs, when Howie would play a lap-steel. And there was something very free about it. I think we learned quite a bit. It was good for me to step back and see what it's like to back somebody up. And it was really interesting to see the whole dynamic of how it works, how you have to really pay attention to what the singer's doing. And it's a whole different mindset than if you're up front. So I think we emerged from that a much better band.

When I saw you, you guys were on fire.
It was so rewarding musically. Just *so* much fun.

The whole band enjoyed it?
Oh yeah. And there were great, great songs to play. Wow. All those songs, and they were all good. And it was just so much fun. It was such a thrill to play "Like A Rolling Stone" with Bob. And we'd sing harmony, and there was only one mike. There was that theory, that kind of goes back to folk music, that everybody is going to sing on one mike and balance themselves. But *God*, it was fun. And [Dylan's] been a good friend for years. And treated us great, really. Treated us great. And it was a great honor. And really rewarding musically.

Did it change the band?
I think it did. It's hard to put it into words. But we became a band that just didn't play the parts from the record. We became a band who could go up there and really express ourselves as to where we were at in the moment. And still stay within a framework and make it all work. But I think it just expanded the horizons. We saw that we could be a better band. And we were honored to be there.

In Dylan's book *Chronicles, Vol. 1*, he writes about touring with you, and I was surprised to read that he said that you were at the "top of your game" and he was at the bottom of his.
Yeah, I was surprised to read that, too. All I can say is that if he was at the bottom of his game, then the bottom is pretty high, because he really could be riveting on some nights. I recently saw a bootleg video of one of the shows, and I was taken back by just how great he was in the show.

You know, artists at times aren't really the best judges of how they're performing. I've had nights where I thought I wasn't very good, and then people who had seen the show would come to me raving about it. I did have the sense of that tour that Bob was searching for something. It's very hard to put into words. We had a lot of long plane rides and talked quite a bit. It was nothing he said in particular, but I did sometimes feel that he was maybe searching for the next step in his career.

But he said in the book that the crowds for the most part were coming in to see me. I don't think that was true. I think they were coming in to see the pair of us, to see us together. And I feel that we had a lot of great nights musically. And maybe because he was in some kind of inner turmoil, he doesn't remember it that way. Maybe I was at the top of my game, but I don't think he was at the bottom of his. I don't think the bottom of his game is that low, anyway. I think he's always good. Maybe, like anyone else, to different degrees on different nights.

In the book he mentions Malmuth, Sweden, where he had a great epiphany onstage that kind of showed him through the next door of his career. And I do remember that happening. I didn't know what was going on in his head, but I remember him stepping up to the mike to sing, and nothing coming out, and I felt really worried for him, like that maybe his voice was gone. And then he dug down deep, and *bang*, it came out, and he was a new man within seconds there. And from that point on, and for the rest of the tour, the shows actually did go up a notch. The energy level went up, and he did seem renewed a little bit. So when I read that in the book, it brought that back to my mind. I do remember that happening.

But Bob is a great artist, and I think that he's always going to be worth the money to come in and see. But artists are like that—they don't necessarily see when they're working at their best.

But I loved his book. I saw it as just one long poem.

I was surprised that during the recording of his album *Oh Mercy*, that he had so much self-doubt. He would go into the studio with only lyrics and no melodies, and try to find the melody while in the studio.

The great thing about the book is that it reveals that he has insecurities like everyone else has. When you're that famous, people don't often give you that benefit of the doubt. They kind of just assume that you understand how great you're supposed to be. [Laughs] But the truth is, you're only a human. And you're still going to go through everything that humans go through.

Was this the time during which your house got burned?
Yes. It was quite a weird time. That was '86 and '87 [May 17, 1987]. Weird stuff happened. And that was when my house got burned down.

Was it arson?
Yes. It was arson. They found the evidence where someone had cut a hole in the back fence on a hill and had been watching the house. For probably a period of time. And really early one morning they came down and set the house on fire. And it was a wooden house, and it went up really quickly. The whole place, just like a matchbox, it went up really fast.

You were there with your wife and kids?
Yeah. Actually, only one of my kids was home. And the fire started really close to her room. [Softly] I mean, I've *never* talked about this ever. Because it was such a shock. To have somebody try to kill you is a *really bad* feeling. And I never really wanted to talk about it in detail, because it frightened me *so* bad. I wouldn't even use the word "fire" in a song or anything. It really frightened me. They didn't just try to kill me, they tried to wipe out my whole family. And it was a hell of a day. It was my wife's birthday. We were planning an afternoon barbecue. So, as the house was burning, guests were arriving.

You all got out of the house okay?
Just. Just got out. I got [my family] out. And it makes that *really* thick smoke and then down at the ground, it was clear. You can't imagine how black it gets inside because immediately the windows are just smutted up, there's no light coming in. So you couldn't see. But you could see clearly at the bottom of the smoke.

The first thing I did was just push my wife and kid out a side door and told them to go to the swimming pool. Just go and jump into the pool, because that won't burn. And then I ran out the back door, and picked up a hose to try to fight the fire in the back. And the hose *melted* in my hands. Just absolutely *melted.* I got kind of burned; standing close to it was kind of like being in the sun for too long. And I remember then I tried to come out of the house, and that's when I realized the whole place was on fire. I hit the ground and crawled on my belly. I knew enough, from hotel safety films, to get on the ground and not breathe the smoke.

I crawled under the smoke, got out through an open door, and at that point I saw that my housekeeper was standing about fifty feet away from me with a hose. And she caught fire. Her head caught fire. Her hair went up. And I yelled at her, "You're on fire!" And she took the hose, and put it on her head, which actually saved her.

Then I went diving down by the pool, pulled my wife and daughter out, went down the driveway. By that time the press arrived. They were the first to get there. Because they listen to those radios. They got there before the fire people. *Just* before. And I was really angry. There was a news crew, and they were shooting everything. And I was kind of crazed. I didn't know what the fuck was going on. I didn't dream at that moment that it was arson. I just thought something had happened. It was a pretty big house, and I couldn't tell. I just thought something somewhere had caught fire.

Literally everything I owned was burned. I think there was one little corner of the house that didn't burn. Luckily, it had a couple guitars and stuff there. That was about all that didn't burn. Everything else burned.

Did the Dove guitar make it?
The Dove guitar made it; it was sitting in the far corner of the house. But everything burned. [Pause]

It was really weird. I didn't have any *shoes*. I had run out of the house in a pair of jeans and a T-shirt. And Annie Lennox helped a whole lot. I remember seeing her out of the corner of my eye. I was running around, and there were a lot of people there. And I'll forever be grateful to her. I sent the family away to a hotel right away.

And I stayed. And at the end of the night, when I finally left and went to the hotel, Annie had gone and bought us all a complete wardrobe of clothes. And that was really the only clothes I had for *weeks*. She went and bought me a pair of shoes. Actually, some pretty nice stuff. Because she was bright enough—she got there and immediately saw that these people are going to need *everything*. So she left and went and bought all the clothes, and then brought them to the hotel. She's really a lovely person.

So Annie was there with the family. And we were all in shock. *Deep* shock.

I remember the firemen got two cars out. One was a Mercedes, and it has that rubber thing on the key. And he gave me the key when he got it out, because the rubber had melted to just this long trickle of plastic. [Laughs] And he gave me the key and said, "That's how close it came."

The studio sprinklers turned on, which kind of ruined all the equipment, but we got the tape out. Whatever tapes were in the studio.

You know, it had a devastating effect on me. The arson guys showed up. And said, "This was arson. Somebody burned your house." And I couldn't *possibly* accept it. I just kept saying, "No, you're mistaken." And then they took me around the back of the house, and showed me where someone had lit a can of lighter fluid, and thrown it into the back of the house. And it was completely clear that it was arson. So when I went back to the hotel I was very scared that somebody was trying to kill us.

Life changed. Suddenly security was going to be around us night and day. And a day or two later, I went to rehearsal. We were rehearsing. I'll never forget, the strangest thing was I drove myself to rehearsal and I was in such a state of shock that after the rehearsal, I drove all the way to my front gate before I remembered the house was burned down. Pulled up to the gate, and then it hit me. [Laughs]

So I've never really talked about that. [Pause] Then you really start to think about fame. It's a good and bad kind of thing. You realize that there are real lunatics out there who may just pick you for, whatever it is, their release or their obsession.

Because they love you so much.
Or they hate you. Or whatever.

So you lived in a hotel for a while?
Yeah, I lived in a hotel. And immediately there were security guards all around us. I've never liked to go around with security guards and an entourage and people. I don't like the idea of servants. And so life changed a bit then. It was necessary to have these people around.

We lived in a hotel for a few weeks, and then I rented a house up on Mulholland Drive that Stevie [Nicks] had been living in. And then I went right on tour, first to Egypt, and then with Dylan to Israel and Europe. Without a possession. Without *anything*. [Laughs]

Did you have your guitars?
The only guitar at the house was the [Gibson] Dove. And everything else was with the other equipment that was being prepared to go on the road. So I didn't lose my guitars. But I lost *so* much. You know, a

lifetime of photos. Everything that I had. I had quite a lot by that time in my life. It was all lost. Completely. The house was just burned to cinders.

Was your family pretty shaken by it?
Oh yeah. Yeah. We were shaken for years by it. It's sort of like being raped, I would imagine. It really took a long time. Because you knew that somebody just went and did it. Somebody tried to off you. So you go through a lot of emotions: Anger, confusion; I think it was fairly therapeutic that we went on the road. The whole family went. For a while. And then they went back to LA and I kept touring. But I think it kind of saved me in a way, because it kept me busy with something to do. It was just so odd to own nothing. [Laughs] You know, you'd go, "Oh, I think I'll pick up this coat here, because I don't have one. I might like another pair of shoes." And you just rebuild your life.

Did you rebuild that house?
I did. I rebuilt. That was the ultimate therapy, because it wasn't even anywhere I wanted to live that badly. I moved to a place on Mulholland, and lived there for a year, and then I moved to Beverly Hills, and rented another house there. Dave Stewart, actually, showed up that afternoon [of the fire] and said, "You're not going to move, are you? Because, you know, I just built my house and you're my neighbor. You're not going to move?"

And I thought that would be the ultimate therapy to build the house back, and to say to whoever did it, "You didn't get me. I didn't move an inch. And I'm still alive. And I'm going to build it back." So I built it back in an even greater way, a more expanded kind of house. So I built it back. Took a few years to build it back.

Did you like living up on Mulholland?
Yeah, it was nice. I think I was just in shock through all that time. [Pause] I was kind of just shocked. I then moved from the house on Mulholland to Charo's house. Charo was this Vegas entertainer, Xavier Cugat's wife. Cugat had bought this big house in Beverly Hills back in the Forties or Fifties. And [my family] moved from Mulholland to there when I was gone. I lived there until I rebuilt the house, and then I moved back.

Were your children okay?

Yeah, they were okay. Kim had this kind of ticking sound [Clicks with his tongue] for about a year after, but that went away. They were okay. Everybody pulled together. And we came very close. And we just kind of went through it. What else can you do?

It's a little confusing to me what happened in what order. The fire happened in the middle of the Bob Dylan tour. I remember telling Bob, when we were in England at the end of the tour, that we were going to have to stop, as far as backing him up. I had to go back and sort out my life and my family, and find a home, and we needed to get back to just being The Heartbreakers. And we had really enjoyed it, and now he needed to get his own band, because we needed to get back to our own thing.

And Bob said, "No, we don't want to break this up, it's too good."

And I said, "It is really good, but we kind of had our own agenda before we got into this." And he thought we could do both. And maybe we could have, but we were really tired. Because we were still trying to be Tom Petty & The Heartbreakers. And we did our own tour in the middle of that, and we made a record. We made *Let Me Up (I've Had Enough)* [1987]. [Laughs] And that title says a lot about that period. So I get it out of order. All I remember about all of it really well is that it ended in 1987 right around Christmastime. I came back. Kind of tired, but happy. I was in a new house, living in Beverly Hills, and I was going to put my feet up for a little while. And, of course, that never happens. [Laughs] And then a whole other chapter of life started.

You and Mike produced *Let Me Up* yourselves. It was the first album you produced on your own. How come you did that?

This album was made on a break during the Dylan tour. It was just before we went to Israel and Europe. We did make this album then, and did a quick tour of the US on our own, and then went back to working with Bob. I think we just wanted to get out from under producers for a while and just produce it ourselves. We're not great at doing that. It taught us that we should never do it again, because we're both too lazy to push ourselves the way we should be. If you hear that record, it's two records in one. There's my stuff, and there's Mike's stuff. And *all* of Mike's stuff sounds completely different than mine does. [Laughs] His stuff is this really produced stuff, like "Runaway Trains." Then you'll hear my side of things, and it's much cruder. I did a lot of songs in the studio and cut them really quick after we'd written them.

"The Damage You've Done" is literally the first time they're hearing the song. [Laughs] We were very bold in that sense, about just going for spontaneity. And I think it worked on some levels and it didn't work on others.

Chapter Nine

Handle With Care

Was it while touring with Dylan that you heard an advance tape of George Harrison's *Cloud Nine*, produced by Jeff Lynne?

TP: Yeah. And I loved it. We played in Birmingham [England] with Bob and then a few weeks later we played London for a few nights. I think we were there for three or four nights in Wembley. On the first night in Birmingham, George Harrison and Jeff Lynne came to visit. And Bob was not feeling well. He was not really around before the show, and then he didn't want to hang around afterwards too much.

It was funny—that first night we were in London, when we had that great time, a hurricane hit. In *London*. Completely unannounced and unpredicted by the weather bureau. I always thought that [hurricane] had something to do with changing my life. This literal hurricane.

The Hindus think that when you meet someone and you feel really close to them immediately, that maybe you knew them in a past life. And that was how it was with George. We met each other and instantly became really close. *Instantly* we became very close. And I remember him saying to me, "You know, I'm not going to let you out of my life now." And it wasn't about The Beatles or anything like that. We really got along well. And shared a sense of humor. And we became very close friends. And Jeff, too.

So we hung out, and one night we really had a nice time, after the gig we hung out for hours with George, and Ringo was there and Derek Taylor [music journalist, former Beatles publicist, and collaborator on George Harrison's autobiography, *I Me Mine*]. And all of their wives. And we hung out, and we had a lot of laughs. And then the next night was my birthday. I have a photo. They brought me a little birthday cake.

And there's a photo of me and George and McGuinn and Bob and Mike, and we're all backstage laughing. And it looks pretty accurate. Victor Maymudes, who was Bob's roadie, was there. We had a really good time. And George gave me this cassette, and said, "This is the album. Let me know if you like it."

So I took it home. That was the last gig of the tour, London. And that was when I told Bob, "I can't carry on because I have to go home and rebuild my life. The house had burned down and all of this, and I've kind of got to put my life back together, so I'm going to have to bow out." Which I think he understood, but he was kind of sad about it.

So I came back, and it was Thanksgiving Day. I was at the house in Beverly Hills, and some people were coming over. And I like to have softball games. And so I was going to have a softball game at the house. But I didn't have enough mitts to play ball. So I was going to drive down to the SavOn in Beverly Hills and buy a dozen ball mitts so everybody could play ball. Which was the only place open on Thanksgiving Day. So I'm at the traffic light, and I look over to my left, and there's Jeff Lynne. Who I'd only just recently seen in England. So I honked my horn, and he turned around, and we pulled over. And I said, "Wow, what are you doing here? And I love that album; the album's great."

He said, "I'm working with Brian Wilson." And he said, "Where do you live?"

I told him where I lived, and he said, "That's weird. I live *really* close to there. So we should get together."

"Okay, let's do—let's get together." Because I really liked Jeff—he's a great guy. And *very* warm, and has a really great sense of humor.

So we fast-forward a little bit. And I think Jeff probably came over after that in a day or two. And we hung out a little bit. And fast-forward a little more and it was right before Christmas. And there were a lot of magical things going on in my life. I was with my daughter Adria, and we were out Christmas shopping. We had driven over to Studio City, there was this one restaurant there on Ventura called Le Seur, a French restaurant that was a *really* good restaurant. It was *really* good, and it was the kind of place you went to on special evenings. It was kind of our special-night restaurant. And I wanted to give Adria a big afternoon out. And we were shopping and buying gifts. And we were driving past Le

Seur and she said, "Wouldn't it be something if you could just eat lunch at Le Seur?"

And I said, "Why not? Let's go."

She said, "You're *kidding*."

I pulled in the parking lot and we came in. I sat down in my chair, and the waiter came over and he said, "There's a friend of yours here and he'd like you to come over to the table." And that's all he said.

I said, "Oh," and I got up and walked around—there was kind of this private dining room—and as I walk in, there's George [Harrison]. And he was having lunch with some people from Warner Brothers. And Jeff. And as I walked into the room, Jeff was writing my number down for George. And George said, "How strange, I'd just gotten your number and somebody told me you'd walked into the restaurant at the same time."

I said, "Yeah, that's far out."

He said, "Where are you going?"

I said, "Well, I was just gonna eat."

He said, "Where are you going after you eat?"

And I said I was going home, and he said, "Can I come with you?"

"Well, I guess so, why not?"

And he said, "Well, I've got my car, but I'll follow you to your house." He said, "I'm staying at the Hotel Bel-Air," which wasn't too far away. He said, "We'll just hang out, okay?"

And I said okay. He followed me to my house, and we hung out that afternoon. And this is kind of strange, because when I talk about George, he's *so* famous, and so much of an icon. But he really had the ability to make you forget about that and be a real good friend, and we had a lot of fun. A lot of laughs, a lot of playing the guitars.

The next day, the door rings, and George is back with his family. We spent Christmas Eve together. Actually, we spent several Christmases to come. He would usually be on his way to Hawaii at Christmas, and he would stop in LA. And our two families became close. Dhani [George's son] became a close friend of Adria's, and they're still good pals.

Did George like LA?

I don't think he really liked LA. He complained a lot about the smog and it being over-populated. But he had a lot of friends here, and he came often to see his friends. You know, Jeff [Lynne] and Jim Keltner,

Mo Ostin, and just many, many more. He had a lot of friends here. And so sometimes he would just come to hang with the guys.

So it was around this time that I showed Jeff one night I had written the song "Yer So Bad." But there was one little bit in the B-section where I didn't know where to go. And he showed me this *E* minor chord. And that kind of opened it all up to me. And he showed me this little part, *E* minor to *C*, and said, "You could do this." And I said, "That's great!" And I was *so* elated, because I had been working on the song for days and I couldn't get from the verse to the chorus somehow. And he showed me this little bit, and I said, "Great! Will you produce this?"

And he said, "Sure, let's do it." And he said, "Where should we record it?" And Mike had the studio in his house, and Jeff said he much preferred working in houses than studios.

And then Jeff came back the next day. We hadn't gone to Mike's yet. And that evening we wrote "Free Fallin'." And that was a pretty big rush. And then he left and I wrote the last verse about Mulholland and all that. And so he came back the next day and I showed him that I had finished the song. And he was really jazzed, and said, "Let's go record it."

So I took Jeff to Mike's. And there was just enough room to get the three of us into the room with the recording console. It was this little bedroom that was *so* small, it was *so* jammed with recording gear and a recording console, that Bugs had to stand in the hall outside the door. Because it was *that* small. It was so funky, nobody would ever believe it.

We ran mike cables out to the garage. Which was a real garage. We pulled the cars out. And we recorded it that way. The first track we did was "Free Fallin'."

How long did it take to record?
One day. Maybe two.

Phil Jones played drums?
Yes. He had been around a long time. He was a drummer, a good friend of ours, and he played percussion on a lot of our albums and on a tour in '81. "Free Fallin'" took one day, maybe two. It was Christmas, so we didn't know where the band was. I think Stanley was in Florida. And so

that became a solo record. And that was a real kind of a weird thing for me, because it was a big deal for The Heartbreakers.

I remember calling Howie because I thought we had better get as many of [The Heartbreakers] as we can. Though we had really made the track, and we had done the bass. But maybe Howie could come and sing, and this would smooth the wound over to have them come in. And I guess they had already talked among themselves, and they were pissed about it. This is pure conjecture on my part, but I think they had probably talked among themselves, Stanley and Ben and Howie. There was a vibe.

So I got to Mike's, and Howie was sitting outside the door of the bedroom. And he seemed kind of preoccupied, like he could be in those days. He was waiting, almost like a doctor waiting in the waiting room. And he said, "You don't really need me for this, do you?" And he said, "I don't like it."

I said, "Well, if you don't like it I don't need you."

Right then I went, *well*, this is going to be a Tom Petty solo record, because *I* like it. And I'm not going to go through this vibe, and there's really no room for them on this anyway. And Mike engineered the track; we didn't have an engineer.

Who played bass?

Jeff.

The next day we recorded "Yer So Bad." So we mixed those two songs. While we were mixing "Free Fallin'," we wrote "I Won't Back Down." Jeff and I did, in a little booth in the studio.

So now George is back in town, and he helped us record "I Won't Back Down." And we're having a ball. We're just having a ball. It seemed like musically we could do no wrong. We were digging everything we were doing. And I was afraid—Jeff kept saying, "I don't know about doing a whole album, 'cause I have to go to England."

And so I really quickly said, "We'll write a song a day and do a track a day. If you can just put off the trip for a week." I was that desperate for him to finish the record with me. And we really did write a song a day and we recorded the next day. We did almost all of it. I think we did nine songs. The last one was "Runnin' Down A Dream." We wrote that around a riff Mike had. [Sings descending riff] And so the record was made really quick. And we mixed it really fast.

Was it a fun experience, working like that?
Yeah, it was a ball. I had so much fun.

Did you have room for drums there?
In the garage. We'd sing in the garage; and we did everything out there. It was cold out there, too. Sometimes you could see your breath [Laughs] when you sang. Jeff kept saying, "Roy Orbison is coming to town." And that was Jeff's great hero. Roy Orbison and Del Shannon were his two favorites. He idolized Roy and Del Shannon. And that was another strange connection, because I knew Del Shannon, I had done a record with him way back when, and so had Jeff. And he kept saying, "Roy Orbison is coming to town, and we're going to do something with Roy Orbison." And Roy came. I guess Roy was living out here in Malibu. And they hooked up.

Jeff lived not far from me, and one afternoon the phone rang and it was him, and he said, "Hey, Roy Orbison's over here, you've got to come over and help me write a song for him. I need some help." So I jumped in the car, I had a new Corvette, and we went over to see Jeff and Roy, and we all went out to look at the car, and we raised the hood of the car. And we were such a bunch of musicians. Non-mechanics, you know. And we couldn't get the hood back down on the car. [Laughs] And I remember my first meeting with Roy, he's got his head under my hood trying to figure out how to get the hood down.

And we wrote "You Got It." [Sings, "Anything you want, you got it..."]

The three of you wrote it together?
Yeah. And that was on that first day. And so I think that went on. We came back the next day too, wrote another song called "California Blue" that he did on his album. So this became a kind of circle of friends. Occasionally Roy would show up for dinner, and George [Harrison] was in and out of town. And Jeff and I were pretty tight, because we were neighbors. So that was the germ of the Traveling Wilburys.

Roy was a mysterious guy, always wearing those dark glasses.
He never took the glasses off. But he was very jovial. Very funny. One of the funniest guys I've ever met. A sweetheart. You couldn't help but love him. He always had some jokes, and he had the most infectious laugh. That's one thing I remember about him a lot; his laugh, for some

reason, was really infectious. Like when you heard him laugh, you couldn't help but laugh with him.

And he was a bit older than us, and he seemed maybe a little wiser. [Laughs] But I liked him a lot. That's who I was hanging with, that year, that Christmas. And the time after that. We were all pals. George came back from Hawaii, and I think he stayed until March or something. He stayed because he had to go to the [Rock and Roll] Hall of Fame and get his Hall of Fame induction—I remember he was in LA before he went to that. [The Beatles were inducted into the Rock and Roll Hall of Fame in 1988.]

George was known as "the quiet Beatle," but I understand he was anything but.
Oh yeah.

Funny, too?
He was so funny, it's hard to explain. He was the funniest guy I ever met. Such a keen sense of humor. A *lot* of fun. A wise person. He really wanted to know the meaning of it all. But at the same time, he was really light-hearted and tremendous fun. [Laughs] Just tremendous fun. And we got along so well. There's really not a day that I don't think about him. Many adventures were to come after that.

You once mentioned that on guitar he would play what he'd call "naughty chords," such as diminished chords.
Yeah. Well, he knew every chord. He knew so many chords. He was a great, great musician. Jeff, too. They were really great. I was in awe of how good they were. And just how musical they were. And there's nothing like that to make you want to step up and do your best work.

So that became my crowd. And I didn't see much of The Heartbreakers during that period. Mike I kept in touch with, of course, because he was working on *Full Moon Fever* with me.

But you knew you didn't want to break up The Heartbreakers?
I never thought of leaving. And I kept reassuring them that I wasn't going to leave. But I think there was some doubt in their mind.

Where did the title "*Full Moon Fever*" come from?
It just came out of my noggin one day. "Full moon fever" was a little phrase for what's happening tonight, it's a full moon—ah yes! It's full moon fever! That was the first solo album, so that was quite an event. Because I always thought when the full moon comes, I get some kind of charge from it. But I think I chose it just because mostly it sounded good.

Were all the songs on that album written with Jeff? Did you have anything pre-written?
Nothing but "The Apartment Song."

You two really inspired each other.
A lot. Denny Cordell came by my house one day, who I hadn't seen in a long time. We were going to call the album *Songs From The Garage*. We had shot the cover, even, which was a photo of me sitting in Mike's garage, surrounded by all these instruments and things.

And Cordell heard the record. *Loved* the record. Which was really reassuring to me, 'cause he didn't hand out compliments easily. And I showed him the cover, and he said, "Oh no, no, no, this is not right. This is *far* too good to be called *Songs From The Garage*." And he said, "Give it a name, man." [Laughs] "Give this thing a name."

So I rethought it and came up with "*Full Moon Fever*." Which was probably good advice. We just completely jettisoned the cover and redid it.

Is it true that MCA didn't like the album at first?
That was the next big shock. I brought the record in, and they didn't like it. Which had never happened to me. I was *stunned*. They didn't like it.

What was their problem with it?
They didn't hear a single!

With "Free Fallin'" and "Runnin' Down A Dream"?
And "I Won't Back Down." But they didn't hear a single. So this is what you're up against in the music business.

Was it just one guy, or a number of guys who felt that?
I think it went all the way to the top. They didn't want to release it. They wanted me to go away and come up with a single. So I was pretty devastated. And I just kind of put it on the back burner. And I was really depressed. Mike and I cut that song "Alright For Now," the kind of lullaby that's on there. We did that without Jeff. Jeff was out of town. And then Jeff came back and I said, "They don't want to put the record out."

For one thing, it was too short. It was only nine songs. And the CD had become really popular. So they wanted it to be a little longer. Then I cut the Byrds song "Feel A Whole Lot Better" just to make the record a little longer.

A Gene Clark song.
Yeah. To which he was eternally grateful. Then, later on, I brought the record back. And the regime had changed at MCA. And I brought exactly the same record in. And they loved it.

They heard singles this time?
Yeah. But this is how the record business is. A guy can leave, or come, and his viewpoint is completely different than the guy that was there. You're just at the mercy of these guys. To some degree.

I would think at your level, that this couldn't happen to you. That if you wanted to put out a record, you could.
I was *so* stunned. I was stunned beyond belief. I'd never ever had anything like that happen.

Especially with such a great album.
Yeah, I thought it was incredible. They just didn't hear it. I don't know why, but they didn't hear it. So it got put on the back burner because the Traveling Wilburys started to happen: It didn't come out until after the Wilburys' album. But it was actually done before the Wilburys. Which used to crack me up, because I saw some reviews that said it had the Traveling Wilburys sound. But the truth was that it was done before there was the Traveling Wilburys.

But it does share that palpable joy of the Traveling Wilburys' albums.
There was a lot of joy around in those days. We were a happy bunch.

Who came up with the name the "Traveling Wilburys"?
George.

Did it appeal to you?
Yeah, I thought it was funny. He had come up with that concept when he was making *Cloud Nine.*

The concept of having you all together?
Of having a band called the Traveling Wilburys. George and Jeff had talked about that a lot when they were making *Cloud Nine.* George had the concept. He wanted to be in a band. He hadn't been in a band since The Beatles.

That was a good band.
[Laughs] Yeah, they were good. He wanted to be in a band, but he wanted to avoid all those pitfalls that a band has. He didn't want it to be so overtly serious that it became a chore. And he didn't want to have a manager. He wanted it to be, above all, an enjoyable experience. But he was smart enough to know it wouldn't be enjoyable if it wasn't good. It had to be good.

The idea was to make the band with people he liked that were good. So I think I remember him talking about the Traveling Wilburys before there was a Traveling Wilburys. And I'm pretty sure that, at least in the back of his mind, he was trying to engineer this band together. He had come out of the garden after a long time and made a record. A really good one. I think he was kind of charged. The record had gone to Number One. I remember him coming over the day it went to Number One and he was really happy. And he wanted to keep playing music. And they were bringing out another single from *Cloud Nine.* And they needed a B-side for the release. And in those days he had a couple of guitars that he always kept at my house, so when he came to town he had guitars.

Acoustics?

I think one was a Gretsch electric. And maybe there was an acoustic, too. And they'd be in my closet. When he came to town, he'd pick them up so he wouldn't have to lug them back and forth on the airplanes. So I guess he had been out to dinner the night before with Jeff and Roy. And he got the idea that "Maybe you guys can help me make this B-side, this track I've got to do." And they were up for it. And he called Bob [Dylan] because Bob had a studio in his house, and he didn't want to go to a commercial studio. And he also liked recording in houses better than studios. So he arranged to cut it at Bob's house.

So he came by my house the night before to get his guitar. And he told me what he was going to do, and he asked, "Would you like to come and play rhythm guitar? Will you come with me?"

I said, "Of course I would. I wouldn't miss that." So in the morning I remember he came in his car with Jeff and picked me up, and we drove out to Bob's house in Malibu. And the night before he had written the chord pattern, pretty much, to "Handle With Care." He wrote it in his room at the Bel-Air Hotel. So, when we got there, Bob was there. And George kind of showed us the chord pattern.

And then he said, "It'd be great if we had a part for Roy to sing in the tune." He didn't want to waste Roy Orbison. So I remember Jeff and George sitting on the grass outside Bob's house and they wrote that middle bit: [Sings] "I'm so tired of being lonely..." They wrote the melody and the chords to that. No lyrics to any of it.

So we started from that. And George said to Bob and I, "You two think of a bit." Because he was like that when he would get energized. And so we came up with [Sings] "Everybody needs somebody to lean on." And we cut the track. We cut the track with just a rhythm box, and all of us playing acoustic guitar. There were five acoustic guitars all at once. And then George looked and saw a road case there, in Bob's garage, that said, "Handle With Care."

George went, "That's good. It'll be 'Handle With Care'." So then we took a break and had some food. And, while we were having dinner, we wrote the lyrics. Between all of us. It was the Wilbury way to say a line. And if everybody agreed, it was, "Yay," and if they didn't it was, "Nay." And then we'd start throwing out lines till one stuck. So that became really good in a way because it takes a lot of guts to say a line. Especially in *that* company. But it was always a warm vibe, a good vibe, and there was laughter. It wasn't overly serious. But it came out to be such a beautiful song, and there's actually such a nice meaning in the lyric, I can't imagine how it happened. [Laughs] Because it did. And we did nearly all of it that night. We did the vocals, and Jeff played the drums.

I always thought Roy wrote his section himself, because it fits his voice and style so well.
I think he wrote the lyric.

How about the lyric, "I've been robbed and ridiculed/In day care centers and night schools." Who wrote that? It sounds Dylanesque.
I think I had the "day care centers and night schools." But I know I had, "Ah, the sweet smell of success." That pleased George quite a bit. It was like that. It's hard to remember who wrote exactly what. It was mostly George's song. So we were very pleased with it. And he took it to Warner Brothers to turn it in. And [George] played it for them, and they went, "My God, this is *way* too heavy to be a B-side. This is really something."

But I remember George the night before saying to Jeff, "Jeff, this is the Traveling Wilburys." And then he explained to me his whole concept of the Traveling Wilburys.

So he arrived at my house that next afternoon after he had played them the track, and he was really excited. Just jumping up and down excited. "We've got a band! We've got to be in a band!"

I said, "Okay. I'll do it."

He said, "We've got to get Bob and Roy in it." And he was at my house and he picked up the phone and phoned Bob, had a conversation with Bob, and when he hung up the phone, he said, "Alright, Bob's in." Next one was Roy. "How do we get Roy in this thing? We've got to ask Roy. Roy's playing in Anaheim."

So we rented a car, all of us piled in the car, Jeff, George, and I and our wives. We drive to Anaheim. We got legal pads, because George wanted us to write down every interesting phrase we heard or saw on the trip to Anaheim and back. And we're all doing that. Any time somebody said something we thought was really good or made us laugh or we thought was interesting, we wrote it down.

And I remember we went in to see Roy before the show, and we threw it out to Roy, and Roy said, "Sure, sure, I'll do it. I'll be in the band." And we rode home just high as kites. A natural high. Like, "Roy Orbison's in our band!" [Laughs]

Was it agreed from the beginning that you would all write the songs together?
It wasn't really said. But we were all going to be in the band. That was the first thing that was said. The rest of it just kind of took shape. "On a certain day we're going to turn up and we're gonna start from there." And it took a little doing, to get that first song off the ground, but we did it, and then we found a way of working, where we could write communally.

Words and music at the same time?
Usually we would have maybe a title or a little bit of words, and then we would write the melody and we'd usually cut the track—this was all at Dave Stewart's house in Encino.

Was Dave involved?
No, Dave was out of the country. But he lent us his house and his studio. So we would go there. And usually, after we had done the track, we'd have dinner. And this was usually where the lyrics started. At dinner. And then when we'd finish the lyric, we'd go up and sing. Sometimes we'd kind of audition to see who sang it the best. "Take a bit—you sing it, no you sing it… Well, okay, this one sounds best with Roy singing," or whoever.

Jeff and George were the producers. That was good, because we had a little bit of authority. Somebody who was leading this crazy thing. And we just pulled it together. We became a group. It lasted for a couple of years.

When George would play those great solos, would he work them out in advance and then lay them down?
Yeah. I think he would usually practice with the tape. And then he'd work it out, and then he'd go for the take.

He was such a phenomenal player.
Yeah, he was an incredible player. His slide work is so unique. It's *so* right in pitch. Today a lot of guitar players don't even pay any attention to pitch. But he really played in tune, in pitch.

Like he was singing.
Yeah. His slide playing almost sounds like a voice at times.

So I think we were all just as happy as five boys could be. [Laughs]

Dylan is such an amazing wordsmith, it would seem he would lead the writing of the lyrics. But it was more of an equal participation?
Yes. Nobody really outranked anybody. It was like a group effort. And anything that got done had to pretty much be the majority of us digging it. But there were few conflicts. I think we almost always agreed on what was good and what wasn't.

It's fun to listen to, and sounds like you all were having fun doing it.
[Softly] We really were. We were having as much fun as you can have. I can't even impart to you how much fun those days were.

I was taking Polaroids through the whole thing. And Bugs was taking a lot of Polaroids. Bugs was also the Wilbury roadie. And I put all the photos in an album as I was taking them. George actually said, "You should put these in an album so they don't get scratched up or anything." And Bugs went down to the drugstore and bought us a little photo album. And I'd stick them all in this photo album. And then George took it back to England at one point, because he thought he might use them for something. And every time I'd be at Friar Park [George's home], he'd say, "Oh, I have your photo album." But I always forgot to get it. And then, just a week ago, Olivia [Harrison, George's wife] sent me the photo album. She put it in this really nice album with a Traveling Wilburys logo on the front. And, to look at the photos, it really says it all. You can just see we're having a ball.

Who came up with the first names of the Wilburys? [Each Wilbury went by a fictitious name: Tom was Charlie T., George Harrison was Nelson, Jeff Lynne was Otis, Roy Orbison was Lefty, and Bob Dylan was Lucky.]
Everybody picked their name. Because we didn't want it to sound like Crosby, Stills, Nash & Young, like a bunch of lawyers. We knew there'd be a lot of heat on it because of who we were. And maybe we could lessen that a little bit by taking on different identities. Because we didn't want the music to be second to the thing. It was a good band; we didn't want to kind of slide on who we were. That was kind of inevitable. We didn't want that to be the main thrust of the thing. And we wanted to keep a sense of humor about it.

What was it like to stand in the studio and hear Roy Orbison's voice?
Oh, it would just give you a chill to hear him sing over your shoulder. It was such a privilege. I mean, standing around a mike and singing and then hearing *that voice* in the blend, it was just a chill down your spine. He had *such* a beautiful tone in his voice.

Would he nail vocals on a first take?
Usually, yeah. In the Wilbury records, who's singing lead isn't necessarily who wrote most of the song. Sometimes George liked to kind of audition us. Take the song, and have three or four of us sing the lead. And then he'd decide who sang that one the best. And that's how that happened. So it would be kind of intimidating if Roy Orbison just sang the song, and then they'd send me out to sing it. [Laughs] But actually, sometimes, they might pick me over Roy, because the song suited me better, or suited Jeff better. Or Bob. What a bunch of singers.

Roy died on December 6, 1988, before you did the second album. Was it tough doing it without him?
Yeah. I mean, he was certainly missed. The second album was a different scene, because by then we were a big successful group. I wouldn't say the vibe was *bad*, it was still good, but it had changed a little bit. That's what success does. We still had a lot of fun on the second one, too.

It's a great album.

I think it is a really good album. It's different from the first one. You know, we just went on. Roy had died. And it was a terrible loss of a friend.

He was Lefty Wilbury?

Yeah. Named after Lefty Frizzell. I was Charlie T. Because Derek Taylor wrote this huge history of the Wilburys. It didn't make the album; I think it was Michael Palin who wrote the sleeve notes. But Derek Taylor wrote *volumes* of history of how the Wilburys came together. And the Wilburys' father was named Charles Truscott Wilbury. [Laughs] And I thought that was so funny that I decided I'd be Charles Truscott, Jr. [Laughs] So it came out Charlie T.

By the second album, I think there were more record company people around, more managers. Maybe a little more tension on that record. Not a lot.

We never intended to replace Roy. The big thing in the media was, "Who is going to take his place?" We never considered replacing him, that I remember. Whoever came around was dubbed the next Wilbury. If McGuinn came over and hung out, you'd read that Roger was joining. Or Del Shannon was one that was bandied about a lot. But I don't think we ever, at all, considered bringing someone else in. We were just going to go on, the four of us.

What was it like recording with the Wilburys? Were those fun sessions?

It was about as much fun as you can legally have. I'm sure it was some of the best times in my life. It was really a joyous time. Everyone was so *up*. The energy level, as far as creativity, was so high. And it was just *so* much fun. I think everyone was grooving on the fact that the whole thing didn't lay on any one person's shoulders. We were all in the position of having to carry the whole thing. Being in this group, where we were sort of equal contributors, all of a sudden, was a *great* relief. And I think everyone really enjoyed that.

And, beyond that, we were really good friends. It really formed some long-lasting friendships. And we were just having a great time. When I think back about it, it's hard to separate the sessions from days we didn't have sessions, because we were all still hanging out, whether we were working or not.

But the sessions were great. George was our leader and our manager. But Jeff was certainly equal as a producer. They did an amazing job. And it was a fairly primitive recording situation, because we were working in Dave Stewart's house. He had a studio across his backyard. But it was the early days, and they'd just put in the board. Just a little Soundcraft board and a little Soundcraft 24-track. And that was *it.* We didn't have any effects, [Laughs] or any of the luxurious things you have. So it was amazing, really, that we pulled it off. But it didn't seem to matter.

So we cut the tracks there—for the first album—at Dave's house. And then we went to Friar Park in England, George's place, and did all the overdubs and mixing there. And that was kind of the pattern for both albums.

Then, by the second album, we had this great big mansion up on a hill in Beverly Hills that was a Wallace Neff home [one of California's most celebrated architects]. He built it in the Twenties. It was kind of a Spanish-style, huge mansion. It was like sixteen acres up at the top of a mountain. We had a big flagpole with the Wilbury flag flying above the home. Even from the bottom of the hill, you could look up and see the flag. So that became dubbed "Wilbury Manor."

We moved a studio into the library. It had this huge library. And we borrowed a desk and a machine, I think, from Herb Alpert at A&M. And really, within forty-eight hours, they put the studio in the library, and we began working.

Jim Keltner [the drummer] should have been billed as a Wilbury. Because he was *always* there, and he played on everything. He called himself a "Sidebury." [Laughs] But he was really a Wilbury. And everyone really loved Jim. He's a very lovable guy. I've known him for many years. Since I was a pretty young guy, knocking around town. Jim's always sort of been there. You'd look up, and there'd be Jim.

I remember when we were recording "Refugee," when we were doing the overdubs at Cherokee Studios, he was in the hallway with a little shaker. I came out into the hallway and he'd been playing the shaker along with "Refugee." And he said, "Go in and dub the shaker on it." And we did dub it on, and it sounded great. I think Stan played it. Because it was his shaker. [Laughs]

Jim's a very soulful person. A deep, deep, spiritual person. And really one of the best musicians I've ever encountered. Absolutely. I think you'll find that a lot of the best musicians, not just in LA but in England, everywhere, they really look up to Jim. Jim is sort of the guru. [Laughs] Everyone's guru.

Who played bass?
Jeff. I think Jeff played bass on everything. And we all played acoustic guitars, and then piecemealed whatever was left. It was kind of spread around. The tracks were cut with Jim playing the drums, and, for separation, we turned the sofa over in front of the drums. And then on the other side we had the four Wilburys with acoustic guitars. And we would track everything with four acoustic guitars, and then we'd build the track from there. But *God*, they were fun sessions. How could they not be? And nobody ever went home when the sessions were over. [Laughs] We hung out all night and all day. We went everywhere. It was a lot of fun. Really a lot of fun.

What was Bob like in the studio?
He was very good, very sharp. He had a lot of good ideas.

He has a reputation of not liking to do things more than once in the studio.
Yeah, a lot of people say that about him.

Not true?
I don't think it's *as* true as the myth. I've seen him work very hard on things. And do a lot of takes. But a myth builds up around people. Because I think on his own records, he goes for a spontaneity. That's my experience with him, anyway. He likes to get a lot of spontaneous feel in the record. But I think he keeps an overview of what's going on, certainly.

I produced a record for him once called "Band Of The Hand," which is a very rare single that I produced for him in Australia. He did it for a movie. I got told about it on the plane. We were landing in Sydney, and he came back and said, "I've got to do this session tonight, could you produce it?" So I really hit the ground running in Sydney, and had to book a studio, and find gear, because our gear was someplace else. And get The Heartbreakers in. And we did a track, and we worked pretty hard on it. We worked most of the night on the song. So, I don't know: I think nobody's exactly one way all of the time.

Did you ever consider having a Wilburys concert?
Many times. Yeah. There was *always* a lot of talk about the Wilburys doing a performance. And then we always talked ourselves out of it.

Why?
I don't know. I guess maybe it was more than we all wanted to take on. I probably would have done it. You know, George *often* talked about it. Especially when we'd have a few drinks, he'd get very keen on the idea. And then the next day he'd be not so keen on it. I think the general feeling was that it was a little more than what we wanted to take on. Taking that out [Laughs] onto the stage. And traveling around. It'd be a little bit of a circus.

So there never was a live Wilburys performance. But it could have been done. When we played the Royal Albert Hall in London [November 29, 2002] for the *Concert For George*, and Jeff and I did the Wilburys' song ["Handle With Care"] with The Heartbreakers and Dhani Harrison, George's son. We saw that it could be done. And also when we did it again at the [Rock and Roll] Hall of Fame. [George Harrison was posthumously inducted into the Rock and Roll Hall of Fame in March 2004. Tom Petty and Jeff Lynne inducted their friend into the Hall and then played Harrison's "While My Guitar Gently Weeps" with several other musicians, including Prince, who was also inducted into the Hall of Fame during the same ceremony.] I remember having a very conscious thought of "Damn, [George] would have really enjoyed this." I think actually George planned for us to get back together and do *a* concert. And we never did get that done, but we were going to do *one* show, and film it. And perhaps do an album of that. But the idea of touring with all five of us—there was just no way.

Why did you choose to mix the albums at George's home in England?
It was just a matter of comfort. I think George and Jeff, who were living in both places, England and America, wanted that. George didn't have a permanent home in America. And I think he was probably anxious to go home. It was like, "Okay, I've been here for quite a while, it'd be nice to go home and have the luxury of working at home." Plus he had a

really nice studio that had all the accessories needed to mix the tracks. And I think, just basically, he wanted to be in England.

It was fun. It was nice going and living in Friar Park and recording. It was lovely. A beautiful place.

I've read that there are beautiful gardens.

The best I've ever seen. [Laughs] Yeah. He really worked on those gardens. He loved his gardens. English gardens, traditionally, are pretty beautiful things. This was no exception. Really quite a place.

He made the statement that he felt most at home inside the gates of his garden, but when he stepped outside, he didn't really feel like part of the modern world.

Yeah. It was this huge, huge compound. I don't know how many acres it was, but you could walk around for days. And just one beautiful garden after the other. And lakes. We used to take a rowboat, or a little boat with a little engine on it, and ride around the lakes. And there were underground caves, and we'd row the boat through the caves. There was plenty to do. Lots of neat little cabins and shacks and things to go into if it suddenly rained. I remember sitting in those in the rain. It was a great time. I went there many, many times. It was a great place to record. A very nice place to be.

Was the writing on the second album the same process, trading lines?

Yeah. Sometimes, even in the first album, sometimes somebody would come in with a chunk of a song. I remember Bob coming in with the song "Congratulations." And he had quite a bit of it written when he came in. That was an exception, when we finished that off.

Or "End Of The Line," I remember George having the chorus. [Sings] "It's all right..." And then the rest of us came up with words, I think Bob and I came up with that verse. And it was like that, piecing things together. There was always a kind of group meeting around the lyrics.

It was something you won't see again, probably. It was a very unusual project. And I just felt really lucky to be part of it.

Did you ever think of doing a third Wilburys album?
Yes. I just don't think we could ever get us all in one place. Especially Bob, who had begun his lifelong tour. We'd all made successful records right after that. We'd all done solo records. I had a responsibility to The Heartbreakers. I'd been gone for a long time. I'd done the Wilburys and a solo record [*Full Moon Fever*]. I felt like I should go back and do that. And Bob went on the road.

So, to the end of George's life, it was always talked about. "Yeah, when are we going to do it again? *Are* we going to do it again?" It never happened, unfortunately. Even when he was attacked, his line going into the hospital, and his only line to the press, was, "Well, I don't think he was there to audition for the Traveling Wilburys." Jeff and George and I stayed pretty close. And Bob seemed to always be traveling.

It was the supergroup of all supergroups, with outstanding people in it. Yet there was always a warmth, humor, and sense of friendliness around it.
Yeah. That was part of our idea. To keep it light. We wanted to take as much heat off of who we were. Which really could have worked against us as much as for us. But we wanted to keep it light, and we wanted it to be something that warmed the heart. We wanted to make something good in a world that seemed to get uglier and uglier and meaner and meaner. The Wilburys was this nice friendly thing. And I'm really proud that I was part of it. Because I do think that it brought a little sunshine into the world.

Chapter Ten

Into The Great Wide Open

After the Wilburys, you returned to The Heartbreakers to make the album *Into The Great Wide Open* which was produced by Jeff Lynne. How was that—combining Lynne with The Heartbreakers?

TP: It's not a bad album. I don't think it was the best way to work with The Heartbreakers.

You called it a "big mess" at one point.

Yeah, it was. It's a good album. I was in this Wilbury way of working. And it was me trying to drag them into that way of working. Which I don't think they were happy with.

How was that different from your usual way of working with them?

Well, there's a lot of overdubbing. And they like to just all play live, and take the tracks live. And there were lots of layers and overdubbing. Jeff was involved. I read somewhere that Howie said he just felt like he was being slapped on a Tom Petty/Jeff Lynne record. Which was probably true, to some degree. I don't think they had the input they were used to having. Because Jeff is a formidable presence. And I think they just felt that it's not really The Heartbreakers. So they weren't really getting along well during that record. But I still think the record came out good.

You said, "I think I made a big mistake that I didn't give The Heartbreakers more say."

Probably. Probably should have just done it on our own. But Jeff and I were so close, we were really hanging out every day. We were really close. We had done a *lot* of records in a row together. And it seemed unnatural for me to work without Jeff. But I probably should have had a better overview of things and said, "Well, I've got to go do The Heartbreakers on my own." But I just thought it could work great. What if it worked out great and they really liked Jeff? It didn't work that great. They felt suppressed. They felt we should be tracking live and making all our own decisions. With all the producers we worked with at that point—Cordell and Jimmy Iovine—we had a lot of input. The whole band always had a lot of input. With Jeff, I don't think they had that kind of input. Which is not to fault Jeff, because he just wanted to make the best record he could. And it was a different way of working. Instead of taking Polaroids, we were oil-painting. [Laughs] It was a different way of working.

You wrote a lot of the songs for that album with Jeff. What was your method of writing together?
We always wrote nose to nose. Two acoustic guitars. Nose to nose from the ground up. Sitting there and working them out. We had quite a thing going. We were a good songwriting team.

So, looking back on it, I don't regret it, because a lot of good music was made. It may have been hard on some people's feelings, and there may have been a little stress within The Heartbreakers, but in the end it was a successful record. Everybody enjoyed that, certainly. And I think it was just another page in our book. It took us down the road to somewhere else.

It has strong material. And it seemed in some ways an extension of the spirit of *Full Moon Fever*.
It was. Which is probably what [The Heartbreakers] didn't like. They thought, "Well, that's a solo record. That's your thing, it's not our thing."

During that time, I think I was trying to do too many things. I think it was when the second Wilburys album was going on, I told The Heartbreakers I could still make a record with you at the same time. And we'll do that on our own. And I remember going to one session. And Mike and I produced the session we did, a song called "Travelin'." That song is actually on the boxed set. They *hated* it. They hated it, hated it, hated it. That was the only session done. It was like, "Forget it, see you down the road. We'll do it another time."

I think that record's *fantastic.* And that was just The Heartbreakers, no outside anybody. But they didn't like working the way I wanted to work. They didn't dig that sound. I don't know if Mike did, but the others didn't like it. They said, "I don't like this. It doesn't sound like us." I didn't see anything wrong with it. I thought, "It is us." And, when I hear that record now, I'm really sorry we didn't put it out on an album. It wasn't even discovered again until the boxed-set project came along, and they started going through the tape vaults. And George Drakoulias found it, and said, "God, this is amazing!" I said, "Yeah, [Laughs] it is."

There was a statement someone made that whenever three or four Heartbreakers were in a room, it was a good time, but when you had all five together, it was work.
[Much laughter] Yeah. All five in a room, it got serious then. To get all five in one place, then things could get really serious. Get three of them, or two of them, no problem. Like I said, we grew up as young men together. We went back, in some cases, all the way to high school. So, you know what that's like, when you get everybody in one place, then it becomes official, right? It's like, we're working. We're here. I think that was what was meant by that.

But there's a deep love between us. Those original five. We were *really* close. As much as we could fight, I'm sure there's a deep respect among all of us. And a lot of love for each other. There was never anything in it that was malicious. We never did anything that was meant to be cruel or mean. But we were under a lot of stress sometimes. [Laughs] And things got really serious sometimes. And the thing got really big. I think it's probably true of most groups in that situation that you've got to handle a lot of people's personalities and egos. It's always a little bit of a balancing act. But, as rock and roll groups go, I think The Heartbreakers got along really well.

You're still essentially together.
Yes. There's still four of us there. So, that's pretty good.

What was it like returning to The Heartbreakers, after being in a group of musicians trading roles? With The Heartbreakers, you're the main guy.

It was different, because The Heartbreakers are *not* as cheerful as the Wilburys. [Laughs] It's not the same vibe. Where I'd come from this gregarious bunch of people, The Heartbreakers are more introverted and not really a slap-happy bunch of people. But it was nice to be back. It was like putting on an old suit of clothes again. They're such a great band, which is what I think struck me. I felt, "*Damn*, these guys are *really* good." It was great to be back with them and to go on the road with them.

These were great times. We were really having a good time. So, as I remember it, when I went back it was great. I think they were happy that I was back. Because I don't think they were completely sure I would come back. I think they had their doubts. I don't think it was ever voiced to *me*, but I think it was voiced to other people, that they weren't sure I would come back. But I always intended to come back.

Did you tell them that?

Yeah. I always tried to reassure them: "Look, I'm coming back." But I think they were a little insecure that I was having a *lot* of fun somewhere else. And I don't blame them. I would have thought the same thing. Especially with the solo album tagged on.

But it was good for me. I needed to get away from The Heartbreakers. I needed to have that freedom that I hadn't had for so many years. To do anything else. It was always having to come up with a bunch of songs, and take them to The Heartbreakers, and practice them, and make a record, and do a tour afterward, and then the whole cycle would start again. That went on year after year. And this was a nice break from that. I think I came back to The Heartbreakers with a lot of new input that I learned when I was away. New recording techniques, I was a much bolder songwriter, I think, in a lot of ways. So I think I learned from going away.

And they learned, as well. They didn't just sit dormant. They did a lot of things. Stan and Mike both worked with Don Henley. Mike wrote "Boys Of Summer" [with Henley], Stan wrote "Last Worthless Evening" and a couple of other ones with Don, and he became kind of a lifelong friend of Don's. That year at the Grammys, all competing for Best

Album, was the Wilburys' album [*Traveling Wilburys, Vol. 1*], *Full Moon Fever*, Don Henley's album [*Building The Perfect Beast*]—and a *big* chunk of that was The Heartbreakers—and Bonnie Raitt [*Nick Of Time*]. And I think we all canceled each other out. And Bonnie Raitt won. Not to take anything away from her, because she's really talented, too. But I was quite proud of that. I thought, "We've really put out a lot of music, these five boys." And at the same time Howie won a Grammy for the John Prine album [*The Missing Years*] he produced, and won the Best Folk Album Grammy. So they weren't really sitting on their thumbs. They had a lot going on themselves.

So, when we came back together, I think it was kind of nice. Everyone felt that it was really good, and we really appreciated it.

Benmont was busy too?
Yeah, Benmont was doing all kinds of session work. I know he wrote a little bit with Don [Henley] and he played on a whole bunch of albums during that period. He played with U2.

They also, all of them, were working on the Roy Orbison album. And Mike was even producing part of the Roy Orbison album. Mike produced a good third of that record. So all of them were doing that. Stan was doing an album with Roger McGuinn. It was this interchangeable bunch of people who were all friends. But there was a *lot* of music going on at that time. For us, The Heartbreakers. There was a huge creative buzz going on. We were making a lot of music all over the place. Just Jeff and I alone, we were singing on people's records, singing with Randy Newman ["Falling In Love," from *Land Of Dreams*]. We played the track to that, sang the harmonies, Jeff produced it. We were doing the stuff on the Roy Orbison album, wrote "You Got It," Roy's single, and cut the track, and sang that. We were doing all kinds of things. Even Jim Horn, the sax player, he played on a lot of the Wilburys' stuff, and I remember Jeff and I doing a track with him. Del Shannon. We were busy guys, but we were happy guys and we were always working with friends. Nice bunch of people.

You've written so many songs with Mike, but Stan was a songwriter as well. Did he ever give you songs to work on?
I don't remember Stan ever submitting a song to me.

Why not?
I don't know. Stan's a curious kind of personality. Stan's not the kind of person you could look at and know right where you are with him. Like, say, Ben. I know right where I am with him. Stan, I don't think I ever knew right where I was with him. But he never brought me a song. And the truth is, I had so many songs, it probably was hard for them to get in the door with anything.

But Mike got in that door so many times.
Yeah. But that was a partnership that went *way* back, many, many years. And even Mike would get two or three a record. But I don't remember the other guys really ever coming up with anything for me. And it was probably because I had so many things of my own. And I don't know if I was that receptive, really.

Ben and I wrote a song once that went all the way to Number One on the Country charts for Rosanne Cash, called "Never Be You."

Did you cut that yourself?
We cut it, but never released it. That's the one and only song we ever wrote together. [Laughs] Though we probably should write more. But I've just got such an overflow of music all the time that I want to get done. But I am open. If somebody had a *great* idea, I would do it.

Look at Howie. Here's a guy who played bass in The Heartbreakers. Until I heard the John Prine record, I never knew that Howie had all that going on. 'Cause he was very quiet, and he was never the kind of person to blow his own horn at all. But he was extremely talented. That's a great, great album.

Oh, you know what else was going on at that time? They did an album [*I Fell In Love*, 1990] with Carlene Carter, Howie's girlfriend. Which turned out to be a hit album. And I think Ben was very involved in that, and Howie produced that, and Ben and Howie wrote another Country hit for her. It was called, "I Fell In Love." So they were plugged into that. Ben, I think, was hanging at Howie's house. The Heartbreakers are big on recording in houses.

So there was really a lot of music going on. And a lot of it really successful. But The Heartbreakers are really talented people. To tap everything that they can do would have been impossible within the framework of one album. So I don't think me leaving for that period of time was a bad thing. We all came back a little broader than we were when it started.

Did Jeff encourage you to do another solo album, or did he like the idea of bringing in the band?
It was kind of like, "It has to be this way, Jeff. I've ignored them for a long time, and I've got to work with them now. I've got to make a record with them. But I'd like for you to be involved, too." And he was very involved, especially in the songwriting.

It does sound like his production style.
Yeah. It does have Jeff's stamp on it. But I don't think it hurt the album. I think we made a good album. And I think in the end they were kind of proud of it when it was done. That's the paradox of the whole thing. I think they were kind of pleased with it. And it did well for us, and we went on to perform everything live. And I know they were happy with things like "Learning To Fly" and "Into The Great Wide Open." So I think whatever their hang-ups were kind of dissipated once the record was done. Then they felt good about it.

It has a continuation of that magic sound of *Full Moon Fever*.
Yeah. Maybe to a fault. We had really done a lot of that sound at that point. If you count two Wilbury records, the Roy Orbison record… We worked together a lot. And I think it was after that that we said we were gonna give each other a rest for a while. But, *God*, it was a long streak of good music.

Absolutely. Did you write all the songs for the album before you started doing the sessions for it?
I think so, yeah. I think I wrote quite a bit before we came in.

The title of the album and "Learning To Fly" both imply that anything's possible. Is that how you were feeling?
Yeah, I think it was like "Into The Great Wide Open." [Laughs] It's a pretty positive, uplifting album. I think I was in a good, happy spot at that time. I wanted to do something, maybe subconsciously, that reflected that. You don't always know exactly where you're headed. You just start writing. And sometimes it's only in retrospect that you look back and see what was on your mind. But when you're in the thick of

it, I think if you think about it too much, you'll just stop cold in your tracks. If you start thinking, "Oh, I'm writing an optimistic album," *boom*, I'd stop. So I try not to give that too much thought and just go with what's coming.

I love the song "King's Highway," which is another optimistic song.
That one we've performed quite a bit. I like that, too.

There's a great acoustic version of it on the boxed set.
Yeah, it works both ways. It's a good song. It'll work just about any way you want to play it. I don't know where it came from, but I know I was pleased with it when I got it. It was a tricky one to record. We went through a few changes trying to get the track to sound the way we wanted. To get the right arrangement. But it came out well with Mike playing that great solo. It's really stirring, with a *lot* of emotion in it. I think that kind of made the record happen.

Of course, there aren't many songs you can point to in which his solos aren't stirring. His playing is phenomenal.
[Laughs] Yeah, that's probably true. He can really just raise the quality of something so fast. And those solos really are stirring. It's almost like another voice. He's a really good player.

Do you leave it to him to come up with the solos, or do you ever suggest what he might play?
We kind of put our heads together a lot of the time. Jeff and I would throw ideas at him. We'd say, "How about something like this?"

And he'd say, "How about something like *this*?"

And we'd usually say, "Oh, yeah, that's much better than what we thought." But we all kind of put our heads together and give the solo quite a bit of attention. But, with someone like Mike, it's good to just let him have his way, and see where he's gonna go. That would be our first approach. To just let Mike go where he wants to go. And then we refine it from there.

Did you and Jeff equally produce the album?
We were both neck in neck. And Mike was certainly involved, too.

Did Stan and Jeff get along during the making of the album?
Yeah. Everybody was very cordial. But I know them *so* well. Without anything even being said, I kind of know how they feel. And it was my feeling that they might have been a little intimidated, or feeling that I'm dragging them onto my boat instead of coming onto theirs. Which was completely true. I *was* dragging them onto my boat. But I thought that was the right thing to do for the band.

Chapter Eleven

Somewhere You Feel Free

You said that *Wildflowers* is the album that is most like you. That it's the closest album to your musical soul.
TP: Yeah, that's probably a true statement. I think it kind of hits every area of music that really speaks to me. It's got a little rock, some blues, some folk. And I think it's maybe my favorite LP that I've ever done. Though I'm kind of partial to a few of them. But, I think as a whole, it's a real long piece of music—it's almost seventy minutes long—but that's the one that really gets me when I hear it. I can kind of go, "Wow, I'm really proud of that. That came out exactly like I wanted it to."

What are the other albums you like the best?
The obvious ones. I like *Full Moon Fever. Damn The Torpedoes*. Damn The Torpedoes I think is a classic record, and will always be around. It really broke some ground as far as sound and creating a style of music. That one I'm very proud of. I always like to hear it. And I thought that *Full Moon Fever* was a really good album. It had a really good sound. And then *Wildflowers* I think was a more mature record than some of the stuff we did early on. But that was us. That was where I'd arrived. That was where I was really at the top of my game as far as craft and inspiration colliding at the same moment. And that one I think I'm most happy with.

***Wildflowers*, maybe more than any of your albums, really reflects what a wide range you have as a songwriter—there are rock songs, tender songs, funny songs, sad ones, all with wonderful melodies and great tracks. It's an amazing album.**
It was a lot of work. Two years. And *She's The One* is almost volume two of *Wildflowers*. There's a lot more than came out. Again. But yeah, I felt right in the pocket there. I was right in the zone, and I got a lot of good work done. We were very determined to bring that thing home. It was a good period of time. I also wrote "Mary Jane's Last Dance" and a few other things during that period. I was demoing everything. I was using an 8-track machine, and doing demos of everything that I did. Then I'd bring in this pretty good picture of what I wanted the record to be. Like "You Don't Know How It Feels," I literally had everything worked out: The bass, the lead guitar, everything, the harmonica. Exactly as it was going to go. And I did that on almost every track, I think. That would be an interesting album to put out—the 8-tracks. They really are close to what came out.

***Wildflowers* has beautifully tasteful orchestrations by the late Michael Kamen.**
Yeah, God bless him, Michael. He was a very talented guy. He was a friend, too. We brought him in to do the string arrangements and the orchestra. And he was really great. We'd go over to his house, and he'd play us his ideas on a keyboard. Then we'd give him our input, and he would make it all work. And then, when we came to record it, right there on the floor, he could make the changes. If something was working or not working, he could make adjustments. It was done really well. I miss him. He died recently. [November 18, 2003, of an apparent heart attack. He was fifty-five years old.] It's a shame. He was a really great musician.

So you were in on the sessions with the orchestra?
Yes, I was there. I was right on the floor. It was a thrill. Anytime you get to work with an orchestra, *God*, it's a *thrill*. Something I could have never have dreamed of in childhood, that I would have that kind of experience. Being in there with all those instruments and that great sound. It's really impressive to write something and then hear an orchestra play it. [Laughs] So Mike and I went to the string sessions. And

we didn't have to have a lot of changes; it was pretty well worked out. He was very good at getting what he had in his head down.

Beautiful arrangements.
Beautiful. "Wake Up Time." God, what a great arrangement he did on that song. Somewhere I have a tape of just the strings from that. I used to play that around the house.

The orchestra is mixed into the track in a beautiful, tender way.
Well, there was a lot of care put into the mix. We were almost neurotic with the mix.

Mike plays bass on much of the album.
Yeah. I played bass on "You Don't Know How It Feels," but he was our main bass player for that.

You spoke of getting to that place where songs start coming in. Does that happen more when you're on a songwriting roll, and writing all the time?
I find if I'm at a session, say, and the session is going *really* well, I've got a lot of adrenaline going. Especially if I'm going to sing. You've got to really work up a lot of adrenaline, just like you would in a show. And when I come home from the sessions, even to this day, I'm really wired. I'm gonna be up for a while. Because there's *so* much energy that's been built up. And I really do write well then. I start thinking, "Ah, this would be fun to do tomorrow." And I can hear how this would sound. And then I tend to write things. It's hard to find that kind of energy if you're not working. Or if the band plays, if we are rehearsing or something, I can come home and be inspired enough to find some music. So it really helps if you've got that kind of adrenaline going. Because you're gonna have to work it up. You can't do it half-assed.

There's been times when I could feel something coming, and I was so tired I didn't even want to do it. Because I knew I was going to be up another four hours if I did it. But I always did it. Because that would just be rude [Laughs] to ignore the muse. But there have been times when I've been really tired, and I say, "Wow, here comes another four hours."

And you can find the energy to get through those hours?
Yeah. And more. Because, if it should go well, you're going to be so buzzed, you're not gonna relax for quite a while.

Having The Heartbreakers energizes and inspires a lot of the writing?
Yeah. They're *so* great. I'm so spoiled to have a group like that. I don't even think I knew it for years, but the truth is that they're almost *too* good. Because they'll give you *so* much. If you play them a progression of chords, they're gonna give you *so* much over that progression of chords that it's gonna take a little time to just sort it out, and pare it back to just what the bare bones should be. They'll give you twenty versions of it in thirty minutes. So what you do is that you take a bit from each take. You go, "Now this was a really great idea—let's cut this back here—but that intro we played there was really great. So let's do that. This wasn't so good." It's like that.

Even Benmont alone. If you just sat down with Benmont alone and played a song five times, he's gonna play it five different ways that are all great. Each time there's gonna be something that you want to keep.

So, yes, they really inspire me, and I count on them a lot.

Getting to that source of the songs, is that different when working on Mike's songs?
Not really, because you've got to come to the same place eventually. It's got to be a good song. It's the old fishing analogy: You can tell the fish story, but if you can't produce the fish, it doesn't matter, right? So you can talk about how close you came with the song [Laughs] but you've got to have it. Even if you had your pole in the water all day, you've got to have the fish. So, with Mike, it's got to come out good. I've got to work up the same energy to make it happen.

You've said Mike gives you lots of tracks on every tape. Do you listen to the whole tape, or do you stop when you hear something that is going to work for you?
I usually listen to all of it. But I usually go for the things that immediately grab me, something that seems immediate, some kind of sense that I relate to this. Because his output is *enormous*. He really does a lot of music. It's a complete different theory from the way I work. I don't write nearly as much. And if I'm writing something that's not

going well, I'll just pitch it. I pitch a lot of songs. I can write a song this afternoon, but it doesn't mean it will amount to anything, so I'll just pitch it.

But will you finish it first?

Sometimes. And then sometimes I feel it's just not that great. I do it all the time. I'll be here in the studio, and I'll have an idea, and I might spend the whole day doing the track. And then I'll feel it's not really that good. So it just goes in the outtake file. But sometimes you'll do that, and maybe it wasn't that good, but one little bit of it was. And so you go, "Okay, let's keep that one little bit. Maybe those two lines, or that one bit of melody was really good." And that can start you on another journey, to where maybe something really good is going to appear. I don't bring [the band] anything until I've really worked on it a lot and feel pretty confident about it. Most of the time. There are times when I've brought in a sketch. But usually I've pretty much hammered it out before I bring it to the band.

Do you tape yourself while writing?

Yes, always. Not while I'm writing, but as soon as I get an idea. Especially these days that I'm old and decrepit, [Laughs] my memory's not nearly as good. So as soon as I have a melody and a chord pattern, I'll tape it with my little tape recorder. And every time I finish a song, I always record it. Because, the next day, you might remember a song. But you might not remember the feel—the space you were in when you wrote it. So it's good to put it down. Even if it's only on a cassette or something. You have something to refer to. So I often refer to the tape that was from the night I wrote it. Let me come back and just see where I was at. Maybe I was phrasing something different. I always say it's a good rule to always record what you're doing.

Roy Orbison used to say to me, "Well, if you can't remember it, who the hell else is going to remember it?" But I don't completely buy that. [Laughs] Because I can forget what I did, *exactly* what I did.

Randy Newman said it's dangerous, while writing, to judge it, because then you are allowing the critic to become bigger than the creator.

Yeah. I only use the tape recorder as a memory device. It's just something that, should I forget it, I can return to. But I don't use the tape while I'm working. Because, it's like he says, all of a sudden you're a critic and not a songwriter. It's best to sit down and try to finish the *whole* song.

All the lyrics, too?
The whole thing. It's best to at least come as close as you can to doing the whole thing. Because when you come back to it, you're gonna be in a different frame of mind and it can be much more difficult to write that third verse if you're doing it a week later.

Dylan told me that reconnecting with an old idea can be one of the saddest and hardest things to do.
It is, sometimes. I've done it successfully. "Mary Jane's Last Dance," I did it. The chorus was written much later.

But that's unusual for you.
It was unusual, and I don't think I would have done it if not for Rick Rubin pushing me to do it. I don't think I'd have drifted there naturally. That one came out good.

You didn't print the lyrics on *Damn The Torpedoes*, but you have on most of your albums. How do you feel about printing the lyrics to the songs?
I never got a Rolling Stones album with the lyrics on it.

The Beatles had them.
True. I should always have them, because my diction's not that good. And my phrasing tends to stretch words, so sometimes people have different ideas of what I'm singing. When Linda Ronstadt did "The Waiting," she phoned me, because she couldn't figure out all the words. It was the line, "No one could have ever told me about this..." She couldn't figure out what the hell it was. And I thought, "Damn, I've got to try to enunciate better."

You have so many powerful melodies that you've written. Any idea what makes a melody work?
I think it's as simple as, can you hum it in your head? Does it do something to you when you hear it? Is it a friendly thing? Do you want to hear it again? Easily said, though not so easily found, sometimes. But

a song doesn't have to have a melody. You can do a song with one note. I like them to have melodies. Somewhat. Some more than others. I think the melody really defines the song. And the chords you find, and the rhythms you find, they're really there to support that melody. Though, sometimes writing, we might work the exact opposite way. Have a chord progression, and then find a melody. But they must support the melody. It's very important.

***Wildflowers* was another solo album; this one produced by Rick Rubin. Why did you decide to make another solo album?**
Rick Rubin.

How did you meet him?
I think he had called Tony and said he would love to be involved with us if we were ever interested. So we invited him over to the studio one day, and we hung out, and we *instantly* got along really well. And I think that Rick and I both wanted more freedom than to be strapped into five guys. We wanted to be able to do whatever we wanted, really, as far as bringing in this guy or that guy. With a Heartbreakers record, you can't bring in a different bass player or a different drummer. So I wanted that freedom, and we did play with a lot of different musicians, and we even did a lot of trial and error with different musicians, auditioned people for the record. And that record really was a great, great time. It was a lot of work.

It's a great record.
It's my favorite, I think, of all of them. I think it's my favorite, just overall. We intended it to be two CDs, and we worked almost two years recording it. And writing it. And I wrote a hell of a lot of songs. And we recorded twenty-one songs or twenty-two. Bugs, at our rehearsal room, has a big chart on the wall that he kept, which used to be in the studio, that has each song title, and then what that song needed to be completed. As bass was done, it would be checked off. And this and that. Orchestra, checked off.

So Stan didn't fit that picture to me. That was when Stan was pissed. He didn't like the record. That's what he told me. And when we got back together to play—we played two nights at this Neil Young Bridge School Benefit [October 1–2, 1994, at the Eighth Annual Bridge School Benefit in Mountain View, California]. And it was just misery. It was *misery*. That's when it all fell apart with Stan. He was *very* unhappy, and we were not digging it. It was the end of the line. It was like, "Okay, if this is going to go on, Stan's going to have to step aside." Twenty years had taken their toll, and that's what had gone on.

Stan didn't want to play the songs from *Full Moon Fever*. He said, "I didn't play these. I feel like I'm in a cover band." And you can imagine how well that went down with us. [Laughs] He was auditioning with other bands. Or placing stories in the press. There'd be a story in *Billboard* that was just so clearly channeled from Stan. A lot of games were being played.

And then the other problem was that Stan had moved out of LA and back to Florida. So every time we wanted to play, we had to orchestrate this trip for Stan from Florida to LA. Which was just a *huge* pain in the ass. And Stan had quit hanging with us. So it was just natural that our circle was becoming independent of Stan. He left the "Mary Jane" sessions without even saying goodbye. We just looked up and he was gone. He went back to Florida.

But getting back to *Wildflowers*, that was *so much* fun. It was the first time in a long time that I had a studio set up. I had a little 8-track studio in my room. And I would just write these songs, and do 8-track demos. Then we would go down to the studio and record them.

Do them over, or use your demos?
No, we did them over. Some of them are exactly like the demo. Like "You Don't Know How It Feels." *Exactly*, note for note, like the demo. With better quality and better players. It was great. That was when we met Steve Ferrone.

Did Rick Rubin bring him in?
No, Mike brought him. George Harrison had done a tour with Eric Clapton and his band. And then George was booked to do one or two shows at the Royal Albert Hall in England. And Eric couldn't make the show. But the band did. And George asked Mike if he would take Eric's spot and play lead guitar. So Mike played lead guitar on those shows. And that's where he met Ferrone, because Ferrone was in Eric's band. So, when it came around to thinking about drummers, Mike said, "I'll tell you—I really like this guy Steve Ferrone that played with me. I think he'd be worth giving a shot."

It's funny, because we had no drummer. And the band actually had bookings. We were booked to go on *Saturday Night Live* really quickly after Stan left. And I got Dave Grohl to come in and do that show. We played "You Don't Know How It Feels" and "Honey Bee." And that was a gas, playing with Dave. And I even discussed with Dave about joining the band. And he wanted to, but he had his own solo thing developing at the time, the Foo Fighters. And, of course, he would rather have done that.

But Ferrone walked in. And his audition was the track on the album called "Hard On Me." And he played that track in one take, and I just went, "Okay, you're the man. We've been through a lot of drummers at this point, and you're the man who's going to make the record." And he's been around ever since. Because he is just a really, really good drummer. It always feels good.

The very next Monday, after we played *Saturday Night Live* with Dave Grohl, we played the Letterman show with Steve Ferrone. [The band played "You Wreck Me."]

Is he as good in the studio as he is live?

He's *incredible* in the studio. He's *so* focused. He's really good at it. He's a pro, and a really good player. I've never heard him bitch about the headphones. I've never heard him make any excuse for anything. He just plays. That was a new one to us. There was no shirking the blame. "I'll take the responsibility for this track, and I'm going to play it."

"Steve, could you play another drum?"

"No problem."

"Steve, could you play this with one hand?"

"No problem."

I've seen that asked of him. "Play this with one hand."

Why?

I don't know. [Laughs] Rick asked him that one time, and he just did it. Didn't even question it. I thought, "*Damn*, that's pretty liberal."

That album was a really long project. It went on a long time. But it was *very* rewarding. It was coming out so good. Unfortunately, it all wouldn't fit; it was trimmed down to one CD, which is almost seventy minutes. On vinyl it was actually a double album. That was probably wise, though a lot of really great stuff didn't make it onto that CD. But

I think, looking back over all our work, to me, it's just one of the most satisfying things. You know, I like other ones. There are some other ones I really like. But that one I think is the most *me*, I think. That's me. That's where I live musically. And Rick did an amazing job. It's the best-sounding record. It actually won the Grammy for Engineering [1995]. It was a really good-sounding record. We worked hard on that record. Mike worked hard on it.

You've got most of the band on it. Mike's on it, Benmont's on it.

Yeah, Howie's a little bit on it. I don't think Howie was there much. And in stages, Ben was there more and more. And then we were just, "To hell with it, Ben's going to play." And I think Howie was beginning to fade on us a little bit. Yeah, he was starting to fade a little bit. He had his big problems beginning then.

So, it was what it was. To me, that's some of the best songwriting I ever did, and some of the best recordings we ever made.

It's got a great range of material—gentle songs like "Wildflowers" and "Crawling Back To You" and rockers, like "You Wreck Me."

Yeah. Ferrone's playing on "You Wreck Me" blows my mind. I mean, I've heard drum machines that can't do that. [Laughs] That hi-hat is *so* consistent. And it's such a fast, hard song to play. And he nailed it really in just a couple of takes. I still marvel at it when I hear it on the radio: "Damn, is that us? Did we do that?"

Did Rick have a different approach in the studio than you had before?

Oh yeah, yeah. He was a lot younger than us. And he *worked* me really hard. He really pushed me and challenged me a lot.

As far as what?

As far as, "Try it again."

I'd say, "What's wrong with that?"

He'd say, "Nothing's wrong with it. Try it again. Do it again." And he *pushed* me, and I really think he got the best out of me. Sometimes he just made me downright angry. And then he'd get a great take. And it was just, "Write, write, *write*! Write more!" And he'd come to my house and want to hear all the demos, and, "Okay, I like this one, I don't like this one, I like half of this one. Finish this. This is really good. Throw that out." He was that way, very song-oriented. And really an intelligent guy. A bright guy. And I enjoyed working with him. We are still good friends. It was a new friendship, which is always a good situation to make a record. So that was a great, great time for me. I *loved* it. I loved all of it. It was hard work, it was really long. But we knew we were working on something great. So the time didn't bother us.

Then, in the middle of it, my deal with MCA was running out. We were going to give them a greatest hits album, but they wanted another track, they wanted a new track. And this had to be The Heartbreakers. So Stan was brought in. I didn't want to give anything from *Wildflowers* to that album. I was adamant that "I will not give one of these tracks to MCA. I'm not going to take something out of the album and put it on the *Greatest Hits*."

Even though you had so many.
Yeah, I wasn't going to do it. So I went and wrote, specifically for that record, "Mary Jane's Last Dance." And, with Rick, we brought Stan in, and the five of us cut that. Stan and Howie.

Also "Come On Down To My House"?
Yeah, it was on the same session. We did a whole bunch of songs on that session. We did a lot of tracks. It was a very productive day. Maybe twelve or thirteen. I don't know how many tracks were done that day. Some of which still haven't come out. So it was a real productive day. But "Mary Jane" was the big one done that day. And that was the one we focused on.

Yeah, it's a great record, and a great song.
Howie's really good on that. The harmonies are good. I remember Johnny Cash was in the studio when we were doing the harmonies, and I got really nervous. [Laughs] Howie and Carlene lived together a long time, so Howie was family to John. And I think John had come down to see Howie. But he was great. He kept saying, "Oh, that's great. Go for it, go for it, that's really good." I remember [Howie] and I singing those harmonies and being really pleased with them.

Was it tough for you to write a song in the midst of making *Wildflowers?*

I had the germ of it. I had written it during the *Full Moon Fever* days. I think one night I had this idea at Mike's house. And Stan was there. And me and Mike and Stan—Mike playing the bass—cut kind of a rough idea of that song. And I was kind of improvising some of the words. So what I did then was take the germ of that. And I sat down and wrote a chorus to it. And then I really struggled with the words right up to the last minute. I was actually doing the vocal and I was still sitting there, going, "No, wait," and then I'd sit down and write, and kept polishing. To where I was almost confused, by the time I was finished, and hoping it was right. [Laughs]

It's interesting you wrote the chorus after, because it has such a powerful contrast between the chorus and the verse.

Yeah. That chorus was probably written two years later.

You played live?

We played live. And that was the end of it. Stan left that session and I never saw him again until the Hall of Fame. [The band was inducted into the Rock and Roll Hall of Fame on March 18, 2002.] It was all over. So that was the last real recording of the original group.

Chapter Twelve

Some Days Are Diamonds

After *Wildflowers*, the next album you made was the soundtrack and songs for the film *She's The One* in 1996. But before that you made, with The Heartbreakers, the great Johnny Cash album *Unchained*. How did that experience unfold?

TP: Right about the time of my divorce, I got a call. I wasn't doing much, and I got a call from Rick Rubin. We had been out to eat a few nights earlier with Johnny Cash. Johnny Cash was someone I had known for probably twenty years; I met him many, many years ago through Nick Lowe, who was a friend of mine, and at the time Carlene [Carter] was married to Nick Lowe. And we had the occasion to go out to their place in Nashville, and have lunch, and we met Johnny Cash at the time. Who is a *huge* idol of mine. And I really loved Johnny. He was great company, and he was a wise fellow. He knew about a lot of subjects, and he was fun to talk to. And he would come to shows from time to time. I remember once being at Madison Square Garden and being just *unnerved*, because when I looked to my left he was sitting in the box just to the left of the stage. And you could see him in the dark; he was such a formidable presence.

So I had been out to dinner with him and Rick. Rick had a record label [American Recordings] and he asked me, "Do you think I should sign Johnny Cash?"

I said, "Are you kidding?"

He goes, "No, I think so, but do you think it would work out?"

I said, "Hell, yeah, it would work out. He's a great guy, and you should sign him." He goes, "Well, I'm thinking I will. I was just running it by you."

They did an acoustic album together. This was during the making of *Wildflowers* because [Rick] would play it for us occasionally during dinner breaks. And we loved it, thought it was great. And so, for his next project, [Cash] decided he would play with a band. So Rick phoned me and asked me if I would like to play the bass. And I think Rick knew I was going through a difficult time, and he wanted to keep me busy. And I love to play the bass. So I was there in a flash to play the bass. And through whatever maneuvering Rick had done (because I hadn't done it) when I got to the studio, it was pretty much The Heartbreakers that were there—Ferrone, Mike, Benmont—and they were augmented by a fellow named Marty Stuart, who is a really great guitar/mandolin player out of Nashville.

So we set about making this record that would later be called *Unchained*. It was a fabulous experience. Just fabulous. I think we felt a lot of freedom there. John had a few songs of his own, but most of them were by other people. So we were interpreting these songs. And we would not necessarily go to our regular instruments. I played the bass a lot of the time. I would also play Mellotron or organ, and Mike might play mandolin. We had a *ball* doing it. We recorded more than what was used on the album, and those tracks recently came out on a boxed set called *Unearthed*.

One night, Carl Perkins came in [to the Johnny Cash session]. *Blew our minds*. Talk about an idol of ours. Carl Perkins was just a *giant*. And he had played with John for years as his lead guitar player. He dropped in and we had the best night of my life, I think. One of them, anyway. We just never laughed so hard. You know when you laugh to where your gut just hurts? The music was all so good, and so effortless. I was really pleased later on when I read the liner notes to *Unearthed*, where [Cash] mentions that night, and said it was one of the greatest nights of his life. Which made me feel good, because it was for me, too. And we went on and did another track with Carl Perkins.

These are the things that are the real bonuses to being in The Heartbreakers. When you get to do something like that. That was a man who we really loved. We loved him deeply. That record is certainly some of the best playing The Heartbreakers ever did. It's funny that it's not one of our records, but, if you go and listen to that album, you really hear what we're about as a band. We really did play our best on that record. And the record won the Grammy for Best Country Album of the Year [1998]. Which is pretty good for a rock and roll band. [Laughs]

After working on that, you turned your attention to the songs and soundtrack for the film *She's The One*. Why did you decide to do that?
I often wonder. [Laughs] I had just gotten divorced. And I was living on my own with nothing to do. And you're in that strange place where suddenly you're a bachelor again.

You moved out of your house?
Yeah. It's a condition of my divorce that I can't legally speak about anything. So I'll just say that I moved out at that time.

Where did you go?
I leased a house in the Palisades. The Chicken Shack. In this place called Peacock Alley, off of Sunset Boulevard. Kind of like a cabin more than a house. Very funky. Chickens in the yard. But I *loved* it. It was really green and overgrown. It was just a small house, and I was living there alone. I thought it was a great place. I had my little 8-track studio in the back bedroom. I wrote the *She's The One* album, the newer stuff for that. I wrote "Walls" and "Angel Dream." I stayed there for a few years. This kind of a log cabin kind of place that actually had chickens. Kind of very rural for being in LA. And The Heartbreakers weren't doing anything. We had just done this long on-and-off tour of *Wildflowers*. I was not in a good head space. I won a Grammy then [1995 for Best Male Rock Vocal Performance on "You Don't Know How It Feels"], and didn't even go to the Grammys. I remember standing outside in the yard when the phone call came and said, "You just won a Grammy."

I didn't have anything to do. There was this guy Ed Burns, the director, a really nice guy, a really talented fellow, who had made this little small independent film called *The Brothers McMullen* that I thought was a really good film. And I got a phone call from his agent that he would really be interested in me doing music for his movie. He sent me the movie, and I thought it was a really charming little film. It wasn't by any means a big, epic movie. It was a small movie. And I met Ed, and I liked him. So, as time went on, I got involved in this project. It didn't happen right away. But the germ was planted.

And so it started out that I was going to do a couple of songs, and I'll be the musical director, and I'll get other people to contribute to this soundtrack album. And then I started calling people, and there were two problems. First of all, I realized that nobody is going to give me anything good. They're holding on to their really good stuff. Secondly, this job does not fit me. I'm really uncomfortable in this role of calling up friends. I don't feel good about it. I don't want to do it.

So I was talking to Jimmy Iovine about it. And he said, "Hell, you should just do it." And I thought about that, and felt, "Well, we could do the album, I guess, because we have all the stuff leftover from *Wildflowers* that is done or almost done. And we could write a few songs and have an album." And so that's what I did. I took quite a bit of that album from stuff that was done for *Wildflowers*. And then The Heartbreakers rushed in and did a few songs to fill it out. And we covered a Lucinda Williams song ["Change The Locks"] and one by Beck ["Asshole"]. Because we didn't have much material. And that became the album *She's The One*. Which was a really kind of confused album for us, because it got stocked in the soundtrack section. It didn't really come out like a Heartbreakers record. So it didn't really feel like we made a record or anything. We didn't do a tour behind it or anything. We just did it.

To me, it's kind of uneven, because it's not really an album. It's just a bunch of things thrown together.

Yet it works as an album.

Well, good, I'm glad. I haven't heard it in a long time. I know I really like some of those songs on it. I like "Hung Up And Overdue." Which I got to do with Ringo. And Carl Wilson of the Beach Boys sang the harmonies. Carl, one of our *hugest* idols. And I also scored the movie. There's not a lot of music in the movie, but I did the scoring. It was a nice project. I thought it was a nice movie.

I also heard recently a great bootleg from the Fillmore [San Francisco] in 1997 of you doing the Stones' "Time Is On My Side."

I've never heard that. The Fillmore, we were there for twenty nights. And over those twenty nights, we played well over one hundred different songs. So it was really some of the most fun I had playing, because we really played a *long* time each night. We did a couple of sets a night, and we had great bands with us, too, every night. The list of people who opened is staggering. We had Carl Perkins, and John Lee Hooker, and McGuinn. And on and on. It seemed like every night there was somebody great who we were pretty jazzed to be playing with. And so we played everything that came across our minds.

One night we played four hours. Which *really* isn't like The Heartbreakers. But we just got into a groove, and it went fine. The encore was an hour and a half. And it was great, because it was intimate. And San Francisco audiences are really good. They are a crowd that's really open to letting you do whatever you want, and they're good listeners. So it was a great environment to do that. A couple of years ago [April 2003] we went to Chicago and did the same thing at the Vic Theatre. We played there for seven or eight nights, and we did kind of the same thing that we did at the Fillmore. Those things are really fun. They really stretch you, and they let people get a really good look at the group and what we're about. And you can do things in a smaller theater that you can't do in a coliseum. So it's kind of liberating.

Is it fun to choose covers to perform?

Oh yeah. God, we know hundreds of covers. We play them endlessly at rehearsal. [Laughs] Yeah. I always like the rehearsals better than the shows. Because we play *everything*. Though we might never play what we're going to play in the show, we play things that we all know, just to keep ourselves amused, and to get our chops up. So covers are a lot of fun, and the band's particularly good at it. Benmont knows every song there is. [Laughs] You can't stump him.

And you must know tons of lyrics.

Yeah, I'm a treasure chest of useless information. [Laughs] I've absorbed this music so much. I really have studied it and enjoyed it.

During the making of *Wildflowers*, you enlisted George Drakoulias to compile your boxed set, the six-disc *Playback*. Who is George Drakoulias?

He's a very talented guy. We met him with Rick Rubin. He and Rick were tight. They were good buddies. The first time you would have heard George was The Black Crowes. He did their first couple of records. He did a lot of different records. Screaming Trees, the Beastie

Boys, Primal Scream, and things like this. I'll tell you what he did, is he came in—George became a good friend—and I chose him to do the boxed set. It was going to be this mammoth project. And he came in and took on that project. And made what I think is a really great boxed set. Six CDs, with two CDs of unreleased material. And he mixed it all down, and he did a *great, great* job of putting it all together. And it actually went on to be a platinum record [more than one million copies sold in the US]. And we were really impressed by his work. And I told him, "Somewhere down the line, we're gonna make a record."

Chapter Thirteen

Angel Dream

Did you meet your wife Dana while living in the Chicken Shack?

TP: No. I met Dana a long time before that. The first time I saw Dana was in 1991 at a show in Texas. And I didn't buy the whole "love at first sight" thing; I had become very cynical of that to that moment, when I saw her. I just *completely* fell in love with her the minute I saw her. And apparently the feeling was mutual. There was immediately some kind of electricity between us. She was at the show with her husband, who she had just married. So we met and we talked. I think we sat in a hotel bar, a bunch of us. And we talked quite a bit, and I was just madly in love with her right away. But we both understood that this obviously was going nowhere, because we were both married. So I let it go. I just didn't think about it much. I didn't think it could ever happen. And then every time we would come through Texas, I would see her. They'd come around and visit with us. And it was never said, but I was madly in love with her. And she tells me she was madly in love with me. It was never really said or voiced. It would have been really inappropriate to say. And we never fooled around or anything. It was just right there in the open.

Did she have kids?

She didn't when I first met her, but then she did eventually have a son, Dylan. So I lost touch with Dana for a while. And then we were going to back up Johnny Cash for one of his LA concerts. At the House of Blues. By this time I was living in the Chicken Shack and feeling pretty down. I was all alone, and it was quite an adjustment to live that way. So

I was at this show, we played with Johnny Cash. And afterwards there were a lot of people mixing. In the backstage area there, there's not a lot of privacy because there's a bar that overflows right into the dressing rooms. So I was just hanging out, because it wasn't really my show. And lo and behold, who walks up but Dana. And *wow*. The love of my life just walked up. And she was in LA visiting a friend. And her dad had lived here in LA and I guess she visited him here from time to time. And, son of a bitch, if she's not separated from her husband, getting a divorce. Well, this was the greatest thing I had ever heard. We got really close right away. But she had to go back to Texas, where she worked and had a son. So that was sad. But she said, "I come to town from time to time, and I'll come back and see you in a few weeks." So she did, and we started dating. And every couple of weeks I'd see her. She'd come in when she had the time.

And we were just madly in love. I never knew what love was. I thought I did. But being in love with that person who makes you *so* happy, that you feel so fulfilled, like you're just standing in the right spot. I had never known that. So we dated for a while. And then, with a lot of urging from me, I convinced her to move out here. Which made sense. Because her brother also got transferred in his job out here. And her mother came. So eventually her whole family was living here. So it all made some cosmic sense, because everybody wound up here.

We didn't move in together. I didn't want to do that. I was still going through a divorce, and I didn't want to take that on yet. And plus she had a little kid, who I really loved, but I didn't think I should step into that position yet. So we dated for a while.

Later, when I moved out to Malibu and bought this place out here, I convinced her to move in with me.

So you moved in alone at first?

Well, for a day or two. [Laughs] Not for very long. Though she still would not give up her apartment. She actually only gave it up a few months ago. [Laughs] She moved in with me, and we were just madly in love, still are. And Dylan moved in. It was fantastic, just fantastic. We were never apart. Even when we didn't live together, there wasn't a night that didn't go by that we didn't see each other and spend most of it together. Even to this point, there's never been more than four or five nights that we've been apart. To this point. All these years later. So she's definitely part of me. If you get one, you get the other. [Laughs]

But she is so wonderful. And she fits me, and she fits my life so perfectly.

She loves your music, too.

Well, that was something that you'd really have to have, wouldn't you, to be that close? And she does love the music. She loves music, period. She's a big music fan. She's an artist, as well, a good artist. We have a lot in common. We have similar tastes. We like old films a lot, especially old films from the Forties. Yeah, that's really what I do a lot of the time, is to watch films from the Forties. So we're both into that, and we have a really happy marriage. It's always been really happy. It took me a while to actually consent to getting married. I didn't see the point in it. Because my divorce lagged on. It was a long, ugly divorce that took three years before it was resolved. And I did *not* want to turn around and sign another contract. I had no doubts I wanted to spend my life with Dana. But I did not want to get married. I think it was six or seven years after we started seeing each other again, and being a couple, that we decided to get married. And that's felt good ever since.

Did you have a wedding?

We had a big wedding here. We got married in Las Vegas [June 3, 2001]. Because here you have to get blood tests and everything, and I didn't want the media on my case. And so our tour finished in Las Vegas. So we went down and did a really quick ceremony there. And got married. Four or five days later, we had the wedding here. Little Richard married us. He was the minister. And we had all our kids and our friends. And Richard did a nice speech. It was lovely. We had a big mariachi band. It was lovely. And I've been really happy since.

I was just thinking about it the other night. That you can be in one room working, and have the security of knowing that the person you love the most in the whole world is right in the next room. And it's great. And she loves touring. And that was a whole new thing for her. She loves the road. It was a whole new world for her, doing that. But, in a way, it made me get interested in it again because it was all new to her. So it was fun for me, introducing her to this life. And I know there are times when Dana goes, "God, this is a lot more than I knew I was getting into." Hooking up with me was really like jumping on a fast train. Coming from civilian life to this is quite a shock. She'll tell me, "I forget who you are, [Laughs] and I don't think about that until we suddenly go out the door and that starts to happen." But I knew she didn't give a damn about any of that. And I just thought she was so beautiful and such a close friend at the same time. It felt like I had finally found my friend. We are very happy. And I've raised Dylan as if he was my own.

Did you like him moving in too?

Yeah. I'd never had a boy. Though he still sees his father from time to time. But he's always lived with me. And I love him just the same. Our family is one now. The girls [Adria and Kim] love Dana and Dylan. Like family. And we're very happy. And I also inherited her extended family. Her mom works for me. She runs the estate here and is also my personal assistant. We get along great. She takes care of things for me. And it's great to have someone who's family doing that job. [Laughs] It's a lot better than somebody who isn't. And her brother and his family live here in LA. And her grandmother. So I have a big family now, which is something I always wanted and never had in my life. It's worked out well.

Has Dana inspired your writing?

Yeah. She certainly inspired "Angel Dream" word for word. Because the first time I saw her, I didn't really know her, but I went to sleep and dreamed her face. It's such a cosmic thing to wind up with that person. When it was really an impossible situation. But life is full of surprises. And that happened. So she certainly inspired that, and I think she inspires a great deal of my work. She gives me a lot of encouragement. She's always very positive about my work, even when I get down and feel frustrated about it, she can kind of pep me up again. So that's great.

Also, when I wrote songs, I went down the hall and locked the door, and *nobody* was around. And nobody heard it until it was absolutely finished. With her, I feel comfortable enough that I will work with her in the room. Recently, I was doing this song and I needed a few lines to finish this verse.

She said, "What's the matter?"

And I said, "I can't get this verse to work."

Recording. Early 1980s. *Dennis Callahan*

Our roadie and crew chief from 1976 to present day: Alan "Bugs" Weidel. *Dennis Callahan*

Stan onstage, 1980. *Dennis Callahan*

Ben's self-portrait, 1981. *Benmont Tench*

Mike at home, 1982. *Dennis Callahan*

Dennis Callahan

Mobbed and torn to bits. Winterland, San Francisco, 1978. These things made my mother terribly nervous!
Photos: Dennis Callahan

"Letting You Go" video set, 1981. *Dennis Callahan*

Record shopping in downtown LA, 1981. *Joel Bernstein*

With Bob Dylan on the "True Confessions" tour, 1986. *Ron Pownall/Getty*

The "True Confessions" tour, 1986. *Ebet Roberts (above left) Dennis Callahan (above)*

A smile for the camera, 1981. *Dennis Callahan*

Showing the boys a new song, 1981. *Joel Bernstein*

With Stevie Nicks, 1981. *Dennis Callahan*

Desert pirates on the "You Got Lucky" set, 1982. *Dennis Callahan*

Recording Johnny Cash's *Unchained* LP with John and Carl Perkins in Los Angeles. Sound City Studios, 1996. *Martyn Atkins*

Onstage with Johnny Cash, 1996.

Howie recording, 1997.
Martyn Atkins

Recording with rockabilly great Carl Perkins, 1996.
Martyn Atkins

And she said, "Well, what are you trying to say?"

And I said, "Something like this..." And she just threw out the two lines, and they were *perfect*. So I took them and I told her she's not getting any publishing. [Laughs]

So it's a happy marriage, and I'm damn lucky. I don't take it for granted.

Was she with you when you were writing *Echo*?
Yeah.

Because that's such a sad album.
Well, that's the paradox. I was happy, but I was sad as well. I had been through a huge divorce. I kind of crashed through a wall in my life. Even though I knew things were going to work out, and I had found my true love, there was a lot of wreckage behind me. And it takes a lot of sorting out when something like that happens, and there's a lot of guilt that you have to deal with and figure out. Am I a good person or a bad one? And I think I did figure all that out. And part of the therapy there was writing that record.

So she was there, and she was supportive of what I was doing, and I think she understood what I was doing. And it was a tough time. She really jumped on a fast-moving train. With *all* of my baggage. And her life had changed, too. She was a single mother. So joining up with my life was a huge commitment on her part. But, it's like I said, it's that mystical thing that I don't know if I ever *really* believed in. That you can just suddenly look at someone and know that that's the person you're gonna spend your life with. But I still wake up every day happy that I'm with her.

You've mentioned how she likes to play you your old albums. Has she connected you with your own legacy and made you see your body of work in a new way?
Yeah, in some ways she has. One thing she was surprised by when we started to hang out was when I said, "No, I don't listen to Tom Petty. We don't play that." [Laughs]

She said, "Well, that's kind of a problem for me, because I really like this music, and I do, I play it."

And I said, "Well, you can play it, you just can't play it around me." And she didn't understand that, why I wouldn't listen to my own work.

And I said, "It's not that I don't like the work, it's just that I spent a lot of time being really close to it. And when I listen to it, I don't really kick back and listen to it. The whole experience goes through my mind again, and I think of what could have been better, or whatever. I really analyze it when I hear it."

She still talks about when music plays, sometimes it's hard to talk to me. If we're riding in the car, and the radio's on. Any music that I get interested in, I suddenly can't hear anybody talking because I'm listening. And she'll be like, "Hey! I'm talking to you."

And I'll say, "Oh, I'm sorry, I was listening to the bass on this..."

But she will, from time to time, say, "Listen, you're gonna listen to this. We're gonna put this on." And it's a good experience from time to time, because listening to an album you've made when you've been away from it for years and you don't even know what's coming next, you do hear it like the listener heard it. And I must say I'm pleasantly surprised by it. I hear it and go, "God, that wasn't a waste of time. We really did do something that is pretty good."

So she does do that for me. She does bring me down to earth a lot. She's very good about bringing me down to earth and saying, "Listen—things are good. You've got a lot going good here."

Has it given you a wider appreciation of what you've created?
I think so. She reminds me that I shouldn't take for granted what's happened to me, the life I live. It's not easy. My life is no easier than most people's lives. Maybe it is in some ways. But success doesn't solve all your problems. [Laughs] It doesn't really change your personal life any. You're still gonna have all the problems that anyone else has, in that regard. So it's good to have someone that can bring you around and remind you that we're okay, we love each other, and everyone's healthy, and the bills are paid, and why are you upset?

She always seems very happy and bright.
She's a very happy and bright person. She's kind of magical in that sense. She's got such a big heart. I'm always worried someone will take advantage of Dana because she's *so* open and up and she won't look for any bad in anybody. She won't ever have anything bad to say about anybody. She gives everybody the benefit of the doubt. Where my life has made me a little more guarded and cynical of people. I'm right away

looking for what this person is after. [Laughs] She's tried to teach me that that's not a good way to go through life. She's pretty bright. Sometimes when a girl is really beautiful, people assume they're not really bright. But she really is. We couldn't hang out if she wasn't really bright. She's really something else. I couldn't get by without her.

Are the two of you able to get off that moving train and have getaways that are peaceful?
I wish we did more than we do. We have done it, and we're striving to do it. Look, we can forget all that. We can have peaceful times when [fame] is not a factor in our lives. Really, most of the time it's like a normal family. I'm working, and we're raising a twelve-year-old kid. It's not unusual spending a large part of the evening trying to help Dylan finish his homework. I've just got an unusual job. [Laughs]

Let's get back to the making of *Echo*.
It was good and bad. I was still trying to get on my feet with a new life. But I was happy, because I had met Dana, and we were going out and we were really happy. But life was very complicated, and I was going through a *really* miserable divorce.

And so *Echo* was The Heartbreakers. We were going to make an album. We'd go in and track something, and then I'd go back [to writing], and when I got another song we'd go in and do that. It was kind of one-off, one-off. And for the longest time, I didn't like that record. I think that my life was such a circus at that time, that I don't think I felt like I was there half of the time. I know Rick [Rubin] doesn't feel like I was there half of the time. But I was.

I thought for the longest time that I didn't like it. And later Dana and I were in the car, and [*Echo*] came on the CD changer, and I said, "Oh no," and she said, "Listen to this. Really listen to it." And we were driving somewhere that was a fairly long drive, and I listened to it, and I really, really liked it. And I went, "*Damn*, you know, this ain't that bad, is it?" For some reason, I got in my head that I didn't like it. But I really did like it that day when I heard it in my car.

One aspect of your songs is their brevity. You usually write short ones—when I mentioned "Echo," you said it was long. As opposed to Dylan or Joni Mitchell or Leonard Cohen, who write extended songs with many verses, do you like songs to be succinct?
Yeah. I like to get in there, get to the business, and get out of there. That's because I grew up listening to AM radio, where the songs were always three minutes or less. I was playing a Beatles album the other day and there wasn't a song on the entire album past 2:40. It was *Yesterday And Today*. There wasn't a song that hit three minutes. Some don't even hit two. It doesn't have to be long to work. Usually 3:00 to 3:30 is good. If I see one come up at 4:00, I really look at it hard. Like, "Is this necessary?" Sometimes it's necessary to go past four minutes. We do that occasionally. But I'm really suspicious of hitting 5:00. It had better be something really good to go to five minutes.

And yet, like The Beatles, you have good guitar solos, even on very short songs.
Ricky Nelson always had great solos on all those records. James Burton, the great Telecaster player was his guitar player. And, if you listen to Ricky Nelson singles, there's always this *great* solo. It's always very succinct and fits right into the arrangement. And it *really* moves you. Yeah, I love to get a good guitar solo.

With Mike's solos, does he play those live, or do you plan out solos?
More often than not, it's either off the top of his head, or he may play it over and over and develop it as he's going. I think it's very rare that he comes in with one worked out. Sometimes I may have a solo worked out. And I'll play my version of it. And he'll take that and improve on it. And that may be the germ for what he does. But I think most of the time it just comes off the top of his head, and then he'll refine it as he goes along.

He's such a fine soloist. Sometimes he'll choose one note, and sustain it, and it sounds wonderful.
Yeah, he's very economical and, just because he can play fast, he doesn't. [Laughs] And he doesn't feel like he has to. And he doesn't feel he has to

use more notes than is necessary. So he's very economical, and a very natural player. These things just come out of him naturally.

It shows how much you love his playing, that even on your solo albums you always have Mike playing.

Yeah. We're almost one as far as the guitar. We make a certain sound, the two of us playing together, that I don't think we make with other people. When he's playing without me, it doesn't really make that noise. And the same, if I'm playing without him, it doesn't really make that *sound*. We've played together *so* long that we can almost read each other's minds as to where to fill the holes and where to leave them.

How was it bringing Ron Blair back into the band?

It worked out okay. Mike had a demo of "Can't Stop The Sun," with Ron on bass. I had played most of the bass on [*The Last DJ*]. And we thought Ron did a really nice job, so we asked him to play on "Lost Children." He did it, and it went great, and we were in the market for a bass player. And I remember we were on the back steps of the studio, and I told him we had this tour coming up, and I asked him what he thought about coming back into the band. And he said, "God, that would be great." He was really into it. And it has been great having him back ever since. He's really diligent about rehearsing, and he works really hard on his parts on the bass. He's a very positive guy, a good vibe to have around. And it was good because it wasn't a stranger coming in. It was somebody we knew, and had a long history with. And he was a *Heartbreaker*. So maybe fate just guided him. That's the way I see it. I'm a big believer in that kind of thing. I think fate just put him right back in.

Scott Thurston sings, and plays harmonica, keyboards, and guitar. Why did you bring him into the band? He wasn't replacing anyone.

He was brought in by Stan. Stan brought him around because I needed another hand. So we could reproduce the records better, around the time of *Full Moon Fever*. We had those layered acoustic guitars. I wanted another guy who could help us out with vocals and guitars. And he showed up, and he was so good. He was only going to do a few songs with us. But he was *so good* that he's been with us ever since. Before us, he had been with the Ike & Tina Turner Revue, and Iggy & The

Stooges in the Seventies, and later on with The Motels and Jackson Browne. And he really is another great, great musician. He's great on the keyboard, great on the guitar, he's played bass with us. *Great* harmony singer. He became like a Swiss Army knife.

There were a lot of numbers where Howie would play the acoustic and Scott would play the bass. Whatever was left over, Scott did. And I love him. He's my best friend. We're very tight. He's got this very charming personality. You have to love him. If you meet him, you'll fall in love with him. He's a downright good fellow. And a very gifted musician. Great slide guitar player. We don't really give him nearly as much as he could do. He doesn't have as much space in The Heartbreakers as he could be doing.

But he's the kind of person who has no ego. He's a team player. So he's usually part of the rhythm section. He also is a really good harmonica player. And if you ever hear some of the blues things we do, he's really good on harmonica. I play harmonica on a lot of the records, like "Mary Jane's Last Dance" and "You Don't Know How It Feels." But I don't want to be bothered with it live. I have enough to do without dealing with the harmonica. So Scott plays it live. He does all the harmonica stuff.

Is he still a Sidebreaker?
He's a Heartbreaker, as far as I'm concerned. I'm not playing without him.

You played a concert at Madison Square Garden in New York City in 1992 honoring thirty years of Dylan's music. Also on the bill were Eric Clapton, George Harrison, Johnny Cash, Neil Young, and others. You played "License To Kill" and "Rainy Day Women."
Oh, that was a great, great night. It was really a high point for me. I really admired everyone on the show. It was so much fun, hanging with all those friends. And people I'd admired for years: Booker T. & The M.G.'s. And then we did a finale where we all did "My Back Pages" and "Knocking On Heaven's Door." And we all got to sing a little bit.

Did Stan play drums?
Stan and Jim Keltner. We had both of them. 'Cause Jim was there. We also had Duck Dunn play bass. Howie played guitar, and Duck Dunn

played bass. And Howie also played with Ronnie Wood. It was that kind of thing where the rehearsals were great fun, and the show was great fun. There's a great film of it. There's a DVD of it and a CD. Me and Bugs heard it the other night. We were driving home, and our version of "Rainy Day Women" from that show came on. And there's a part before I start singing, and it's playing, and we both said, "Hey—is that us?" And he was like, "I don't know." And we were listening for a minute. And then suddenly a vocal came in, and we went, "Yeah, it is us." But that show was so much fun.

There have been a few times like that that were really memorable. *Concert For George* was kind of like that. I was scared to death at that show.

Were you?
Yeah, I was really nervous. Something like [*Concert For George*] had quite a heavy lineup of people on it. And we wanted to be really good. And we hadn't had much rehearsal. [Laughs] We'd only played those songs a few times. So we wanted to shine, and fortunately we got away with it.

There are a lot of times you just remember. The other night I remembered one time when we played the Forum [in LA on the *Full Moon Fever* tour], and we came back for the encore and Bob Dylan was there. And he wanted to play. And he came out. And then the next thing, I looked up, and Bruce Springsteen had come out. So there's all three of us playing at once. And the crowd was just *insane*, they were just *insane*.

What did you play?
We played "I'm Crying," The Animals song. And I think Bruce sang "Travelin' Band," the Creedence Clearwater song. And Bob did "Leopard-Skin Pill-Box Hat." But none of it was rehearsed, because we didn't know it was going to happen. We literally got into a huddle, planned it out, came out of the huddle, and started the song. And huddled up again. But that was something I had forgotten about, but the other night something triggered that memory. And I thought, "Damn, that must have been a real treat for the audience."

We've had so many wonderful things happen. So many wonderful moments. But those are my favorite shows, the ones where there are a lot of acts on them. I love those things, because there's a backstage kind of camaraderie that's really nice. And you get to know people that you didn't know. Like playing with Prince. I never would have played with Prince in my life. And I never would have known that he's a fan. And he's somebody that I really admired. We got to meet him, and we really had a great time playing together. [At the Rock and Roll Hall of Fame induction ceremony for George Harrison in 2004, Prince played guitar on "While My Guitar Gently Weeps" with Tom, Jeff Lynne, Dhani Harrison, and members of The Heartbreakers.]

What an astounding solo he played that night.
Oh *man*. It really just blew it out there. You see, those things are so much fun to me. That kind of collaboration. And something that you don't do that much. Not that I don't love playing with The Heartbreakers. I have just as much fun some nights. But I love those shows that have a lot of people on them. They're really fun.

You played the White House, along with Stevie Nicks, for Clinton and his family in 2000. What was that like?
That was a gas. Who would ever think these kids from Gainesville would be playing to the President? The President and the First Lady were sitting right down in the front row. I've been to the White House a few times, and met the President, and gone to the Oval Office. That's just happy stuff. You don't dream when you're a kid that that will ever enter your life. You just like being in a band, and playing a guitar. [Laughs] And, you know, you walk into the Oval Office. And Al Gore looked up and said, "I was just discussing the Traveling Wilburys with the President." [Laughs] And the Wilburys got a good kick out of that. But there are so many great things that have happened.

Chapter Fourteen

Howie

Howie, as we know, sadly died of a heroin overdose on February 23, 2003, at the age of forty-seven. Do you mind discussing his decline?

TP: Howie had always been the kind of lone ranger of the band. He was the loner. Not that he wasn't close to us. He was. He had a distance. Ben was very close with Howie. He socialized a lot with Howie, went over to Howie's house. I really didn't go over there much. I only saw Howie when we worked. I didn't see him much. I knew that heroin was around. I knew, as early as *Southern Accents*, I remember seeing heroin in the studio.

Did you try it?

I think we all probably tried it one night when Howie offered it to us. [Laughs] We all had a little bit, and that was it for us.

You didn't like it?

I think we all liked it a *lot*. And we knew we could start liking it a *whole* lot, so we didn't have any more of it.

You didn't shoot up?

No. We just smoked some. I don't think Howie was a shooter. I don't think he liked needles. But I knew from seeing him bust that out that night that it was around. Heroin, not a good thing. But I don't moralize, and I wasn't the kind of person to tell someone how to live. Now I think I would, but then I wouldn't tell somebody how to live. Now I think I would be very vocal about it. But that was his business, so if he could do his job, that was all I was interested in, and I wasn't going to say anything.

So I didn't know if he was addicted to heroin. But I knew that it showed up from time to time. Then, as the years went by, I started to realize, as we all did, that Howie's a heroin addict. And all of us in our way talked to him. And we said, "You're gonna have to quit this. It's gonna get you. You just don't win with heroin. You die or you go to jail. There's no middle ground. There's no other options. There's not one more choice. That's it."

He was always receptive, like junkies are. They always tell you they are gonna straighten up, and then junkies start to lie. And they really start to lie. They can't help it. They have to constantly cover for their lives, so they become professional liars. And we loved Howie so much. But he was always the one who was two hours late for rehearsal. Like junkies are. They're just late. And the dangerous thing about it is that he could play and sing.

So it didn't affect his abilities to perform?
It didn't affect his ability for a long time. Heroin can be like that with musicians; I think that's why you see so many musicians drift that way, because you can remain musical for a long time. But I think, without exception, they all hit the wall eventually and the creativity goes. We knew that [heroin] was around. We weren't bold enough for a long time to tell him how to live. We probably should have been. Though eventually that changed, and we got very vocal about it.

Because I didn't know if it was something he did on the weekend, I didn't know if it was something that he did and then he stopped it. He lived in his own world in a way. He had his home studio. He spent much of his time in his house, being up in the evening hours and sleeping in the day. I think the only one of us who went over there a lot was Benmont. Carlene Carter, his girlfriend, was making a record that Howie was producing. And they were really happy because Ben had been working with them, and they got a hit song for Carlene that Ben played on, and they had been trying for years, and it finally came through. And they seemed to be very upbeat, really happy about it.

Did Ben have any inkling of Howie's problem?
I'm sure he had an inkling, but I don't think any of us realized for a while how serious it was.

And then [Howie's] appearance started to tell you how serious it was. He started to look bad. Really bad.

He lost a lot of weight?
He lost an *intense* amount of weight. His face seemed to physically change. He didn't even look like the same person. The shape of his nose changed. If you see photos of him early on and then later on, it doesn't even look like the same guy. And then he would come to sessions and we knew it was going on in sessions because we could smell it. You smoke heroin and it makes a really distinct odor. He would drift away into the back room or wherever he went, do this thing, and come back. It was starting to let him down as far as music. He wasn't all there in the studio. He started to make mistakes. The studio will magnify anything that's not going right. And we became very concerned that he couldn't pull his weight at that point.

All of us had talks with him—on more than one occasion—about quitting heroin, and how serious this had become. It was jeopardizing his position in the group.

So on many occasions we would talk to him, and have really long talks about how that has got to stop. It would always be answered with, "Yes, I completely agree with you, and I'm gonna stop." This went on for years. He died in 2003, so this went on from the middle Eighties until then. And, in that time, some of us had drug problems and drink problems, and overcame them. Not all of us, but some of us. We had overcome them. I remember telling him, "This can be done. You can overcome this." And he was a little ambivalent about it. Sometimes he would seem to take it really seriously, and then other times he was almost annoyed at being pinned down.

Then the big warning flag, the big day, was when he was arrested. He got busted in New Mexico. We were starting a tour in Pennsylvania. It was an outdoor show, out in the woods somewhere. We were flying there from LA that morning to play that night. And we all got out to the airport and got on the plane, and that's when they broke the news to us that Howie wasn't going to make the plane. They said he got arrested the night before with Carlene. He had a goodly amount of heroin.

I assumed that was probably his stash for the tour. And they were in a stolen car, which I still, to this day, don't understand. Howie didn't even drive. He didn't have a driver's license. So why he was in a stolen car I don't understand.

So they got arrested and thrown in jail. And the band's lawyers got somebody to go to New Mexico right away. We were told that this was gonna be worked out, and that they would have him at the show by 9:00 that night. Which seemed pretty far out.

So we went on to Pennsylvania. And on the plane that was the topic of discussion, and everyone was kind of fed up. Because he had gotten to where he was turning up later and later for rehearsals. We were always waiting around for him. We got to the gig, and Howie wasn't there. We did the sound check without him. Scott Thurston, for some time, was always on alert that he might have to pick up the bass. He was in the dressing room practicing the bass, because we didn't know if Howie would show up, and what shape he would be in if he did show up.

So, twenty minutes before the show, *voilà*, there [Howie] is. They drive him in. He looks *really* bad, like somebody who has spent some time in jail without any dope. He was shoeless.

This paints a very bad picture of him. This is a guy we loved with all our hearts. Who never wanted to cause any trouble. He had the *biggest* heart, and was so sweet. It would really kill us to see him kind of leaning forward on the plane with only his seatbelt holding him up. And he just looked hammered to me, all the time, like he had been through a terrible experience just to make it to the plane. I didn't know what it was, but I could tell something really bad had gone down every time I saw him.

I talked to him after the show and said, "Howie, you know, this is it. This is the big wake-up call. You're gonna have to change. And when we get to the end of this, you're gonna have to clean up, or it's gonna be your gig."

He said, "No, I absolutely agree with you, this is it, and I'm gonna clean up."

So the tour moved on to New York City. We were based in New York City and playing a few gigs in that area. So we'd go out and play the show, and come back to New York at night. We were traveling by plane and by bus. We had a chartered jet, and then we had tour buses as well that would take us on the shorter jumps. And Howie had his own bus. Which wasn't a good thing. Because, even sometimes if we flew, he might make the whole journey in his bus just so he didn't have to associate with anyone. We knew what was going on in that bus.

The next day, when we went down to ride the buses out to New Jersey, Howie's bus didn't pull out. I asked the tour manager what was going on, and he said, "Look, Howie's really sick. He's not gonna make the sound check. And, honestly, I'm really hoping that he makes the gig. 'Cause he's really sick." I guess the supply had run out, and he was really sick.

Again, there's much discussion about this. And then again, maybe half an hour before the show, Howie arrives. And he's *really* in bad shape. Even worse shape. I can't see how he's going to play. I'm really mystified about how he's gonna get through this. This was a man in a lot of pain. And I felt really sorry for him. And I did my best to try to console him and tell him it was gonna be okay, that he would make it through this. And we went on. He played the show somehow. The audience didn't seem to notice anything was wrong, but we did. We knew he was *really* suffering bad. And he wasn't playing very well.

Could he sing his harmonies?

Not very well. Scott really was singing most of Howie's parts. Howie was very weak. He wasn't in good shape at all. I saw this *real* big look of relief when the show ended, that he made it through, but he was almost doubled over, cramping up. It was just sad. Really, really sad.

Of course, I had to answer questions from the press. His bust had hit the wire services by then. Howie wasn't talking. So I had to talk for him. And I didn't know what to say. And I brought all of this to his door and said, "Look what you've done. It's time now. You don't look good. You're gonna have to change, or you're gonna lose your job. And where are you gonna be then?"

So he agreed to go to a rehab in Florida after the last show. The jet is gonna drop us in LA, and refuel, and take him to Florida. On the way back to LA, he starts telling us he needs a day in LA before he goes to rehab. Now we're not buying that at all. I remember saying to him, "Howie, you're gonna make me look like an asshole to the band if I say okay." And he was saying that he needed a day to shut up his house and get his affairs in order. But I didn't buy that, because we'd been gone all that time, and it didn't seem to me it would take a lot of effort [Laughs] for someone to look after his house. But he was adamant that he was gonna go home. So what are you gonna do? He got off the plane and he took off. We didn't see him again.

Then he went to New Mexico. He had bought a ranch in New Mexico and spent most of his time there. So we sent a trusted roadie to go to New Mexico and put him on a plane and physically take him to rehab.

What was done, and after many tries, they got him on a plane to Miami, got him to Miami, got him into rehab. He called me from there a few weeks later, really up and happy, and saying he had detoxed, and he was clean, and everything was good now.

I said, "I'm really proud of you," and he said, "I'm gonna come home. Could you guys maybe send a plane for me so I can get home?"

And I said, "No." All of us knew that being detoxed is only one part of the battle. Then you have to go through some rehabilitation and some therapy. I said, "No, you should stay there and go through the whole thing. We're not accustomed to sending planes for people, anyway. You're gonna have to finish the program."

So this doesn't happen. The next thing I hear is that Bugs has been called and told to pick up Howie at LAX, and he's taken a commercial flight back. And Bugs was very annoyed about this. Because he loved him, too. I remember Bugs grabbing Howie by the lapels at that last show and just shaking him and said, "Straighten your shit up." Or something to that effect. But it was done out of love.

So Bugs had to go pick him up. And, as it was told to me, Howie wanted to go to a motel, he didn't want to go home. Why, I don't know. And Bugs reported to me that he didn't think things looked good. He thought the backslide had already begun.

So what do you do? We all didn't know *what* to do. We didn't hear from him. And then we had a meeting, and we were talking about it. And we felt we were basically financing Howie's drug habit by letting him be in the band. We should kick him out of the band, just if for no other reason than to wake him up. But we didn't.

Then, around that time, we were being inducted into the Rock and Roll Hall of Fame. And when you're inducted, they want all the original members to get together and play at the ceremony. So we hadn't seen Stan Lynch in a long time. But it was set up that we'd rehearse for two days in LA and Stan would come. We were gonna do "American Girl" with Ron Blair [on bass] and Stan. And then we would do "Mary Jane's Last Dance" with Howie and Stan, because Howie had played on that record.

So we hadn't played with Ron for a long time, either. And on that first day we played with Stan and Ron, and it was a lot of fun. It really sounded good, and it was very nostalgic to have the original five all in one room and playing together. It was very nostalgic, and really nice. It sounded great.

And then, to completely turn the card over, the next day Howie came in. But he was very late. And we wound up waiting and waiting and waiting. And when he came in, Stan was just *mortified* at the way Howie looked. [Stan] came to me and said, "Why don't you guys do something about this?"

I said, "Look, we've done everything we know to do. What else can we do?" And he said, "This is really bad."

And I said, "I know. I know it's really bad."

And then, to make things worse, when we started to play, it sounded like shit. It really didn't sound good. And we were coming off the high of having the day before, of having this great day of playing. And then I don't think the rehearsal lasted more than twenty, thirty minutes. Where we'd played all evening the night before. We were only gonna rehearse one song, but we were having so much fun playing, we just kept playing on and on and on. The next night, I think we just did the one song twice and that was it.

Did you nail it down?

No. It didn't sound good to me. So we go to New York for the induction ceremony, and we made it through the show. Though, on the TV show, they cut Howie's number and just had the number that Ron played on.

Howie *really* didn't look good. And he didn't have much to say. He hadn't seen us for a while. I think he was probably embarrassed that he didn't do what he said he was gonna do.

When the show was over, we went up to my room in the hotel. Dana was there, and my daughters were up there, and some of the band, and Stevie Nicks was there, and we were in a warm, nostalgic mood, as those things will make you. [Laughs] And we were singing a little bit, and playing some music on the stereo. And having a nice conversation. And somebody said, "Let's call Howie. Let's tell him to come over here." And the call was made, and sure as hell he came. He had a kind of smile on his face, but he was very quiet. He stayed for a while, and then got up to go. And I knew inside, sure as I was sitting there, that I would never see him again.

You could sense that?

Yeah. I knew it. I knew he didn't have many more days.

So he left, and when we got home, we were all too chicken to do it, but I told Tony to call him to fire him. The band had made that decision. They call it "enabling." We were just enabling Howie to carry on with this lifestyle, and *maybe* this was a last-ditch effort to wake him up. And he was fired with the words, "If you get yourself clean and sober, come on back. But we can't go through this anymore. And we love you, and we don't want to see you destroy yourself." So he was fired. And I never saw him again.

He had a dog named Dingo, a German Shepherd, that he was very close to. He had him for years and years and years. He was very tight with the dog, he took him on tour with him, he wouldn't be apart from this dog. And I heard, through the grapevine, that he had broken up with Carlene, and that he was staying in New Mexico full-time. And the dog died. And the next day Howie died.

I can't even remember how the word came to me. I think Dana told me, I think she took the call. And I could tell from what was going on that this had happened. I've never gotten a complete story of what had happened. He wasn't at home, and he got some bad dope, and it killed him. And it was hard to believe. Even though I expected it, and we all saw it coming. But it's still really hard to believe when it happens.

So then we had a memorial for him at McCabe's, in LA, which is a little music store which has folk concerts in a small room, and a nice warm atmosphere, and it would have been a place he liked. We had some Indians come down and bless the room. And all his pals came down. And everyone got up and told a Howie story. And it was very upbeat, and a lot of laughs, and a good closure. I think we walked away from that night feeling, "Okay, we've put this to rest. And we can move on."

But I still can't believe he's gone. I saw a rerun the other night of *Saturday Night Live* and there he was, and he looked so vibrant and healthy, the way I really remember him the most. And he was just the sweetest person. I never heard anything but positive statements from him. He was never negative. And he always looked for the good in things. And it's weird, because he hasn't become like a photograph to me. He's still 3-D to me.

Chapter Fifteen

Joe

Your next album, recorded in 2002, was *The Last DJ*, which was co-produced by you, Mike, and George Drakoulias.
TP: When *The Last DJ* came up, I approached George about it: "Would you be interested in this?" And so he was, and he threw himself into it really hard, and I think he did a great job. He's a lovely guy. A very talented guy. And he did a really great job on that record. And that was one where he got us all in there, and tracked us live, with me playing the bass.

Yeah, you played the bass on all but two tracks on that one.
Yeah, Ron [Blair] came back into the band right at the end of that record. Howie was out of commission. Howie never showed for that record. So I played the bass in lieu of a bass player. Which I *loved* doing. I hadn't played it in years. So he tracked us that way, with everyone playing live. And then I came back over and did my guitar part.

You played bass live? While singing?
Yeah, well, I'd sing a guide vocal. Because of the leakage. We had so much leakage on the microphone. Which, for the layman, is where the sound of the drums is coming into the vocal mike. It makes this really dirty sound. There may have been a time or two where we kept the vocal from the live track. But I usually went back and overdubbed the vocal after we cut the track.

I thought *The Last DJ* was really good. It's different for us, and it was a step forward, I thought. I'm really proud of it. I think it will endure. I think it will be around a lot longer than its detractors seem to think.

It's a powerful album.
It was ambitious. [Laughs]

Another concept record.
A loose concept, yeah. [The idea] came to me when I kept seeing these billboards for radio stations that said, "No Talk." And I thought, "God, that's sad. There's *no talk*. They don't tell you who that was [playing each song]." And, when I was growing up, there were disc jockeys that seemed like people you knew. And they actually did a show. And they played a great range of music. And radio was *so* magical and so interesting. It played such a huge role in my life. And I kept seeing these billboards that said, "No Talk." [Laughs]

And then I saw it as a parallel, a metaphor, for what was going on in the world. So I kind of devised this kind of moral play. If the record is about anything, it's about morals. And how far do we go in the name of money. And what's gained and what's lost. Then I decided I would make this record about the music business. I'll use that as my metaphor. Which, in some areas, I paid dearly for that.

How so?
Well, the record was *banned* when it first came out. It was banned on some stations.

People thought it was anti-radio.
And it was absolutely pro-radio. It still made Number One on the *Billboard* Rock chart. The [title] song did. But it was banned. And I saw a lot of editorializing about this record. Some people thought that I was being bitter. Or "Where has he been—under a rock? This has been going on for so long." Well, I haven't been under a rock, and yes, it's been going on so long, but I still think it's worth addressing. [Laughs] And I don't think the record was bitter. I think there's redemption in the record, and there's hope in the record. The song wound up being read into the Senate record, in these hearings on the Clear Channel and the monopoly of the radio business. And I know Don Henley took it to Washington and handed it out at a Senate hearing. It's caused quite a ruffle. Which I'm kind of proud of. [Laughs]

People assumed you were writing about Clear Channel and their monopoly.

I wasn't. I'm afraid that I live in such a bubble that I didn't know much about Clear Channel. Believe it or not, the only thing I knew about the Clear Channel was that they promoted concerts. I saw the enemy as something much greater than Clear Channel. I wasn't talking specifically about music or radio stations. I was talking about the state of the world, where our moral head has gone. How the world has gotten meaner and meaner and meaner, and almost applauds evil. That was what I was trying to say. And the saddest thing about that album to me is that the lyrics got *so* much attention, that all that music got overlooked. And there's really good music on that record. And there's beautiful playing, and really good melodies. And I took a lot of time on those songs. I think all I ever read about it was the lyrics.

Do you think its poor sales were because it wasn't promoted well?

I don't know, but I think that the record will live on. I think it will endure, and it will ultimately prevail. Because it's good. And I've had more and more people coming up to me and tell me how much they liked it. I even had Bob Dylan tell me recently that he really liked it. And that made me feel really good.

I guess I bit off more than I expected to bite off. I didn't think it was that big a deal, that it was going to ruffle that many feathers. I just thought it was a fun way to say something. An entertaining way. It was meant as entertainment, that also said something. And I think maybe it was taken too seriously by some people.

The art direction for the album was done by your daughter, Adria Petty.

Yeah. Adria is very talented. She's actually a filmmaker. She's been doing some videos. She was just out here, and she showed me a press kit she'd done for an artist. She's *so* good. I'm really proud of her. She's turned out to be quite an artist. She's twenty-nine, and my other daughter, Kim, who is twenty-two, she's an artist as well. And she just got a deal with a big makeup company. She's drawing all their logos and things like that, and also studying acting. So they've both gotten into the arts, and they're both having some success. So I'm really proud of them. And that Adria, she's just a pretty magical person. She's pretty damn talented.

Was it a happy time for you when you were making *The Last DJ*?
Yes. We had bought another house. Though we kept the big house, and bought kind of a cottage on the ocean. And we were spending more and more time there. We did that to get away from this place. Because this house can get so busy, and there's always so many people in and out of it. A number of people work here. My personal office is here. It can get busy. Sometimes it's good—we go there, and you have to make your own bed, and it's an escape. So we were spending more and more time there. And the ocean is there, and the ocean is great. Both of us love the ocean. That's why we live out here. Being able to just go out and walk the beach every day, it's really idyllic, it's really a wonderful thing. I think I was doing that quite a bit during that period. I felt creative and I felt up. And I don't recall any real stress in that period.

Some people see it as an angry album, so they assumed you were angry then.
I wasn't. I was happy as a clam. But I had something to say. I think the concept had been in my mind for a while. I wanted to write an album about what everybody thought but wouldn't say. And some people are still criticizing me for saying it, but I thought it was worth saying, and I knew they wouldn't like it. But I'm still happy I did it. I think it's good in our body of work. I think it's a good, little different album. It's not just a collection of songs.

These days you're doing your own radio show, a show for XM satellite radio called *Tom Petty's Buried Treasure* on Deep Tracks channel fifty. How do you choose the songs you play, and is it fun?
It's a *gas*. I'm addicted to it. I love doing it. The way I do it is that I have this large collection of CDs. And I've downloaded a lot of it, at least a few thousand songs, into my iPod library on my computer. And so I just make files and, with that equipment, with the computer, it's really easy. It's the only time it's gotten me into using the computer, because I never have before. And that's a really good way to assemble your shows, because you can move things around and see what flows. So

I look around the library, and pick out things I like, and throw them into the files. See if they segue together nicely. And try to make a nice balance. Most of them are just over an hour. And then, when I get the music done, I have a producer who comes here. We record it here in the studio. He guides me through the talking bits, the song introductions and whatever else we do. We get a few jokes in and read fictional mail. [Laughs] And it's so much fun. I love doing it. And I guess the show's doing really well. People like it, and they have us on three times a week now. It's a gas.

I don't do much current music. I do a little bit. The idea of the show is to turn people on to stuff they may not have heard. So I don't go with the obvious choices. I stay in the Fifties and Sixties and a little bit of the Seventies. R&B and rock and roll. There's a lot of *great* music to choose from those eras. So, I've got to admit, I've got fourteen shows done, and I have to really hustle. I'm running out of music. I have to keep buying more CDs. [Laughs] But I haven't enjoyed anything like that in a long time. I really love doing it. I used to always have this dream in the back of my head how cool it would be to be a late-night disc jockey. And this is kind of like that.

The last DJ.
The last DJ. Yeah. But it's a different kind of show. It's a specialized show. I hope people like it, and I'm told they do. But it's really a guilty pleasure. I do it for myself.

Are you always nervous before concerts?
Yeah. Look, if you're going out in front of twenty thousand people, and you're not nervous, there's something wrong with you. You know? You're not plugged in somewhere, if you're not nervous.

Even though you have such a solid supporting band?
And you know that [the audience] all love you, and they've all come to see you. But you still have a degree of nerves. That adrenaline thing that comes. I've gotten more and more used to it.

Do you have a routine for the day of a gig? You wrote "the waiting is the hardest part." Isn't waiting until the show starts nerve-racking?

When you're on a tour, it becomes very routine. Tours are very organized. Everything's done by the book. You get a sheet of paper the night before that tells you where you're going to be at a specific time and everything that's gonna go on that day. You have to have your bags ready to go by noon, and then at 2:00 you leave the hotel, at 3:00 there's a sound check, at 5:00 there's a meal. The opening band goes on at 7:00 and you're on at 9:00.

After the show, you'll be driven by police escort around the traffic to the airport, get on the plane at such and such a time, arrive at the next city at such and such a time, where you'll be met by a car to take you to such and such a hotel, and then you go to bed, and you get another sheet in the morning telling you what's going on that day. So you're living like this.

What do you do during the day to prepare you for the night's show?

I try to stay pretty loose most of the day. The sound check's where I really concentrate. I want to make sure the sound's gonna be good onstage, so we can have a good time. And I want to make sure the sound's gonna be good in the hall. So we work pretty hard for an hour or so in the afternoon, making sure everything's going to be right. Then we usually go and have a meal. There's a meal served backstage for the crew and the bands. And then I might hang out with The Heartbreakers or whoever's around—the crew, or whoever's hanging.

And I've always got Dana there. She really kind of looks after everything for me on the road. And then, about an hour before the show, I need to be alone. Or it cuts down to just me and Dana. And then Dana leaves maybe a half an hour before I'm going to go on. She'll say, "Okay, I'm going to leave. You get yourself together. Have a good show, see ya." Then, for thirty minutes, I just kind of concentrate on what I'm going to do.

With your guitar?

Just in my mind, usually. I'll go warm up my voice about fifteen or twenty minutes before the show. There's usually a shower back there, in these big locker rooms. Team showers. I like to go into the shower, because it has all that echo. I'll take a cup of Throat Coat tea. And I'll go in there and slowly do these exercises I do to warm up my voice, and make sure my voice is kicking. I'll warm up my voice, and get dressed, and hang out till it's time to go.

But I met this racecar driver once named Emerson Fittipaldi. It was the day of the Long Beach Grand Prix. I wasn't that in touch with car racing. It was George Harrison's passion. He loved it. So he took me to quite a few races. And that's how I met Emerson. We went out after the race, and I said, "How do you prepare for these races?" Because I watched him. We were backstage, and I watched him getting ready and into his racing suit. I thought, "This is heavy shit. This guy is going to be going *really* fast for a long time. And if you fuck up, you're dead." So it's a heavy gig.

So I said to him, "How do you prepare for this?" And he goes, "What I do is I go through the entire race in my head before I go out there. Because I know the track, and I think it through, and I think what I'm going to do, where I'm going to be, and I see myself doing it."

And I took that advice, since then. I'll look at the set list, see how it's going to go, I can picture what we're going to do, and that kind of puts me at ease. It's like, "Okay, I know what I'm going to do. And I can see it working. And now I'm just gonna forget it all and relax. And go up there and have a good time."

The secret, really, the most important thing, is: *Have a good time*. Don't take it too seriously. You've got to take it seriously enough that it happens. But don't let anything throw you. You can't be thrown by something breaking, or this or that. You've got to remember that they all came to see you, they like you, [Laughs] all they want to do is see you and hear you play some songs. If you keep it on that level, and be sure that you're enjoying it, then that will carry and they'll enjoy it. But you've got to walk into the middle of an arena and command everyone's attention at once. So it's an art doing that. You have to learn how to do it. But if I go up there and really enjoy myself, it's going to travel, and they're going to pick it up in the furthest regions of the room.

You have to learn how to play a big place. It's a different art than playing a club. We've gotten pretty good at it over the years, if I say so myself. I enjoy it. Sometimes I have to overcome being really tired from traveling, or singing forty nights in a row. [Laughs] But I always try to enjoy it. And the audience sustains me. That's the truth.

So I go through the whole thing in my head before I go out there.

All the songs?

Yeah. Just what's going to happen. I get a mental picture of what's going to happen. And it's not an exact science, because there are going to be spontaneous moments. There's going to be something that surprises you. But if you have some basic confidence of what's going to go on, I think it helps.

It's a funny job. I never thought we would be doing it at this age. I never planned for that. I'm in my middle fifties, and there's girls throwing their panties at me. I never planned for it to go on that long, but here we are, still going on.

In terms of sequencing a show, is it different from sequencing an album?

There's a real art to sequencing a show that's entirely different from sequencing an album. With an album you can do things like put a ballad second. It's a different mentality; the audience is in a different frame of mind. Whereas the show is really about energy levels, guiding the audience into a place where you can give them a certain kind of thing, and they'll take it in. If I came on the stage and played a ballad first or second with my audience, I don't think it would get heard very well. So it's really all about sequencing to me. It's all about how we're going to lay this music on the crowd, and where that's going to take them, and how they're going to receive it. Over the years, I think we've gotten better and better at that. I think we have really well-sequenced shows.

Is that something you do yourself, or with that band?

I do it myself, 'cause I've got to sing it. The singer's got to really do that. The musicians are a different head. Mike will complain a lot: "Oh, I don't want to do that again, let's change this" or "Let's change that." But he's not really focused into the whole thing. He's just thinking about his guitar playing. But I've got to think about how am I going to *sing* this thing. I've got to be up there for two hours, and I'm going to sing for two hours. How do I pace that?

So they leave it up to me.

Is it hard to choose an opening song?
Not really. A good opening song is something that usually hits a pretty good tempo and a good amount of energy, and is something that you haven't opened with before. But you don't want to open with the same song, year after year. I think the first two or three are very important.

Do you rehearse in sequence with the band?
Very rarely. We might have a rehearsal early in the tour where we work things out, and we do try a little bit of the sequencing stuff. Once we have those basic songs down, if we rehearse anymore, we might not even play those songs, we just play whatever comes to mind.

It's kind of like working out. Just to build your muscle. I have to get myself into that head where I don't have to think about my hands. My hands are going to go to the right place whether I think about them or not. That way I can concentrate on the singing. 'Cause usually, if I've been off for a year, and I come back, I may have forgotten the chord changes. So I've got to get my mind to where my hands are going to do the right things. And, once you've got that down, then you can start to think about singing, and lose yourself in the singing. But if you try to think about both, it's a little hectic.

So a lot of it is physical memory, in terms of playing all those chords.
It's a very physical thing. The whole thing of performing for us is that it's a very physical show. It takes a *lot* of energy. I lose a few pounds every time I go up there. You've got to really be in shape and in condition to do it. I have to get plenty of rest the night before, and be really clear when I go up there.

That seems like a true challenge while on the road, to get sufficient rest after coming down from these big shows.
It really is. It's a challenge. But you learn, if you've done it a long time; we've done it thirty years now. So I kind of know how far I can push it, and when I should lay it down, and when I'm talking too much. You just kind of get in a regimen.

You mean talking too much onstage?
No, offstage. You don't want to talk all night. [Laughs] But it's hard, because you've got your adrenaline up, so it's easy to stay up all night and just *talk*. But you have to know when to pull the plug and go to sleep.

Are you talking to The Heartbreakers? Does the band hang out together after the show?
Sometimes they do. Sometimes they have other pursuits. Most of the time, we're traveling after the show. Immediately. By the time the last chords die, we're in a moving vehicle. We usually have a police escort right from the stage right to the airport. We're on our plane and off. And then, when the plane lands, you're in another van and they take you to the hotel. So most of the evening after the show is spent traveling. Unless you're there for a couple of nights.

What do you do during the encore breaks when you're offstage? Do you listen to the crowd?
Yeah, we're usually not too far away so we can usually hear the crowd. We usually just breathe really heavy. [Laughs] Maybe have a smoke. A joke.

You don't usually do more than one encore, do you?
No, we don't. I hate these groups that keep coming on and going off and coming on and going off. Because the audience knows you're coming back. We could do fourteen encores, you know, and they're not going to leave. We come back and do two, three songs, and we leave. But [the audience] is really sure you're coming back. [Laughs] They'd be very disappointed if you didn't.

At least once.
Yeah. We kind of make it a set. That's our last set. When we come back for the encore, we're going to do several songs. And that's really going to be the highest energy point of the night. The encore's fun, because you're really so in the groove by then. You've had a few minutes to rest, and then you can *really* hit it hard. That's *fifth* gear.

So what do we do? We just kind of stand around in a bunch and laugh and have a smoke, and then go back.

You mentioned that you drink Throat Coat tea before the show.
Slippery elm. It's from the bark of the slippery elm tree. There's even slippery elm root that you can chew. It's just a nice coating for the throat. It's not going to work any miracles or anything, but it does coat your throat and toughen it up a little bit.

Because, on tour, you have to do an immense amount of singing. Is it tough to preserve your voice throughout?
Not if you're sensible. If you get sick, it's really hard. There's *nothing* harder. It's a *nightmare* to go up there sick. That's a nightmare.

You've done that, rather than call off the show?
You've got to go. [Laughs] I've called it off when I'm so sick that I can't make a sound. When it's a nightmare is when you're borderline sick, and you know you can do some of it, but you're not sure you can do *all* of it. And your voice might crack at any moment. That's walking the tightrope. You really want to avoid getting sick. But, if you don't worry about it much, it usually goes okay. If you worry about it, you can make yourself sick. I do little things, like I don't get into any air conditioning *ever.* I never step into a car or a van that is really cold with air conditioning. 'Cause that's bad. If you're really wet, and soaked through, and you jump into a car that's really freezing, that's not a good idea for singers.

I stay in hotels where the windows open. I'm really conscious of that, of having the windows open all the time. And getting real air, instead of piped-in. So there's a lot of little things that are force of habit. But truthfully, the best thing's just not to worry about it much. It's only a rock and roll show. [Laughs]

Reminds me of your line "Most things that I worry about/Never happen anyway."
That's true. That's somewhat of a mantra for me. [Laughs] I keep that in my mind, and I still use it a lot.

Sometimes in shows you'll talk between songs, and sometimes you don't talk at all. Do you like talking onstage?
If I feel like I've got something to say, I don't mind talking. And some nights I just feel more like playing, and let that do the talking.

Today is John Lennon's birthday. Do you remember where you were when you heard he got shot?
Yeah. I was in Cherokee Studios [in Hollywood]. And the weird thing was that I was working with Jimmy Iovine, who was a friend of John's. He worked with him on *Walls And Bridges* and *Rock 'N' Roll.* And Ringo was working next door that week. The talk right around that time was John was coming to sing on Ringo's album. So we were kind of jazzed up, thinking that we'd get to meet John. A call came. It seemed like the early evening. A call came and said John had been shot. We just thought it was nonsense. And then a call came right back in about fifteen minutes that said that John's dead. So we stopped work. And went home. We were working on "A Woman In Love" that night. We were singing it. If you ever see a vinyl copy of *Hard Promises,* etched in the run-out groove, you'll see, "We love you, J.L." We etched it in the groove at the mastering plant.

It was a terrible day. It was just damn unbelievable, wasn't it? You know, you just can't fathom something like that. It's strange, you know, The Beatles paid such a huge cost. They were people who could have done anything, and they chose to do good.

And John was murdered. George was *viciously* attacked in his house, stabbed many times. That really upset me. I feel it had a lot to do with George's death, really. *I* feel that. I think that he was on his way up, recovering, and it really took a lot of wind out of his sails. I know he was very disillusioned about the whole thing. So I've always found it odd that they were paid back so maliciously.

Do you still have security?
When necessary, but I don't like to walk around with a big gorilla. [Laughs] You've got to have a little bit. Just to be safe.

You have an extensive fan base throughout the world. I know that fans have listening parties in which they send out compilation CDs of your songs, and then listen at the same time in their homes, discussing them over the Internet. Does it sustain you to have such an immense network of fans?
Yeah. God, you know, you just feel so grateful to all of them. You've got to love them for being there *all* this time. I don't think we've ever answered a fan letter or anything. [Laughs] But you go to these shows,

and they're *so* frantic. I don't know if everyone realizes it, but these shows, they're downright *frenzied*. It's *so* loud that sometimes you can't really do quiet songs. It's *so loud*. The audience is so loud sometimes that they can almost drown us out.

I'm really grateful to them. The live show *completely* depends on the audience. The more you give us, the more you're gonna get.

I'm just *amazed* that they're still there. And that they're on that kind of level. It's fabulous.

And God, what a gift. That is *so* great. It really does sustain us. You can be *so* tired on the road. *So* exhausted. Just whipped beyond belief. Nobody in that audience can picture what you've gone through in the last twenty-four hours. Maybe this is your third city in a day, and God knows what's gone on by the time you've hit the stage. But when that audience starts up, it really does just lift you up. You forget everything else, and you become involved in this moment. And that's just pure magic.

PART TWO

Songs

Chapter Sixteen

The Records

TOM PETTY AND THE HEARTBREAKERS. 1976

With your indulgence, I'd like to name many of your songs to get your response to them. Your first album, *Tom Petty And The Heartbreakers* (1976) started with "Rockin' Around (With You)." Written with Mike.

TP: Yeah. That was off a riff that Mike had. I remember he had this little guitar riff. And we got into this harmony thing, holding one note for a *long* time. [Laughs] But it *worked*, it was fun.

You wrote "Breakdown" during a break in a recording session?
Yeah. We had a little time, and I wrote it on the piano there in the studio. So sometimes those are the best situations to be in. I get particularly inspired when the mikes are all up and there's a great sound up in the studio. You want to do as much as you can, 'cause it *sounds* so good. You've got this great sound in there, so I like to use it. And that was the first record we made, so we were still really new to the studio. "Breakdown," I wrote that, and we cut it. It was really long. Maybe seven or eight minutes.

Really? Now it's only 2:42.
I didn't intend it to be seven or eight minutes, we just got on the groove and played a long time. And then I listened back to it, and I was going to extract the best bits from it. And somewhere near the end, [Mike] played that lick. [Sings famous descending riff] And Dwight Twilley was there with his band; we kind of shared that studio, Shelter Studio, in Hollywood. And it was quite late, it was eleven or twelve at night, and

Dwight Twilley came in, and when that lick went by, he goes, "That's the lick! Oh, man, that's the lick!" So we stopped the tape, rolled back and listened to that lick. And I said, "Yeah."

This is how crazy we were in those days. By now it's one or two in the morning. And I called [The Heartbreakers] and had them all come back. They had all gone home. I called them, and they came back at two-thirty or three in the morning, and we cut the song. The version you now know. So that could never happen now. [Laughs]

That wouldn't happen now?
No. But that's how passionate we were. We were passionate kids.

That descending riff Mike plays really ties together the whole song.
It does. It's kind of a really perfect little record, isn't it? I hear it sometimes on oldie stations, and it really stands up. It really holds up over the years.

It has a great drumbeat, too.
Yeah, that was a drumbeat that I got wrong. There's a Beatle song called "All I've Got To Do." Which has a great drumbeat. [Sings drumbeat] So I was thinking that would be the drumbeat. Though I think I kind of translated it wrong, 'cause it's not really that beat at all. So that's what Stan did with it. And he really played a great track there. Ron [Blair], too. It was a really good little track. Maybe because we played it all night, and we really explored it. So it really had to be a feel. You had to get into a certain groove with that song. And we cut it live, with all of us playing.

Was that typical, that you would come up with a drumbeat and give it to Stan?
Sometimes. Because I wrote the song and I had a really good picture of how the rhythm should go. So I said, "The beat's gonna be like this. I hear the kick and the snare like this."

And he was cool with that?
Yeah, he was cool with that. I don't think that is that unusual. And he would often expand on that, and find other things I hadn't thought of.

Did that title come to you right away during that break?
Just flowed out of me. [Laughs] It just happened. Pretty much, top to bottom, it just happened. Grace Jones did that song, and I wrote her another verse. She has three verses on her version. Because they were recording it and phoned and said, "The song is so short. Is there any chance of getting another verse?" And I can't remember what it is, but I did sit down and write another verse. And she did a pretty good version of it. I've heard a few covers of that. Suzi Quatro. Remember her? She did it. I've heard different people do it, and I never really liked their versions much. But I liked the Grace Jones one.

The song "Hometown Blues," which is also a very short song, was cut at Leon Russell's house, with Duck Dunn on bass, Randall Marsh on drums, and Charlie Souza on sax.
Yeah, that was the dying days of Mudcrutch. Mudcrutch's last hurrah. And that's why there's a couple of them on the record. And the record didn't really take shape until Duck Dunn played his bass line. That was the last throws of me being a solo artist, was how that track started.

I did bring The Heartbreakers in, and they overdubbed to the track. But the basic track was Randall Marsh, Mudcrutch's drummer, and Duck Dunn playing the bass. And Charlie Souza, in the last few minutes of Mudcrutch, we brought him in to be the bass player. And he didn't know how to play the sax, but he was playing it. And it got this really authentic kind of Stax sax sound.

It was on a tape at Leon's house that someone already used. So I erased that tape and recorded over that. [Laughs] And I actually engineered the basic track. Because there was nobody around.

And Duck Dunn had ancient strings on his bass.
Yeah, I don't think he ever changed his strings.

There's "The Wild One, Forever," which is in *D* major, and has that great building melody over that riff of the *D* going to the *D* suspended.
One of my wife's favorites. Dana loves that song. She says, "Why don't you ever play that song?" But there's *so* many songs. I can't play every one that everybody wants us to play.

I think we did play it at the Fillmore during that long run. [The band did play the song at the Fillmore on January 31, 1997.] Yeah, that was another one written during a break in the studio, perhaps the same night that "Breakdown" was written. I wrote two songs in that long break. And Ron played a cello on that. He doesn't play the cello. But he just fashioned out enough that he could play the chorus part. So, if you listen closely, you'll hear the cello.

I think, with that chorus, we were trying to make it sound like The Rascals, to have a chorus like The Rascals would have.

I thought "The Wild One, Forever" was somewhat Springsteen-inspired.

No, because I hadn't really heard Springsteen much in those days.

Was he an inspiration later?

No. I don't think any of my contemporaries ever influenced my work. I've always been more interested in music that came before. I think very little of my music would have been influenced by anyone after, say, 1974. [Laughs]

Not that I don't like them; I think Bruce is a great songwriter. And he's a friend. But he probably doesn't listen to me, either. I have never really soaked that up. I listen to it, and I appreciate it, but I think my influences come from somewhere further back.

I know he does listen to you—he liked "Straight Into Darkness," among others.

Yeah, we're friendly. We've been friends for many years. We don't see a lot of each other, but we've been friends for a long time. I think he's a really good writer. But I kind of feel the things that influenced me came before. And when I hear the guys that were coming up the same time as me, I think they were probably influenced by things before as well.

I certainly wasn't influenced by anything from the Eighties. I hardly ever even *heard* the Eighties. It's like Ben said, "We completely missed the music of the Eighties, because we were so immersed in what we were doing, we weren't listening to anything else." I missed all that. I wasn't tuned in to that stuff. I was more into what I was doing, and our music is all influenced by music from the Fifties and the Sixties, and some of the Seventies.

That could be one of the reasons your songs have such a timeless quality about them. Even your early songs still work and don't sound dated.

We go to a lot of trouble to make sure it has a kind of timelessness to it. Even the way we make the records. We don't use a real gimmicky instrument. Like there was this synthesizer called the [Yamaha] DX7 in the Eighties. Everybody put these DX7s on their records. [Laughs] These kind of bell sounds that I thought were *terrible.* And I hear them now, and it really does say that time period to me. I wouldn't have used an instrument like that. I try to make it sound like no particular time.

There's the song "Anything That's Rock'N'Roll." Mike said he saw Kiss and realized if you put the words "rock and roll" into a song, it would make it work.

I never knew he said that. I liked the phrase "rock and roll" and I was kind of afraid it was dying out at the time. I used it in a couple of songs around those days. That song's really naïve; it's something I couldn't sing now. It's a kid singing that song. "Your mama don't like it when you run around with me... You don't dig school..." But that was our first hit record. It was a hit in England. So we often played it on television when we were over there. That was our big hit. [Laughs] It was like a Chuck Berry kind of thing, just a good rocking song.

"Strangered In The Night"?

I remember writing that one. Again, right in the dying days of my solo career. I started that song with Jim Gordon playing the drums. From Derek & The Dominos and a million records. And one of the greatest drummers ever, I think. Now in jail for killing his mother. But he was a really great drummer. He played the basic track on that. There were actually two sets of drums; he overdubbed himself. I've never seen that done in my life. He did the track and said, "Let me have another track," and he overdubbed that and he played exactly a carbon copy and doubled the drum sound.

That was the first session I brought The Heartbreakers down to. They were watching that go down, and they did the next song, and I overdubbed them onto ["Strangered In The Night"]. And that's when I stopped being a solo artist.

Was that the right move to make?
Definitely. [Laughs]

"Fooled Again (I Don't Like It)"?
That was The Heartbreakers. We recorded that out at the old Warner's studio on the Warner's lot. Denny Cordell. We moved [to a different studio] for that record because Denny liked that studio at Warner's. It was very strict. The engineers took a break every three hours. It was like really union, and the engineer was a really older guy, and not a rock and roller. And Cordell was frustrated with that. That was the only track we did there. We didn't stay there long, because it was just too grown up.

"Mystery Man"?
I remember the session, which was at A&M studio. We went in there for one night and we cut "Mystery Man." We cut it live, the vocal and everything.

A&M's studio was originally Charlie Chaplin's movie studio. Did you like being there?
I always thought there were good vibes at A&M. I liked the old studios. Jimmy Iovine went in there and tore the studios down and built new ones. And they were pretty terrible, I thought, once they changed them. But I really liked the old ones that were there.

It was kind of an interesting place. You could stroll around—there were a lot of studios in that complex, and you could stick your head in the door, and just hear all kinds of artists. I remember seeing Johnny Mathis do a track there. He was there, wearing a sweater, looking just like an album cover. And I saw the Carpenters do a track there. I saw Donovan.

I always do that when we're in a studio—go around and visit the other studios and see what's going on. It's a good way to gauge what you're doing. [Laughs] Because, if you walk into a place, and you hear, "Oh well, we're way ahead of this," or "Hey, this is really cooking," it will give you a little energy to go back to your session.

"Luna"?
That was the last song done in Tulsa, where we went to Shelter's studio. It was in a church. When they made the Shelter studio in Hollywood, they took all the gear from the Church Studio, and moved it out here.

And me and Stan, for some reason, flew to Tulsa, and they were going to rip the stuff out of the church. And Noah Shark, the Shelter producer, said, "Hey, why don't you guys fly down and we'll cut a track before we take the gear out. Because no one's around and we can do it for free."

So Stan and I, just on a lark, flew to Tulsa. There was a tornado, and we had to land and wait it out. And we had this really bumpy plane ride to Tulsa.

So it was an empty studio. We got there and it was just empty. We got there, just the four of us, Noah and his second engineer Max [Reese], and me and Stan. But there was a Hammond organ and some drums. And I made that song up on the spot, and we cut it with me playing the organ and Stan playing the drums. And then we brought the tape back, and finished it at Shelter Studio in Hollywood. Put the guys on it. But we cut the vocal and the organ and the drums, and we played it live together. So it's very improvised, especially the ending. You hear all these weird stops and little licks. It's just us jamming together. And there's a string sound on there. This kind of a bendy string sound. And the first string machine was an Arp, and there was an old Arp there, and Stan played those strings, bending the tuner on the Arp, bending it up and down. He did this really cool part. So that's what we came back with. The Arp, and the organ and the drums.

And you came up with the words on the spot?
Yeah. I just sat down and wrote them out. And roughed out a chord progression and we cut it.

"American Girl" is on your first album. Do you remember writing it?
I don't remember exactly. I was living in an apartment where I was right by the freeway. And the cars would go by. In Encino, near Leon's house. And I remember thinking that that sounded like the ocean to me. That was my ocean. My Malibu. Where I heard the waves crash, but it was just the cars going by. I think that must have inspired the lyric. I know it was in the bicentennial year. When there were a lot of American things going on. Super red, white, and blue things going on. And we actually made the record on the fourth of July, 1976.

You wrote it on an acoustic guitar?
Yeah. I would have written that on my Gibson Dove, because I wrote everything on that then. It was the only guitar I had.

Did you intend a Bo Diddley beat for it?
Yeah, right. It was supposed to be like Bo Diddley. That was Stan's version of the Bo Diddley rhythm. It was recorded on one track. The drums are all on one track, which is really unusual. These days, most people put the drums on about ten tracks. With the bass drum on a separate track, and the snare on a separate track. At least to have two. But, for some reason, Noah wanted to try this experiment and put them all on one track. So they're in mono on one track.

We had forgotten that until we did a documentary for the Disney channel years ago. And part of the documentary was to take tapes out of the vault, bring them up on the camera, and listen to them. And Mike and I were really cracked up when we pulled the tape up. Because the drums were on one track! [Laughs]

They sound surprisingly good, considering.
Yeah. They're damn present. And it's a wacky-sounding record. I heard it in a shop the other day. I went in to get a cup of coffee and it was on the radio in the shop. I was standing there listening to it, and I felt it was really good production on that record. It sounded good.

People assume there's 12-string on that record, but there is none.
No. It's Mike and I on two 6-strings.

There's the story that the song was based on the suicide of a girl at the University of Florida. Any truth to that?
Urban legend. It's become a huge urban myth down in Florida. That's just not at all true. The song has nothing to do with that. But that story really gets around. I'll meet students from Gainesville. And they'll say, "Yeah, we party in your old house on Halloween." There's this tradition that they go to my house, whoever's renting it at the time, and have this big party. But I never lived in a house in Gainesville. I lived in apartments. I lived in my mom's house, where I know they're not throwing a party. So that's also a myth. Someone got a house and said, "This is where he lived." That tradition has gone on and on. And every

time I tell them it's not true, they go, "Aaah…" [Laughs] I almost am tempted to go "Oh great," because I don't want to pop their balloon.

It's a rich thing about songs; people can bring their own significance to them.
Yeah. And that's happened with a lot of songs. But really extremely in that song. They've really got the whole story. I've even seen magazine articles about that story. Is it true or isn't it true? They could have just called me and found out it wasn't true. But that song has really been around for a long time now. And I'm very proud of it.

Then there's that story that McGuinn heard it in his car, and thought it was one of his own songs.
Yeah. He said he thought that it was a Byrds song. I don't think it sounds anything like the Byrds to me. People ask us if we were trying to sound like the Byrds. We would never have *dreamed* that we could sound like the Byrds. We would have *wished* we could sound like the Byrds. But we certainly weren't thinking that. But McGuinn did record it, very soon after our record came out.

Even in the jangly sound of the guitars, you didn't have the Byrds in mind?
Yeah, we might have had that. But not on that song. On that song, we certainly weren't thinking Byrds. I think later on there may have been things like "Listen To Her Heart" or something like that, where we were thinking of getting that 12-string sound. But not on "American Girl."

YOU'RE GONNA GET IT! 1978

Your second album was *You're Gonna Get It!* (1978). You said that you felt it was done hastily, and that you were trying to do something different than the first album.
[*You're Gonna Get It!*] is a quirky, weird, little record. It's a very strange almost eccentric record. But I kind of like it now, because it's so off the wall. It's kind of an offbeat kind of record. It's very short. It was done quickly. The first album was breaking almost a year after we had recorded it. And we were tired of playing that first album; we wanted to

get some more product out there. So we really quickly did that record. Wrote it and recorded it really quickly. And it did pretty well for us. It had some good songs. It had "I Need To Know" and "Listen To Her Heart." Which were both pretty popular songs at the time.

I understand you recorded "I Need To Know" very quickly. Two guitars live, recorded in just a few takes.

Probably, yeah. You know the inspiration for that song was Wilson Pickett's "Land Of A Thousand Dances." Listen to that song and you'll hear that kind of rhythm. [Sings rhythm] And that's where that came from, I'm sure.

You also mentioned "Listen To Her Heart," which really holds up.

Yeah, it had that kind of Byrds or Searchers kind of riff. A 12-string riff. I think by then we'd gotten Vox Phantom 12-string guitars. And I'm sure that had a lot to do with that sound.

Your record company tried to get you to change the word "cocaine" to "champagne"?

Yeah, that record company, they're always sticking their nose in there. Of course, we didn't [make the change]. Because it would have made it a different song. I didn't really see the character as caring about the price of a bottle of champagne. Cocaine was much more expensive.

My ex-wife had gone with Cordell to Ike Turner's house. And Ike Turner had locked them in the house. [Laughs] And there was a lot of cocaine and drugs around. When they told me this story, I thought it was really funny. I think that had something to do with the cocaine line. The story was related to me, and I think it probably had something to do with that line. I thought it was a pretty funny story.

Such a beautiful, visceral melody.

It came out really good. I remember going to the rehearsal the first day I had it, and playing it with the band, and really being knocked out with it, because it was one that really suited me and Mike when we played that riff. And when the song kicked in, I thought, "Oh God, this is great." It was really good. We were doing it in the show before the record was out. Actually, we played it at a show in Chicago at the Riviera Theater with Elvis Costello & The Attractions. This would have been '77.

He opened for you?

I think he did, yeah. I think it was a buck to come in, it was a thousand-seat place, and we didn't sell it out. It didn't quite go clean with us and Elvis Costello. And Elvis Costello stole the ending of that song. And he admits it. [Laughs] He remembered it. He watched us do the ending, and he put it on this song he just wrote called "Radio, Radio." If you listen, it's the same ending. I heard him say that in an interview one time. I thought that was humorous, because I remember thinking, when I heard that song, "*Damn*, that's exactly like our ending." And he admitted that he took it that night at the Riviera Theater.

It's a good song, "Radio, Radio."

Yeah. Great ending. [Laughs]

The phrasing of "Listen to Her Heart" is so good. And Dylan once said that, if you get the phrasing of a song right, the rest of it will fall into place.

Yeah. It's extremely important. I have my own kind of phrasing. When I hear people cover my stuff, I'm sometimes disappointed in the way they phrase. Phrasing is really important. A phrase can really convey a certain amount of emotion. If you change that phrasing, you can sometimes lose the emotion. Though Dylan can rephrase his stuff every night and still make it work, because the songs are so durable. But, yeah, I think phrasing is really important. And so is meter. That you sing in meter and time. And even the way you sustain a line, or clip a line, is gonna really have an emotional impact.

The song "You're Gonna Get It" is a good song; it has a really soulful vocal over the piano part.

I played the piano on that. I wrote it on a piano and I played it on piano on the track. I remember doing that, and I remember bringing in the string quartet to play the string part. It was just a small, just a little bit of strings, that are doubled with an Arp string machine that Benmont played.

Did he mind playing the Arp?
No. We liked the Arp, we thought it was really cool, especially if you put it through a Leslie or a phaser of some kind, it sounded really cool. We liked the Arp; Benmont didn't like synthesizers because there were a lot of really bloated rock groups at the time using synthesizers that were really not creating interesting music. So we wanted to go away from that. I personally have nothing against the synthesizer; I think it can be used really well if it's used right. So many people have used them wrong that you don't tend to go there.

How about rhymes? Sometimes you have real rhymes, sometimes false ones. Is rhyming important to you?
Yeah. Not as much as it used to be. I've gotten to where I just don't give a damn anymore. [Laughs]

How come?
Because I'd rather just deal with what I want to say, as exactly as I want to say it, and I don't want to compromise it for a rhyme. Sometimes, though, if you don't rhyme it, it don't feel good. So, it is the great thorn in the songwriter's side that you've *got* to pretty much rhyme what you're gonna sing. So that's part of the trick, getting that rhyme to say what you want.

I've talked about this with really good screenwriters. They have *so* much more room to get across what they want to do. I've got three and a half minutes. If I'm gonna tell a story, I have three and a half minutes to get it across. So sometimes a single word is Act II. [Laughs] I don't have that kind of space. And then, when you come in with rhymes as another rule, it really makes it difficult. I feel good when it does rhyme. But if it's something that I'm *really* attached to, even if it doesn't rhyme, I just don't care anymore, I'm gonna put it in.

I do get annoyed though, with near-rhymes. When people do things that don't rhyme.

You do that sometimes.
Oh yeah, I'm as guilty as anybody.

Is rhyming ever fun for you?
I wouldn't say it's particularly fun. It's just something that comes with the craft of writing the song. You gotta do it.

Do you ever set up a rhyme, and then work backwards—coming up with the second rhyme first?
Well, sometimes. I think probably all songwriters come up with that great line they want to hold for the second part of the verse. So that sometimes happens, where you've got your line, and then you come up with one to come in front of it. And then *often* you'll come up with one better, just trying to do it backwards like that. But I'm not conscious of these things when I'm writing. I'm just trying to get it across somehow. And there just aren't any rules. There's so many ways of doing it. And I'll go to any length that I have to to get it. And, really, there's never two that come in the same way. And there's never two that follow the exact same rules.

Craft is a good thing to know, as far as writing. But you don't want it to get in the way of things. It's something you want to learn and then forget. I hear a lot of crafty songs that aren't really very good. They don't really stick with you very long. You can hear a really crafty song, but unless it's got something to say it might not be around very long. So it's the kind of thing you learn and then forget it. You use it to make your life easier, but you certainly don't want to count on it.

A craft element you use really well is the use of song structure—verses, bridges, and choruses. You always have great verses with very strong choruses. And you've written some great bridges, as well. Do you enjoy working with those structures?
Yeah, I do. When I started working with Jeff Lynne, he really taught me a really good rule: If you have a verse that's not as good as the chorus, you don't have a verse.

Musically and lyrically?
Yeah. If this bit isn't as engaging as that bit, there's no point in having it. And especially with middle eights or bridges. If you go off somewhere just for the sake of giving the song relief from the verse and the chorus, if that bit isn't *really* good, if it isn't absolutely as good as the rest of it, you don't need it. And I've taught myself that. I can always write a middle eight. But I can't always write one that's gonna be as good as the chorus. And, if it's not, I just throw it out.

You've written so many powerful bridges.
Been lucky with bridges, yeah. Had a few good ones.

Quite a few. You call them "middle eights," but they're not always eight measures long.
Well, that's a term we picked up from The Beatles, but they can be any length. I didn't really know anything about music—I still don't, really—but I know I always heard The Beatles refer to them as "middle eights." So I just thought that's what you called one. And they're still people who have different names for verses, bridges, and choruses. But we always call it "verse, bridge, chorus." "Bridge" is something that's a departure.

You seem to have an innate talent for building up to the title in the chorus, which is something you've done powerfully so many times.
That's just something you hope happens. Sometimes the title is a big refrain. And sometimes it's a punchline. Sometimes it isn't as significant as that. I like having the title in the song. I never have understood these songs that have a different title that doesn't appear in the song. I think you're trying to be overly clever. I'm old-fashioned that way. I like to hear the title.

Do you often get the title first before writing the song, or does the title emerge during the writing?
I went through a period of doing that, of looking for titles. "Southern Accents" was one. And after that, a little bit. I got into that idea. You don't always have that luxury. Especially if you've started something. Like right now, I've started something, and I have this beautiful song, and I don't know what the title is. I don't know what my big line is. And so you don't always have the luxury. If you do have the title, that's great. If you've got the title and you know where you're going, that's great. But it isn't always true.

Do you remember writing "Hurt"? It's another collaboration with Mike, and it has the lines "Thank God for California/ Thank God I'm going home."
Mike wrote the middle bit, the guitar bit. I wrote the verse and the chorus. I wrote it on an airplane. I had it in my head, and we were on an airplane coming back from somewhere to California. I wrote it out on airplane stationery. Then, when I got home, I put the music to it, and figured it all out. And then Mike had that *great* guitar bit. And we

met up and put it together. And we cut it. Denny Cordell was producing and he made a great kind of percussion loop of us on acoustic guitars, where we would just comp on the guitar without playing any chords. And maybe a bongo, too. And then we'd make a loop, and the band would play live to the loop. And that was done in that song "Hurt."

Great chorus. I love the chorus in that one. I had a Dolly Parton idea in my head. I wanted it to sound like a really good Dolly Parton song.

One of my favorite songs on the album is "Magnolia," which is beautiful.

Now that was one [Laughs] written and made to order for Roger McGuinn, who had recorded "American Girl" and had requested another tune. And he declined to do it. So I did it. I wrote it in Tony Dimitriades' apartment. It was one of those situations where [Tony] said, "You need to write a song for Roger McGuinn. I'll be back in a few hours." And I just *made* myself write a song. I wrote it with Roger in mind. Maybe to a fault. I really did an imitation of Roger. I don't know why he didn't like it, but he didn't want to do it.

That's amazing, because it's such a strong song.

It would have been good for him. But for some reason he didn't want to do it. I did the same thing for the Everly Brothers once. I wrote this song called "Keeping Me Alive." Which I think is just a killer song. We never really did it. It's on the boxed set. They didn't like it. [Laughs] Phil Everly came over to my house, and I thought I had done this great song, and I played it to him, and [Laughs] he just didn't go for it. And I always thought it would be this great song for them. So you never know.

One thing I've learned is usually when someone asks you for a song, they don't want one that sounds like them. They can make the ones that sound like them. Usually, if they're looking for an outside song, they're looking for something that is away from what they normally do. I've learned that, over the years, that you don't sit down and write one that sounds like Johnny Cash for Johnny Cash. They want something that's more like you, or more away from what they're doing. I think.

“Magnolia” is one of your story songs. Did the title come first?
I think it probably did. I was just trying to write a Southern romantic song. Magnolia trees are predominant in the South and they give off this great odor at night. So that’s probably what it was.

You treat the woman of that song tenderly, and your treatment of women in songs is generally pretty tender. You’re not ruthless with them, as are many rockers.
I like women a lot. Always have. I was always the man who loved women. Not in a lascivious way. I grew up surrounded by women more than males. My dad was never around much. And my grandmother, my mother, my aunts, my cousins—I was in that world a lot. And somehow I came out of it respecting women in kind of an equal way. There’s a lot of people in rock and roll who don’t. I don’t know if I’ve always been that good to them, but I think I have for the most part.

The song “Too Much Ain’t Enough” is another with a powerful drum groove that powers the whole song; it’s almost rockabilly.
Yeah, a good track. And a great solo. Campbell just burned that solo. Just great. I wrote it after seeing Fleetwood Mac, and they played that song “Oh Well,” that has this great bluesy lick. I was trying to find a riff like that, or like what Muddy Waters would have. That’s what *started* the song. I think I had written the title down when I was in New York. I saw it on a building somewhere, and I wrote it in my notebook.

So I came up with this blues lick. And then I made my own thing out of it; made it my own kind of phrasing, my own kind of chord pattern. And The Heartbreakers were really kind of thrilled with it when I brought it in. They were, like, “All right! We’ve been wanting something like this.”

And I have a memory of [Mike] playing the solo. And all of us going, “Wow! That’s great.” We did it a lot on the road. We even did it about two tours ago. We brought it back. And it *really* went over big. [Laughs] It’s a fun song to do live.

Do you always keep a notebook of song ideas?
Yeah. I always make notes if I hear something that’s interesting, or appeals to me in one way or another. When I’m going to write an album, if one’s coming up, I might make it my business to keep my ears

open and listen. I'm the kind of person who sits in a restaurant and listens to everyone talking around me. I'll write things down. I'll get out of bed at night and write things down. I still do that. Sometimes during that little time right before you fall asleep, your mind gets into a certain place, and you get a lot of ideas. So I keep a notebook by my bed, and I do a lot of leaning over and writing things down. And maybe they never come to anything, but sometimes they do. Sometimes I'll look at my notebook and I'll pick something up.

It's nice the way a song can take a line, or a title, and bend it with music, so it's heard in a new way.
Oh yeah. It can lead you into great things. Sometimes the simplest of phrases can lead you to something really cool. It's a strange thing. And sometimes you hear a kind of poetry in what somebody says.

I don't go for the Nashville way. I don't like those songs that have some clever line for the title. I hate that. You based a whole song on this catchphrase.

It's like a cheap joke.
Yeah. It feels cheap to me, like you're trying to trick me. And they do it *all* the time, and it's just dreadful. I can't stand it.

I read that the song "When The Time Comes" reminds you of the New Wave.
It might have started the New Wave. [Laughs] Maybe that was the one. [Laughs] I don't know where that came from. It's very Byrds-like, too, especially the chorus.

"No Second Thoughts."
The track was based on a tape loop. That was Denny Cordell. We had a lot of percussion: We had everybody banging on congas and whatever was around. Maybe even acoustic guitar. And we looped the tape, and then we played to the loop. I always saw that as a kind of UFO song. [Laughs] That's how it appeared to me. It was almost a UFO experience. I didn't have one, but that's how I saw that song.

Another use of the phrase "rock and roll" is "Baby's A Rock'N'Roller."
Yeah, that's us following up on "Anything That's Rock'N'Roll." [Laughs] Bugs and I were talking about that song the other day. I heard it somewhere. I always had in my head that I didn't like that song, that it was just this cheap throwaway. But it sounded so good when I heard it. [Laughs] Again, it's not a song I would sing now, but pretty indicative of how we were back then.

DAMN THE TORPEDOES. 1979

The song "Refugee," from your third album, *Damn The Torpedoes*, was made in 1979. It's one of your many classic songs. Did that start with the title, or did the title come while you were writing it?
It came while I was writing it. It was a very easy song to write. Mike had the chord progression.

Which has a nice sound, that repeating *F#m-A-E* pattern.
Yeah. He sent me over a cassette of him playing that progression. The memory I have of it is walking around the room with his cassette playing. And I started to sing to it, and really right away I got the tune, and most of the words. And it was really quick. 'Cause there are only two verses in it. The third repeats the second, almost. [Laughs] It didn't take long at all to write it. But it was a difficult song to record. But well worth it. It's really one of our best records; certainly one of the best singles we ever made.

That's an example of a song where the chord progression doesn't change, but the chorus builds up to a great climax.
Yeah. There's a middle eight. I'm just proud to have been there on that one. I hear that on the radio still. And Jimmy Iovine did a *really* great job of making a great record out of that song. It's really just a beautiful sound. Jimmy *really, really* believed in the song. He wouldn't accept less than greatness, [Laughs] which is the way he is. And he got it.

Mike's playing on it is tremendous.
Yeah. And Benmont. It's an organ solo. All of them really shine on it. That's the epitome of The Heartbreakers, of that original five.

It has such a nice opening, with the drums first, then the keys, then the rhythm guitar, then the lead guitar, and then the vocal. You introduce each element separately.
That arrangement wasn't remotely like what Mike did originally. We took the chord patterns and The Heartbreakers came up with that by playing it over and over. We really played that a lot. And a change here and a change there. Until it got the way it was. And it did work like that, in layers.

But it's the kind of song I can't picture anyone else ever singing. I've never heard anyone else ever do it. It's so uniquely us. I don't think I've ever heard anything like that.

The line "you don't have to live like a refugee" is powerful.
Sometimes you can't see these things coming. They just appear. That was a case in which I didn't see that coming. It just appeared, and there it was. So I didn't question it. I just went with it.

It's a great example of a song where the verse leads us so strongly to the chorus. The phrasing has such great rhythm built into it: "Somewhere, somehow, somebody/Must have kicked you around some..." And I love the line "Tell me, why you wanna lay there/Revel in your abandon."
Yeah. I remember all of it coming very quickly. I don't know *why* or *how*. Sometimes you can't look too deeply at these things. I'm almost superstitious about it. It's like I say, you don't see it coming. Sometimes you can, with some kinds of songs. But this one just appeared as I was just kind of pacing. I remember pacing around the room, and I started singing to the cassette. And, within twenty minutes, it had all appeared. I think I worked a little longer filling in the bridge. But I'm not even sure of that. It really came quickly. There was no effort at all. It was just very easily done, as far as the writing.

Isn't it unusual that you will work with the cassette on one of Mike's tunes instead of learning to play it yourself?

In that instance, it didn't go on long enough to learn it myself. It was over really quickly. But I will usually do both. I'll sing along to the cassette. But then, if I'm going to change any chords, or change the arrangement or something, I'll transfer it over to the piano or the guitar, and I'll learn it. And I'll often add something to it or change something. But it's not unusual to pace around to the cassette. [Laughs]

That's in a minor key, and some songwriters have remarked that writing strong melodies in a minor key is easier than writing them in a major key. Do you agree?

Well, [minor keys] are spookier. And kind of romantic-sounding. I don't know if they're any easier. Especially if you're working with an LP. You can't do *too* many minors or you'll really drag down the whole. I always think that I'm only going to get so many minor keys in the framework of twelve songs. If I do six, I might create a mood I don't want to create. So, yes, when you strum a minor chord, it's got a more exotic feel to it than a major chord. But I don't think it's any easier. There's a lot of drivel written in minor chords. [Laughs] And in major.

The song "Century City" is a great blues song in *A*. And it's got a cool bridge, which comes twice.

Yeah, the bridge is kind of the chorus in a way. I wrote that on piano. During my lawsuit phase, when I was being sued, and had to go to Century City often. And, if you've never seen it, it's kind of an acre of skyscrapers, a really modern-looking place. It's full of lawyers. And they take you up to big glass conference rooms. Just *completely* a *million* miles away from where I was at at the time. I dreaded going there.

Did you?

Dreaded it. Legal stuff. There's nothing worse. I went quite often, because there were a lot of legal meetings. We were in a huge lawsuit that had the kind of horizon of being a precedent-setter in the music business, and they tend to take those things seriously. And I was just a kid, and I was just dropped into the middle of it. And I think that song was just a way of letting off steam.

It's great you got a song out of a dreadful experience.
Yeah. I remember writing it on the piano. The house I rented at the time came with a piano. The same one I wrote "You're Gonna Get It" and some other things. I remember I came up with it on the piano.

The song "What Are You Doin' In My Life?" is cool. I like the way it stays on the *E* chord for a long time before it changes, and it just keeps building. And it has a great chorus that builds harmonically and rhythmically and melodically. Great piano on it, too.
Yeah. Benmont. I remember that. It was very early on. Written about an annoying groupie in New York. But it was a good track. We played it not long ago. We hadn't played it in about fifteen years, but we did an AIDS benefit show about a year ago. And for that show, because it was just a one-off, we hadn't been touring, we did a number of songs that we hadn't performed in a long time, and that was one of them. And I really enjoyed singing it, it was a lot of fun. [Tom and the band performed at Art for AIDS III: The Concert for Stephen in 2004, raising more than $500,000 for the Laguna Art Museum and AIDS Services Foundation Orange County. The concert was dedicated to the memory of Stephen Cy Costick, Dana Petty's brother, whose life was claimed by the disease in 1993.]

It's a good song.
Better than I realized at the time. I wasn't that knocked out by it at that time, but when I played it at that show I realized it was pretty durable. It held up really well.

You've said that about a lot of songs and albums, that at the time you didn't think they were very good, but in retrospect you've realized how good and durable they are.
That's nice when that happens. They're some that at the time I know are really good. I'll be really knocked out by it. And then they're some that have something drawing me to it, but I'm not really sure what. And that song was good. But it was up against "Refugee," "Here Comes My Girl," "Even The Losers." You know, it's pretty stiff competition. But it did hold up.

You have to compete with your own work, and your own hits. Is that a challenge?
Always. Yeah, it is a challenge. You're always competing with yourself, even a hundred songs later.

And you've managed to pull it off.
But you've got to stick to a standard. It's in the back of your mind. I don't have it in the front of my mind. But it's certainly in the back of my mind that I have to compete with myself on some level. I have to stay up to a certain standard. So, even within an album, everything has got to be as good as the thing before it.

There are so many instances of songwriters whose first albums are great, and then they never manage to match that quality in subsequent albums.
Well, you've got all your life to write your first album. And then you've got nine months to write the second one.

And a lot of people don't succeed.
Well, it's hard lonely work. That's what I said to Scott Thurston recently. He asked me what I was doing, and I told him I was doing that ugly, hard, lonely work. Writing songs. There's nobody there but me. And most people don't want to do it. Especially once they've been successful.

It's much more fun to run around being a star than going home to your room and sitting there, sweating it out hour after hour. Fortunately, I was much more interested in writing the song than going to a movie premiere. And then I just got into that discipline. Because I always knew I had to come up with ten more for the next year. So it usually took a year to come up with ten that were any good.

Is it always lonely, or does the music sometimes give you sustenance?
The music does, but you're kind of off by yourself most of the time. Most of the evening and the day. I'd stick with it. I've learned over the years that once it's not coming anymore, put the guitar down and walk away. Don't beat yourself up. So it is kind of lonely work, sometimes. But if it's coming good, if it's coming fast, that's great.

Do you have any routine where you write at the same time each day?
A little bit, if there's time booked, and you know there's gonna be a session on such and such a day. I kind of block out some time to write songs, because I've got to come in with something.

Have you ever had writer's block, where nothing comes for a long time?
I'm sure every writer's had that. But it's just a lack of confidence. You have to remind yourself that it's a lack of confidence. If you did it once, you can certainly do it again. If you start doubting yourself, you can get in that frame of mind. But you've got to remind yourself, "This is what I do. And I've done it a lot. And there's no reason I shouldn't be able to do it again." So, yeah, I bet everybody's gone through a period when they couldn't write anything.

Have you had any long periods of that?
Not really. I've been pretty prolific. I'll tell you what happens: If I'm doing a record, and I've written ten or eleven, it's almost like the well just needs to be refilled before any more is going to come out. I'm *out*. I'm out of ideas. Where I can come back in eight months and, *boom*, there it is again.

When you've written an album, and you've written nine or ten things, then you've really restricted yourself, because you can't go back to a rhythm that you've already used. Or a beat that you've already used. Or maybe a certain mood. If you're written a number of minor key songs, you know you've got your quota on minor keys here. So there are those restrictions that come down late in an album. But the best thing to do is to *ignore* that. Because you may write a minor key one that's *better* than one of the others. So it's a little bit of a mind game.

When you write ten or eleven songs, do you stop for a period of time before you write again?
I tend to. I tend to stop completely. The pattern is usually that I stop and go on a lengthy tour.

And you don't write on tour?
Never. Writing on tour has never really happened. Maybe in a very one-off situation. There's just too much going on. And you can really

fool yourself in that kind of situation, because even after a tour it takes me a while to come down and get back to the reality of what a record is. 'Cause it's *so* drastically different than what a show is. Or what will work in a show and what won't work in the studio. They're drastically different animals. If you write at the end of a tour, you might think that anything with a good beat that would go over live is worth recording. But it's often not.

"Here Comes My Girl" was also written to a track Mike gave you.

That was quite a tape. I got that tape, and "Refugee" was the first song. The second was "Here Comes My Girl." And, in that instance, we religiously copied his arrangement of what he had done. And I struggled with that song for a little while. *Until* I hit on the idea of doing narration. And then it really came through to me.

I struggled with it, because it's not an easy song to sing over. And I kept listening to it. I remember Ron Blair came by my house one day and he said, "You know, that's *really* a great piece of music there." And that stuck in my mind. I felt, "I have to learn this thing. I'm not going to let it get away from me." And then I got the idea for the narration. And once I started that, it started falling into place.

I read that you got the idea from a Blondie track.

That might be true. But I don't know if Blondie ever did a narration track. I know we'd been playing gigs with Blondie, and maybe I heard [Deborah Harry] do it in a show. But I'm thinking, maybe not Blondie, but the Shangri-Las, or somebody like that. Blondie sort of reminds me of the Shangri-Las. You used to hear [narration] done like that on those girl-group records from time to time.

It's a great sound, when you talk, and then burst into the singing.

Yeah, it's kind of an R&B vocal. It's kind of weird. It's kind of like our whole vision of the Stones and the Byrds and all that wrapped into one. Where it sort of goes from narration into R&B and then the chorus is almost Byrds-like. But wrapping it all into one bundle, you come up with something that's original in itself.

It's got the great line "Yeah, I just catch myself wondering, waiting, worrying about some silly little things that don't add up to nothing..."
Yeah. There's that theme again. Yeah. It comes back from time to time. Yes.

You said with "Even The Losers" that you had the song, but no words for the chorus?
That's the weirdest one ever. I still have a hard time believing that happened, but it did. I had everything but the chorus. I had the *tune* for the chorus. And I had the chords. And I was bold enough to say, "Let's cut this thing." But I had no idea what I was going to sing when I got to that point. And *boom*, divine intervention, it just came out. "Even the losers get lucky some time." The whole thing. I don't know if I even told [the band]. I don't know if they even know that. But I was kind of wondering what I was gonna sing when that came. I was really happy. I'm not even going to question where that came from. [Laughs]

But I will: Any idea where lines like that come from?
In a spiritual sense, I think they're all out there. They're all out there. It's just a matter of you getting yourself into a place where you can receive, where you can get your antenna out there where you can get that signal. I think, if you get your antenna out there and you get into that space, a *lot* will come in. You never really get the results if you try to force it that you do if you just let it come in. But it can be frustrating if you've got session time booked, and you've got to come out with something, it can be tough.

There have been times, such as with "Magnolia," where you forced it to come in, and you got something great.
Well, there I had to make it come in. I had to. And I think maybe I've been in two minds about that song, always have been, because I forced it to come in.

Is that so?
I know we never performed it. There're still guys who hold up signs that say "Magnolia" in concerts. [Laughs] To this day, you'll see the signs that say "Magnolia." But I think it will be a cold day in hell [Laughs] before we ever play "Magnolia." I doubt we know it.

It's not something I would put on. But I think I'm in two minds about it, because a), I forced it, and b), it was for McGuinn, so I was really trying to do an imitation of McGuinn. So I never felt it was really me. So I never chose to perform it.

On "Shadow Of A Doubt (A Complex Kid)," Mike said it was the band bashing in the studio, and that it didn't take very long, and was cut pretty much live.
As I remember it. It was in open-*A* tuning. I think pretty much all of *Damn The Torpedoes* we cut as a group. Playing together. I kind of have a picture of us doing that song. I remember thinking it had some humorous lines in it. "Sometimes she sings in French/But in the morning, she don't remember it."

Yeah, it's a good rock and roll song. We put that in the show in the last tour. We hadn't done it for years. And we put it in the show, and it worked really well.

"Don't Do Me Like That" was an old Mudcrutch song. I read that you didn't have a piano, so you rented a little recording studio and wrote it there. Is that right?
Yes. It was in North Hollywood. A place called the Alley. It's kind of dingy. Mudcrutch had rehearsed there. I wrote the song when I was in Mudcrutch. So I didn't have a piano. But in my head I could hear that rhythm. The piano playing that right-hand part: *Ding ding ding ding ding.* It was only about eight bucks an hour. It wasn't much money to rent the studio, but it was the *loneliest* feeling, walking in there by myself, sitting there, and playing the piano. And I didn't stay long. I think I only stayed an hour or so. And I wrote that song pretty much there. And then I went home and finished the words. That was something my dad used to say. "Don't do me like that." I always thought it was a humorous [Laughs] thing he said. So it was kind of an R&B idea. I was trying to do an R&B song.

It has a cool bridge, which shifts tempo, and really rocks.
Yeah. Yeah, it's all-out rock. And it was a big hit for us.

Your first AM radio hit?
Yeah, the first big, big AM hit. Yeah, probably the first one to make the Top Ten.

How about the song "Louisiana Rain"? It's one of your oldest.
Yeah. I wrote that while I was in Mudcrutch. I wrote it in Leon Russell's house, while I was keeping his house while he was on tour. I first cut it at the Warner Brothers studios with Jim Gordon and Al Kooper. And Mike. And that version is on the boxed set. And it was Jimmy Iovine who heard that version. He came to me. He had gone down to the publishing office and went through everything I had ever written when we started *Damn The Torpedoes.* And he came to me with "Louisiana Rain" and "Don't Do Me Like That." And wanted to re-record them. And I was less than keen on it, because I felt like I had already been down that road. But he did wind up making a great record out of it. I think we only did a few takes of it, and it came out really nice right away. Which was unusual on *Damn The Torpedoes*, because most of those songs were really worked on, and there were a lot of takes.

HARD PROMISES. 1981

"The Waiting" is from your fourth album, *Hard Promises* (1981). Is it true you got the title from a Janis Joplin line, "I love being onstage and everything else is just waiting"?
That's where I think I got it from. McGuinn *swears* that he said it to me. Maybe he did. I don't think so. I think I got it from the Janis Joplin quote. That's where it stuck in my mind. I don't think she said, "The waiting is the hardest part," but it was something to that effect: "Everything else is just waiting..." And so that's where that came from, I think.

That was a long, drawn-out process. It took a very long time to write the song. I had a *really* good chorus, and I had to work backwards from the chorus. So that's always hard. But I was really determined that I was going to get it. And I got it, it just took me a long time. It took weeks of working on it.

And during those weeks, would you work only on that song?
I'm afraid to say I worked *only* on that song. So I had to work a little while, take a break, and come back, and work a little longer. But I knew I had something. And I was determined I was gonna get it. I just had to get the whole fish in the boat. I knew I hooked it.

There is that challenge in songwriting when you have a piece of a song, and you know the potential for a great song is there. And you have to hold up that element of it that will keep it alive, like holding up a tent with one hand and knowing you need the other pieces.
Sometimes that is the case. If you're not lucky enough to get it all in one burst, but you know you've got something there, and there's any number of ways of getting it, any number of ways of completing it. But only one's gonna be right.

Is it unusual for you to have a chorus before having a verse?
Yeah. It is unusual. I usually kind of work linear, from the beginning. It's a whole lot harder to work back from the chorus. It is for me.

"Woman In Love (It's Not Me)" is great.
Yeah, that was one of Mike's. Those were his chords. And again it was where I wrote the tune and the words, but he had the chords. But we didn't use his arrangement. As I remember it, we kind of hammered it out in the studio. And we used Duck Dunn playing that *great*, great bass part. Because his bass line was so good, we just went, "Let's just sing over the bass line." And that's really the verse. There's not much more playing but a bass.

Why did you use Duck Dunn?
Because he's just *so* damn good. [Laughs] I think maybe Ron had left. He left during that album. So I knew Duck. And he'd *always* been one of my musical heroes. I'm such a fan of Stax, and those records out of Memphis. And Booker T. & The M.G.'s, I still just fall apart when I hear them. That's my *ultimate* drummer, Al Jackson. And Duck Dunn on bass. And he's a lovely guy, and he was nice enough to come play with us on that. He's a *great* bass player. His bass line was so good that we just had Stanley keeping time very quietly, and nothing else. And that kind of made the song. Then the chorus falls down, and it's this *big, huge* thing.

That's another one that we started doing live again. That we didn't do for a decade or more. We started doing it in the last tour, and it *really* goes over big.

That bass line moves around the vocal and leaves the space for the singing; he was really basing it on your phrasing.
He played *brilliantly*. We did it live, and he's playing to me singing and vice versa. So it was really something. It was a lot of fun to do it.

Years later, Nirvana came out with many songs that have a similar pattern—a soft verse with a chorus that just explodes. Which is exactly what you do in "A Woman In Love," among other songs.
Yeah. It's been done. It's a good trick. It's a good thing when you can make that work. It can really move you. In a show, a lot of times it's very effective to just suddenly bring a roar to a whisper. And it always moves the audience.

And it takes a great band to do it right.
[Laughs] I think so, yeah. Doing it wrong could be really awkward. [Laughs]

"Something Big" is a great use of a title. "He put up with it for a little while, he was working on something big."
Yeah, that's like a little short story.

Was that fun to write?
Yeah. It was tremendous fun. 'Cause it was kind of a little movie. And it was one of my first attempts at making characters. So I got into it, and it was fun. "Speedball and the night clerk."

You played electric piano on that one, with Benmont on organ. And it's all based on your groove on the piano.
Yeah, I wrote it on piano, so I wound up doing that on the session, and played the electric piano. Which can happen, from time to time. If I wrote it on piano, I'll often play the piano and Benmont will play the organ. I played it that way because the only way I knew it was on piano. I played it on a Wurlitzer electric.

Dylan said it was one of his favorite songs that you've written.
Yeah, he did tell me that. He also told me he liked "The Last DJ" a lot.

On "A Thing About You," Mike said he loved the interplay of your two guitars.
That's typical of us, how we would play live. How we would listen to each other, and fill in each other's gaps. That's just an instinctual thing we have from playing so long together. We're *really* lucky to have Mike, because that's a real precious thing, when you get two people who can play together and create *a* sound. And we always make a certain sound when we play together.

It reminds me of the Stones, the interplay of two electric guitars.
Yeah, it's kind of like that. But I'm more of a rhythm player. I don't play much lead. They let me play a bit. But I'm more concentrating on the rhythm guitar. Which is kind of a lost art these days. I don't really see a lot of people really working on playing the rhythm guitar. I really want to be good at playing the rhythm guitar. So we don't really weave lines that much. It's a chordal thing, and a voicing of chords. If I use a certain voicing, and he uses a certain voicing, it makes a sound. Like maybe he's gonna play a barre chord and I'm gonna play an open chord. It's just a natural thing that we do that creates this certain noise.

Is it just natural, or do you work it out?
We don't really work it out. We just do it. And sometimes if I've got the solo, Mike will just say, "You should do it. You've got the gist of it."

When you're playing rhythm, do you generally play the lower root chords?
It depends on what sounds good.

Emmylou Harris recorded a version of the song with the band Southern Pacific [on the album *Southern Pacific: Greatest Hits*].
Yeah. I love Emmylou. Just hearing Emmylou sing one of my songs was a real thrill. And it was kind of cool to hear it in a country setting, because it was such a rock and roll song. I was honored that she sang the song.

“Insider” is a cool title. Was that one you had before writing the song?
No. It came as I was writing, if I remember correctly. It just came out of the verse. I wrote that on my own at home. I remember spending a good day on it. And I was just knocked out with it when I got done. And Iovine was really knocked out with it. Extremely excited about it.

Did you tell him it was for Stevie Nicks?
Yeah. He asked for a song. He was going to produce [Stevie’s album *Bella Donna*]. He wanted one desperately. I remember bringing it to him, and he said, “God, when I asked for a song, I didn’t expect this!” And I was really attached to it. And it really *hurt* me when I did the track and the vocals. And I said, [softly] “Stevie, I can’t give you this.” And she said, “Well, I can relate to that. I completely understand. I’ll take something else.”

Was there any thought of making “Insider” a single?
No, they always wanted something more upbeat for singles. Very rarely did they put out a ballad for a single. I don’t think ever. “Free Fallin’” was the first time, I think, that I ever had a ballad out for a single. And even then it was the third single from the album. They didn’t want to do it because they didn’t think anyone outside of Southern California would relate to it. And I said, “No, you’re wrong, they will.”

And you were right.
Yeah, I was. [Laughs]

Did you have the title of the album “Hard Promises” before the song, or did it come from the lyrics of “Insider”?
That came from the song. It was a stressful period; I was fighting a battle over the price of the LP.

And yet it showed your fans that you were one guy who cared more about them than making an extra buck per record.
I was young and idealistic. [Laughs]

You’re still idealistic, aren’t you?
Maybe not as much as when I was in my twenties. I try to remain idealistic.

"Nightwatchman," which you wrote with Mike, is another story song.

That was in the days when it had come to the point of living with security guards. I found that kind of disgusting and amusing at the same time. [Laughs] That I was forced to live with someone guarding the house and the door. This guy used to sit outside of the door in a little cage. Like a little security gate between that and the front door. And he sat in this cage every night. It was cold as hell out there. It was the wintertime and I used to look out the window at him, and I'd feel really bad that there was this guy sitting out there, guarding the door.

I think that was the inspiration for the song. That particular guy would show up right about dark, and go home at dawn. And I was always up all night. So I would wind up going out there and talking with him a lot. [Laughs] Really, he was the only other person awake in the house. So I think he inspired the song.

On "Nightwatchman" you thank Bugs for his "wild dog piano" playing.

I think there's a piano note in the middle. There's a break, and a drum thing, right before the lick comes back. And there's a piano note. I think Bugs hit that note because no one else could. We were all busy with other things, so we had him hit that note on the piano. He's always been handy. [Laughs]

There's a cool, spidery guitar part on that song.

Yeah, that's Mike. It's a great track. There's good bass on that track, too. Ron Blair played a really good bass part.

It's got some great lines. I like, "Yeah I got a permit to wear this .38/But listen, my life's worth more than the minimum wage."

Well, that's what I used to say to the guy, "You know, if somebody comes here, are you gonna shoot them?" [Laughs] 'Cause he had a *gun*. I'd ask him, "Would you get into a firefight with somebody here? For what we're paying you?" [Laughs]

And he'd say [in a low voice], "Well, you know, it's my job, you know, I take my job seriously."

I said, "Well, you know, I hope you never have to shoot a teenage girl..." [Laughs] It seemed like overkill to me.

That one has two choruses. The words change in the chorus, which is something you do from time to time.
Sometimes, if you do that, it can give you a really nice build. Even a *slight* change can really lift things all of a sudden. It's a good thing. I wish I did it more often, now that you mention it. It's an old songwriter trick. But it will raise things up. It's almost like a key change.

Speaking of key changes, that's not something you do very often, if at all. They can tend to sound pretty corny.
It's very hard to do and not sound corny. It can be done, but it's very hard to do and not sound silly. There's a Buddy Holly song I heard the other day, "True Love Ways," that Peter and Gordon did. And there's a key change in that, and I thought they did it really clever. They did it as the band stopped, and then sang the punchline, and went up a key. So it worked. But we don't do that much. Because it's just like you said, it can sound very corny.

"Kings Road"?
That was a direct result of going to England, and going down to Kings Road in London. We'd always go there every time we went to London, because that was where all the crazy clothes were. You could buy great clothes there. Maybe what Carnaby Street was in the Sixties. This was where all the giant green mohawks were. This was where people paraded, the punks were all out, and that was a fairly new thing then. It was kind of like a carnival. You could walk down the road and just see all kinds of things. Vendors. I remember we used to go buy snakeskin boots, and things that you just didn't see here. It's just kind of a light-hearted song.

The song "Letting You Go" has a great melody.
I remember writing that. I wrote it on my Gibson Dove guitar. I was trying to do a Buddy Holly kind of thing. I do remember that lick at the top. That wasn't on the record. It was a very last-minute afterthought. We'd already mixed the record. So what we did was make a 2-track stereo copy of the master. And, as we made the copy, we actually recorded the lick onto the 2-track copy as it was going down. We've never done that again. It was very unusual.

On "Letting You Go," it shows what a large vocal range you have. It goes from very low in your register to very high.
I only realized that recently. Someone was talking about another singer and said they only have two octaves. And I wondered how many I have. And I sat down at the piano and realized I have quite a few. [Goes to piano, and sings four octaves.] I probably have four.

That's exceptional. Most people have about two.
Yeah, it's nice to be fifty-four and still be able to do that. I find that it's a trick. Maybe you can hit the note, but how much tone can you hit it with? So, with some keys I notice that I get up high, but I'm losing tone. It all depends on the key the song is in. Each song is a little different.

And you sing those high notes in your chest voice, instead of going into falsetto. Which is not easy to do.
Yeah. I did a lot of harmony singing when I was coming up. I used to sing a lot of high harmonies in the band. In garage groups. And I think that helped me quite a bit. I still do a lot of the harmonies on the records.

How about "The Criminal Kind"? It's based on a nice guitar riff.
Yeah, that was Mike's riff. It was a good bit of filler, really. It was okay. Just a little blues.

It's got intense lyrics on the bridge, "That little girl you used to know/She don't come around no more/Now she ain't there to watch the door/She don't wanna die in no liquor store…" You also have "They're calling you a sickness, disease of the mind."
[Laughs] I forgot that. That's probably better than I remember it. I think it was inspired by Vietnam veterans, who had been back for quite a while, but they got no respect at all. And I had been reading this thing about how they had been shoved over to one side. Agent Orange had made them all sick, and the veterans' hospitals weren't treating them. I think that inspired that line, and probably a lot of the song. "Dog tags on the mirror, hanging down on a chain." That was that, Vietnam vets.

I love "You Can Still Change Your Mind," which you wrote with Mike. It's a beautiful ballad.
Yeah, really mostly his. He wrote that whole arrangement. I think I might have made a slight adjustment in it to bring the bridge back again. I did write the melody and the words. But it's really his baby. It's a great piece of music, and it would have to be laid at his door.

You called it "Mike's tribute to Brian Wilson."
I thought it sounded like something that could have been in the Beach Boys' catalogue somewhere. *Very* different from what we normally do. But that whole album [*Hard Promises*], we were trying to find some different ground. We didn't want to make *Damn The Torpedoes* again. We were experimenting with different things. And that was one thing he played me that I felt was really different.

"You Can Still Change Your Mind" has Stevie Nicks on it, as well, singing with Sharon Ceylani.
They just happened to be there that day. And [Stevie] came over and said, "Hey, let me just have one shot on the mike, I've got an idea." And I guess she and Sharon had been singing it over in the corner of the control booth. And I let her have one pass. [Laughs] And we loved it.

I understand you wanted it to be a single.
That was when I was realizing a ballad couldn't be a single. And they were probably right, because there's not a lot of rhythm to it. But I just thought it was so beautiful, it would have sounded great on the radio. But I was probably wrong. I don't know if it's a single. It doesn't really have a beat. [Laughs]

You know, a lot of our best work isn't on the *Greatest Hits* album. A lot of our singles, which were really successful singles, weren't the best songs from that album. But you're just grateful that you have hits. But I don't know if our best work has always been the single.

I would agree. You have many songs that could have been hits, but weren't released as singles.
Yeah. When I did it, I always thought the song "You And Me" from *The Last DJ* was a smash single. And they never released it. But I still think that song could be a hit song. So you never know. You've got to deal with that business side a lot. Which can be [Laughs] very

disappointing in some ways because they're looking at it from a whole different place. They're not looking at it in an artistic way, they're looking at it as something which fills the bill.

Have you ever purposely written a song to be a single?
I did, when I did "Don't Come Around Here No More," with Dave Stewart. We set out to write a hit. 'Let's write a hit song. And make a really interesting single." And we worked for an entire month on it. And we succeeded. But I haven't done that very much. I think it would intimidate me a little bit to do that.

Did you ever release a single that didn't become a hit?
There must be. Not many. They usually found some level of success. "Room At The Top." I didn't think it would be a hit. I think they chose the wrong song. It's pretty down. There was another one—"All Mixed Up," which didn't hit at all.

LONG AFTER DARK. 1982

***Long After Dark* starts with "A One Story Town." Is LA the one-story town?**
Well, no, it could be LA or it could be a small town. I thought it was kind of a play on words where you could have a town where you didn't get above one story. Literally. Or it just had one story! [Laughs] That was what intrigued me about the title. I don't think it was specifically about LA.

It has a cool bass line in it, which anchors the whole track.
Yeah. I remember liking that when we did it a lot. Nice organ, too.

"You Got Lucky" was based on a track by Mike. Do you remember writing that?
I know when we recorded it, we made a drum loop and, again, we played to the loop. And that created a certain groove. I think Stanley actually played his drums *again*, with the loop going. So, by pulling it out here and there, it created a certain feel, a certain groove.

Benmont was really angry about the synthesizer. It was one of the only times we've used a synthesizer. He didn't want to do it. We don't ever really use the synthesizer much. But I don't see them as taboo. I don't see *anything* as taboo. I think if it's getting the job done, it's okay with me. But he *begrudgingly* played it. And I'm glad he did, because it was a hit record. [Laughs]

You've said it's not one of your favorites.
Not really. It's not that I don't like it. It's nice. It was a hit single for us. It's a popular one. It's not about a lot. It's just kind of a love song. But it doesn't have to be about a lot to be good. "Tutti Frutti" is not about a lot, but I like it. So I think it was kind of good—there's some nice textures in that song. The guitar, and the synthesizer that he's [Benmont's] playing.

And the drumming is great.
The drumming is really good, Stan is on that song. You know what that song is? It's a perfect little single. It's just a perfect little single. When I hear it on the radio I think, "Wow, we really just filled every little space in the right way." And the groove is so good. Stanley was really good on that.

The song "Deliver Me" is one you wrote alone. It's got a beautiful chorus: "Take this heart, set it free/Deliver me."
Yeah, I liked that one. We played that one quite a bit during that period. It was fun.

Do you remember writing "Change Of Heart"?
I was trying to write an ELO kind of song. I think the inspiration was "Do Ya." [Sings chordal pattern] I was a fan of ELO. And I knew of Jeff Lynne when he was in The Move. We used to listen to The Move. We'd get the records imported from England. Benmont would get them.

So I actually wanted Jeff Lynne to produce our second record, *You're Gonna Get It!* I don't know why it never happened. I think it was that he was too busy, and he didn't do outside productions at the time. But I wanted to bring him in then and do a record with him. I always had this hope that we could get to work with him.

You sensed that coming.
Well, I guess I did. I certainly wanted it to happen. And then it just happened by accident, long after I'd forgotten about it.

I loved the way [Jeff Lynne] used chords. So I was trying to write my own kind of riff like that [on "Change Of Heart"]. [Sings riff] And I think the words came later. I don't think I had the title till later.

"Change Of Heart" begins and ends with a big crunchy guitar, and you said you considered doing it live, but you and Mike said you didn't want to go back to that place where the song came from.

We didn't want to do it live. But we did play it live. We played it so much in those days. And we did do it live later. We did it just out of the blue when we did *The Last DJ* shows. For the encore we did a few oldies for the people for sitting through the new album. So that just came out of the blue one night and we played it. I think it just kind of took us back—as Mike said, "It feels like I'm in Germany"—we played it through Europe, we were playing it every night, and we got really sick of it, and ended up not playing it anymore. But, yeah, I think I wanted it to sound like "Do Ya." [Sings crunchy guitar chords] I wanted to do something that had that kind of guitar, and that was the kick-off point. Not one of my great songs. But it's a good rock song.

You wrote the song "Finding Out" with Mike. Another one with great drums.

Yeah, great drums. Stanley played really good on that album. I remember Howie doing harmonies, and he sang some really good harmonies on that.

It's got some good lines: "I don't think pain is so romantic/ I'm just a working man/I feel each day go by..."

Yeah. Well, [pain] is not that romantic. Though it's certainly been romanticized. In songs and in literature. Sometimes the idea that you have to suffer to create a good piece of art is a really dangerous idea. It's not true. I don't think so.

Many songwriters have said when their life is in turmoil, that's when they write their best work.

It's not necessary. You don't want to beat yourself up just to write a song. Even if I'm writing a sad song, I'm usually happy when I write it. When you're sad, you don't feel like writing. I don't. There are probably people who are different. But I tend to write when I'm really up. And not when I'm down. I don't even like playing music when I'm down.

That song ends with, "I have to thank you baby—honey I must confess/You have pulled me from this river of loneliness."
Yeah. The song is about finding out, and finding something you didn't know. So maybe that was the punchline. It's about self-realization.

How about the song "We Stand A Chance"?
I wrote it on the piano, though strangely enough I wound up playing the guitar, the only guitar on the track. And, if you listen closely, that's me on this really distorted guitar. And Mike played the organ on it. Jimmy Iovine was really keen on that song, and we thought it might be the one that people focused on, but it turned out to be "You Got Lucky" instead.

"Straight Into Darkness" is a powerful song.
That's a good one, yeah. That was in that same period. I remember it really came to life when we turned it over to the piano. We let the piano take it.

It's got a beautiful piano intro.
Yeah. We were trying to do it more guitar-based, when we first started recording it. When it got turned over to the piano is when it really started to show what it was about.

Sometimes it really takes a lot of work. To me, the song's as good as the record. If I can't make a good record of it, I'm not interested in it. Sometimes the songs won't reveal themselves to you until you find the right sound and the right recording of it. And that was one like that. You couldn't really get everybody grooving the same way until we went over to the piano, and then everybody instinctually found what to play. But that's part of working with a group.

That was always my idea with The Heartbreakers: Good or bad, we keep the same people together and that way we'll create a thing that's unique to us. We don't hire five new guys for each record. Sometimes that has its faults. And it's a little bit of a struggle. But that was when that song came to life, when the piano took over.

It's a dark song, about darkness of course, but it ends optimistically: "I don't believe the good times are all over/ I don't believe the thrill is all gone."
Yeah, there's some hope in it. It wasn't just a downer. [Laughs]

"The Same Old You" is another Mike Campbell collaboration.
It had a good beat and a good groove. Not a real serious thing, just a good time.

You wrote "Between Two Worlds" with Mike. It's got a cool intro: Before the drum kicks in, the piano hits chords on every beat, and then the guitars are woven in, and then the drums enter.
That's a good example of The Heartbreakers as a live group, just finding their way. We cut that at the old RCA studios on Sunset Boulevard. That was where [the Stones] cut "Satisfaction." A lot of great records were cut there. We cut "Between Two Worlds" and "We Stand A Chance" there. And that was a totally live track. And that intro just kind of happened. It wasn't rehearsed or planned. It just happened. And it was a killer intro. And I actually played some lead guitar on that track. That solo going out at the end is me. Which was really rare for those days. And I remember playing the riff at the beginning. I'm playing through a very little ten-inch amp that was really over-driven, so it had this particular distortion. I think I played on both those tracks with that amp. That intro was just something that happened. And that's the kind of band we are. If you let us have our way, sometimes we can just stumble into something great.

The song "A Wasted Life" is a very tender song, with a really sweet melody.
[Sings song] Yeah, that was another one where the record turned out to be an entirely different arrangement than what I came in with. I can't remember exactly what it was. I did a demo at home, and it just wouldn't work, the way I had first sort of realized it in my mind didn't translate. And really late in the session, somebody just said, "Let's play it *completely* different. Let's look at it in an entirely different way. Let's just start to play and see what happens." And that's what happened. We just played it once, with Benmont out in front. And that's the way it came out.

It's an affirmative song: "Don't have a wasted life/I love you too much."
Yeah, it's very positive. There again, it has something to say. It's a friendship song, just kind of being sweet.

SOUTHERN ACCENTS. 1985

"Rebels," from Southern Accents, is a classic, and has that great visceral feeling of moving from the *I* chord to the *VI* chord, the *C* to the *A* minor. How did that one come together?
That is a good progression. You can do a lot with that. That was a tough song to record. We really struggled with that. The horns on it. I had this idea that it should have horns on it. And that was new ground for us, and it was *hard*. Finding room in the arrangement for the horns. And I think that the demo I made, with nothing on it but me and the guitar, was much better. And then there's the whole story of me smashing my hand, which we've discussed.

It has some beautiful lines in it: "Even before my father's father/They called us all rebels/While they burned our cornfields/And left our cities leveled/I can still feel the eyes/ Of those blue-bellied devils/Yeah, when I'm walking round at night/Through the concrete and metal."
I did like the lyric. I really did. I liked "one foot in the grave/And one foot on the pedal..." And there's the whole story about the guy getting picked up in jail by his girlfriend. I had this whole little movie of it in my head.

Some people have seen "Rebels" as a song about history. Some critics said it was a muddled history.
I don't see why. It isn't, really. It's a story song, about a guy being arrested for being drunk and disorderly. And his frustration at basically what a screw-up he is. And he's trying to blame it on his heritage. And it's not really working. And, in the last verse, it talks about the cornfields and the cities being burned. And they were. And, in the South, to this day, there's a little bit of that grudge still being carried.

If you think about Atlanta, it was certainly burned to the ground. Even in the album, I wasn't trying to cover the entire South and its story. I was trying to use it as a jumping-off place. It's a well-written song. But it wasn't meant to be the theme of the South or anything. It was just a story, really, that dealt with this person who had problems and was trying to lay it on his heritage. You know, I only got two or three minutes to get it all in. So I think I did a pretty good job of it.

Yeah, it's a very powerful song.
It's another one Bugs won't listen to.

Why?
Because we worked on it for a year. I was never happy with it. I never felt it came out good. I felt I could have done a much better vocal than I did. I have a demo that's much better than the record, because I sang it better. I sang it clearer. And I think cocaine was popular at that time. And I think we were taking cocaine. It was one of the only times in the studio that we were on drugs. But there was cocaine going around, and I think it affected my judgment. I don't think I sang that song as well as I could have.

The horns work nicely on "Rebels" but they are mixed very low. As opposed to "The Best Of Everything," also on Southern Accents, in which the horns are really bright and prominent in the mix. And you had the late Richard Manuel singing harmonies on it.
He was one of my favorite singers. But I wasn't there when he did it. Robbie [Robertson] did that.

You originally cut "The Best Of Everything" for *Hard Promises*?
Yeah. There wasn't space for it on that album. We usually cut more than we needed. I'm glad we didn't use it, because I think it was a much better record after Robbie Robertson got a hold of it. I think he really made a much better record by the things he added to it.

It may be one of the best songs I ever wrote. It's a really good song, and he really did it justice. I'm still quite proud of that song. We had the song, and Robbie was the musical director for a film, *The King of Comedy*, and he asked me if I had something, and I told him I had this real good song which would be perfect for it. He said, "Well, would you mind if I took it and added some horns?" And I said, "Sure, give it a try." 'Cause I always liked The Band's horn arrangements. And he took it, and he edited it down a little bit. There was one more verse, which was kind of superfluous. And it came out great. I was really pleased with it.

So he finished the whole mix and all without your input?
Yeah. He didn't even want me coming in the studio. I gave it to him with the understanding that he could take it away and finish it. And then by chance one night I was working across the hall from him. And I was gonna walk over and look in, and he actually barred the door. He said, "No, no, no, don't come in. Stay away until I'm done. Then, if you don't like it, we'll change it." And I didn't change a note. When I heard it, I thought, "*Damn*, this is great." [Laughs] I wish they were all that easy.

He actually edited the song down a little bit. I don't remember what he cut out, but he made the song a little more concise. I don't think he took any lyrics out, but he made the song a little shorter. And then he had that beautiful arrangement of how he did the horns, and had Richard Manuel sing that verse with me in harmony.

Did you like that sound, of your voices together?
Oh, it was a dream come true. I *really* looked up to him as a singer. I'm kind of glad I wasn't there, because I might have screwed it up. [Laughs] Robbie did a great job. I'm in his debt.

It's amazing to me that within the period of craziness which was ensuing that you wrote the title song "Southern Accents," which is such a gorgeous and spiritual song.
I remember writing it well. It was around four. Really, really late in the morning. Or early in the morning. I was all alone in the studio, everybody had gone, and I was playing the piano. And *boom*, here's this song.

In *F*?
In *F*! Yeah, on the piano. One of the best songs I ever wrote. It just appeared. I did it all real fast on the piano. And I had a cassette deck, and I remember I taped it on the cassette deck. And I couldn't go to sleep, I was so excited about it. [Laughs] So that was a lot of fun. I got Jack

Nitzsche [arranger/composer], who's one of my heroes, I got him to do the strings. That was the first time we ever used an orchestra.

Beautiful string part.
Yeah. And that was a track I was really happy about. I thought it came out really well.

Some people have said it's your "Let It Be." Have you heard that?
No, but that's a pretty good analogy for that one.

It's got that beautiful bridge. The bridge is great.
I *loved* the bridge. The bridge was what made it for me, when I found that. I hit those chords. Sometimes you have a lot of tries for a bridge. I actually just hit those chords on my first pass through. I just went, "Oh *boy*, I got it!" It was such a great feeling. That's what makes you keep doing this. You get something like that. So that was a really, great, great moment for me, when I wrote that song. I remember it really well. I don't remember a lot of them, but I remember just playing that cassette over and over, and I stayed up all night. I couldn't possibly go to sleep. I was so excited. I wanted to play it for somebody. [Laughs]

You were in your home studio?
That was in the home studio. I couldn't wait for the guys to come over. It was like, "Wow, I've really got this thing *down*." That was exciting, man. Everything was taped on cassette in those days. And I had a little cassette player that sat on the piano. And luckily I just turned that on and got it all on the cassette. So we made the record the following day. We made it right there in my studio. I think it's Ben and me on the piano. He liked the way I played it. Because I have this kind of primitive way of playing the piano. So I have my own way of doing it. I think on the bridge, that's me on the piano. Because he said he liked the way I played the bridge, and he wanted me to do the piano. But I wanted him to do it. So the compromise was we did a pass with Ben, and a pass with me. And then they used my pass just for the bridge. And there's not much else on it. There's a bass and side stick on the drums. And that's about it.

It's one of the things that makes the album great.
Oh yeah. You couldn't have done the album without it. You had to have that.

Did you have that title before you wrote the song?
[Pause] I think, when I started working on it, I had the title. Because that's what got me off on that trip, that title. I thought, "Ah, this is a great idea, because the South is so rich. It's just this mythic kind of place."

It's one of my better songs.

I love the line about the drunk tank in Atlanta.
I'd be lucky to write even one more on that level. That song really came to life when I heard Johnny Cash's version. The "drunk tank" line. I *really* believed it when I heard him sing it. [Laughs] "Think I might go work Orlando, if those orange groves don't freeze..." 'Cause that used to put people out of work, when the frost came in.

It was just one of those magic moments, writing that song. It's really gratifying, if you're a songwriter, to get one of those. It really does make it all worthwhile. To me it did. This is a payoff for me.

The song has the dream about your mother appearing. Did you really have that dream?
[Pause] No, I don't think so. Maybe it was. I don't think so.

How about the song "Make It Better (Forget About Me)"?
I hate that song. It's just trash. It was Dave just trying to get me to knock a song out. Just write a song for the sake of writing one. And I think that's what it sounds like to me. It's one of the few that I just *don't like.* I like a lot of our work. I'm pretty proud of most of it. That one was the result of some misguided people. We didn't really know what we were doing.

Yet you included it on the album.
Yeah. A mistake. There were better songs that should have been on the album.

How about the song "Spike"? It's a funny song.
I like that one. I assumed the identity of a really kind of ignorant redneck guy who is kind of shaken up when he sees a punk rocker. I sang it from that point of view. When you do that, you've got to be really careful, because there's a certain part of the audience that really thinks it's you and your point of view. They don't get that you slid into a character.

Unless you're Randy Newman, and you do it in every song.
Yeah, he does that a lot. And I've done it some. But not as often as he does it. But I thought it worked in that instance.

A very late-night session on that one. I remember we cut that very late at night, really stoned. We were all pretty high. [Laughs] Higher than we would normally be. And so it has that kind of feel to it. But it's a funny song. "Hey Spike, you're scarin' my wife... tell me about life..."

It's low in your register.
Well, I was trying to be a different guy. So I went down low for it.

You have a number of different voices and different tones that you use. You have an Elvis quality that you use sometimes.
Well, if you're gonna sing every song, you have to find a lot of voices. [Laughs] I like the idea that you could be a number of voices, so I have had some success at doing that.

Was Elvis an influence on your singing style?
Oh yeah. I don't really hear it that much, but as a child, when I was eleven, twelve years old, I absorbed all of Elvis' recordings up to that point. This was about 1961. I really hunted down everything he'd ever done. I was just *fanatic* about it. So I'm sure that had a lot of influence. One of my favorite records that probably no one would ever think about is in the boxed set, when we covered his song "Wooden Heart." I *love* our record of that.

I think we did it better than Elvis. That's saying a lot, but I think we did. And that was a one take. I had *no idea* I was going to do it. I just said, "Let's play 'Wooden Heart'," and I just started it, and we played it. And that was the only time we did it. But it was right from the heart. We just did it, and sang it live. And when I hear that, I'm really touched by it, because it reminds me of being young and listening to those records. It doesn't sound like Elvis, really, but I'm sure there's some of that influence.

You wrote the song "Dogs On The Run" with Mike.
I think he had some of the chords, and I wrote some of the chords. I liked it a lot. Not one of our more well-known songs.

Did you like "Mary's New Car"?
Yeah. It's got Marty Jourard on sax. We recorded that in my house. It's based on the trusty Mary Klauzer. And I think she got a new car. Or we thought she should get a new car. [Laughs] So it was just a light-hearted thing. [According to Mary, she had just bought a used 1980 gold Honda Accord, which she proudly showed off to the band in the parking lot of a church at the wedding of a friend.]

Mary's a great person. I love working with her.
She's wonderful, and we love her so much. She's definitely been the den mother of The Heartbreakers. She manages every crisis in all our lives, right down to the kids' toys. Everything.

PACK UP THE PLANTATION: LIVE! 1986

***Pack Up The Plantation: Live!* was your first compilation and it included five covers, including "Needles And Pins" (a duet with Stevie Nicks), "Don't Bring Me Down," "Shout," and "Stories We Could Tell." You guys also did a great version of "So You Want To Be A Rock'N'Roll Star."**
Yeah, that was a live recording. Where Mike put elements of "Eight Miles High" into the arrangement. And we were particularly pleased that when we saw McGuinn play it, he kind of copied our arrangement. [Laughs]

McGuinn said, about the Byrds, that if it wasn't for you they would probably be forgotten.
He did say that to me. I don't know if that's true, but they felt that I reminded people of them.

LET ME UP (I'VE HAD ENOUGH). 1987

***Let Me Up (I've Had Enough)* was recorded in 1987. Where did that title come from?**
Stan. I don't remember how, but it was his line "Let me up, I've had enough." I wrote a song with it.

You said to *Rolling Stone* about *Let Me Up*: "The number one characteristic is that there are only the five Heartbreakers on this album. There are not outsiders on it whatsoever. Most of it is just off-the-cuff stuff. I like the feel of it so much. It was just really meant to be a good rock and roll album."
Yeah, well I guess that's fairly accurate. There were no producers, it was just me and Mike, and we were doing whatever we felt like doing. We had been on the tour with Bob [Dylan]. I think it was made on a break in those tours. Some things are ad-libbed on that record. "The Damage You've Done" is ad-libbed completely. You can hear on the boxed set, there's "The Damage You've Done" country version. And that was the first take. It was like a George Jones kind of thing. And the very next take is the one that's on the album. Where I just started to play a different rhythm, [the band] fell in, I ad-libbed the entire song. *Boom.* That was it. Thank you very much, that's the record.

I did that again on two other songs. They were ad-libbed right off the top of my head. One called "Think About Me." Another one called "How Many More Days." That was a *complete* ad-lib. Count four, let's see what happens. Very bold. Very much flying by the seat of my pants. Can't imagine doing that again. But I did it. I had the band set up, had a sound up, let's try this. Not having any idea at all. But just started to sing, and seeing where it took me.

"Jammin' Me" is unusual in that you wrote it with Dylan and Mike, and you have modern references, whereas most of your songs have timeless imagery. This one has "Take back Eddie Murphy," and also "Vanessa Redgrave" and "Joe Piscopo."
That was all Bob, that verse about Eddie Murphy. Which embarrassed me a little bit, because I remember seeing Eddie Murphy on TV really pissed off about it. And I had nothing against Eddie Murphy or Vanessa Redgrave. [Laughs] I just thought what [Dylan] was talking about was media overload and being slammed with so many things at once. And

times were changing; there weren't four TV channels anymore. It was changing, and that was the essence, I think, of what he was writing about.

We wrote a version together at the Sunset Marquis Hotel. We wrote a couple of songs that day. There was another one called "Got My Mind Made Up." That was on one of his albums—*Knocked Out Loaded*, I think. I produced the track. We had done a version of it for *Let Me Up* that didn't get used. It's on the boxed set. So we wrote those songs, and then I took really just the lyrics to "Jammin' Me," and completely rewrote the music with Mike. And then I sent it over to Bob to see if it was okay, and he said, "Yeah, sure." So that's the extent I talked about it with him. [Laughs]

So you changed the whole melody?
Yeah, we changed the melody and the chord structure somewhat. Mike had the idea of the chords, and how the track went, and I wrote the melody and used the lyrics I wrote with Bob. And it was successful. It came out really well, and they released it as a single.

When you write with Bob, is that something where you're exchanging lines?
Yeah, just like you'd think. I remember we would write a lot more verses than we needed. We did that in the Wilburys, too. It's a great honor to work with someone so great. And more than an honor; it was fun, because he's really good at it. So anytime you can work with somebody that's really good at what they do, it's going to be a good experience.

We've spoken about the use of unusual keys, and "Runaway Trains," which you wrote with Mike, is in *F#*. And I know you've said it's not one of your favorites, but it's a great song.
I heard that on the radio not long ago. And it is good. I was pleasantly surprised. Somehow I got it into my head that I didn't like that. But I did like that when I heard it.

You've said that about some of your albums, such as *Echo*, and then you hear them later and change your mind.
Well, I don't listen to them. Usually by the time I'm done with it, I never play it again. So it's only on the radio that I hear them. But Dana

likes to play them. And with *Echo*, she actually made me listen to it again. So sometimes that's true, that with time gone by, I'll hear it, and it's like a revelation to me. 'Cause I've forgotten the sequence of it, or a song. 'Cause we've done *so* many. But I'm pretty distanced from them once I've done them. Unless we're playing it in a show. But even that isn't the record. I don't remember the record that well, unless I hear it. But I always listen to them when they come on the radio.

You talked about using only two chords in a song, and "The Damage You've Done" is basically just *G* and *F*. Two chords, but with the melody rising and falling inside them.
It was an improv. And I think there's probably a bridge in there, too. What I'd do is yell, "*G*!" And everyone would go to *G*. Then "*F*!" And everyone would go to *F*. And then I'd go back to the tape, and take out those instructions. But while we were playing I'd yell, "*A* minor!" And everyone would go to *A* minor. They had that much precision as a unit, that you could call out the chords and [the band] would change. So that's how I was doing that. [Laughs]

And the other side of the coin on that record were the things that Mike was more involved in. And they tend to be more production pieces, where we really buckled down and made more serious-type records. Things like "Runaway Trains."

Another song you wrote with Mike is "My Life/Your World."
Yeah, that's an overlooked one. That's a really good song. I had a good set of lyrics for that one. "They came out here with a dog on a chain/Came and took my little brother away..." I liked that one. That's one of Mike's really good chord patterns.

It has that great line "His generation never even got a name."
I was thinking about my brother, who is seven years younger than me. He's in that generation that didn't get a name. He's not in the X generation or anything. They were just dismissed. [Laughs] They came right after the Sixties and nobody really called them anything.

"Think About Me"?
That was another one that was improv right from the start. They had to actually go back and find another chord for the very first chord; it was clipped, because the engineer wasn't rolling. And he turned the tape on

right as I started to play, so it clipped the front of the track. So I think they had to find one later, and edit it onto the front. But that's completely ad-lib, with me yelling out the chords.

It's got some funny lyrics in it.
Yeah. God knows where they came from. It wasn't very serious; it was just meant to be a rock and roll song.

You said of the song "It'll All Work Out," that it was one your favorites, and that it's a "durable song."
It is durable. It still holds up. It was one that I really liked. Which, strangely enough, the record was all Mike. But I wrote it. But I was going through a crisis at the time with my marriage. My first marriage was on the rocks. I was separated. Though it was later reconciled. So I had more on my plate than I could handle. I had written "It'll All Work Out" and I sang it into a cassette. And I brought it to Mike's house, giving him the cassette. He had a studio at his house. And I said, "Could you just make this a record?" [Laughs] "Because I don't have time, I can't deal with it mentally, but I think it's a really good song." And I gave him the tune. And when I saw him again at the proper sessions, he brought in the track, and he had done the whole track, and I sang it, and we were done with it. That's never happened before or since.

It's got beautiful instrumental acoustic guitars on the intro.
He's playing a Japanese koto. Which you don't hear in rock very much. But he found a way to bring it into the track. But I don't play on that at all. I don't think any of us are on that except for Mike.

The song "All Mixed Up" starts with clapping and singing and laughing.
[Laughs] Right. It was another light-hearted one. Wrote it with Mike, too.

It has a spoken bridge, which is not something you do very much.
Yeah. I remember it has a catchy chorus.

You once said you saw your song "A Self-Made Man" as a B-movie starring Johnny Cash.
[Much laughter] That's pretty accurate, yeah. Later on in life, I tried to get Cash to do that one. But he couldn't deal with the major seventh chord. [Laughs]

Too pretty for him?
I guess so. He just said, "I can't sing over that. My voice doesn't sound right with it. Can you find another chord?" And I couldn't come up with another chord that sounded right. But I always wanted him to do it, and almost got him to do it, because he *liked* it. And he wanted to do it; he just couldn't get over that major seventh chord.

"Ain't Love Strange"?
I wrote it on electric piano at my house. That was all in that rocky romance period I was in. "Make you string barbed wire/Around your little piece of ground..."

So that was a time you were writing, although your life was in turmoil.
Life was really interesting during that period, yeah. It kept getting interesting. But for me it was like a "Where did I wake up today?" period. [Laughs] One of those times in life.

"How Many More Days"?
It was ad-lib. That was ad-libbed completely. And not a bad song. Our wardrobe girl, Linda [Burcher]—Queenie, we call her—she's been with us, God knows, since the early eighties. She always requests that one. And we always laugh, because we know damn well we're not gonna play it. [Laughs] We'll always be back there during an encore, waiting in the hall, and Queenie will run up and go, "'HOW MANY MORE DAYS'! Do 'HOW MANY MORE DAYS'!" [Laughs] But we never do it. We don't know it. Just that she thinks we would know it is hysterical.

FULL MOON FEVER. 1989

On to *Full Moon Fever* now, which was released in 1989. You wrote "Free Fallin'" with Jeff Lynne?

Yes I did. It was, I think, the first thing we wrote together. When we really got nose to nose and wrote a song. Jeff came over, and I had a little electric keyboard that Bugs had bought. I really gave him hell about buying it. I said, "Why would you waste money on this? I would never play something like this."

He said, "Well, look, take it into the house, if you write one song on it, it will pay for itself."

And I thought, "Well, okay," and Jeff was over and I had the little keyboard. And I started playing on it, and I hit this riff. This little chord pattern that we would know as "Free Fallin'." But I had a couple notes more in the riff.

And Jeff looked up, and said, "Oh, that's good. Can you leave out that last chord there and see what it does?"

And, when I did that, it made this nice round of chords. And so I was just trying really to make Jeff smile, as I was ad-libbing these words. You know, "She's a good girl/Loves her mama/Loves Jesus and America too." And Jeff smiled. I kept going. And I got right up to the chorus bit, and I didn't know what to sing, and he said [in a British accent] "Free Fallin'." And I tried to sing it, but I couldn't get "Free Fallin'" to fit into the line. So I just sang "Free..." And then in the next line I sang "Free Fallin'." And then he perked up and said, "That's good—that's great! But take your voice up an octave when you do it, when you go to the chorus." And *bang*, there it was. "Free Fallin'." I was very excited. I loved the song.

So Jeff went home and I sat there for a while and I finished the last verse alone, the one about flying out over Mulholland and writing the girl's name in the sky. And he came around the next day, and I played it for him. And he said, "Man, you stayed up and finished the song. That's incredible, it's great." And so this is how these things happen. And it's turned out to be probably the most famous song I ever wrote. And there's not a day that goes by that somebody doesn't hum "Free Fallin'" to me, or I don't hear it somewhere. It's become synonymous with me, I guess. But it was really only thirty minutes of my life. [Laughs]

You also wrote "I Won't Back Down" with Jeff.

We wrote that as we were mixing "Free Fallin'." We wrote that in the next room. In a little glass booth, where I could actually see into the control room, I could see them working on the mix. So we went in next door, where the piano was, and came up with that. We came out really excited. It was hard to keep our mind on the mix because we already wanted to cut this other song.

Jeff showing up was such a lightning bolt from the gods. It was such a big deal. It had such an impact on everything we would do after that. Literally, I think everything we've done since then, it's always been, "What would Jeff think of this?" It's always been like that.

I'd always admired Jeff so much. And I got to hang out with him a little bit when we were in England on the Bob Dylan tour. He'd come down with George Harrison. Jeff came out to Birmingham when we played there. And then we were in London for a week. They would come down pretty often in the afternoon, and hang around till late after the gig. So I became pretty tight with him and George right away. We had a marvelous time.

But Jeff was *such* a genius in the studio. Just *so* good. He made things that had been really difficult seem so easy all of a sudden. Like getting a good take. It just all came so *easy* with him. He taught me a lot. A lot about singing, a lot about harmony, a lot about arranging. Everything.

What could he teach you about singing?

He'd say, "Here's where you sound best. Here's what you do really good. And here's what you don't do really good." It's hard to put your finger on it and put it into words. But he had just such a great perspective. He could sit back and see everything. Hear the record, and guide you though it so effortlessly. Where things that had been really hard—sometimes making those records would really bring us to our knees emotionally, it could be really hard—and with *Full Moon Fever* everything was a breeze.

Even the writing?

Even the writing. We made it *so* fast and did it so effortlessly that it was done before you knew it. There it was! I remember coming home after we cut "Free Fallin'" and "Yer So Bad." And having those two tracks on cassette, and I must have played them for two hours, over and over, just sitting there on the bathroom floor, feeling, "*Wow*, this is *so* great." It was really exciting.

With Mike you always write to tape, but with Jeff you would write nose to nose.

Yeah, we did. We sat there with our acoustics and wrote together, nose to nose.

And who would guide those sessions?

Both of us would. Whoever had something. We were great friends. We had a lot of laughs together. We would just start playing, and then one of us would say, "Oh, that's nice, that's a nice bit." And we'd say, "Okay, let's work on this bit." And I did all of the words. He didn't want to get involved in the words. He said, "You're gonna sing it, so you may as well write the words." So I did.

It is that way: If you're gonna sing the song, it's good to write the words yourself, so you can believe it and get behind it. And we would just throw things around. He was good, too, about that we're gonna finish the thing. *Completely* finish it.

Mike remembered that when you wrote "I Won't Back Down" you didn't have all the words, so you went to the piano and finished it. And then you did harmony vocals with Mike, Jeff, and George Harrison.

Yeah. George was around a lot during that time. Just socially, just hanging out. His family would come over, and we became close, the two families. So George would sometimes come to the session to hang out. That was a particular time that he was there, and he wound up singing with us.

I played the piano. Jeff had the melody for the verse, and then I came up with the main riff. We got together, and with all this synergy, we pretty much finished the song—all but one line. Which was "There ain't no easy way out." I didn't have a line for that. And I was singing, "I'm standing on the edge of the world." [Laughs] And when we were recording it, George said, "What the hell is that—'I'm standing on the edge of the world.' Surely there's got to be something better than that." [Laughs] And then I came up with "There ain't no easy way out," which seemed so obvious. But that was George going, "That line's dumb." And so I'm really glad that I got all the dumb lines out, because it's a song that apparently a lot of people have been inspired by. I get a lot of people telling me, either through the mail or in person, how that song has played a role in helping them in some way in their life. How it's given them conviction to get over a certain obstacle in their life. It's really gratifying. I even saw an article in a paper about a girl coming out of a coma listening to that song. It had been her favorite song.

There was a pro-choice doctor who was murdered, and they did a rally for him, and Eddie Vedder of Pearl Jam phoned me and said, "I'm gonna sing 'I Won't Back Down' tonight and I wanted to make sure you wouldn't mind." And I said, "No, the song is there to be used." And I later heard Pearl Jam's version of it, and it was really good. [On March 10, 1993, Michael Griffin murdered Dr. David Gunn outside a Pensacola, Florida, clinic. Pearl Jam appeared at a Rock the Choice event at the Pensacola Civic Center on March 9, 1994, and sang "I Won't Back Down" in memory of Dr. Gunn.]

I've heard a lot of different versions of it. I heard a church choir sing it. My brother told me he's heard marching bands do it at football games. And I just heard a gospel record of it, where the guy was doing it as a shuffle. So, when I first wrote that song, I thought, "This might not be right, because it's so blunt. There's not a lot of metaphor in it, there's not a lot of hiding behind anything. It's very blunt." But I think that bluntness may have been what inspired people. One of my more well-known songs. I just *have* to do it in shows, or people feel let down. So I'm really happy to have written that one.

"Love Is A Long Road" was written with Mike; he said the music was inspired by motorcycles.

I didn't know that. I remember writing it. Mike had a track that was close to what we used, but it had a very different rhythm. It had a lot of drum fills, and was a little more chaotic. And we began recording it without Jeff, because he had gone to England for a week or two. When he came back, he helped us straighten it out. He really was the one who made it work. And Jim Keltner played the drums. But it was basically, musically, Mike's idea. I wrote all the melody and the lyrics to it. And then all of us had a hand in the arrangement. It's a really good one. We still play that a lot.

"Runnin' Down A Dream" is something you wrote with Mike and Jeff?
Actually, all Mike wrote was that one descending riff.

Which is the engine of the song.
Yeah. He had that riff, but in a different time signature. It was kind of a broken beat, much slower. I liked the lick a lot, and I'd sit around, playing it on my guitar, experimenting with it in different ways. I came to think it sounded good in a really straight beat, really fast. And I played it for Jeff, one night when he was over at my house, and he said, "Oh, that's good. That might be one of those last riffs left." [Laughs]

So we sat down and came up with some chords. Just blocked it out. Didn't have any words. I had the lion's share of the chords. He [Jeff] may have helped me with the chorus. I remember writing the bridge and all that myself. So we had a vague tune that we kind of blocked out, and hummed it into the tape recorder. And, over that weekend, I worked on it for two different afternoons. I didn't feel completely confident about it. Because I was singing in a low register. I remember saying to them, "Do you think we should change the key?" Jeff said, "No, no, no, it's perfect, it's perfect the way you're doing it."

Del Shannon was around. He was running around with us a little bit during that time. That's why I threw in that line: "Me and Del were singing, 'Little Runaway'." I put that in for him. He was very pleased. I got a big smile from him on that. And "Little Runaway" fit the whole concept. So that was that.

The most incredible thing about that one to me, which to this day amazes me, was the solo at the end. Mike played that. There was no one there but me, Mike, and Jeff. And Mike was engineering. We were in Mike's *tiny* little studio in his house. Four people could *barely* fit in. If any more came, they had to stand in the garage. You had to pull the cars out to work.

Mike was just sitting there with his head down. And that bit came, and he started to play. And he played that *incredible* solo. But he looked like a stone statue. He didn't ever blink or move. And he had his back to us. I remember Jeff looking around his shoulder and looking back at me, and making this face, like, "Is he really doing this?" It was one take. One take. And he played that incredible solo.

That song is longer than most of your songs—over four minutes.

That was because he got on that roll at the end, and he just kept playing, and I wasn't going to edit it out or fade out, because it was just so good what he was playing.

"Yer So Bad" has some funny lyrics: "My sister got lucky, married a yuppie/Took him for all he was worth..."

Black humor. I was stuck on the little turnaround and couldn't figure where to go. The "Not me baby" place. And Jeff said, "Well, put an *E* minor there." And, when I put the *E* minor in, it led me right through everything.

One of the most haunting songs on the album is "Face In The Crowd," which is in *E* minor. Written with Jeff. A beautiful song.

It's held up well. I went to Mexico not long ago and there was a male flight attendant. And he didn't speak much English. And he came over, and said [with Mexican accent], "Oh yes, Tom Petty. 'A Face In The Crowd'!" [Laughs] "'A Face In The Crowd'!" That was the one he keyed in on.

And I do like that song. I think it's a really sweet song. A nice sentiment. Very simple. Extremely simple. It's not complex in any way. Just *E* minor, *C*, *D*, *A* minor seventh.

That was one of the first CDs I ever got. And I would hit "repeat" to hear that song over and over.

It's on that CD where I put, in the middle, "Hello CD listeners. We've come to the point in this album where those listening on cassette or records will have to stand up or sit down and turn over the record or tape. In fairness to those listeners, we'll now take a few seconds before we begin side two." Yeah, CDs were getting big around that time.

Do you like having your work come out on CD as opposed to LPs?

I miss the covers [of LPs]. Because it was such a huge part of the experience. It was something you held in your hands as you listened. And it was an art form in itself. Which really is pretty much gone now.

We still have covers.

But they are really insignificant though, aren't they? They are so tiny, and your eyes hurt trying to read anything on them. I miss the jackets. I'm glad I got to be involved when records came around. I'm glad I came up that way, because it was a lot of fun.

Do you still listen to LPs?

Yeah, I do. A lot. It was different, because you had a beginning, and a middle, and a second act. I miss that. You could only get about twenty minutes on a side. So you planned it out where you had two twenty-minute sides, usually. Now we don't think that way. Time is unlimited. And I think once we had the luxury of all the time we wanted that records got really long, maybe too long. *Echo*, I think, is too long. Some of those songs should have been held for later. When you sit down for a listen, seventy minutes is kind of a long time to really pay attention.

The song "Depending On You" is one you wrote yourself.

That was really fun to do. We should play that song. We've never played it [in concert].

That whole album [*Full Moon Fever*] sounds *so* good. I mean, the *sound* of that album—sometimes you get lucky and a little magic happens and you get this magical sound going. And that album really has it. It intimidates me a little bit. How will I ever do that again? It's such a magical sound, I don't know how it happened. I mean, obviously, there were a lot of talented people working on that. But it really had something beyond that. Maybe it was because we just had such positive energy. But there's *such* a good sound to that record.

It's amazing you did it crowded into Mike's little home studio. Did that contribute to the magic?

It must have. That period of our life, speaking for me and Jeff, that was the best time of my life. The Wilburys, *Full Moon Fever*... The music was coming with very little effort. Deep, deep friendships, and a lot of laughs. Between Jeff and George and I. And everyone else.

Olivia [Harrison, George's widow] was over here last week. They're doing a film on the Wilburys, and she showed me a lot of video that Bugs shot. George had Bugs shooting us all the time. I didn't know it. I knew that some video existed. But I guess that, every time we left the control room and went into the studio proper, [George] handed the camera to Bugs and had Bugs shoot. And there was a lot he shot himself. But we are having such a good time. You never saw a bunch of guys having a better time than we are having. It's really something to see.

I've never seen any film of Bob in the studio. And we're there, and we're writing. There's a point where Bob has a paper in his hand, and says, "Let me do this again, there's too many 'I's' in this." [Laughs] "Too many 'I's'." He just scratched them out. But, God, it was a great, great time. Just great friendships. A really nice time.

"Apartment Song" made the album, though you wrote it long ago.

Yeah, I had written that for *Southern Accents*, and it had laid around all that time. We were going through songs really fast, and [Jeff] said, "Have you got anything laying around?" And I said, "Well, I've got this one thing." I cut a demo with Stevie, just the two of us. That was the only thing I had, that demo. Jeff made it into a great record.

It's nice, after the second chorus, the way the guitar and drums kick into a different rhythm.

Yeah, that's us doing our Buddy Holly thing.

"Alright For Now" is a gentle, lovely lullaby.

Yeah. That was written late at night, with my kids in mind. That was when Jeff wasn't there. He was gone, and Mike and I did it. We dubbed everything on it.

Beautiful acoustic finger-picking on that one.

Yeah, we did that live, the two of us, just playing together.

How about "A Mind With A Heart Of Its Own"?

[Jeff and I] heard Connie Francis singing "My Heart Has A Mind Of Its Own." And we were both in two cars driving to the studio, we used to listen to this AM station playing oldies. And I got out of the car, and I said, "Did you hear that Connie Francis thing?" He said, "Yeah, I just heard that. But what if you sang that the other way? Then it means an entirely different thing."

So I kind of put that in the back of my mind, and then the next day I came up with this Bo Diddley idea, and then we knocked it out pretty fast. There's one verse that's ad-libbed, where I didn't have the verse lyrics. And I was doing the vocal on the other one: "I've been all around the world/I've been over to your house/You've been over sometimes to my house/I've slept in your tree house/My middle name is Earl." [Laughs] And I was so pleased with that. And my middle name really is Earl. And it just landed perfectly with "world." So we kept that in.

Sometimes songs seem to just fall together for you, if you're in the right place.
Well, that one did. Because I had a couple of verses, but I couldn't come up with the third one. So [Jeff] just said, "Come out and do the ones you've got." So, when it came to the third one, I just threw that in.

I understand that with "Zombie Zoo" you heard that name from a Mohawked punk in a diner.
Yeah. It was when Jeff and George and I went out to Anaheim to ask Roy Orbison to be in the band [Traveling Wilburys]. We were working on *Full Moon Fever* at the time. We were writing everything we saw. One line I remember that we saw on a billboard was "Every day is judgment day." That later turned up in "End Of The Line," the Wilburys song. We stopped at a restaurant on the way back, and these punky-looking guys recognized us and came over. And I said, "Where have you been? Where are you playing?" And they said, "The zombie zoo," and out came the pads! [Laughs]

It's a very light-hearted song. Nonsense, really. There's no great statement. It was just for the fun of it. I kind of wondered about "Zombie Zoo" really. I don't think I would have had it on if Jeff hadn't really campaigned for it. I would have cut it out. But there it is.

INTO THE GREAT WIDE OPEN. 1991

***Into The Great Wide Open*, from 1991, has the great song "Learning To Fly."**
That's been one of our most popular songs. We still get a lot of requests for that in movies, and people always want to hear it in the show. People embrace it.

You said once that you heard a pilot say that learning to fly is easy, but coming down's the hard part.
True. That was the inspiration, and I took it from there. Jeff and I wrote that together. I think I started it, and pretty much had it going, and then he came in and helped me with the chords. We finished it off together. I still like that song. I like to perform it. I've gotten a lot of different mail on it; different people that were inspired one way or the other in life by that song, and they send me letters about it. I'm proud I wrote that song. And it's a good-sounding record, it's a good sounding single.

Did it come quickly when you and Jeff were working on it?
Yeah, I think we wrote it in an evening. It came quickly because I had written most of the words, and I had gotten a tune in my head. So I had this idea, and we sat down and spent a whole evening on it. But that's fairly quick, if it comes in a day or two. I just had this little tune in my head, and I sang him this tune, and he said, "Let's see what fits nicely under it." And he played a big part in the chords.

The song "Into The Great Wide Open" starts with a great slide part that Mike plays. Sounds very George Harrison-inspired.
Well, it might have been. George really liked Mike's playing, as well. They had a mutual admiration for each other on slide guitar. There's a lot of good guitar on that track. The 12-string he plays on that track is really good. He added quite a bit to that album.

Was that one of the first songs you wrote for the album?
Yeah, it was.

You called it a "very funny song and a very true song."
[Laughs] It's a narrative. It's a story. And I think it has some truth in it. It's light-hearted in a way. With a kind of black humor to it. The video was the great thing with that song. The video was as good as the song, I think. It's a rare instance where they really complemented each other. And we actually had to extend the song for the video. The video is seven minutes long. Because we shot so much, and we didn't want to lose it. So we went back and did a re-edit and remix of the song to make it fit the video. [Laughs]

The key line is, "The sky was the limit."
Yeah. Well, that's what people think when they come out to California. Strike it big. Some people hit it, some people don't.

Did you just fall into that story, or was it one you intended to write?
I just kind of fell into it. You don't know where those things come from. I was just playing those chords, and this little story started to appear. I carried it around in my head for a while, and refined it a little bit. And I had it pretty well written, and then I played it for Jeff, and he helped me, and he added a few ideas, too. Like that chord turnaround. [Sings chords] Jeff's idea. And we added that in, and we altered a couple chords. Gave them a little bit more exotic treatment under the melody. But it was pretty much all done. I pretty much had it when he came aboard.

I was happy to see you included "Two Gunslingers," which is a wonderful song from *Into The Great Wide Open* but not a hit, on the Anthology album that was released on October 31, 2000.
Well, with that *Anthology* album, I didn't see the point in that record. But we were under a contract where we had to deliver. So what we did was to pick our favorites. As many of them as we could get in. Because they insisted on having all the hits. But, since it was a double CD, we were allowed to pick more songs. So we picked our favorite ones and put them in.

So "Two Gunslingers" is one of your favorites?
Oh, definitely.

Mine, too.
I love that song. I was really proud of that when I got it done.

It's a funny song, but also meaningful.
Yeah. It's a really good anti-war song.

Do you remember writing it?
Yeah, I remember. I have a picture of where I wrote it. There was a poster that Jim Lenahan had given me. He's a movie buff. And, back when we were in Gainesville, he was always telling me about movies.

And I would kind of wind him up by giving him a really bad movie. Like I'd say, "How about *Hostile Guns*, now there's a movie." [Laughs] And it was this terrible Western, and I thought the title was so funny. He'd be talking *Citizen Kane*, and I'd say *Hostile Guns*, and it would really wind him up. So, many years later, he came upon the movie poster for *Hostile Guns*, and he sent me the poster. Gave it to me. And it was on my wall. I'm pretty sure that's what was the germ for that song, the poster of the gunslingers.

"The Dark Of The Sun"?
Now that's one, if I had the chance, I would play that song. We've never played it [live]. It got lost in the shuffle of that album. There were so many songs on it. I thought it was a good little song. I haven't heard it in years, but I bet I would like it if I heard it.

I think you would enjoy the entire album. You should have Dana put it on in the car.
[Laughs] Last time I heard that album, I checked into a hotel somewhere. Might have been Santa Barbara. We were on one of our getaways. And the room had a CD set-up and then they have a few CDs which are standard with the room. Mantovani, or Johnny Mathis. And then there was me, and it was *Into The Great Wide Open*. And I put it on, and listened to it. That was the last time I heard that album.

Did you enjoy it?
Yeah. I remember enjoying "The Dark Of The Sun." And I think, for the most part, I enjoyed it. I always get pretty critical. But I was pleasantly surprised.

"The Dark Of The Sun" has some great words: "I saw you sail across the river/Underneath Orion's sword/In your eyes there was a freedom/I had never known before..."
Constellations. Orion is one of the few I can easily pick out when I look up there. That was another song that came from a staring-at-the-sky kind of thing.

The song "All Or Nothin'" has a compelling melody.
It was Mike's thing. It was mostly Mike's track. And I don't think we made many changes to it.

That also has a great slide opening.
He's so good on the slide guitar. George [Harrison] just thought that Mike was right up there with the best of them on the slide. He told me time and again. He said, "There's Ry Cooder, and then there's Mike Campbell..." He really loved his slide playing. And it's a different kind of instrument. It's kind of not within the notes. It's more like a voice. It's all about vibrato, and how you ring the note out of the guitar with this piece of metal. Or glass. Something I've never really tried to do.

It's not easy.
No, it's not easy. It's an acquired thing. You have to work at it. But it's very natural to him. He has a perfect vibrato, and a perfect pitch. It's really about pitch. It's a lot like singing. You've got to come right up to the note, and sustain it. But he's just a marvelous player. Somebody I've known my entire life, and I still marvel at his playing. I've really known him longer than I haven't. And I still marvel at his work.

You could almost take Mike for granted, because anything you asked him to do he did it. And more. I don't remember ever throwing anything his way that he couldn't do. He could do it, and do it better than you thought. He will give you back your idea better than you had it in the first place. *That's* a great musician.

Benmont is quite the same way. It doesn't seem there's anything he can't do.
I was going to say he's kind of the same way. If you give him an idea, he'll give it back to you better than your idea was. So they make me look good. But we do count on each other. And it's very much a collaboration between the three of us. It's probably the biggest part of the records we make, is those three of us, the collaboration we make in tone, in texture, and in melody. That's what creates that sound.

You said that you wished "All Or Nothin'" got radio play instead of "Out In The Cold."
Yeah, I think it might have been a better song. Time plays tricks on you, though. I went around for years thinking "Out In The Cold" wasn't that good. "Out In The Cold" got a *lot* of radio play. And I was kind of irritated with it. I thought they were going after it because it had the big beat. But, the last time we played, we rehearsed that song and played it and I was really fond of it.

But it has been frustrating to you sometimes that certain songs which could definitely have been hits don't get that chance to be singles.
Well, in that case we had two singles that got a *lot* of play: "Learning To Fly" and "Into The Great Wide Open." And "Out In The Cold" got a lot of FM play. I think I wanted people to hear the versatility on the album. There was a lot of different kinds of music, and I thought, "Oh, they've gone over it." But that's really a small point. It wasn't something that wrecked my world or anything. How much can you get played off an album? There are some albums where they almost played everything off the album, and then some albums where they only played one. But truthfully, you've got to be thankful if they play any of it.

You wrote "Out In The Cold" with Jeff Lynne. But you said you were never completely happy with that one.
I think I struggled with that one. I struggled with the lyrics quite a bit. It was one of those things where you struggle, and you always wonder if you got everything out of it that you could. Thinking back, when I played it recently in rehearsal, I was pleasantly surprised by the lyrics and I liked them. I liked to sing them.

It's got some nice counterpoint harmonies on it.
Yeah, that was all Jeff's idea. That is his arrangement. He started that song and then brought it to me. Which was unusual. He came in and said he had an idea. It went through a lot of changes from where he brought it in, like from major to minor. But he kicked it off. It was his basic idea. It wound up being a good rock and roll song. It's nothing earthshaking, but it's a good rock and roll song.

Again, Mike's playing on that one is great.
Yeah, well he's always good. He really stepped out on that one. I remember the things he played in the stops. There were some stops where he really wowed us all. *Shazam!* How did he do that?

It must be fun in the studio when he's playing such great stuff.
Hell, yeah. I feel really lucky to be involved with somebody like that. [Pause] It's quite a band. And he plays no small part in it. He's really good.

One of my favorite songs on the album is "All The Wrong Reasons." The music is beautiful, and it's got a great lyric.
Benmont likes that song. He brings that song up to me a lot, saying why don't we do that one.

I remember writing that one. I was inspired. There was a family we knew through one of the kids. And they were a very wealthy family with all the trimmings. The big cars and the big house. And then suddenly the economy started failing and all their money went. They had to pack up and go. And I think that was the germ of the idea. "The big ol' house went up for sale/They were on the road by morning." 'Cause they were *gone* overnight. *Gone*. From the top of the world to gone.

It was the Gulf War period, Bush, Sr. was president. I felt that a lot of things were going on for the wrong reasons. It was a pretty grand thought, but I just thought that America itself was becoming kind of a cheap place to live, morally speaking. The value system was changing. The culture was becoming celebrity-driven and empty.

It's still like that in a lot of ways. But there was a change, and you felt it. Things that wouldn't have been tolerated suddenly were almost celebrated. So that was really the inspiration behind a lot of that album. "The rocks might melt and the sea may burn" was from seeing oil fires on the ocean. So it was a reflection of those times. There was a war, and there was a bad feeling in my gut in a way. I wanted to make a positive album, but I also wanted to reflect those changes. It was the end of the decade. And I wanted to try to make some comment on that, on where we're going. We're going into the great wide open.

We spoke about memorable melodies, tunes you can sing along to, and "All The Wrong Reasons" definitely has that. It's a wonderful melody.
There's a lot of melody in that tune. It's a lot like "Free Fallin'," in a way. The chord pattern is just this simple three-chord thing that repeats over and over. The tune is nothing like it. But I remember Mike playing a bouzouki, the Greek instrument, on that opening riff. [Sings riff.] The lick at the beginning is on guitar as well as bouzouki, and it made this real neat timbre. That's the kind of thing he'll do—he'll pick up some odd instrument and incorporate it into the thing he's doing. So, yeah, that's a good record. And if Benmont ever gets his way, we'll play it live.

You should listen to him.
[Laughs] I cracked up when reading Bob Dylan's book. There's a bit in there about Benmont pestering him to play certain songs. [Laughs] God bless him. Benmont keeps the vigil. He keeps us honest.

"Too Good To Be True"?
I like that song. I don't know if people know it, but that was another, in our last gig, where we were purposely looking for the odd things to do, and that one came out, and we played it for a bit. And I really like it. It's kind of modal-sounding. It's all around these one or two chords that kind of repeat a lot. I just like the imagery of the girl, and things she was thinking. And I think it's an uplifting thing, in the end. At the end of the song she's sitting in traffic, and she thinks, "You don't know what it means to be free/It was too good to be true." I was lucky with that one. [Laughs] That came out good. I liked it.

It has a false ending on a cool chord, which I can't even figure out. And then it picks up again, and has a really nice solo.
Yeah, that's one of my mystery chords, of which Jeff says, "I didn't even know that chord existed." [Laughs] And if I was a good musician, I probably wouldn't have used it. But I just hit things, and if it sounds good, I use it. I use a *lot* of variations on chords on the guitar. I've got my own way of doing it and playing it and voicing the chords. Which is very important, if you're going to do our stuff. People play my songs, but they don't get the voicings of the chords right. And the voicings are what it's all about.

I think I just hit that chord. And it's probably not a proper chord, but it made the right sound. Somebody could probably sit down and go, "Oh, yeah, it's a diminished eleventh or something," but it just made the right sound, so I kept it in. If it makes the right noise, that's what I'm looking for. I honestly don't know the names of all those chords. I don't know exactly what a ninth is. I'm learning it, and I'm getting better at it. I know sevenths and sixths. But once I get into elevenths or diminished chords, I don't know the names. I know where my fingers should go to make the right sound, and I go with that.

The same on the keyboard. Sometimes I make these accidental chords that were just a mistake in the first place, but it sounded so good, I put it in. That's the fun thing about music: Wherever your hands drop, you're gonna create something. Sometimes there are really happy accidents. I'm sure that's what that chord was, just a happy accident.

Can Benmont figure out what those chords are?
Oh yeah. There's nothing he couldn't figure out.

You wrote "You And I Will Meet Again" alone, which is a song about faith. And it has some beautiful imagery: "A red-winged hawk is circling/The blacktop stretches out for days..."
Yeah. In Encino we lived on this wooded hill. There were a lot of big oak trees. To be in the middle of LA, it was kind of a rural setting. You'd see these hawks all the time. I'd actually watch them dive, and come back up. And I wouldn't be surprised if that's where the reference to the hawks came from. You find yourself drawing on things that you never would have expected. Like a simple thing like watching a hawk circle. Later on, it enters your mind, and you use it as a metaphor.

That's a lot of the fun of writing songs, or being a writer at all, is that you've got the luxury of grabbing anything around you. It's all floating around, and your job is to get as much of it in your net as you can. So, when someone says, "I'm blocked up, and I can't write," the truth is that if you take a deep breath and look around, there's probably something really close that you could write about. It's just having the confidence, sometimes, to go after it.

There's the song "Makin' Some Noise," which you wrote with Mike and Jeff. And it has a nice riff.
Yeah, that's Mike's riff. Most of that was Mike's. I wrote the tune and the words, and Jeff may have come up with the verse pattern. That was something Mike brought in, and we thought it was really great, and we put our heads together and wrote it. And I really love that one. It's a great song to perform. It's really a lot of fun. He used some kind of odd tuning to play those notes. I think his guitar is tuned lower than it normally would be to get that riff out.

It was inspired—when I was writing, I was in this canyon. And in canyons you can hear the other side really well. You can pick up a conversation that's going on over on the other side really well, sometimes. I was playing my guitar, and then suddenly I heard another guy playing his guitar on the other side of the canyon. And in my mind

I thought it would be really funny if we could play something together. So I incorporated that into the last verse.

"Built To Last" written with Jeff, has a cool groove, like an old Motown beat.
Yeah, that was another one that I struggled with a little bit. That was one I wrote at the studio. And I didn't really know where to take it. And it went through a few versions before it wound up with that beat. But I think it was the only one that I wrote while the album was going on. And it was the very last thing we did. That was the end of it. Because I remember, when we got it done, there was this sigh of relief. I don't know if I really like that one.

Is it true that you were annoyed because the Grateful Dead had a song with the same title?
Yeah. That happens sometimes. You look up, and you think you've come up with something, and you realize somebody else has done it first. You try not to let it bug you. What bugs you the most is when you write something and then realize it's somebody else's song. That'll happen to me two times a month. I'll be working with something and then realize I'm channeling this melody from somewhere else, and then I have to abandon the idea. But there's only so many words and so many notes, so sometimes you do cross somebody else's territory. [Laughs]

Have you found that, as the years have gone by, you're better at knowing when you're using somebody else's melody?
Yeah. And, when that happens, I just have to throw it away.

Throw it away or change it?
Well, I just usually pitch it. And start over. Because, if I change a note or two, it's still going to be in my head that it's that other song. So I think every songwriter must have that problem from time to time. You play something and you realize it's Beethoven, or The Beatles. I have this theory that in open tuning Keith Richards got everything you can do. [Laughs] He got there first and he got everything there was to get.

He uses that unique five-string tuning.
He's *so* good. You don't really hear him mentioned as a songwriter much, but *God*, he's a good songwriter. He's really, really a great, great

writer. He's a great player and everything. But, it's like I said, if you get an open-tuned guitar, you'll find that everywhere you go, he's been there first.

It's interesting with Jagger and Richards, as opposed to you and Mike, that they will write everything together, whereas you write most of your songs alone, and only some with Mike.

It was just the way our relationship built itself. I was always the writer. And when we started out, Mike didn't write that much. And then he'd come in with the odd thing, and I'd say, "Okay." But the way he would present it to me would always be on a tape. So I just got into the practice of doing that.

We have tried writing together in the same room, but we didn't like it. It kind of hung me up. I can't go all over the map with someone sitting there like that. [Laughs] And, with his stuff, I might really go all over the map before I find what's going to work. Like we mentioned, a lot of times what he thought was going to be a verse ends up to be a chorus. And, if we're in the same room, that's gonna be brought up. And it's better if nothing is brought up for me when I'm working with his stuff, and that's just the way it evolved. So we stuck to that way. Though there's always gonna be a meeting of the minds when it's done. I've got to play it to him, and at that point we're gonna discuss what's good or bad about it. And it always makes me happy if he likes what I did.

Is he generally happy with what you've done?

Yeah. He's usually happy about it.

How do you present it to him?

Whatever way. I might make a little demo of it, or I might play it on guitar. It just depends. Sometimes, if I've changed chords, I can't really sing over his track, so I'll just learn it on guitar or piano and play it for him.

Does he comment on the lyrical content that you bring to his songs?

Yeah. More and more. As time has gone on, more and more. He'll single out things that he likes. But he goes along with the same theory that I do, which is that I've got to sing it. So it's good that I write the words. Because I just can't sing other people's words. It's really hard for me to believe it and get behind it as much. If I wrote it, then I know what character to get into to sing it. So he lets me have my way with words.

GREATEST HITS. 1993

One song the fans love is "Mary Jane's Last Dance." You included it on 1993's *Greatest Hits* album, but you actually wrote part of the song several years before.

That was one I wrote during the *Full Moon Fever* sessions. I wrote all but the chorus. I just had the loop going around and around and really had most of the words and everything. And I played the tape for Rick [Rubin] and he liked it a lot and suggested I write a chorus. So I tried to finish it up while I was making *Wildflowers*, and there were maybe five years between the writing of the verses and the chorus.

Is "Mary Jane" a marijuana reference?

I don't think I was writing about pot. I think it was just a girl's name. I can't imagine that I'd write a song about pot. I don't think there's enough there to write about. [Laughs]

WILDFLOWERS. 1994

Next comes *Wildflowers* in 1994. The title song, "Wildflowers," is such a gentle, acoustic number, and such a sweet opening song for the album.

I swear to God it's an absolute ad-lib from the word go. I turned on my tape deck, picked up my acoustic guitar, took a breath, and played that from start to finish. And then sat back and went, "Wow, what did I just do?" And I listened to it. I didn't change a word. Everything was just right there, off the top of my head.

The production of it is so nice. It has no drums and is very tender.

It's a very sweet song. It's got really good intentions. It clears my head. That's why I like that music in that album. It's got a purity to it that clears your mind when you hear it.

The production of that record intimidates me. It's *so* well done that I find myself in competition with it all the time. Trying to do something that's on that level.

And we were all very pleased with it. Rick Rubin and Mike and I. We worked *so* hard on it. We worked two years on that record. And I mean working five days a week. Really concentrating really hard. Very few breaks. Just determined to do something really good. And we were pretty successful. We were getting off on what we were doing. And it was a new friendship, having Rick there. And it's very much his album, too. Because he bled like the rest of us. [Laughs] He put a lot into it.

It was going to be two CDs. And we were just determined to do something *great*. We wanted it to be great. I think we succeeded on that level, because it's a piece of music I think will be around. I think that people will continue to buy it and listen to it. And that's a really good feeling. That's the best feeling that I can get. That I made something that has a timeless quality to it. So it was a very good feeling when it was received so well. 'Cause sometimes you can work on something and maybe people don't get it. But this was great because we had that great feedback, that great reception of it. So, *God*, it was a wonderful feeling.

I know many people who consider it their favorite album of yours.
I can understand that. It's certainly my best work of the later period. I like it quite a bit.

I love the way the track swells up in "You Don't Know How It Feels."
Yeah, that was something Mike got. I think it was a Magnatone amp, and he got this great swell that came up. And it was so cool we kept it. because it wasn't planned that way, it just happened.

That's such a great song—I love the line "And turn the radio loud, I'm too alone to be proud."
[Laughs] Well, that guy's pretty down. He's out for adventure. [Laughs]

"Time To Move On"?
Dana and I heard that on the radio a few days ago, driving home from Santa Monica. I had forgotten the lines, and there's a really funny line in it: "Nauseous adrenaline/Like breakin' up a dogfight." [Laughs] I was

really pleased with that. To get those lines into a song that's pretty was really hard. [Laughs] But it worked out really nice.

The song "You Wreck Me" was based on a track by Mike. I know you worked a long time to get the word "wreck" in there.

I had "You rock me." I had that down as something to sing; I never thought I'd use it. Because you wouldn't use that. But I had to scan something for the melody, so I had "You rock me, baby." It was so obvious to change "rock" to "wreck" and the whole thing made sense. Because I really wrote every other word. I don't know why it took me that long. Suddenly a lightbulb went off and, I went, "Oh, it's '*wreck*'." And we really held off for a long time, and didn't record the song until very late in the album, because I didn't think I had the line. And, when I got the line, it just all fell into place, it was very easy to record. Steve Ferrone *really* played *amazing* on that track. That's a live track.

So, yeah, that's a great one that we nearly always play live. That was a good one. That was one that I really felt like it paid off. When you're writing a fast rock and roll song, that's one of the most difficult things to do.

Is it?

Oh, yeah. They're really hard to do. It's not where you're drawn to when you're gonna write. You tend to find yourself going to the minor chords, and going to the slower tempos. But to write an uptempo rock and roll song, and have it work, God, that's a huge payoff.

Did you change that much from Mike's original conception?

No. Not at all, really. I think he had completely mapped out the chords and the arrangement. I just had to find a tune and lyrics for it.

[Laughs] That's all.

[Laughs] Yeah. And I did. We were all very pleased when it worked out. But I did hold out a long time. I wouldn't record it until I had every single thing in place.

"It's Good To Be King" has a great melody, and funny lyrics.

It's one of my favorite songs I ever wrote. "Excuse me if I have some place in my mind/Where I go time to time..." I love that. And I liked all the verses. I thought it worked really well. I was very pleased with that song. That's just the truth. I thought it was one of my best things. That one had something to say.

The ending is nice—the orchestra changes chords, and keeps going up.

Yeah, that was Michael Kamen's idea, to have that note at the end go up. And I thought it was a great idea. That was just another good case of having a lot of talented people, and you've got a good piece of material, and then, when you bring in all those people and they fully realized what I want to do, it really works. And that doesn't always happen *exactly* like that. But that was just a case where I sat back and felt, "Wow, this is so nice." And Benmont played the piano on it, just this simple little thing [Sings four notes], but it really made the verses work so well. Yeah, that one was very satisfying.

"Only A Broken Heart"?

I liked that phrase "It's only a broken heart." Like you can throw away the most serious ailment known to man. Like saying, "It's only cancer." It's a pretty song. And kind of a bittersweet one.

The song "Honey Bee" is another rocker. It starts with some funny muttering. And then some very distorted guitar before the drums kick in.

Yeah, that's me playing the guitar there. It's kind of like a blues-based song. And I got the idea to do that walk-up verse, where the chords kept going up and up. It was just kind of fun. It was meant to be a release from getting overly serious. Because some of those songs get pretty deep, and I think it's good to have something that clears the mind for a minute. Let's rock for a second, and not get overly serious here. And that's what "Honey Bee" was, and that's another one that *so* many people want to hear live. I get *so* many requests for "Honey Bee." People just love it.

It's got very funny lyrics: "She give me her monkey hand/ And a Rambler sedan/I'm the king of Milwaukee/Her juju beads are so nice/She kissed my third cousin twice/I'm the king of Pomona..."

[Laughs] Where does it come from? I don't know where I got "I'm the king of Pomona." But I wanted it to be like that. I wanted it to be one part gibberish. Where it would be clear to anyone that I'm not taking this too seriously, I'm just having some fun here. So it was just a little fun with words. "Kissed my third cousin twice..." [Laughs]

You wrote "Don't Fade On Me" with Mike, which has a really pretty, somewhat spectral melody.

Yeah, he showed me that tuning. I think what he wrote was just those chords in the chorus. He showed me how to do that on the guitar one night during the sessions, and I thought, "Oh God, I love that sound." And he said, "It's really simple—you do it like this." And I went home and wrote the song. And then I came back with it, and he said, "Well, I didn't really write it," and I said, "Well, no, you did, you wrote that bit, because I wouldn't have known that if you didn't show it to me." So I wrote that, and then I made the record. It's just two guitars and a voice. It's very sparse. It's just me and Mike playing in drop-*D* tuning.

It's interesting with that song, that you sing between those chords that Mike showed you, instead of singing right on the chords.

Well, I loved the sound the voicing of those chords made. That inspired me to write the song. I don't think Mike had thought of a melody or anything, he just had that chord pattern. And he played it really good when it came time to do the track. The little solo thing he does in there is just great.

It's a nice sound, just the two acoustic guitars.

Yeah. We practiced that quite a bit. We would play it from time to time. Took a lot of passes at it. It was one of those things we would try every day at the end of the session. So, by the time we got it, we had practiced it quite a bit.

The song "Hard On Me" is another one with a really beautiful melody. It has a cool structure, too, with two bridges.
Yeah, it does. That's Rick Rubin's favorite. Both of us were a little sad that it didn't become the big song from the album. Both of us thought that this was gonna be the thing that everybody picks up on. But it wasn't. But Rick really loves that song. And it was the first song written for the whole album. Probably the first thing I did. "It's all I can do/To keep that little girl smiling/And keep my faith alive..." That's what I remember.

"Cabin Down Below"?
It's blues and rockabilly mixed. And it was another one that I saw as a relief in the sequence of things, that it would be a moment of semi-nonsense for a minute. "Okay, we're gonna party for a minute here."

But it's not a nonsense song.
No, no, it fit in really well. But it was light-hearted. I think I probably ad-libbed a lot of it and then refined it from there. I had the skeleton from an ad-lib and then I took it and polished it up.

It seems connected to "House In The Woods," which is another strong song.
Yeah, it is connected. I loved "House In The Woods," too. That's got a good chord progression.

Yeah, it does. And no real chorus—it has the title in the verse.
It's one that we built with horns and pedal steel. I really loved the texture that that made. Because I had this hunch that, with those kind of dirty guitars that we did, if we put a pedal steel in it with a very clear, clean sound, it would work. At first, I was worried about how distorted the guitars were. I thought, "No, this is not the way I want to go with this." And Rick and Mike said, "No, it is. So let's put a really clean sound against that. We'll take four baritone saxes, and have them all playing in unison, and then play pedal steel with those chords, with a walking bass line under it." And it started to turn into this really beautiful thing there at the end. And I mixed the horns where you hardly notice they're there. They just kind of come in as a texture.

"To Find A Friend" is one of your story songs. It starts, "In the middle of his life/He left his wife/And ran off to be bad..."
[Laughs] I like the way that guy gets mad, and everybody's quiet. Like a family suddenly being turned over to a new person, who's a tyrant. It's scary.

That one has Ringo playing drums.
Yeah, I love Ringo's playing. He was kind enough to come in and play a few things on the album.

You've played with George before, of course, and also Ringo. How is it to have a Beatle play on your music?
Well, it's a luxury to have musicians of that caliber. And Ringo can really just play perfect time all day long. Yeah, God, that's as good as they come, isn't it? I've always been fortunate to have really, really good musicians. I don't know why, but I've been *very* fortunate in that I really have the best musicians around.

To have Ringo come in was a real honor. I've had him on a few things. And he knows he's always welcome to come play. He did a really good job of playing. The feel of that song is so good. Many drummers today wouldn't know how to play a song like that. But he knew exactly where to go with it. He plays with a lot of nuance. Just one of my favorite drummers of all time.

I think he's an incredibly creative drummer. A *lot* of feel. I just knew he would play that song well. And I was right. He played it perfect right away. I demoed it without any drums, and we thought, "How would a drum pattern go to this?" And I thought, "You know who could play this would be Ringo." I've known Ringo for years. So I called him and asked him. And he was gracious enough to come down and play.

We tracked it with just three of us—me on acoustic, Ringo, and Mike on bass. And singing it at the same time. Benmont overdubbed his little piano solo later.

It's got a beautiful chorus: "And the days went by like paper in the wind/Everything changed, then changed again/It's hard to find a friend."
It was those days. I was getting stuff. Like I said, I think I was really at the top of my game. Things were coming to me with very little effort.

The material was coming in. And God, that's what a record's about, the material. And so you get the material, and that's just a sheer luxury: I've got the material. Then you just try to bring in the best people and really concentrate and make a great record.

How about the song "A Higher Place"? Benmont plays organ, piano, and Vako Orchestron, whatever that is.

The Orchestron is an old keyboard where you actually put in a plastic disc, which is string sounds. And, when you hit the keyboard, it activates this plastic disc, this record, and the record plays the note that you were playing. Very shaky. Extremely shaky. I think one take on the record was *all* we could get out of the Orchestron. But for *one* moment there, it all synced up, and it worked. I'd never seen one before, or since. I never would have dreamed that there was a thing like that. I remember us just going, "Wow." Almost the first time he played it, he got that great thing. But then we couldn't get it to work anymore. We couldn't get it to do what we wanted it to do.

On "A Higher Place," you do all the harmonies yourself.

I do it from time to time. It was a very high part. And I could get it, so I just did it. Sometimes I do the harmonies myself just to get a certain blend.

The album closes with two of your greatest songs, "Crawling Back To You" and "Wake Up Time." "Crawling Back To You" has lyrics and music which are both phenomenal.

That one ["Crawling Back To You"] took a little work. I wrote that song in three-quarter time. Where it had nothing to do with what came out. And then that wasn't going to work, but I knew there was a song there. Then I brought it over to four-four, but I still couldn't get it to work. I couldn't really find where the accents should be. And I remember us tracking it all night and being really frustrated that it wasn't working. Then they came on the idea of having us all walk out, and "Play this like we've never heard it before. I'm just gonna start playing, and whatever we fall in on, we'll go that way." And that was the take. It worked. I started to diddle on guitar, we went around a couple of times, Ferrone dropped in on that beat, and *bang*, we had it. But we would have never had that feel if we hadn't have done that.

That's the value of a live group in the studio. I'd have never come up with that without them. And it was a very tricky song to find the feel for, but once we found it, it was really, really right, and it was very easy to sing and very easy to make the words believable.

It's got some wonderful words in there, including my favorite lines, "I'm so tired of being tired/Sure as night will follow day/Most things I worry about/Never happen anyway."
That's one of my favorite verses, too, that I ever wrote. 'Cause it just rings so true.

My cousin gave me that line. She sent me a little book of phrases once. I opened that book, and saw just that phrase: "Most things I worry about never happen anyway."

And it works so well coming after the Indian shooting-out-the-lights verse. You have the specific imagery, and then the abstract reflection.
That's a good thing to do. If you get too specific, you kind of want to pull away from it. Because now things are getting almost narrative, and you don't want to do that. So you give them a little taste of that, and then back away. Into something that's not as nailed down. And it creates a nice mixture, and does a certain thing in the mind. So that was an instance where that kind of thing actually worked really well.

And then comes the song "Wake Up Time," which is such a poignant way of closing the record. It has sparse production—just you on piano and vocal, Mike on bass, Ferrone on gentle drums, and the orchestra.
Yeah, I wrote that on guitar and we cut it that way. And then we weren't quite satisfied with it, though it was pretty good. And then Rick said, "Why don't you play it on piano?" And I thought, "Well, damn, I've never played it on piano." And he said, "Go out and see what comes if you start to play it on piano." So it took me a little while to figure out how to play it on piano, because I'm not so great on piano, in terms of playing it on a track. I worked it out, and he said, "Okay, we're gonna cut it with you on the piano."

And I said, "Well, Ben's here." So then they got Benmont out. And they thought, "No, he plays it too good. Like, we don't want it to be *that good*. We want it to be like you play it. Very simple." So I did it—with me on piano, and drums, and Mike on bass. Mike sat in the control room and played the bass.

So, God, you talk about your shortlist of things you've ever done. That song is just one of my best songs. I was very pleased to get to play that to Denny Cordell, not long before he died. I hadn't seen him in many a year. And he came down to the studio and he listened to the album and when he heard "Wake Up Time" he was really taken by it. And he said, "You know, TP, that's not like *anybody*. That's your thing, man. That's your thing. And you should be really happy, because you've created something which is your thing and nobody else's." And I kind of felt like that. That he's right, and I felt really good about that, and I'm glad I got to come full circle with my mentor, who really guided me into this business of writing songs. To get that approval from him, so many years later, meant a whole lot to me.

The song has an absolutely beautiful melody, one of your greatest ever. I love the way you extend the word "home" in "a long way from home..." It's a perfect match of music and words.

We came back to playing that on our last tour. We only played it a couple of times. And I just thought it was too delicate a number to try to play it in an arena. And then I rethought that, years later, and I thought that I could come out with a guitar, just me and guitar, and get that song over. So we came back and that's how we did it. For the most part, it was just me alone with the guitar. And it really worked. It was easy to sell it in the arena, because bringing it down to one instrument really got everyone's attention. So when the band finally did fall in, it really made a big impact. So it worked that way.

But I am very happy with that one. It will always mean a lot to me.

It's touching how you speak the title in the song, instead of singing it. It's your only song that I know of in which you do that.

I don't know why I did that. But it seemed to work better than singing it. You know, you write so many of them, and you hope for something like "Wake Up Time." [Laughs] And now and then you get it. And that's enough inspiration to keep going. I'm going to keep doing this, because I want something else like this.

Did you write that late in the album?
No, it was fairly early on. I wrote it around the time I wrote "It's Good To Be King."

Did you know at the time it would be a good closer for the album?
I always did think it would be the end. I wasn't sure what would be the beginning, but I knew that was going to be the end, and that I was gonna work toward that. And that would be the finale. Of the double album. So that was kind of a good thing to have in your back pocket, knowing where you were going.

Was *Wildflowers* the title of the album from the beginning?
I think pretty early on I started to think that would be a good title. I'd written the song, and I started to think, "Yeah, this would probably be a good title, and this song will hold up to that."

And then Jim Scott, the engineer, he came to me and said, "I think that would be a good song to start with." Because we were talking about how we should begin this thing. And he said, "'Wildflowers.' That's how you should begin this thing." And I thought for a minute if you could start with a song like that. "An acoustic song. Can we come in on that?" But then I thought it would work: especially when the orchestra comes in halfway through, you know everything is gonna be okay.

PLAYBACK. 1995

Now on to *Playback*, the boxed set. It's got many of your greatest hits, but also is a veritable treasure trove of unreleased gems. Many of them are so good it's amazing they never got released on albums, though a good deal of them were B-sides.
[*Playback*] came out after *Wildflowers*, but was limited only to a certain date, the stuff we did for MCA. So it was gonna go that far, and that was *plenty*, because we barely fit it all onto six CDs. From going through the vaults and finding all the unreleased stuff, the B-sides, and all the things that the boxed-set buyer would want. I'm *so* pleased with that boxed set. I really love it. I think some of our best work is on there. The last CD ["Nobody's Children"], I really like. And you don't always get that

'cause a lot of boxed sets can be really dull and boring and you go, "I see why that didn't come out. I can see why they didn't release this." Or it's nine versions of the same thing.

So, for this one, George Drakoulias was the producer and overseer of everything. And he did *such* a great job in finding the best stuff. 'Cause we weren't going to do it. We weren't going to get too involved in it, because we were on the road, and it was too big a job. I once came down to one of his sessions, and he had a room that was *absolutely* full of tape. There were tape boxes to the sky. Just *packed* with tape. He was really going through all of that tape. Big job. And he did such a good job. And that was such a good feeling, because I really think it was a lot of stuff that should have been out, that we just didn't have the presence of mind or the space to put out.

It's an unusual boxed set, in that there were so many great songs you never released. It's like getting many new Tom Petty albums all at once.

Yeah, it is. You get all the old stuff, and then you get a whole bunch of new stuff. It's still around. It still keeps selling. They did such a nice job of packaging it. They gave every record its own cover, and a nice little booklet with notes by Bill Flanagan [editorial director for VH1, the author of several music books, and Zollo's editor at *Musician* magazine years ago] It was a really satisfying thing.

Fortunately for us, you included "Peace In LA" on *Playback*, which you recorded very quickly and got on the radio.

Probably within twenty-four hours of recording it. I came back from Europe, and the day I got back, the LA riots started. We had been on a tour in Europe, and we got back, and all that broke loose. And I just had the feeling that the word "peace" needs to be on the radio. We just need to hear "peace, peace." I quickly got on the phone, arranged the session, and went into my little room and wrote the song. Really fast.

You arranged the session first before writing the song. That's bold.

Yeah, it was bold. And so I got all of them down to the studio. All of them that I could get there—I couldn't get Howie there. So we called him on the phone, and recorded him over the phone. Just talking. I think we thought we could get him to sing over the phone on the track, but it wouldn't work, for some reason. So, for the end, we just kept a little bit of him talking.

He says, "What's burning? Is there smoke everywhere?"
Yeah, and it seemed to fit the situation. I think he was talking about something on the stove. It fit the situation, so we kept it in. The one that's on the boxed set is actually the B-side. It's called the "Peace Mix." We did a different mix for the B-side. It got on the air quick. We sent it out over satellite. And *bang*, it was on the air fast. We gave all the money to different good causes in East LA. To this day I still get letters of thanks from missions in East LA because the money keeps coming in, it ended up on the boxed set. So they still keep getting royalties. So it was something I felt good about because it did some good. And I was going down the road, and I saw somebody had graffitied the wall, and it said, "Peace in LA." And I thought, "*Damn*, that's something. [Laughs] We had an idea, got it on the air, and now it's painted on the wall." So I felt really good about it.

[The Los Angeles Riots began in the late afternoon of April 29, 1992, upon the acquittal of four LAPD officers accused of beating Rodney G. King. When the officers were acquitted, unrest broke out in South-Central Los Angeles, and then spread to other areas of the city.]

The song "I Don't Know What To Say To You" was recorded at one of the first Heartbreakers sessions, and was released as the B-side to "Listen To Her Heart."
That's got John Sebastian on that. Playing a baritone guitar or a 6-string bass. He finger-picked it with a thumb pick. It was something that the guys were playing, and Cordell said, "Oh, that's good. That's a good thing. Why don't you guys turn that into a tune?" And I wrote it on the spot. Part of it I was lifting words from Cordell's racing form. He had a racing form and I was lifting names from horses. But it's just another fun-with-words kind of song.

Seems very Dylanesque.
Oh sure, yeah. It is. And it mentions Road Turkey, which was Stan [Lynch] and Marty's [Jourard] old band. So there's a line in there: "Road Turkey's in the lobby." It was just fun with words. But it's a really cool little track.

Then there's that great live, acoustic version of "King's Highway." And the vocal is so passionate on that one.
I think we recorded that in Oakland, California. Mike on mandolin. 'Cause we like to do that in the shows: We'll do a little section and Mike'll pick up the mandolin, and we do just an acoustic section, a kind of no-drums section. And that was just a case of where the song lent itself to that arrangement and really worked that way. It got slapped on a B-side somewhere.

The song "Depot Street" dates back to Mudcrutch. You did that full year of recording, and then released it.
Yeah, that was the only thing that ever came out. It was a single, with "Depot Street" on one side and a song of mine called "Wild Eyes." That was very early upon our arrival in LA [1975]. That was done at the Village Recorder in Santa Monica with Denny Cordell producing.

Is Depot Street a street in Gainesville?
Yeah. I think it's Depot Avenue or Depot Road. But I called it Depot Street, and based it on that. It's just a little story that I made up. But somehow I got that street in my mind.

Did you try to work a reggae rhythm into it?
We did. We tried to put a little reggae rhythm into the chorus. We were trying to get that kind of ska beat. I'm sure that was Cordell's influence. Because he had gone to Jamaica, and signed up a lot of reggae groups. So he was exposing us to it all the time, from the time we got to LA.

How about the song "I Can't Fight It"? That was another Mudcrutch song.
Yeah. That was one we recorded for that album which never came out.

It's about a girl, but it could be about the dream of making it as a musician. You say, "But this dream has become an obsession/'Cause I've held it inside so long/All my friends say I should use discretion/But I know I'm just not that strong." We've talked about rhyming, too, and every line in that verse has a perfect rhyme.
That's a long time ago, that one. I think I was just trying to write a rock and roll song. I doubt I had that grand a thought about it. I played bass on it. That was back in my bass-playing days. I love playing bass. I still do.

The song "Since You Said You Loved Me" is from your first, unreleased solo album. It has Emory Gordy on bass, Al Kooper on keys, Jim Gordon on drums.
Mike on guitar.

Mike said it was a great track but kind of a "sappy song." But I don't find it sappy.
[Laughs] A lot of major sevenths. [Laughs]

Is that what makes it sappy? A lot of musicians don't like major sevenths. They think they sound too pretty.
Well, you have to be careful how you use them. But I don't think it's sappy, either. It's almost like an R&B song to me. And I was just learning to be the lead singer proper. In Mudcrutch I wasn't always the singer. So I was trying to do my best.

It's got a soulful vocal.
I thought it was kind of a nice R&B thing. It never really came out until the boxed set. But I thought it was kind of cool. Jim Gordon's great on it. Wow, he's amazing.

And so is Al Kooper on organ.
Yeah, he's just terrific on the organ. And Emory's great. Emory has played with a lot of people: Elvis. And on that great Gram Parsons album *Grievous Angel*. He's an old pro, and he was really good. It was a good little band that we put together.

The song "Turning Point" sounds inspired by Buddy Holly. You said, "It's kind of an ominous song, but I think an optimistic one."
I think that was done for *Long After Dark*. And left off. There were a couple of things from that album that didn't make the final cut. I think Jimmy thought it was too country or something. [Laughs] But I didn't see it as country at all.

You sent that to the band Lone Justice and they didn't use it.
Oh yeah. They had recorded "Ways To Be Wicked." Another outtake. And I sent them "Turning Point" for their next album, but they didn't use it. I thought it would have been good for them.

"Ways To Be Wicked" is another one with a great chorus.
Yeah, that was one that Jimmy kind of stole. Took it to Lone Justice and gave it to them. It goes as far back as *Damn The Torpedoes*. It was one that Mike and I wrote, and we couldn't really get a hold of it. We couldn't really find a way to record it. But [Jimmy] took whatever attempt we made, and gave it to Lone Justice. He never even really asked me. I found out later. Though I didn't mind. But I mean I found out later that they'd done it. We released a version on the boxed set, but until that time that was the only place you would have heard it, was through them.

Did George put the whole boxed set together before you heard it?
No, we came in from time to time. Checked in on him, to see what he was doing. Sometimes we'd come in for a few days. But I think we were on the road a lot of the time he was doing it. So we'd come in and out.

He did such a great job.
He really did.

Are there a whole lot of songs we haven't heard that he left off?
Yeah, there's stuff that didn't get on. That there wasn't space for, or just didn't make the grade. I think he got the best of what was in the vaults. There may be more stuff, but I don't think it's of that standard, of that quality.

It's genuine proof of how prolific you've been. Six discs of great songs.

Well, we've been in the studio a lot. The Heartbreakers, probably up to this year, were always real workaholics. That's what we did. We lived rock and roll. We were not part-time guys. We did it twenty-four hours a day. It's all we did. If we weren't actually on tour playing, there would never be more than a week or two, then we'd go straight to the studio, and we'd stay there until we went on the road again. And then there was the proliferation of home studios. Mike, me, Howie. So that kept us going for a while.

The Heartbreakers never ever rehearsed a record. Which is unusual. We came to the studio and we put it together there. And whatever rehearsing was gonna be done, was done there. We never rehearsed a record, like "pre-production." That's something that we didn't know anything about. That's a term that never applied to The Heartbreakers. [Laughs] We went into the studio and we did it there. It was kind of an expensive way to do things, but it was the only way we knew how to do it. We never had an A&R guy. We never, *ever* had anybody on the scene from a record company, or that had any say whatsoever in what we did. We just did it and turned it in. But we've never been one of those bands who had some guy hovering around from the record company giving his two cents. That would never, *never* have been tolerated. So we were unique in that respect. And we were lucky that we were trusted. The label just trusted us. That was the only way they knew. The whole history with us had been that we bring in a finished master. And so we were really never interfered with. There was never anybody that tried to assert any kind of creative input. They just let us find our own way.

It worked. Part of not rehearsing is that the tracks are so live, so of the moment. They are not overworked at all.

That was our theory. If you're gonna rehearse it, maybe the great magic take will go by and there won't be any tape rolling. So we recorded everything. I mean, *really* everything. We had this rule that, if the band's in the room, you roll tape. Because you never know when something's gonna be played that can't be played like that again. We really used up a lot of tape, because we would have them roll from the time *anybody's* in the room. It got down to that. "What if I'm in the room and I play something?" So the tape always rolls.

Even if Stan was just tuning up the drums?
Whoever. If anybody's in the room, the tape rolls. It's essential. And if you're changing tapes, you roll the 2-track. Always. Don't miss nothing.

I love the song "U Get Me High."
[Laughs] That was another improv. Just a joke, really. But we really weren't like big high guys. That song, actually, I remember improvising that onstage in Europe. I just started playing and led the band through that onstage one night just as a goof. And we thought it was cool, it went over really well, [Laughs] so we hung onto it and recorded it.

That's pretty bold, too, to do it in concert.
Yeah, I can't *imagine* doing something like that now. But something came over me, and I did it.

It's probably one of your most overt references to smoking pot.
Yeah, I get the label "Mr. Pot," but I don't smoke pot at all now. No. I don't think we were ever as interested in it as people believe.

You mention it in "You Don't Know How It Feels"—"let's roll another joint."
Every time that song starts in concert, the sky rains joints. People throw joints at us and they're all over the stage. Every time it starts up. And you'll see them light up. But pot, I don't think it's a bad thing if it's not done to excess. If it's done casually, it's not a bad thing. I think it's better than alcohol, for sure.

Has it ever helped you with your writing?
Probably. It's not a rule. It's better, if you're in a session, to save the pot for the playbacks at the end of the night. You can't get a lot done if you're smoking pot and getting smashed. You're not going to work as well. So I tried to look at it like that; if I wanted to smoke some pot, I'd do it at the end of the session when we were going to listen to things back.

How about during the mixes?
No, not at all. Because that's too important. You want to have your senses about you when you're mixing. That's surgery. You scrub up for that. We actually almost play tag team in mixing, where there's someone out of the room all of the time. So, when somebody comes back into the room, they're fresh, and they can hear what you won't hear. We always keep somebody out, between me, Mike, and whoever is producing the record. Somebody'd stay out of the room. And usually, if I stayed out of the room, and then walked in, I'll go, "Hey, the tambourine's too loud." They'll go, "Oh, God, I didn't notice that." But if you're sitting there playing a song a hundred times, you're gonna make some mistakes if you don't leave the room. So it was just a natural thing, but it proved to be a good method.

I remember on *Wildflowers* with Rick Rubin, somebody would go in and steer the ship for a while, and then somebody else would go in. And then when we'd do the first mix, we'd take it out on a cassette and play it in the car. And listen to it in the car, and then go back into the studio. And we got so attached to this one car, [Laughs] this one rental car, that there was this panic one day when we couldn't get it. [Laughs] Somebody had turned it in. We had to go find the right car, because we were used to that cassette player. That's how neurotic we got about it.

McGuinn even came down once and he built a radio, where he could broadcast from the studio. He could broadcast to the parking lot. And he actually broadcast it from the studio to the radio in the parking lot, and we'd listen to it on the radio. We were nuts. [Laughs] Really nuts. We wanted it to sound really good on car radios.

Would you hear things on the car radio that would cause you to change the mix?
Oh yeah. We'd listen in the car and go, "The bass drum's not loud enough," or this or that. And we'd go back in and make the adjustment.

It seems to be a very fine line to get the vocal in the right place, where it's out front, but you still hear the band well. The Rolling Stones often have the lead vocal way back in the mix, but you don't do that. How do you get that right balance of track and vocal?

It's very hard. Over the years, I think I've put it louder and louder. It's a different kind of mix. Some people don't mix the voice that loud. I like Beatle records where the voice is *way* up there. The voice is what you've got to build the record around. For *us*.

That's our kind of thing. So we tend to put it right up there, and then build everything around it. But it's not always easy to find *exactly* where it should be, because if you put it too loud, you can make the band sound very small. So you want to find that happy balance of where the track still sounds big, but the voice is present, to where you can get all the tone and the intricacies of the voice. So you can hear all the little subtle things. Because a lot of the feel is in the singer. But I listen to everything. Rick Rubin told me I was one of the only artists he ever worked with that listened to everything. Most people only listen to themselves. But I listen to everything, I listen to everything playing, and I'm very astute about every little thing.

Do you like a lot of effects, like reverb, on the voice?

We usually don't put anything on the voice. Just leave it. That started around *Full Moon Fever*. And then Jeff said, "Don't put anything on it. Just leave it dry. Leave it alone." And we liked that so much, we've stuck to it ever since. Now it drives me nuts to hear reverb. We don't use reverb at all, unless we use it for an effect on a particular instrument.

Because it muddies everything up?

It tends to make everything go back in the speaker. We used it so much in the early Eighties. But, to me, it makes everything wash out. I don't like it. I like tape delay. And I like compression. We'll use compression and limiters. But I don't like reverb on the voice. I like a very dry microphone, and maybe turn the compression up on the mike. It gives you a good sound. But you've really got to sing! There's no hiding behind anything. But it sounds so much better.

Yeah, it's very clean. Is there a specific mike you like to use for your vocals?
I like this Neumann mike here, which is a C12. It's been around for ages. And I also sing on a Neumann 87. But I *usually* use that C12.

The song "Come On Down To My House" is a real rave-up, starting with a scream from you.
Yeah, that was us trying to do a really punk rock pedal-to-the-metal kind of thing, where the speakers were turned up really loud. That's a good one. I like that one. It makes you feel really refreshed when it's over. It's good therapy to sing that one.

You did it as an encore a lot.
Yeah. We did it as an encore because it's not a thing you can do in the middle of a show, because it would be hard to do anything after it. It's pretty high velocity. So, it's one of those where you have to really work yourself up, and then, when you do it, you just let everything out.

Stan's playing is explosive on that one.
Oh yeah, it's *ferocious*.

I love the song "You Come Through."
Yeah, that's a good one. Lenny Kravitz played drums on it.

And he also did vocals and bass.
Yeah, he did. We did as much as we could [Laughs] and it was Drakoulias' idea, because the track wasn't finished.

So there were no drums on it?
No, there was just a click track. So we gave it to Lenny, and he did that: He put the drums, the bass, and the background vocals on it. There might have been a little bit of background vocal that I did. But he added quite a bit to the song. He made it a really good track. That would have been a good single to put out.

We talked about how wide your vocal range is, and that really shows it off. You sing really low, and then you go really high.
Yeah, I was trying to do a thing like Sly Stone used to do. Go down really low and come back. So that was probably the inspiration for that. That was Mike's arrangement.

There's a false ending on it, where it fades down and then comes back up.
Yeah, that was George Drakoulias' idea. Which kind of puzzled me for a minute. [Laughs] The first time I heard it I thought, "Why?" Then I got it later on. I got it that you're in this groove and it goes away, and then it comes back, and you feel paid off.

I love that track. I really love it. I just kick myself that I didn't put it out. I don't know why. I think I had something about it being too pop, or something. And I didn't put it on the record.

Too pop? It's pretty soulful.
Yeah, it is. I don't know why I didn't put that out. It doesn't make any sense.

Do you play it live?
No, we never have. Yeah, it's a good number. I just never got around to it.

George did a great job with the boxed set, because it stands as its own album, whereas so many of them are just additions to people's existing work.
I think it's a special one. Of course, I'm prejudiced. But I'm really glad he did it. I'm grateful to him forever, because all that work would have been lost if he hadn't got it down as a document of what went on for all those years. There was a lot more than what came out on record, and it sort of reflects our lifestyle. We spent a lot of time in studios. Our mission was always to get that great track—to a crazy extent. We were just crazed with it. When I look at it now, you'd have to be nuts to work that hard. God, those boys worked. We worked a lot. We were gonna do something great. And we *damn* well were gonna do it. Or die trying. And a lot of it paid off. A lot of it's really worth hearing.

"Casa Dega" is a wonderful song.
Cassadaga is this really odd place in Florida that is filled with fortune-tellers. There are all kinds of psychics and fortune-tellers in the whole town. It's this really small place. And I wrote that by putting myself in the mind of someone who went to Cassadaga. Though I spelled it wrong. It has a double "s". Poetic license, I guess. But it was the B-side of "Don't Do Me Like That," done during *Damn The Torpedoes.*

You wrote it on an airplane?
I did. I wrote it on an airplane. You know everything.

Music and lyrics?
Yeah, I think I had the lyric and a little bit of tune, and then I put it to one of Mike's tapes. We pulled it together from there in the studio. We did a rearrangement and everything, basing it around the bass guitar. It was all around the bass guitar and the drums.

The chorus is great: "I'm starting to believe things that I've heard/'Cause tonight in Casa Dega, I hang on every word..."
[Sings chorus] Yeah. Well, it was full of fortune-tellers and psychics. It's a strange idea. I guess that's just where they hang, and that's where people go to get their fortunes told.

A fun song is "Heartbreaker's Beach Party."
Yeah, it was just nonsense. The kind of thing we would do if there's a break in the session. Oftentimes the band will start playing while we're waiting. And that was one of those things that we just improvised. And it's just silly. It's funny to me how many people come up to me who like that song. It's just nonsense. I just made it up as a joke. It's all ad-libbed. But you'll still see people at shows holding up signs that say, "Heartbreaker's Beach Party." [Laughs] And Cameron Crowe did this documentary on us in 1982, and he called his film *Heartbreaker's Beach Party*. We've given a lot of filmmakers their first break. [Laughs] I still joke with Cameron about it, because that was his first movie.

I like, at the end of "Heartbreaker's Beach Party," you say, "Another modern classic."
Yeah. "Another modern classic." That sums it up. But it was just a joke.

The song "Trailer" was the B-side to "Don't Come Around Here No More." You wrote that for *Southern Accents*?
Yeah, it was a huge mistake not to put it on the album. I don't know why we didn't. That just shows the amount of confusion going on at that time. Between broken limbs and whatever. But it should have been on the album. I think it was an important song, and part of that trip. It should have been on the album, but it got put on a B-side. We like to always do a B-side on the singles that wasn't on the album.

Why?
Just so you got more for your money. And also because it gave you a reason to buy it, if you had the album. I always liked that, that if I got a single, you gave me something that wasn't just two things pulled off an album. So we always tried to put things on the other sides that weren't on the album.

You said of "Trailer" that it "was something that we really lived and understood very well. It's where we all came from."
Yeah, it was. We knew a lot of people who lived in trailers. And that's kind of the tragic story of the high-school sweethearts who strike out and get married too fast, move into a trailer, and it doesn't work out. "I could've had the army/I could've had the navy/But no I had to go for a mobile home/...I kept up with my payments/I kept up my interest..." It's kind of a sad song. "We used to dance to Lynyrd Skynyrd/Boy she used to look so good at times..." But it was a shame that we didn't put that on the album.

Another fast, funny song is "Gator On The Lawn."
Yeah, that would go in the "Heartbreaker's Beach Party" category. Just something that was ad-libbed. It was funny enough to survive. It's like rockabilly.

I understand there are gators everywhere in Gainesville, and one got on the lawn of Marty Jourard's home and ate his dog.
Ate his *dog*! Yeah. We thought that was so hysterical. Obviously, he didn't. It was kind of tragic, but it was just so *hysterical* to us that this alligator ate his dog. [Gators] are everywhere there in Gainesville. They're just all over the place.

Is that why you called your publishing company Gone Gator music?
Yeah. We were gator-influenced: "Every other day I got a gator on the lawn." That was certainly about Marty's experience. Because his family lived right on kind of a lake. It was an inlet, or a lake. And it's just *filled* with alligators. So you can just walk up on the shore and see them. And we just found that so hysterical that they would be on his lawn.

The song "Make That Connection," was that another ad-lib song?
Pretty much, yeah. I think I had the idea and then we walked out and ad-libbed it. You can probably hear me running out of words at some point. It had a lot of fire. It really got going. Howie's singing kind of a falsetto part behind the chorus. And I think he was doing that live on the track, just making it up as we went along. It was just one of those fun things to do.

The bridge is funny—it just goes up to one chord only.
[Laughs] Probably didn't know where to go. Again, that was probably me yelling, "*A*!" and everyone went to *A*, and then we didn't know where to go.

"Down The Line"?
We just took a basic drum and bass part and then just kind of made up a song there. And then we put Marty Jourard on horns. Stacked him up.

Did Mike come up with the chords for that one?
He did. I wrote the words and Jeff [Lynne] helped us make an arrangement.

Were you trying to make a Heartbreakers album while you were making *Full Moon Fever*?
For a moment. There was a moment where we tried to do that. But it was just overload. I couldn't handle all of that workload. We did one song, "Travelin'." That's all Heartbreakers. Jeff wasn't there, and it was just me and Mike producing. And I like that song a lot. It's got a cool sound.

It starts with the chorus, and then has a great verse over descending chords.

Yeah, they didn't like it at the time. We did it in a day. I wrote it in the car driving to the session; I was completely out of songs. And I actually made it up in my mind driving to the session, because I knew I'd better come in with something. 'Cause The Heartbreakers are all gonna be there. And I came in, and went over to the piano, and quickly put together what I had in my head. Then we set about making the record. And we really made it in one day and one night.

And I loved it and I got the feeling that they didn't really like it. They weren't really glad to see me. [Laughs] It was like I was in the Wilburys, and I was doing the solo record, and they felt, "*Damn*, we're at the end of the line here. And we would like to be working." Though they were working on lots of different projects. They wanted to know what's up with the band. So I said, "We'll do a band record, too." But I overextended myself. So we called it after that session. We said, "We'll just have to come back later." But then that song got lost in the shuffle. Because it was a one-off thing.

That song seems very Elvis-inspired.

Very much so. It was another one that George Drakoulias found when he was doing the boxed set.

The boxed set has a wonderful home demo of "The Apartment Song" with Stevie Nicks singing the harmonies.

[Stevie and I] used to do that from time to time: just sit around and sing. And sometimes run a tape recorder, and we'd play it back, have some drinks. She used to visit me quite often. Come over, and we'd always wind up singing. So I love to sing with Stevie.

You recorded that song for *Full Moon Fever*. Was there the thought of bringing Stevie in to sing on it?

No. I think, at that point, I wanted it to be a solo. I had never *really* pictured it being a duet. But Stevie was there, and I showed her the song I'd written. And she liked it, and sang along on it. Probably only got recorded once.

You recorded "Can't Get Her Out" for *Let Me Up (I've Had Enough)*.
Yeah, that is obscure. It was probably written and recorded in the studio. And we probably just hashed out the arrangement on the floor of the studio. There's a great organ on that. That's what I remember about it. It's amazing. And I played the guitar solo on it. I also liked Howie's counterpoint singing on that. He was good on that.

It's got a catchy chorus: "Can't get her out/Can't get her out of my mind…"
Yeah, very primal. Very basic. But it gets the job done.

The song "God's Gift To Man" is a nice blues in *A*. Was that improvised?
Yeah, completely. That's just count to four, start to play the guitar, you can hear the whole thing, everybody drops in, we get faster and faster, we're not really holding the tempo very well, and I'm just improvising the lyrics. That was another one that George Drakoulias found and thought was worthy of release. But we would have never given it a second thought. It was just something that took five minutes to write and record. It's not bad for what it was.

The last song on the boxed set is "Up In Mississippi." Mudcrutch's first song from '73.
Oh God. That was the first time we ever went into the studio. We put that out as a single in Gainesville on Pepper Records. Did pretty well for us around town, got us some gigs. [Laughs]

It sounds good. It's a good mix.
Well, I think George remixed it. It was cut on 8-track. George remixed it for the boxed set. Yeah, we were a pretty good little band. For not knowing anything about what we were doing, and only having a few hours to do the track, which is all we could afford. I think we were only in there for four hours. So it's not bad. We did two sides really quickly.

It's got a good sense of place—up in Mississippi.
Yeah, which is kind of strange, because you'd have to be really south to be up in Mississippi. [Laughs] But that's just how naïve I was then. I think it was okay for the time. It's a cute little way to end the boxed

set. Those were just boys, you know. Very young boys trying to do something.

SONGS AND MUSIC FROM SHE'S THE ONE. 1996

You mentioned that many of the cast-offs from *Wildflowers* wound up on the *She's The One* soundtrack, which followed it. You have two versions of "Walls" on it.

"Walls" was new. I wrote that for the movie at the Chicken Shack. I think the inspiration was that I was supposed to write a song for this movie, and that came into my head. I think what kicked it off was that Johnny Cash said to me one day, "Some days are diamonds and some days are rocks." And I took that line, and wrote the song.

Good opening.

Yeah, I thought it was a great line.

You have one version of it called "Walls (Circus)" with amazing vocal harmonies by Lindsey Buckingham.

He's amazing. He was kind enough to come down and sing that.

Was it your idea to call him?

Yeah, yeah. I'm a big fan of Lindsey's. And I called him and was really knocked out that he came down and helped me with that. [Having two versions of "Walls"] was Ed Burns' idea. He wanted one version of "Walls" to start the movie, and another arrangement to end the movie. So I did two different arrangements of it. And Lindsey's just amazing on that track.

Did he come up with those harmonies?

Yeah, it was all him. He came down and did it all in one session. I kind of just sat back and watched him go. Just going, "Yep—that's what I would've done!" [Laughs]

It's cool you've worked with both Stevie Nicks and with Lindsey.

Yeah. I worked with [Lindsey] again on *The Last DJ*. He sang on "The Man Who Loves Women."

How did you happen to choose "Asshole" by Beck for *She's The One*?
I like that song. Rick [Rubin] played me that. And there's a character in the movie who was a real asshole. And I thought it really fit the movie. Though I think Ed Burns was a little uncomfortable with it. [Laughs] I don't know why, but he was a little uncomfortable with it.

Are you a Beck fan?
Oh, yeah. I think he's one of the few who have come along that's really going to be around a long time. He's got a lot of range. And a lot of integrity, I think.

"Angel Dream"?
"Angel Dream," I wrote for Dana when I first met her.

There are two versions of that—"Angel Dream (No. 4)" and "Angel Dream (No. 2)."
[Laughs] There is absolutely no reason for those numbers. [Laughs] That was just a little joke. Yeah, I wrote that as I fell in love with Dana.

"Supernatural Radio"?
That was a new one. We did that for the record. But the album was done that way, with some new songs, but mostly songs from *Wildflowers*. There are still some tracks from *Wildflowers* that haven't come out. So [*She's The One*] was a patchwork kind of thing.

"California"?
"California" was *Wildflowers*.

"Hung Up And Overdue" is such a strong song. I'm surprised you left it off of *Wildflowers*.
Yeah, we didn't use a lot of things. Almost all of that *She's The One* stuff, like "Hope You Never," that was for *Wildflowers*. I'm really happy with "Hung Up And Overdue." That might be the best song on the album.

ECHO. 1999

***Echo* is a thoughtful album, with some really good songs.**
Yeah, it's got some good songs. It's got "Billy The Kid." I love that song.

And "Counting On You."
That's great. That should have been a single. I don't know why they didn't put that out as a single.

"Room At The Top" is a compelling song about being solitary, cut off from the world. Was that how you felt at the time?
Yeah, I think that pretty much sums up where I was at at the time. It's still hard for me to listen to. We cut that track straight through, very much like the first and last verses, which are soft and tender and almost countryish. We cut it all like that straight through. And then Rick had this idea of having Mike slam this really heavy guitar over the second verse. That was really Rick's idea. And so Rick and Mike tried this guitar and we all got really excited, it sounded great. So we went back and changed the bass line through there and added a couple of other things, I think the piano, just to accommodate the heavy chords. And then we had a whole different record.

Then, in that section, I took my own acoustic out. We also had Scott Thurston playing some kind of electric guitar there, I think through a Leslie. And I took my acoustic off, though we had cut to the acoustic. When we took the acoustic off, it had a whole different feel, which was less common than the acoustic strumming all the way through. And we just kind of did a reshuffle on it.

But we were all tremendously pleased with "Room At The Top." [Laughs] I still think that's one of the better moments of the album. I was really tickled by how that came out. It was a great example of The Heartbreakers at work. On my own I would have never arrived at that arrangement of the song. But they really took it somewhere that I would have never got to by myself.

You wrote that on piano?
Yeah. In the only key I'm really good at on the piano: *C*. [Laughs] Actually, I've been playing the music to that song on the piano for about a hundred years and I never knew it. I'd go in and sit down at the piano, and I would just start noodling that music, to "Room At The Top." Those chords. And I was going to write songs with Jeff Lynne one day, and he said, "Do you want to do that one?"

And I said, "What one?"

And he said, "That one you keep playing on the piano." And I wasn't aware that I was playing anything.

I said, "That's not a song. I'm just moving around chords."

And he said, "No, you *kind* of do the same thing every time." And I think that night I caught it finally, because I was just unconscious to what I was doing, and I was playing it at the piano and had my little cassette deck on and was singing along. And, later on, I realized that that's the song I always sit down and play in the key of C.

It has such a beautiful lyric, too. The room at the top of the world in some ways is an escape, but also seems like a necessary exile.

It evolved into more than what it was when it started. That was really a joke on VH1's *Storytellers*, to say that this is a song about escapism called "Escapism." [Laughs] [The band recorded an episode of VH1's *Storytellers* on March 31, 1999, at a Los Angeles-area soundstage.]

The guitar solo on that one is pretty wild. That is two guitars, yes?

No. It's clavinet and guitar. It alternates between Ben playing clavinet through a guitar amp and Mike on guitar. Though, you're right, there are two guitars playing. He had done another pass, and by mistake someone had both of them on once and I thought it sounded great. So we just mixed in a little bit of the extra part in just two places.

We actually cut down that solo section. That was much longer—it was twice that long. And I hated to do it. They really played some great stuff, but I felt that it was really a little bit too long. It just unbalanced the song a little bit, so I had to cut it down. But they're such great players, it's scary sometimes.

And Steve Ferrone's drumming on that one and the whole album—the way he kicks the band into gear—is so solid.

Yeah, he's so good. And we're teaching him to never play drum solos. [Laughs] "Steve, *no*. Just play this."

And he'd say, "Really? That's really all you want?"

And I'd say, "That's all I want. I don't want you to ever play anything else." But he has such a good natural feel. And he's really good in the studio. He's really quick and his time is immaculate. We can really count on him to hold the time.

You posted "Free Girl Now" on the Internet as an MP3. You were the first major artist to do so, which was revolutionary. Many felt this would dismantle the record industry.
They thought that radio was going to dismantle the record industry. They thought no one would need records any more. They thought blank tape was going to do the same thing. And DAT was another one. I don't think that this is the case, that this is going to dismantle the record industry. I understand their concern with protection, but I think if you can turn people on to music, in the end it's only going to sell more music. This "Free Girl Now" thing happened because it had been explained to me that singles don't sell. They break even, at best. The pop singles chart now is just an airplay chart. They don't take a poll on what singles sold. They're just promotional tools for selling albums. So, if this is the case, I thought why don't we just put it on mp3.com and allow fans to download it? It will be a great promotion for the album, and everybody can hear the song if they like. And they had such an overwhelming response to it—hundreds of thousands of people in a day just downloading like crazy—and then I was politely advised that it would probably be a good idea not to do that. [Laughs]

By your record company?
Yeah. I must say, because we didn't ask permission, we just did it—they were really polite about it, they weren't jerks at all. They kind of said, "That's funny, Tom..."

Did they say, "Don't do it again, Tom"?
No. They said, "We really think you should take it off. It's time to give it a rest."

And did you?
Yeah. I had to. [Laughs]

Did they see the value of using it as a promotional tool?
I would think so, but I didn't really ask.

"Lonesome Sundown" is interesting musically, in that it's got a shifting tonal center, so it's not clear even what key it's in.
Yeah, I'm not sure, either. I don't know what key it's in. But I love to do that, if I can bust into another key from one, and then somehow get back. It's not easy to do, as we have discussed.

"Lonesome Sundown" has some of your most beautiful lyrics—"Redemption comes/To those who wait/Forgiveness is the key..." Do you recall what triggered that verse?
I think I was thinking kind of deep there. I had gotten in that zone and it all just started coming. I was going through a lot in my life when I wrote that. I went through a divorce the year before, and I was trying to get just settled into a new life. And so some of that is reflected in the songs, I think. And my relationship with my children. But I didn't want to write one of those "I just got divorced" albums. So I consciously tried to stay away from it. But some of it creeps in.

There are definitely many sad moments throughout the album.
Yeah, it's down sometimes. It's kind of bleak.

But with hope. "Lonesome Sundown" is a hopeful song.
Sometimes I noticed that even within one song, because I may be thinking about different people or different things within the scope of one song, one verse might be happy and the next verse might be a little bit melancholy [Laughs] because there's a lot of *good* things going on in my life, too. Actually, I'm pretty happy now. I've been skating along pretty well now, I think. So there is hope in the songs.

The words changed several times in that song. But I finally got it to where I liked it. I think I worked on that one a lot more than any of the others.

It also has "Swingin'" on it, which is a cool song.
"Swingin'" is a good one. I actually ad-libbed it completely. That is the writing of the song. Yeah. It's a complete ad-lib. I played that first round of chords, the band fell in, I ad-libbed the lyric from top to bottom.

Good ad-lib.
Yeah, good ad-lib. [Laughs] Lucky. It was the easiest one to write for the album. We got down to the end of the album and we started thinking

we were going to do a recut of "Free Girl Now." We were thinking we could make a better record out of this. There was *some* school of thought that we could make a better record, and some of us thought that it should be just as it was. Because it's a real shaky record in a way, it's like…

It's raw, but it has a great feel.

Yeah, it's *very* raw. So we got down to the studio and went back at the very eleventh hour of the record to see if we could make a better track. And really our hearts weren't in it. Everybody knew we already had it. So we never actually played it. [Laughs] But, while we were plugging in and sitting there, I came up with these chords to "Swingin'."

I just started playing them, actually, underneath what they were doing—they were all jamming, and there was this feedback and this noise. And I was playing against them. I think they were even in a different key, and I just kept playing. And there was no real beat going on. It was just chaos. Dissonance. The noise of everybody getting plugged in. And I felt, "Oh, this sounds good," with the guitar sounds I had up, and these chords sounded good. And I just kept playing it because I had no other way to communicate it. [Laughs] So I just kept playing those chords over and over. And then finally I could hear them one by one pick up on this chord thing.

And then *koo-koo-a-bam*, the drums fell in and we were on our way. And I just ad-libbed the whole song. Top to bottom.

The lyric is funny: "Swingin'…/Like Benny Goodman…/Like Glenn Miller…/Like Sonny Liston."

Yeah. Those were all ad-lib things that just came out of nowhere. I wish I'd have gotten Dizzy Gillespie in there. [Laughs]

And then, after that, Rick Rubin was looking at what was going down, and said, "I *think* that is a really great song." Which seemed hard to believe, because I'd just ad-libbed it. We not only ad-libbed it, I mean Howie sang that back-up part live, and it all just came down. There were a few chords I was calling out. So we listened to it once again, and cut it one more time, and that was it. So there's *that* done, and *I don't even know this song*. It was really a thrill. I didn't even *know* this song, and it was done. It was a record.

Do you mistrust the songs that come that easy?
Well, *yeah*. Because you don't know where it came from. Where did that come from? But I'm getting better about just accepting it as a gift. Let's just be happy you got it.

You didn't have any of those words before?
No. I didn't have the song before. We just started playing it.

"Accused Of Love"?
"Accused Of Love" took about two days. Two days of thinking that through. And what it was, was getting the title, was getting the punchline, to fall into place just right. Because I didn't know what it was. I knew what I wanted to *say*, but I didn't know how to say it yet.

And I was actually with Dana. This was before we were married. [Laughs] About five in the morning, I kept playing her this song. On guitar. And I'd just put in anything where the title goes: "Can of beans," or whatever. And then suddenly, *poof*, "Accused Of Love" fell down, and I just fell all around the room laughing. I got *so* elated.

"Accused Of Love" has kind of a British, early Beatles sound.
Yeah. It's funny how you see these influences go round and round, because I was thinking of Don Everly, that sort of melody. But it does have a mid-Sixties British sound. And he was obviously influencing them.

Like one of those old songs, it's very short—under three minutes.
Yeah. It's great when you can get it all in, in that amount of time.

The bridge is an instrumental. Did you ever think of singing words there?
No. I thought about that for a minute, but I felt the song would get too wordy if I put in a big thing there. So, in some of those British Invasion records they sometimes do that, they just hammer out some variation on the chord progression for the bridge. And that works.

The last verse is about judicial proceedings—with the defense flying out the window and all. Did you write that after finding the title?
Well, I did have a different last verse, but finding that title did inspire a quick rewrite in the last verse.

Does it feel more like a process of discovering what works, of finding that puzzle piece, rather than inventing it?
I always feel that way. Like it's already been done, it's just gonna come. I enjoyed writing those songs. I really enjoyed doing the album. I wrote them at my own pace and there was never any real pressure to hurry up. So it was really pretty enjoyable. I was kind of sad when it all wrapped up. [Laughs] I just feel like I'm really getting good now. [Laughs]

That enjoyment is reflected in the melodies and chord changes you often choose. The changes are often unusual, but they always seem inevitable.
Oh yeah? Thank you. That is thorough, when you learn the chords. There were some good chords. "Lonesome Sundown" has some good chords—that weird turnaround at the chorus. I really liked that. I was kind of tickled with those chords. Another one was "One More Day, One More Night." I liked those chords. I originally wrote that as a skiffle. Like really fast. [Sings, in fast tempo, playing rhythm with his hands on his lap] "One more day…" But then I thought, "I've done so many skiffles," so I took it to a more R&B thing with the band. We did it once as a skiffle and no one said anything, but they had this look of "I think we've been down this road." So I said, "Let's try it as an R&B thing."

The title song, "Echo," is a beautiful song.
Long. [Laughs] But it's good. It's a long song and it's funny because it doesn't hold any particular tense. [Laughs] It's being sung to many different people. It goes into narrative and then it goes out of narrative. But I just thought that I would leave it just as it came out. There was no editing on this album at all, or any rethinking too much. I just let it come out the way it was. And sometimes that song is kind of scary. But it's a good one. And I thought we got such a tremendous sound on it. The intro just falls in, and the piano is beautiful. Upright piano, we used.

But I like this other rock and roll song on there called "About To Give Out." I thought they played really great on that.

It was funny, because I listened to the album, and there was a song that came on, that I had *completely* forgotten that I had ever done it. And I have no memory of writing it. Called "It Won't Last Long." [Sings] "I'm down, but it won't last long..." And I thought, "What a cool song." I had no memory of writing that song. And I actually forgot that we ever made it. [Laughs] And it was such an odd feeling when it came on, because I was listening to it really as somebody who was hearing it for the first time.

But that was *Echo*. There was a lot going on then in my life. Howie was disintegrating before our eyes. That was a big issue. Not the happiest time for The Heartbreakers. We did a tour behind that record. We did a pretty long tour, for us. That's what I remember most about it, doing the tour. And the tour went on and on and on. And we played quite a few songs from it. But I was kind of glad to get to another place after *Echo*. [Laughs] I was kind of glad to get somewhere else. I don't know why, but I kind of felt like we came back into the sun after that.

"Billy The Kid"?

I wrote that on the drive to the studio in Bugs' truck. My trusty roadie Bugs was driving me to work—and I got this idea for this song, "Billy The Kid." I pulled out a pad as we were going over Topanga Canyon with all those curves, so I was really writing on the edge of the paper, and back and forth in the truck. And I wrote it all out on the way to work, and I had the tune in my head.

The tune just came from nowhere—no guitar or anything?

No, I just had it in my head. So I got in there to work, and I said, "Boy, I think I got a good one."

They said, "How does it go?"

And I said, "Well, wait a minute, I've got to figure it out." And they were looking at me kind of like, "What?" And I got the guitar out, and I started to figure out the chords, because I knew the tune in my head. And that was another one where I *swear* I didn't know how the song really went. I put the lyric sheet up and I ran over the chords with them on an acoustic. And I changed the key right there, because where I was humming in my head was a little higher than where I was playing. And if you hear "Billy The Kid" you hear this *brrrrrng* at the beginning...

Yeah, what is that sound?
What it is, is that Mike did all the engineering on the tracking dates. There was no other engineer. It's Mike hitting record while the band is playing. Because the band started to play and this *great* feel came down and I yelled to him, "*Hit it, hit it!*" And he turned around and he hit record, and then you can hear his guitar slowly kick in because he's just getting his guitar on.

And so, there's "Billy The Kid." We did it down, and we're tremendously excited at the end of this. And then we'd go, "Well, wow, this is going to be great." And then we spent *all night* playing it, and it never got as good as that *very first pass-through*. So we wound up using the one with the noise on the front of it. And then we got used to that sound on the beginning of it, so we left it on.

"I Don't Wanna Fight" is a song written by Mike Campbell alone, without any help from you?
You know what I wrote? I wrote "I'm a lover, lover, lover."

That's the best part.
I put that bit in. [Laughs]

That's the punchline to the whole song. It makes it work.
I thought so. But he had really done the whole song, so I didn't think it was fair to take credit for it. But I did help with that one line.

I also love "Rhino Skin," which is both a funny and a sad song.
Dark, yeah. It's dismal and humorous at the same time. There were some people in the group that thought the "elephant balls" line was offensive.

To elephants?
[Laughs] I don't know. I didn't find it offensive at all. Rick [Rubin] couldn't stand it. He wanted me to take it out. I couldn't take it out. I tried taking it out and it didn't sound good to me. So I just said I was gonna have it in. "I'm gonna have it in because that's the way I sing it, it sounds right to me, and I don't think it's offensive or anything." And

he couldn't tell me why he felt it was offensive. Actually, I think the whole group, at one point, on one evening, everybody said, "You ought to change that line. It cheapens the song." And I got kind of intimidated by it. But, in the end, I'm glad I left it there.

I agree. Because it sounds like something a guy might say to another guy after having had a few drinks in a bar.
That's what *I* thought. "You need elephant balls/If you don't want to crawl..." I just thought it was a conversational line. I'm glad you got it that way.

And the title, "Rhino Skin," is such a perfect way of expressing that need to develop a thick skin.
Well, you do sometimes need it these days. [Laughs]

In "One More Day, One More Night," you wrote, "God I've had to fight/To keep my line of sight on what's real." Can you keep some perspective, being within the music industry, on the meaning and impact an album can have to some guy who is far outside of the system?
I hope I do. I mean, I know what they meant to me and still do. I know how a record to me is so important, you can't even weigh up the value, because you're being inspired by something. I hope it's still like that. I hope people still get albums and get inspired by them. I know they do. Because too many people tell me about it.

I make them for me. And, if I get off on them, I feel that somebody else will feel the same way.

ANTHOLOGY: THROUGH THE YEARS. 2000

***Anthology* was a compendium of your previous work, and it also included two bonus tracks: "Waiting For Tonight" and "Surrender." Did you record "Waiting For Tonight" around the same time you recorded the song "Travelin'," which ended up on *Playback*?**
No. It was *near* that same session. It was probably me and Mike picking up the ball after The Heartbreakers were called off. We had the studio

time, so the two of us did "Waiting For Tonight." But it wasn't The Heartbreakers; it was me and Mike. And The Bangles.

The Bangles' part on that is great.
Yeah, they were great on it.

That could have been a single.
Should have been. Got a lot of airplay. If we had done a video, I think it would have pushed it over the top. But there was a feeling that we had overextended ourselves. We had so much product out that they thought it was overkill. Because we had had a lot of product out in a row for a couple years straight.

That's one of my favorites. That we *ever* did.

Great harmonies.
Yeah, great. I sometimes wonder if we could play that live, because I really like that song.

You never have?
No, we never have, because we don't have The Bangles. But if we could figure out a way around that, to arrange it right, I think we could play it. But I'd love to play it. I like that song.

I read that, when The Bangles were in the studio, you had all four talking at once, and it was rather chaotic.
[Laughs] Well, having girls there was kind of different for us. [Laughs] I think a lot of people saw The Bangles as disposable pop music. But I kind of like disposable pop music. And I thought they had a real good sound. In a way like The Mamas & The Papas had a certain sound, they had a certain sound. And I was really excited to work with them. I was really glad. And those arrangements came from what they just naturally sang. I just put the track on and let them sing. And they put their heads together and came up with these nice parts.

Yeah, it's a nice counterpoint to the melody.
Yeah. It's great when you have an experiment like that in your head and it actually works. You *can* do that and it won't work, sometimes. Sometimes you'll have this brilliant casting in your head and it won't

work at all. But that was an instance where it actually worked. It worked really well.

There are some great lines in that song. I love the opening: "I went walking down the boulevard/Past the skateboards and the beggars..." Sounds like Venice Beach.
It might have been Venice Beach.

Was that one ever in the running for *Full Moon Fever*?
It came in the very last days of *Full Moon Fever*, and Jeff wasn't there. It was while he was in England. We did that and we did a track called "Alright For Now," the lullaby track. So it was really going to be between one or the other, and we chose the other one because we really didn't have a song like that. And, by the time we got onto the next record, I'd already written a bunch of new songs.

Like many of your songs, it shows you don't need a lot of chords. The chord progression repeats, and then the melody will rise and shift above the repeated chords. "Waiting For Tonight" is in *F#* minor, and has such a good feel.
Yeah. I learned that from listening to Buddy Holly. He could take the simplest chord structure, where it really never moved, and find these incredible melodies. I really think Buddy, from what I've read and from what I've listened to, really got hooked on this song, "Love Is Strange," by Mickey & Sylvia. You listen to that song, you can really hear the influence it had on Buddy Holly. I think it had a *huge* influence on him. Because he wrote every derivation of "Love Is Strange" that you could write. He turned those chords inside out, around, backwards. And his melodies are kind of in that same range. He did a lot with just those basic chords. Sometimes you can play two chords. And, if you're patient, you'll find a melody that will work over those chords—verse and chorus. If you arrange the record right, you can make it entertaining. "Free Fallin'" is three chords the entire song. It's not because we don't *know* any more chords, it's because that was all that was needed. You have to sometimes watch yourself that you don't do more than is needed.

Too tired to stand, 1993. *Robert Sebree*

Martyn Atkins

Mike and me onstage at The Fillmore. San Francisco, 1997.

Steve, myself, and Scott, 1999.

Me and Dana with my hero Bo Diddley backstage at The Fillmore, 1999. *Photos: Martyn Atkins*

The Last DJ tour, 2002. *Ebet Roberts*

Getting our star on the Walk of Fame. Hollywood, April 28, 1999. *Lester Cohen*

My lovely daughters, Kim and Adria. Malibu, June 21, 2001. *Robert Sebree*

My dog Chase, my son Dylan, and me in Dana's red Mustang, 2004. *Dana Petty*

Me and Dana on the street in New York City, 2002.

Me and Dana at the Rock and Roll Hall of Fame Awards, New York City, 2004. *Startraks/Shutterstock*

Taken by the author at Tom's last ever show, September 25, 2017, the final night of the 40th Anniversary Tour at the Hollywood Bowl. One week to this night, Tom left to start his next great adventure. *Paul Zollo*

You're good at that. You said to me once that, if a chord doesn't sound like it fits into a song, it's probably not meant to be in the song.
Probably not.

It's not the chord progression that will impress people about a song, it's the song itself—the words and the melody.
Yeah, it always makes me laugh when I read that my music is *simple*. Because, if you think it's simple, try to do it. It's not simple. There's a lot of nuance. And light and shade. It's not a simple thing. It's sometimes much harder to do, really. But I've got this thing where, if you wrote a bridge, and it's not as good as the verse or the chorus, it really shouldn't be there. And the verse has got to be *as* good as the chorus. If you look at it in a modular way, you want all those sections to be equal. So that's a pretty handy tool: if you're writing, and you have a middle eight, and you're only using it to get from one place to the other, and it's not doing anything else, you might as well throw it out.

I think your songs seem to be simpler than they are.
They're *not* simple. I was in a music store recently, and a guy was trying to impress me and he was playing all our licks. Saying, "Hey, look at this!" And he had *every* one wrong. He had the right *root* of the chord. But we use a lot of variations of chords. For example, I use a lot of variations of G. I don't play, necessarily, a straight G. There's a lot of variations on those chords. And this guy was playing everything straight. So he thought it was right, but it wasn't. [Laughs]

Also, the bass line can move against those chords, and it creates chords just by the way it's moving across the chords. So the records have an awful lot of nuance in them. And, the more you listen, the more you'll hear it. And that works on a subliminal level. You may be asking yourself why you're recording something, "Well, is this something somebody is even going to hear, that you're putting into the song, the arrangement?" But these little things all add up on a subliminal level and they just equal, "Hey, I like that." But that's kind of the fun of doing it.

It's true that your songs will often work in a modular sense, in that your verses have strong melodies of their own, and then will often build up momentum and just explode into the chorus.

Yeah. Different people do it different ways. When I wrote songs with Roy Orbison, he had a completely different way of doing it, which was really unique, and really fascinating to me. He didn't really care about things being modular at all. He might not ever return to where he started. He was all about melody. And you just move the chords to follow the singing. So they were like small operas. It fascinated me that he might *never* return to that first verse, if you listen to some of those songs. [Laughs] So everybody has their own way of doing it.

When you were writing with Dylan, was he writing in a modular way?

Yeah, I think so. I think he likes to put down a pretty basic chord pattern, often almost a descending or an ascending scale. And then put his melody around that. But the few things we wrote were very simple.

Another song that didn't make it onto one of your albums, but is on *Anthology*, is "Surrender."

Yeah. That's a really, really old song.

Written in 1977.

Right. We opened all our shows in '77 with "Surrender." It was always the first song. Like Bugs said, "We recorded it on the next six albums." [Laughs] We recorded it and recorded it, and *never* got a version of it we liked. We tried on every album. And when they were putting out the *Anthology* album, they, again, wanted another new track. So then I thought that would be a good thing to do, because it would fit into the *Anthology* theme, and *maybe* we could do it now. And we took a shot at it, and it came out pretty well. Howie's amazing on that, those high harmonies. 'Cause we did it in the same key that we wrote it in when we were really young. [Laughs] Singing really high. So, yeah, that came out really good.

That's in *E* major—do you think that's the best guitar key?

Oh, there are many of them. Sometimes getting into the flat keys on guitar can be tricky, but we use capos. You can do about anything on guitar. [A capo is an accessory that changes the location of the "head" of the guitar to any place on the neck. That way, one can change keys without changing fingerings. The capo also "brightens" the sound of the guitar.]

Do you use capos while you're writing?
Sometimes, to make the guitar sound a little different, and see what happens.

Do you ever use different tunings on guitar?
We have. We've used the drop-*D* from time to time, where the *E* string goes down to *D*. And I know we've used open *A* on "Shadow Of A Doubt." Mike used them quite a bit. I might be playing in a straight tuning and he might be in an open tuning. On "Blue Sunday," everything was tuned down a step. My guitar was tuned down a whole step.

Why?
[Laughs] I think it just sounded good.

THE LAST DJ. 2002

Your next album, *The Last DJ*, has the song "Joe," which is a biting indictment of a record company CEO.
Every word of it is true. And the truth hurts sometimes. I saw him also as an impresario. What I was trying to say there was something about pre-packaged pop stars. And how they come ready to assemble. And TV shows that make pop stars for you. How it's gotten *so* cold that they're actually just created to fit certain market demands. There's an element of artist out there that doesn't really have much to say about anything. They're just presented as pop stars. I don't mind that. I think that's fine. But I wish they weren't presented as musicians. They're *not*. They're not musicians. And I think the public is short-changed by that.

I think there's a lot of talent out there that, maybe because they don't fit a certain marketable slot, they're just overlooked. I don't think things were always like that. But marketing has become more important than product, I think. It *seems* that way to me. And that's what I was trying to say in that song. I wasn't trying to sing about any actual living person. I wouldn't do that. But I just thought it said something about how cold it's become.

And, if I'm perceived as being bitter, so be it. [Laughs] Maybe I am.

The song has the great line "He gets to be famous/I get to be rich."

My favorite line in that is "Some angel whore who can learn a guitar lick/Hey! That's what I call music!" [Laughs] And that's true. It's before our eyes. I wasn't trying to be profound. I just thought it was funny. It was humorous. It was entertainment.

And there are so many young girl pop stars now who fit that description.

Yeah. They're created to fit certain markets. But the truth is, there's one very popular one that we were on a television show with, and I saw her, and it was so bad that I thought to myself, "If this kid was playing Pizza Hut, they'd say, 'Look, we're sorry, but you can't play here, because we can't really sell pizza with you playing here.'"

It would be like that. [Laughs] "We really can't sell any pizza with you playing out in front of the shop here, you've got to go." It was *so* poor that we were slack-jawed by it. We were open-mouthed, just in amazement, that that's what's being passed off as rock music.

It's *insane*. It's Fabian. It's *worse* than Fabian. We've gone full circle back to the days of the early Sixties when pop stars were just created, when all the Bobbys were out, and they went from leather jackets to sweaters, and they tried to say that they *aspired* to be something more than rock. That they weren't just rock, but they were aspiring to be more. Be real entertainers and actors. And we didn't learn a lesson from that? That it's just suddenly swung *right* back into that. That's your popular entertainment.

And that's fine, if people like it, that's fine. *I* don't like it. I just think there are a lot of people who are good—there *must* be people that are better than that—but, because they don't have the right face or haircut or stylist, they don't fit this marketing slot that the industry has for them, so they're overlooked. So we can only hope that that changes or gets better, or something comes and just completely knocks it out of the park.

You think that's a possibility?
It's always a possibility. I mean, in the Sixties, The Beatles came and *completely* knocked that out of the park. The only other time I've seen that happen is when Nirvana came and suddenly all those fake hairspray bands were completely out of work. The next day. It was wheat before the sickle. But Nirvana couldn't sustain it. It was too much for [Kurt Cobain] and it destroyed him. So I think you need something on that level to come along. Something that's really pure and honest to become popular. Then you'll have people who want to imitate honesty. [Laughs]

Because of the content of "The Last DJ," "Money Becomes King," and "Joe," people missed some of the other really special songs on that album, such as "Dreamville."
"Dreamville" is one of the best songs I ever wrote. That was about innocence.

It starts with you going to a music store to buy guitar strings.
I'm innocent. Before all the corruptions hit me. And how pure it could be. I think that it was missed because of that. I loved that song. I wrote the orchestration with Jon Brion [songwriter, arranger, producer] and did the whole thing.

I love this music, this rock and roll. And it's meant a lot to me. And I do take it personally. It changed my life. It sustained my life. It's absolutely the embodiment of the American dream. It made things possible for me that could never have been possible. And, even if it hadn't, I loved it in such a way that I really respect it. And I really care about it. I care *passionately* about it. And people call me bitter. I'm not bitter, I'm just *sad*. [Laughs] I'm just sad that there's such a great, wonderful thing, and it's being denied a whole audience. It's going to be hard for them to ever discover it.

I don't care. If it all ends tomorrow, I'm fine. But I just think it's sad that there's such a wonderful thing there, this music thing, and integrity in music and in art should be *respected*. And maybe the struggle has always been there. But I don't think it's been there in quite the ratio it's at now, where it's nearly buried. So, we just have to hope that maybe it will turn around at some point, and there will be another way of looking at it. That the audience will actually demand quality. But I think you can only pick from what you're offered. And, if you don't offer them anything, they can't possibly pick it.

And I think it's cheaper for the record companies to manufacture artists who aren't going to make any waves, who aren't going to demand anything—they're going to completely play the game—than it is to deal with somebody who comes along with a point of view and some integrity. They're not always easy to deal with. [Laughs]

There's also "Like A Diamond," which is a haunting song.
Yeah, I like that song, too. It's such a positive song. I think there's redemption and hope in that record. And it has a good positive thing to say. But, to make that point, I had to show the bad guy ["Joe"]. [Laughs] But, unfortunately, that was so sensational, I guess, that that was where the focus went.

I love the song "Blue Sunday." There are great details in the lyrics, like "Her backseat could've been a hotel/I slept for a thousand years/Every now and then she'd laugh out loud for no reason/I pretended not to hear..."
Yeah, that's kind of a story song. It's kind of a little short movie, that one.

Do you enjoy writing story songs?
Sometimes, yeah. If I'm lucky. They're hard to come by. "Something Big," on *Hard Promises*, which we've spoken about, is the same kind of thing, it's just a quick, short story. And the trouble with them in songs is you don't have a lot of space to get it in. So you've got to be lucky enough to get the lyric where it hits, and it has a pretty wide scope, where maybe one line can create multiple images in a person's head. And, that way, you can kind of squeeze a movie into three minutes. It's a lot trickier than writing a whole story out, like a narrative. So I don't usually set out to do that, but when it starts to happen it's a lot of fun to follow it down the road and see where it goes.

And it is more a sense of following it than leading it?
I think so. With me, most of those come in and I am literally following it and writing it down. And then I don't really know the ending, and then the ending appears before me.

A lot of novelists have said they write their books that way, following the story, but unsure where it's going to end up.
I have to. I don't think I've ever written one where I knew how it was going to end up. So the endings sometimes are kind of ambiguous. But I think in song it's got to be. You don't want to nail it down too much. In songwriting, I think the better ones have some element of ambiguity, where it allows the listener to create his own picture. And those are the ones I like.

I also like the song "The Man Who Loves Women." Which starts with ukulele, which is nice. And reminded me of George Harrison, who I know loved the uke.
Yes. I actually wrote it on a ukulele that he gave me. I like the chords in that. I really came up with a lot of good chords that I don't think I would have hit on guitar. George taught me to play the ukulele, and he taught me a lot of cool chords and inversions on it.

Is it easy to play?
Yeah. If you're a guitar player, it's not a big leap to learn the ukulele. Because it's really just the top four strings of the guitar. You have to get into a different head to play it. But you do find yourself going into different kinds of chords or different progressions than you do on guitar. I love the ukulele. You can't be sad and play the ukulele. [Laughs] It always brings a smile into the room.

George was playing one all the time, wasn't he?
Yeah, he was mad about them. Loved them.

Another song from that album which is really nice is "Have Love Will Travel," which has three sections to it.
Yeah, it was almost a summary. We're getting farther down the line in the story. The DJ comes back into the picture. And there's a girl named Maggie, that shows up, which is a little hard to understand, because I'd written this whole song that introduced her, but I didn't use that in the end. [Laughs] It got kicked out. So I kind of sweated, that they're not going to know who Maggie is, because [Laughs] she's never really introduced. She's kind of the girl in "Blue Sunday." But there was another song that really explained her. But it never got into the record.

Because in the end we just didn't think it was good enough. I kind of overwrote that album. I wrote several things that didn't make the final cut.

"Have Love Will Travel" has that beautiful second section, "Should I lose you in the smoke..." That's really lovely.
Yeah, that came out good, that song. I love playing it live. And I love that last verse. The audiences always love it: "How about a cheer for all those bad girls/And all the boys that play that rock and roll/They love it like you love Jesus/It does the same thing to their souls..." They love that.

"Can't Stop The Sun" is also a strong song. And one you wrote with Mike.
Yeah, that was mostly Mike's. He even wrote some of the lyrics, which has never happened before. He had written that out completely. One of the rare times he gave it to me with a vocal on it. I swung it around a little differently. I rewrote probably ninety percent of the lyric. But I did keep the title. He had that lick: "Can't stop the sun from shining." And I thought it was a good way to end the album. It was a good "up" song.

Unusual that he would have the title, isn't it?
Yeah, it is. Though I think he was calling it "Can't Stop the World," which I didn't think was right. [Laughs] But I kind of twisted it around. But he agreed with me. He wrote the melody and the chords, everything. So it's mostly Mike's song.

When you finish a song, does it give you a feeling of triumph?
Yeah, I *love* it. I love it.

How long does that feeling last?
It can last for years, if it's really good. Yeah, sometimes I'll hear something on the radio and I just can't believe I wrote that. I'll say, "*God*, that was a good one." [Laughs]

It always feels good to finish an album, because I've done it long enough to know these things are gonna be around a lot longer than me. It's something that wasn't there and now it's there. That's what is great about music and composing in the first place. Something that wasn't there a few minutes ago is there. I *love* that about art. You just created something, and now it's here and it could be here longer than you.

As this book was about to go to press, I received a phone call from Tom. He was in a happy place… just having come off a successful summer tour and having recorded several songs for his forthcoming solo album, Highway Companion. *He was thrilled with the music he, Jeff Lynne, and Mike Campbell were creating and he invited me to come have a listen to their work in progress. It was the eleventh hour in the production for this book, but I couldn't resist the opportunity to hear a few new songs. So, I headed to Malibu, listened to some songs, and asked Tom a few more questions.*

HIGHWAY COMPANION, 2005

You just started work on an album with producer Jeff Lynne. It's another solo album, tentatively titled *Highway Companion*. Did you write all the songs and then start recording, or are you writing during the sessions?
I think I wrote most of it before the recording. I had a good chunk, maybe eighty or ninety percent of it, before we started recording. I think I only wrote one completely while we were in the studio, "Damaged By Love."

"Turn This Car Around" is a great opener. It's a powerful song.
Yeah. It says "opener" to me.

It's got a great chorus, and a different use of the title than usual. Did that come while writing?
That was one of those nice gifts you get where it just really just fell into place. I started singing it, and I think I got a verse and a chorus. Then I spent a little time working on the lyrics. I wrote more verses than I needed, actually, so I had to sit down and pare it back a little bit. It came out beautifully. And it was one of the first couple we did. And I remember Jeff saying, "I've really never heard anything like this." [Laughs] And we were pleased with that. He said, "I really wouldn't know what bag to put this in. I've never heard anything like it."

It's cool in that it's in *E* minor, but starts with a complex chord.
It's a very odd chord. Jeff said he'd never seen it used before. I don't really know what chord it is. It's almost an *E* minor seventh, but with something else in there. [Picks up guitar and plays an *E* minor seventh with a suspended fourth.] I just started playing that one day, and I loved that chord.

Did you write these all on acoustic guitar?
Yeah. I think so. It was all on the acoustic.

The theme of time passing reoccurs throughout the album.
It does. I don't know why. I guess it's just subliminal. Subconsciously, I did it. I didn't intend to do that. Maybe it's just getting older. You start realizing that you have a certain amount of time to deal with. And I'm at that age where I realize time is really precious. Maybe that was in the back of my mind. It was not something I set out to do.

The slide solo on "Turn This Car Around" by Mike is so languid and nice.
Incredible, isn't it? He's just incredible. He does it so effortlessly. He just makes that sound. He was very clever with how he used the guitar. He went after different textures. He used different amps. Sometimes he used a stereo amp. Sometimes for one track he'd take [the amp] out into the big room and mike it at a distance, to get a bigger sound. He's just a genius with guitar sounds. Beautiful sounds, he got.

He felt that maybe we were doing too much slide guitar. But I urged him to keep doing it, because I thought it gave the album a character. I wanted the album to have a somewhat similar sound throughout. I didn't want it to be one of these, and now one of those. We'd *done* that before. I wanted this to have a thread of character sonically. So I urged him to do the slide a little more than I think he naturally would have done. But I liked it. It became another voice to me.

The album does have a beautiful sonic character.
Well, that's Jeff.

Yet it doesn't have the typical Jeff Lynne sound at all.
I think it's *certainly* the most different thing he's ever done. You'd never even know that it was Jeff necessarily. He doesn't have to put his classic

stamp on it. But I think he's really stepped forward in a way as a producer. It's some of his best work, I know that.

It's much sparser than his typical work.
I wanted it to sound like a combo. I didn't want this to be a big production. I wanted it to sound like it could be played by a combo. Like five guys could do this. And therefore that helped us maintain a lot of space in the music.

Jeff played the bass?
Yes. And he's a really good bass player. Sometimes you don't really even notice how good the bass is, because it's doing its job, and you're not paying attention to it.

Yet it's anchoring the whole song.
Yeah, like crazy. With a bass, even knowing how long to let a note ring is so important. It's not just that you hit the right note. It's how long you let that note ring, and where did you cut it off. He's just a genius at that. He's so good at that. He plays that great bass solo at one point, too.

Yeah, on "Night Driver."
[Laughs] He said, "I'm sorry, I didn't mean to go off on that."

And I said, "No, we're keeping that."

He said, "Really? I thought maybe I was being overindulgent. I'm sorry, I didn't mean to take off on that."

I said, "No, it's great. It's beautiful."

And nice to have a bass solo.
Yeah, you never hear one.

And you played all the drums throughout?
I did. I think I could play these songs. I mean, you would never see me onstage playing the drums. But these days, with the luxury of all the equipment you've got in the studio and the engineers, they can really forgive a lot of sins. [Laughs] But I managed to get through it. Jeff encouraged me to do it. At first, it was done just out of necessity. We were there, and we didn't have a drummer.

But I've got to admit, I really enjoyed doing it. I don't think I'd do it a lot. But for this project I really suddenly thought "I'm gonna try to do it all." It probably could have been done better by a real drummer, but I did my best with it. And I had fun doing it. But, like I say, the engineer forgives a multitude of sins. Because they can fix all my mistakes. So I would never try to do it live.

Though I'm not that bad. I practiced a lot. While we were making the record, I would go in the drum room and practice a lot, just to try to get used to being a drummer.

You did it to a click track?
Yeah.

You put down guitars first?
Yeah, we'd do the guitars, and maybe even the bass sometimes. And then I'd do the drums.

Did Jeff play keyboards?
We all played a little bit of keyboards. We split them up. Jeff played most of the piano and a bit of organ. In the things we did here, I played all the keyboards. And I played that electric piano on "Night Driver." That's me. So that was just whoever had a good idea, though Jeff did the lion's share of the piano. We'd all put our heads together and figure out the piano part. And then whoever could pull it off could play it. [Laughs]

And did you do the vocals before finishing the tracks?
I did the vocals very early on. Because I don't like the idea of building a track and then having to glue it all together with the vocal. So it's better to base it around the vocal. So I usually did the vocal as soon as we had a rhythm guitar down.

The harmonies are very subtle, and so gently mixed into the track.
That's just Jeff mixing them in the right spot. He's very good at that. Better than I am at placing the harmonies in the mix. Sometimes we might turn them up and down depending on the song. He and the engineer would do the mix for most of the day, and then Mike and I would come in for the last few hours of the mix. And then, if we heard something that they hadn't heard, they might make an adjustment. But

[Jeff] is quite good at putting them in the right spot. And I *love* singing with him. We have so much fun singing.

Did you do any demos of these songs?

I did one for "Big Weekend," but I never played it for Jeff. I just played it on guitar. And there were a couple of things I started, and they just took that track and finished it, rather than starting again. Things like "Square One." I did that here [Tom's home in Malibu]. "This Old Town," I did the guitar and the vocal here. And "Jack," I did most of that track here, and they finished it up.

"Square One" is a beautiful song. Very tender, with no drums.

It's funny. It came together when I was here in the studio with my engineer. And I had that song, and I sat down and recorded it, and then I didn't like the way the verses were going. And then on the spot, just because I thought it didn't matter, I changed the chords around in the verses. And we did another take, and that was it. So the unfortunate thing for the producer was that I didn't realize I was making a record, and I played the guitar and the voice into one mike. So it was nearly impossible to separate them. So [the engineer] had to do a bit of editing to get it all right. And I did sing some of it again. But I think most of it is the track I did here.

I just wrote that one night. Kind of late at night, just thumping on my guitar, and that came to me. And once I got the chords for the verse, then it all fell into place.

It's a beautiful chorus: "Square one, my slate is clear..." And I love the line "Always had more dogs than bones."

Yeah. I know a lot of people like that. It's a good song in a way. I guess it's about finding some kind of redemption, and getting back to square one, and feeling good about it. Starting over, I guess, is the simplest way of saying it.

The song "Night Driver" has a haunting opening: "There's a shadow on the moon tonight/I swear I see your face up there with the satellites/Looking down from outer space..."

I saw the album in that way, in a loose way, about traveling and about driving. I've done songs about driving in the past. But I wanted this to have a different mood. And the driver in that song is going through a lot in his head. And I thought that would set the mood: "There's a shadow on the moon..." Really, it all kind of came easily after I had that.

I was lucky. I didn't really struggle a lot with these songs. I looked up one day and I had ten songs. I was surprised by it. Because I would write them, and I'd have them in my head, but I wasn't sure if I'd *really* written something or not. But when I got to Jeff's, I did have that song done. And "Night Driver" was the first song we did. And then I thought, "Wow, this is really working." And then it was just a natural move. It was like, "Hey, we should record something." So we went over to his place, with Mike, and we recorded that, "Night Driver." And then I was like, "Okay, we're pitching our tent here. This is going really well." And then we did "Turn This Car Around." And I remember them saying to me, "Do you have any more songs?"

And I said, "Yeah, I think I have about ten." And I did. So we just went to work, finishing them off.

The songs have great lyrics, and some beautiful melodies. The chorus to "Down South," for example, is such a sweet melody.
I wrote two different choruses for that song. The other one was pretty good, too, but it was too long. It's a wordy song. And then it hit me that the chorus has to be more or less a turnaround, instead of going into this big long thing. And that got me onto the other chorus, which is so much better. But I did have a little bit of a holdout on that song, because I knew I was onto something, but until it was perfect I didn't want to try to record it. About midway through the album, I got the chorus, and I was really excited.

The other chorus has different words and music?
Yeah, it had different words and music. I think it said the same thing, basically, but with different words. So I found a way of quickly getting it in there, and it's *so* much better: "If I come to your door/Let me sleep on your floor..." It made a much better picture.

I have to admit I'm very fond of that song. I read this book [*Dusty Springfield's Dusty In Memphis*] on an album that Dusty Springfield made, *Dusty in Memphis*, which is a classic R&B album. In his book the author really didn't write about the album as much as he wrote about the South. It's a very romantic place, but it's also a spooky place. You'd think a lot of ghosts still linger down there. And I enjoyed reading his book, and that got me thinking about the South. I'd written about the South years ago. And I wondered, "What would I write now? Now that I've been gone so long?" Then I got my head into thinking about, "What if I went back? What would be my impressions?" And then it came pretty easily. I wrote all the lyrics before I wrote the music. It's the only one on this album that I did that way. I wrote all the lyrics. And I think, as I was writing them, I heard the tune in my head. And then it was just a matter of picking up the guitar and finding what chords were under it. It took me a little time to get a melody, but I got one. 'Cause it's very wordy. But I think every word counts. So, once I had the chorus, I was really happy. [Laughs] I'm still happy about that song.

Jeff made *such* a great record of that song. And Mike played so beautifully on it.

There's a nice recurring riff that holds it together.

Yeah, that's Mike with his Magnatone amp. It's got a wobble on the amp that makes a tremolo, but something even more bizarre than that. That's how we made the record. He got that killer sound, and we just based the record on that.

It's got beautiful lyrics about digging up your past, and confronting the ghosts of that past. You have "Sell the family headstones/Drag a bag of dry bones..."

"Make good on my back loans..." "Live off Yankee winters..." Which they do down there. I think my favorite verse is "Spirits cross the dead fields/Mosquitoes hit the windshields/All documents remain sealed..." That's when I got really excited.

I love the part about "Impress all the women/Pretend I'm Samuel Clemens/Wear seersuckers and white linens."

It's funny, I was playing it, and there are people who didn't know who Samuel Clemens [Mark Twain] was. It frightened me. [Laughs] Younger people. But he's one of my great heroes. So, yeah, that was a bit of luck, getting those nice lines. I've rarely written something that I felt so good about. It's up there in my Top Ten of things I ever did. And that's great. It makes me feel really good. It makes me feel like I want to keep doing this.

It's interesting that you wrote all the words for it first. Did you have more lyrics that you didn't use?
Yeah. I wrote a lot. And I edited it down. I got on a tear there. I just started writing and writing.

It's got some good rhymes in it.
That's a good feeling, when it all rhymes. Though I wasn't really concerned with the rhymes when I was writing it. It worked out, so what I did was to take the most important verses and use them. But I had more that I didn't use. I'm a wealth of information on that subject. 'Cause I did grow up there, and, once I got on the theme of what it would be like if I went back, *everything* started springing up. [Laughs]

I really like that song. I think it's up there with anything I ever wrote. I hope people see it that way. I was so happy to get that chorus.

"Big Weekend" is a fun song. It's a story song, being in a hotel, leaving a tip for the maid, packing up your guitar, and going to see your friends in the bar.
My favorite line was "I may shake your hand but I won't know your name/The joke in your language don't come out the same." [Laughs]

What inspired that song?
I don't have the damnedest idea. I just started playing and it appeared. Almost like a word game. It was along the same theme of "If I went back, what would I do?" And you'd probably look somebody up, and go out on a big weekend. It's a little bit of fun, that song. I tried to hammer in a little more into it. Like "You can look back, but it's best not to stare." So maybe there is a theme somewhat, of readdressing things.

It was nice writing these songs, because I didn't feel I was under any pressure, or had any deadline. And I didn't. I did it just to amuse myself. And like I said, I looked up, and *boom*, there was a lot of songs.

"Around The Roses" is a nice song.
That's a good melody. I wrote that in Mexico. I checked into this hotel. There's English, but it's not the best English. When I checked in, the guy said, "Anything we can do for you, let us know." I started thinking that I would really like a guitar. I called the concierge and asked him if

he could get me a guitar. And he was kind of thrown by that. I said, "It doesn't have to be an expensive one, but it's got to be one that tunes up."

And I didn't know how well he understood all that. And then I went out and rode horses for a while. And when I came back, there was a guitar. A nice Spanish guitar, nylon string. And I still have it. I brought it home with me, because I really liked it. But I thought it was so great that I called the front desk and they brought me a guitar. We were about thirty miles from Puerto Vallarta, and I guess somebody drove into town and bought me one. And it tuned up.

So I wrote "Around The Roses" and I finished the chorus to "Down South" when I was there. And I was really happy with that melody to "Around The Roses."

So I came back, and I had that song, and [Jeff and Mike] just dove right in on it. I love Mike's solo on it. God, it just got me when he played that solo. 'Cause he did part of it on regular 6-string, and on the turnaround he did that slide. Which I thought was so nice.

It's an odd little song. It's not normal. But I like it. I don't think it's one people are going to be drawn to immediately, but the more you hear it, the more it will grow on you.

It's revealing to me that, even when you're on vacation, you want a guitar, and you want to write.

It's better than TV. [Laughs] It was a wonderful vacation I had. I had a hammock outside the door, and I would lie in the hammock with my guitar.

I love the beginning of the song "Home": "Left town in a hurry/Blackmailed the judge and the jury..."

Yeah, I like the song. I don't know if it's as deep as the other ones. And [Jeff] made a great record of it. Maybe it will make the cut, I don't know. The only reason it wouldn't make the cut is because I'm trying to police myself on the length of the album. I was very vocal with everybody that I only wanted to do twelve. Because I think it's hard to remember more than twelve. I might wind up breaking up my own rule. Because I really like the songs. It would be painful to cut anything.

"Home" has that great line "Sometime everything's nothing at all." Which ties into bigger themes throughout your work.
I have to remember that. Everything, in a tangible sense, can add up to nothing. You've got to keep your head to where you realize what's important and what isn't. I think that's what I was trying to say.

And "Honey, your arms/Feel like home" is such a romantic line.
Well, we've all felt that. That's home, isn't it? When you're with the person you love, and you can go anywhere and still feel at home. That's an important thing to find in life.

"Flirting With Time" has such a catchy chorus, almost like an old Motown hook.
It's almost too catchy, isn't it? [Laughs] I played that for Jeff, and I was kind of worried that he might say, "That's too catchy. It's too obvious." I was worried it was too light. But Jeff and Mike liked it. That was another one that I wrote, and the chorus emerged right out of the verse. So I'm still not dead sure what that song's about. I just followed my nose until the end of it.

It's on that theme of realizing that time is precious, and you've got to really use it every day. It's not a song I would have written as a kid. It's like a little letter to myself to remember to do that.

The song "Golden Rose" is beautiful. About a boat.
Yeah. Probably like a riverboat. That's what I saw. I wrote that song way back before the album. And I actually did a track of it with The Heartbreakers, which didn't quite come out the way I wanted. So I remembered it during the sessions, and I played it for Jeff, and he wanted to do it. So it's really just a little riverboat story. A guy's stuck on a boat. The captain's nuts, and the son is worse. [Laughs] He's left someone behind.

The chorus is lovely.
Jeff and I sang that in unison. We had a lot of fun singing it. And we did the harmonies together in unison on one mike. We went out into the big room, so we could get a nice ambient room sound on it. And it made a really good sound. Then we put a piano through a Leslie speaker with some tape delay, which makes that strange sound at the end. I tried

playing it a few times, and I couldn't get it. And then Jeff took a go at it. I think he came up with a really nice melody for the ending.

"Ankle Deep In Love" is about a horse.
It's a story about a daughter that steals her dad's prize racehorse. And it's got a little bit of humor in it.

I love that line, when the girl says, "Daddy, you've been a mother to me..."
[Laughs] Yeah, that was a good way to tie it up. I don't know where that came from. That just came into my head, and I followed the story to see where it would go. It's like I've said, you don't have a lot of room to write a story in a song. So you have to be economical with your lines. But I like that one because I was able to do it, and get a chuckle out of some of the lines. This girl runs off with a field hand, and they steal a prize racehorse from her father. So you kind of get the picture that the father's wealthy. And the field hand isn't. "Found her hiding high in the family tree." I liked that one.

The song "Jack" is cool. It has a different feel than the others.
Yeah, that's a bit of rock and roll. It was fun playing the drums on that.

It's got great drums on it, especially on the turnarounds.
Yeah, I was pleased when I found that part. I had a good time doing the drums. I did the drums here on that. I did a lot of that track alone, and then they helped me finish it. Jeff did a bass. It's not the deepest song in the world, but I thought it would be good to have a nice rock and roll song. Fun to sing, too. It's got a good melody. I also played lead guitar on that one. Where it was actually so bad, they kept it. They said, "No, that's too authentic, we're not gonna touch that. Leave it the way it is."

"Damaged By Love" is a nice song about time. With another beautiful chorus.
I could hear the Everly Brothers sing that song. It is about time again. Love is a funny thing, because it can really damage someone, as well as redeem them.

Dana actually helped me with two lines in that song. In the last verse. I was kind of stuck. It's not something I would ordinarily do, but I said, "Hey, what would you put here? What would you say? I know what I want to say, but I can't really find a way of saying it." And that was her line, "In a crowd all alone/Walking round in a song." That was hers.

"So young, and damaged by love." I see that all the time. Parents can damage a child, too. So it's kind of a serious song, but it's a very beautiful song. I played that tremolo guitar. It's basically just an electric guitar with a tremolo and an acoustic. It's very sparse, but it's a great song. I love singing that, the chorus especially. It's one of my favorite ones, I think. It was done late in the album. I really love that kind of song. We were finishing the album, and I wrote it at home. It was the last one I wrote, and I played it for Jeff, and he said, "Damn, how do you do this? You're on a roll. You should run this out as far as it can go." And I think that's as far as it went.

It's funny, because I wrote all those songs, and it's probably been about four or five months since we quit working. And I haven't written anything. So it's weird, you get in a space, and things start coming in. But then it quits. So I'm just sitting around, waiting to write another song before I go back to the studio. Because I don't want to go back with just one song. But nothing's coming. I may just have to say that that's the way it's supposed to be, because nothing's coming.

But part of my goal with this album was to have something that is of a piece, and it's got a certain vibe, and it keeps it throughout.

How about "This Old Town"?

That was written in the middle of all the other things. It's a little bit of a story about someone who is somewhere they don't want to be, and feels the town is closing in on him. I hear a lot of people say that when they're unhappy where they're living.

Was it LA you were writing about?

No, not necessarily. I think it could be any town. The bridge was good. And it was another song that was fun to play the drums on. I got to do a little bit more in that one. I got to do some fills and stuff. I think maybe that's one of the best tracks. Just as a record. That's one of the best ones on there. I still haven't figured out where to put it in the sequence. Right now I have it at the end, but I don't think it's the perfect ending.

I like the chords. The chords have a nice turnaround in them. I like that one a lot. That was another one I did here. I did the vocal and the guitar and voice, and then took it over there and did the rest there.

Where did the title "Highway Companion" come from?
It just came to me, that this would be a nice highway companion. Like a good book that you could take with you on a trip. I liked that. It's good traveling music. Something you could go on a journey with, and it would be a nice companion.

I'm pretty proud of this album. I think I've done something that I'm particularly proud of. I hope people get to hear it. Because it's hard these days, with the way radio is, to get a lot of exposure for rock and roll. I think those that do will enjoy it. I keep thinking I want to go back and do more. I'm struggling so much with this song I'm trying to write now. But I don't know if I'm gonna finish it in time. Because I know I've got something there, but I can't seem to get it all to tie up. It's just a huge headache trying to finish it. It's just a nightmare trying to finish it.

Is that unusual for you, to struggle to that extent?
This much is unusual. But there's something that makes me not want to give up on it. Because I know the bit that I've got, as much as I've got, is really good. But I can't quite find the line or two I need, melodically and lyrically, to tie it all up. So I'm at a point where I'm almost tired of working on it. So I'll take a break of a few days, and then come back and work on it again. I think that, if I could pull it off, it could be really good.

Does it have a title?
No, that's the tough part. I don't know really where to hang my hat. [Laughs] I know what I want to say, but I don't know how to say it yet.

PART THREE

Additional Interviews, Articles And Reviews

"Lonesome Sundown" is interesting musically, in that it's got a shifting tonal center, so it's not clear even what key it's in.
Yeah, I'm not sure, either. I don't know what key it's in. But I love to do that, if I can bust into another key from one, and then somehow get back. It's not easy to do, as we have discussed.

"Lonesome Sundown" has some of your most beautiful lyrics—"Redemption comes/To those who wait/Forgiveness is the key..." Do you recall what triggered that verse?
I think I was thinking kind of deep there. I had gotten in that zone and it all just started coming. I was going through a lot in my life when I wrote that. I went through a divorce the year before, and I was trying to get just settled into a new life. And so some of that is reflected in the songs, I think. And my relationship with my children. But I didn't want to write one of those "I just got divorced" albums. So I consciously tried to stay away from it. But some of it creeps in.

There are definitely many sad moments throughout the album.
Yeah, it's down sometimes. It's kind of bleak.

But with hope. "Lonesome Sundown" is a hopeful song.
Sometimes I noticed that even within one song, because I may be thinking about different people or different things within the scope of one song, one verse might be happy and the next verse might be a little bit melancholy [Laughs] because there's a lot of *good* things going on in my life, too. Actually, I'm pretty happy now. I've been skating along pretty well now, I think. So there is hope in the songs.

The words changed several times in that song. But I finally got it to where I liked it. I think I worked on that one a lot more than any of the others.

It also has "Swingin'" on it, which is a cool song.
"Swingin'" is a good one. I actually ad-libbed it completely. That is the writing of the song. Yeah, it's a complete ad-lib. I played that first round of chords, the band fell in, I ad-libbed the lyric from top to bottom.

Good ad-lib.
Yeah, good ad-lib. [Laughs] Lucky. It was the easiest one to write for the album. We got down to the end of the album and we started thinking

Chapter Seventeen

Interview For Tom's Website

When I suggested the idea to Tom—via Mary Klauzer, of course—that we do a full book of conversations, he liked the idea, and said the timing was right, as there was no book about him in the world and his fans wanted one. But, as a kind of audition, and also to create some new content for his website, which was still pretty new then, he invited me over to the Malibu home to do an interview. Except for use on his website, it has never been published before.

The California sun is shining. It's the final day of March 2004, and Tom Petty is in the recording studio of his Malibu home, talking about the experiences he's had making music with his classic band The Heartbreakers and also with famous friends that include George Harrison, Bob Dylan, Johnny Cash and others. He also expounds about the late Howie Epstein, a founding member of The Heartbreakers, who died in 2003 of a heroin overdose.

A week earlier, Petty was in New York to induct George Harrison into the Rock and Roll Hall of Fame, performing two songs for George along with Jeff Lynne and even Prince, who was also inducted and who contributed a fluidly blistering five-minute guitar solo to the end of "While My Guitar Gently Weeps." But now Petty is happily back at the home by the ocean he shares with his wife Dana, who comes in to talk about fish and chips for dinner.

Tom's taking the time these days to do a lot of things, the kind of things he doesn't have time to do when he's on the road touring. But he's not touring this year, one of the few years in which this is so, and is using this period instead to tend to many aspects of a tremendously busy life, including the creation of a live album, and the design and expansion of his own website (for which we conducted this interview).

I loved seeing you and Jeff Lynne at the Rock and Roll Hall of Fame induction of your friend George Harrison.
TP: It was a lot of fun. That whole weekend we had a lot of fun. It was a good crowd that year.

Did you choose the songs to do? You played George's "While My Guitar Gently Weeps" and also the Wilburys' "Handle With Care."
No, since they televise the whole thing [Laughs], they have this habit of choosing the songs. They pretty much always tell you what they would like you to play. It was okay.

Had you ever performed "Handle With Care" live before?
We had performed "Handle With Care" in London at the *Concert For George*. We did three songs, with Jeff Lynne and Dhani [Harrison, George's son]. We've done it on the road from time to time.

Jeff Lynne really sang the Roy Orbison part well. He's got a quality in his voice that sounds a lot like Roy.
Jeff's amazing. Took a little coaxing to get him to do "While My Guitar Gently Weeps." Because he never appears live. Ever. He just doesn't do it. Hasn't done it in years and years. So it took a little coaxing to convince him. [Laughs] On everybody's part. And I think he was really happy that he did it.

His harmonies with you were really nice.
Yeah, we practiced a lot on those harmonies. We came over here and practiced that.

It was quite a band for the Hall of Fame. You had your drummer from The Heartbreakers, Steve Ferrone, on drums.
Yeah, he played drums and we had Scott Thurston, who actually played bass, which he doesn't usually do, and harmonica, which is an odd thing to do. [Laughs] And then we had Steve Winwood on the organ. Dhani played acoustic too, and Jim Capaldi played percussion.

And Prince played that amazing five-minute solo at the conclusion of "While My Guitar..."
Yeah. He was really terrific.

Did you rehearse with him?
Yeah. He was really inspiring.

"Handle With Care" was the first song by the Wilburys. Did George Harrison start it?
Yeah, it was mostly George's. He had the frame of the song. And we recorded that just across the road [from here] at Bob Dylan's house, in his garage. And we all wrote the song there. We wrote the lyric together. Mostly George and Bob and myself. Jeff sat down with George—I remember them sitting down in the grass, and working out that middle-eight section. There's an augmented chord in there. A "naughty chord," as we call it. They worked that out.

Bob and I came up with that other bridge: "Everybody needs somebody/To lean on." That was Bob and me. And then the lyrics are just kind of a communal thing.

George took the title off a box, a packing box, which said "Handle With Care," which is the actual title, and he took that off the box because he just needed a title.

It was a good day's work. 'Cause the song was all finished and recorded that night. Almost. Pretty much everything. I think we did an overdub or two the next day, but for the most part, it was finished.

That middle section—"I'm so tired of being lonely"—is so perfect for Roy's voice. Did George and Jeff write it for Roy?
Yeah. They wrote it specifically for Roy. Because it just turned out that everybody was there that day. I think George always had that idea in his head of the Traveling Wilburys. Actually, we had all been hanging out for some time by then. We had all been hanging out socially. I think maybe we had already done part of *Full Moon Fever* by that point. Probably recorded part of it. Roy had just come on the scene, because Jeff was going to do a track with Roy.

The first day I met Roy, Jeff and I and Roy wrote that song "You Got It." "Anything you want, you got it..." We had written that song. So everybody knew each other. We had been hanging out. And George decided—'cause he was just trying to do an extra track for single—so he thought, "If we're all here, let's design something for each of us to sing on." And when he got the record on, he felt it wasn't really a George Harrison record, it's more of a group. "So what do you say we have a group?" So that's how that ball got rolling. It was a great band. It was really fun being in that band.

And now with George and Roy being gone, we see how historic it was to have the five of you together.

Yeah. And to stay together that long. There were a few years of it. It's pretty amazing when you look back at it. [Laughs] But the truth is that it was friends. It was really just a friendly thing. It was kind of like we were going to hang out anyway, [Laughs] so we might as well make a record.

When all of you would work on lyrics, how did that happen? Would you all sit around with guitars and just toss in lines?

Yeah. We often did. It was like a community kind of thing. I had never done it that way. Usually somebody would find the thread. Like, okay, here's what this is. Here's the title, and here's the idea. And we all had usually sketched out the track. Like, here's how the music will go. Not always but sometimes. And then somebody would say a line and somebody else would say a line, and you'd kind of get this thumbs up or thumbs down. Like "Yes!" or "Noooo!" [Laughs] "Yes!" And then sometimes that would carry on.

I remember being at dinner and the writing pad going around the table and discussion about the lyrics. "How about this line, how about that?" And, of course, Bob [Dylan] was really good at that. It was a real eye-opener just how brilliant he is. It was great to see him do it. He just has a really good sense of the craft of writing a song.

Usually it didn't take too long. Sometimes we would struggle with words, and it would take a while to finish something off. But if I remember things right, usually things were written pretty quickly. Usually within a day. The lyrics anyway. Sometimes more. Sometimes the music and the lyrics.

Would you usually finish the music first and then work on the lyrics?

Yeah, usually music first. Though sometimes they came together. I remember George having that song "End Of The Line." We were all sitting in a room singing, "It's all right..." And George had the ending of the line, "We're going to the end of the line..." He had that much together on that song. I don't remember it all. But it was quite an experience. We probably will never see anything again like that.

Does Jeff Lynne sing a lot on the album? His voice is the hardest to discern of the five of you.

Well, see, to me, I hear him really clearly. George and Jeff produced the record.

Jeff had a *huge* contribution to all that. And, as far as arranging the harmonies, because it was really a harmony group. That's what we did the best. Jeff was the one who would figure out the harmonies, and what we were going to sing. His contribution was enormous to the Wilburys.

One time you told me you learned a lot of new chords from hanging around with George. Were there actually new chords he showed you that you didn't already know?

Sure, yeah. He showed me a lot of things on the guitar. Not only new chords, but different ways of playing them, or simpler ways to find them. Little tricks on guitar. It would be amazing—things that I thought were really hard, like things in Beatles songs that I thought was a real hard thing, he'd show it to me, and the way that he did it was really simple.

He was a really good chord man. He really knew his chords, and different ways to play them. But that's really what I picked up the most from him. We did a lot of casual playing, and he was quite good at showing me, "Oh, you know, there's an easier way to do that, or there's another way you can make that chord."

George was a great, great musician. One night we were at my house, and it was really late. And I had a bass for some reason. And it was just the two of us there and it was really late at night. And he started playing electric guitar, and he started playing the blues. And he just played the *shit* out of the blues. And I had never heard him do that. I asked him, "Why have you never done that? I had no idea you could do that." And he said, "Oh, that's Eric's thing." [Laughs]

He could really do that. He could really play the blues. And he said something like, "It didn't occur to me that when Eric came out with that kind of thing that everybody would leap on it and try to do it. I always looked at it as really Eric's kind of thing."

It was nice seeing you with Dhani, George's son, who looks so much like George. Is he a good musician?
Yeah. Dhani I've known since he was just a little boy. And my girls, especially Adria, kind of grew up being pals with him, and they're still very close. Our families are close. And we've remained that way. We're still very close friends.

Dhani is a good musician. I think he told me he has a group together. And they're going to make a record.

He looks so much like George, it's kind of haunting.
It is, isn't it? It's like George just traded bodies or something. [Laughs]

I just read the passage in the new *Rolling Stone* you wrote about the Byrds.
Did that come out okay? I haven't read it. David Wild of *Rolling Stone* interviewed me, and kind of took me off-guard. Time to think about the Byrds. But that's another friend of, *God*, twenty-five years. [Roger] McGuinn. So I'm pretty steeped in the Byrds, too. But I've always liked the Byrds.

You said that you wanted The Heartbreakers to be kind of a cross between the Byrds and the Rolling Stones. You said, "What could be better than that?"
Yeah. [Laughs] That's how we saw what we were going to do as a group. We wanted to have a sensibility that was kind of a mixture of the Rolling Stones and the Byrds. So we had the kind of R&B rock and roll thing, and then a kind of a nice harmony song sense. And a lot of other influences, but that's probably the simplest way to break it down. We wanted to be a mix of those things.

Were The Beatles also a big influence at the time?
Oh yeah. McGuinn got the idea of the 12-string Rickenbacker electric from seeing George play one in *A Hard Day's Night*. The Beatles were an *enormous* influence. A *huge* influence. But then they were on everyone, I guess. I still love The Beatles. And listen to The Beatles a lot. I just rotate around the albums, you know. [Laughs] I love The Beatles. You don't really hear people say it much, but if you came out of the Sixties like we did, there were the two big obvious ones: the Stones and

The Beatles. Everything else was another road. And the Beach Boys was another one that we really loved.

Did you?

Oh yeah, we adored the Beach Boys. And Mike [Campbell] and I had always liked Fifties rock and roll: Chuck Berry, and Elvis, Little Richard. When we met, we both knew all that music. Very few people played it. It's kind of odd when you think about it, but the truth was that in 1970 there wasn't that many people playing that kind of music, like Chuck Berry.

Yeah, it already seemed old by then.

Yeah, I think it was that group Sha Na Na that made it seem kind of gimmicky, with poodle skirts and jukeboxes. I think they were trying to make it into that. But we knew that music, and I think that also played into what we were doing. Still does.

When you formed The Heartbreakers, was it always Tom Petty & The Heartbreakers?

I think it was always Tom Petty & The Heartbreakers, because Mudcrutch, the band that Mike and Benmont and I had just before that, got burned so bad. We made a record, and then we put a single out, and the band broke up. And I thought, "If I'm going to start another group, I'm going to put my name into it, so at least I get something out of this." [Laughs] You know? And I wanted to have a lot of say in what went down. In the other group, I felt I had to stand silently by and watch it self-destruct. So I really wanted to be the leader.

Were you writing songs from the start when it became The Heartbreakers?

Yeah. I was really the only songwriter. Mike wrote a little bit. I think he might have co-written one or two songs on the first couple albums. Where he really blossomed as a writer was *Damn The Torpedoes*. That's when he really started bringing in the great stuff. But he was learning. In the very early days of the group, it was up to me to come up with the material. And it was so easy then. [Laughs]

Was it?
Yeah. *Much* easier than it is now, five hundred songs later. It was so much of a kind of fresh, clean palette. All those songs came really quickly. Most of them were just written to have something to do.

Did you write them on guitar from the start?
Mostly. I wrote a few on the piano. I remember, it was during a break while making the first album, that I wrote "Breakdown" on a piano. I wrote "Breakdown" and "The Wild One Forever" on that break. These were just strange days. I wrote the whole songs, words and music. It's something I wouldn't really think I could do now. But I guess I could. But when you're young, and just so innocent, it was just something that happened. You know, we weren't going to sit around for two hours and let them fix the mikes or whatever without doing something, so we did that.

You wrote "Southern Accents" on piano?
Yeah. I've used the piano a lot. "Don't Do Me Like That" was a piano song.

Do they come up differently when they are piano songs?
Yeah, because you have the bass line with your left hand. So you find different chords than if you were going to play guitar, and sometimes a different feel. I've used the piano quite a bit.

Do you enjoy playing piano?
Yeah. *All* of *The Last DJ* I wrote on piano. I think almost everything. I know it's always there, [Laughs] and it always figures in to some degree all the time.

Do you ever do both, and switch back and forth between guitar and piano?
Yeah. Sometimes if I've got something going on the piano, I might switch over to guitar and play it on guitar just to see if something else might happen. Sometimes it sets me off into a new direction. I'm not the greatest piano player. I've become a lot better [Laughs] over the years.

Do you use a drum machine when you make demos?
No, very rarely. I can play the drums a little bit. I can lay down a click, and then do one thing at a time—or sample and make a loop of the bass drum;

play a little pattern and then loop it. Sometimes, if it's not too fast a song, I can do it, I can play the whole thing. [Laughs] I'm not Steve Ferrone.

His drumming is so good.
He's *incredible*. Just an amazing musician. He can do anything in one take. He's just amazing.

He has such a great feel for your music.
He never plays anything that doesn't feel great. That's what I liked about him *immediately*. Every time, every take, feels good. Somebody might make a mistake, or you might want to change the arrangement or this or that, but it doesn't take really long to get a track because he's so rock solid with his feel. And he's a really bright musician. He actually can read and write music, which I can't do. I see him in the sessions just making little notes, sometimes writing on his floor tom. And so he gets the arrangement down really quick. Yeah, he's terrific. I just had him over here the other day doing some stuff with me. And I still am in awe of him. He went with us to New York.

And, funny enough, I met Steve Ferrone through George [Harrison]. [Steve] was in Eric Clapton's band; George did a tour of Japan with Clapton and his band, and did one show in London. But Eric couldn't do it. So George got Mike Campbell to play lead guitar, and they played the Albert Hall. And Mike came back from that saying, "Listen—this drummer, Steve Ferrone, is really a good drummer." [Laughs] And we were in the market for a drummer…

Stan had already left?
Yeah, Stan was going. We had done one television show and had used Dave Grohl from Nirvana. And Dave came *close* to joining the band. Kurt Cobain had just died. And I really discussed Dave joining the band. But Dave had his own career going. He had just done his Foo Fighters album. So it clearly wasn't going to work. And Steve came along at the perfect time.

And you've replaced Howie Epstein, who died last year?
Yeah, Ron Blair has replaced Howie. He's always been kind of an official Heartbreaker, so that was pretty seamless, adding him to the band. He stepped right in.

The Heartbreakers are an amazing band.
Yeah. They're ridiculous. I think they're one of the best rock and roll bands there is. For sure. It's kind of like you feel guilty if you don't play. [Laughs] Because they're *so* good that you want people to see them. So we've worked a lot over the last four years. We've really done a lot of touring. And this year we're *not* touring for the first time in a long time. We decided to give it a break and try to live life for a while, and have a semblance of a normal life for a year. So there's not going to be any real touring this year.

Are you going to write new songs during this time?
Yeah, that's the plan. We're going to make a record. [Laughs]

Do you already have new songs?
Not yet. I'm just starting to work on them. So it's too early. But I'm just starting.

Your last album, *The Last DJ*, was somewhat of a concept album. Do you think you would do that again?
No. [Laughs] No, that album was a shame, really. My idea with that album was to sort of do an album about morals in the twenty-first century. It seemed so obvious to me. And I guess as a framework, I took the music business, which is something that I was close to. And then I wound up really being hammered over the head for it. You know, I really took a beating.

Did you?
Yeah. [Laughs] From a lot of people. And the day the song came out, it was banned from a lot of stations. Which in a way kind of pleased me, it made me feel good. But that wasn't the idea. It was just a little work of fiction. It was almost a sci-fi film.

But there's been so much written about that album. It even got taken to the Senate. There were Senate hearings on radio monopolies, and my songs were being read into the record. You know it became much more that I intended.

The drag about it to me is that it's a really good piece of music. And the music became so overlooked because of the lyrics. The lyrics became the focal point, and I think, in reading about the album, you'd never know that it's got this really nice music, and melodies, and humor. That kind of got pushed aside.

I saw people say things like, "Where has Tom Petty been? Has he been under a rock for thirty years? I mean, this is not news." No, I *haven't* been under a rock, and that wasn't the point. *Everything in the record is relevant.* And I think time will bear me out on that. I wasn't trying to make an up-to-date study of the record business. I was just using it as a *tool*, as a metaphor. And the whole record isn't even about that. But in this day of really short attention-spans, [Laughs] I think the focus really went in on the first few songs, and it didn't go much past that.

The record actually has a lot of hope in it, and ends that way. So it was a record I worked really hard on, and it was kind of a concept record. But I don't think I'd do it again. I don't think I would take on a concept record. At least, not in the near future.

Were you surprised, when writing about the record business, that people would conclude that this is your statement on the industry?

I guess not. I guess I was naïve in a way to think that they wouldn't see it that way. I have a problem in that I can go into a song as a character, and write as a character, but the audience always sees it as me. And I forget that.

I think I was kind of naïve to think that people would take *The Last DJ* as a book, or as different characters per song. And they *didn't*. They took it as me *literally* taking a stand. And in all the promotion I did for the record, I could never get past these points. I could never talk about the *record*, it was all about what was going on in the record business.

It made it seem as if you were pissed off.

And maybe I'm a *little* pissed off. But I've got far more to do than be pissed off at the music business. It's such an easy target. It wouldn't have been something that I wanted to make my life's work. So I found myself in this kind of merry-go-round of that's all that anyone wanted to talk about, and the more I talked about it, the more pissed off I looked. So it was kind of a disappointing trip [Laughs] all the way around.

You've always cared about maintaining the meaning of your songs, and the connection with your audience. You've always been careful about keeping your ticket prices reasonable for your concerts.

Yeah. I've done the best job I can at that. You can go [Laughs] and see those year-in polls about who made the most money on the road. And we've seen a lot of situations where we actually sold a lot more tickets than people that were in front of us in the poll, because their ticket price was so high that their gross was much higher. So that's a really hard thing, too, because all around you the prices are going up, up, up to even mount a tour. As with everything else, I guess, it just gets more and more expensive.

But the audience wants to keep the ticket price in the same spot. And it's hard, because we have seen our prices go up a bit over the years. But I try to be just as decent as I can. Without getting too greedy.

There's one group that I know of—I won't mention their name—but we played the same venue—I think it was a 20,000-seat venue—we played it back to back one night.

We both sold out the venue. They made *500,000 bucks more than me.* [Laughs] I don't know if people realize this, but we kind of walked away from that going, "Hmmm, this is a lot of money."

I guess it doesn't matter, if people want to see it, to pay that kind of money. But my audience—and I've done a lot of research about this—my audience, which kind of makes me happy, is the salt of the earth. They're not wealthy people. For the most part. Even at our age, our audience is a rock and roll audience. It's a rock and roll crowd.

They're great audiences. They're downright *frenzied* audiences. Then I can go and see The Eagles, and the crowd is a completely different kind of crowd. They seem to be much more well-to-do. Maybe it's just my imagination, but they seem to be wealthier people and they're on a nice night out, and they're enjoying the show that way. But I kind of have the flatbed-crowd. [Laughs]

For a long time, you were on a songwriting roll, where songs kept coming.

Yeah. I haven't written in a while. I'm kind of excited to do it again. I've been touring so much that, since *The Last DJ*, I haven't written anything. But I'm just now getting my mind around that, to say, "Okay, I'm going to sit down and try to write some songs."

Where do you start?

I usually just play my guitar and piano a little bit, and let something drift in.

There are days when the instrument feels friendly, and days when it doesn't. I just kind of get some kind of regimen of, "Okay, I'm going to spend a few hours today to play guitar and piano, with the mind of writing something. And maybe something will come in."

Maybe some ideas will come in. And sometimes they do.

Also, I spend some time, when I get in that mode, writing things, writing lyrics, writing whatever interests me at the time, whatever feels right. And sometimes I'll sit and write lyrics. I'll just write in my notebook. I'll jot down ideas or titles or something that seems interesting to me. And then there's the other side of the coin where [words and music] both come at the same time. Those are the ones I really like, where I'm just playing and start to sing and a song starts to appear.

Many have said those are their best songs, when words and music come together, but that it's rare. Is it rare for you?
It's about fifty-fifty. It used to be that that was the *only* way I did it. I didn't really know any other way to do it. And then we became more and more professional, and so much of my life became about having to come up with twelve songs here, or you've *got* to have another hit single. You've got to have one every year, or every six months. [Laughs] You've *got* to have another hit song.

So when you get into that situation you really have to organize your time and your energy. I can't go off fishing for six months. I have to pay attention to this.

So I think, as I came up doing that, I learned a lot of craft. And a lot about the craft of songwriting, and how to do it, and how to apply it to making a record of the song. Because the song, to me, is really a record. First, I want it to be a great record, or there's not much point in me doing it. So that's where I began to kind of stockpile lyrics and ideas. You write them all down, so when it comes time sit down and write a batch of songs for an album, you've got a little help. You're not just going from nowhere to do it.

But I do love them when they just appear.

Any examples of ones that just appeared like that?
Probably most of my earlier work.

"American Girl"?
Certainly, yeah. Yeah, "American Girl" kind of all came at the same time. "Breakdown."

When you had that pressure to write hit singles, was that from the record company?
Well, it was just to stay in the game. I don't know if it's different now, it's probably not. But radio was a really important part of what we did. And then MTV. You had to have a hit song to stay in the game. So, you know, I stayed pretty much on the job.

[Drummer] Stan Lynch was out meeting girls, and I was home writing songs. [Laughs] I was the one who had to come up with another song. So it's kept me pretty busy.

Did it add pressure when you were thinking a song had to be a hit?
I didn't really think that way. I just thought, "I've got to come up with some more music." You just kind of hope and pray that one of the batch, or two of the batch, sometimes three and four of the batch, will be hits.

The funniest story of hits to me was the *Full Moon Fever* album. I think there were five hit songs on that record. When I first brought it to the record company, they *rejected* the album, saying there were no hits.

Is that so?
I'd *never* had that happened, before or since. I'd *never* had a record rejected.

Imagine: I did that record, and brought it in, and they *hated* it. They said, "Uh, *sorry*, we don't want to put this out. We don't hear any hits." And this had "Free Fallin'," "I Won't Back Down," "Running Down A Dream," "Yer So Bad." I was completely, *really* depressed. I went away *completely* depressed by it. So I waited six months and brought the same record back. And they loved it. [Laughs]

Did they know it was the same record?
I didn't bring it up. [Laughs]

It's amazing that they could hear a song like "Free Fallin'," for example, and not hear a single.
I think it was one of the biggest-selling records I ever had. But they didn't hear it. After six months, I guess personnel had shifted. And so I went right back with the same record. I said, "Hey, what do you think of it now?" Giving the impression that I'd been working on it, [Laughs]

trying to make it better. And I *did* try. I thought, "How could I make it better?" And I *couldn't*.

Finally, I thought, "This is *crazy*. Just put it out as it is and I'll take my chances." I just brought it back and said, "Hey, what do you think?" And they said, "*Great*." These are the things [Laughs] that you come up against from time to time in this business.

That was one of the first albums you made that came out as a CD as well as an LP. And in the middle of it, you have that funny passage in which you say, "For those of you listening to this on LP, you can stand up now, or sit down, and turn over the album. We'll give you a moment to do that."
[Laughs] I forgot that. You know why I put that in? At that point I had always thought of albums as two parts. It kind of bugged me that there was no break between the two sides [on a CD]. So I think I put that in for pacing, actually.

Did that change how you made albums?
Yeah, it's changed. Though I think I still think, pacing-wise, when the first half's over, and it's time to move into the second half. I really struggle with the idea anymore that anybody's even going to listen to it all in order. Or that people are oriented toward the record as one thing. Especially now that you can so quickly just dash from track to track, or that you can sample or download the songs you want without even hearing them. And I'm guilty of that, too.

Are you?
Oh, yeah. I'll go up on my iTunes and say, "Let me hear thirty seconds of this, oh, I don't want that." [Laughs] And the drag is that I've had albums where, maybe on the first play, I didn't like it this song or that song. But, as I lived with it, I really came to love that song.

Sometimes songs take a little while. You have to live with them to get them. And I think we're losing some of that, because the technology has made everything so much quicker and there's so many more choices. But all you can do is still make them as good as you can. That's what they are, and so I keep my blinders on and say, "To me, I'm making this as a piece of music. Whether most of the audience hears it that way or not, I don't know."

You said you're concerned with making each song into a good record...
Well, you just can't make a good record without a good song. You just can't do it. If you don't have a song, you don't have a record. You can have all the best production, all the best musicians, even the best arrangements. But if the song isn't good, it just won't fly. And a good rule that I've always stuck by is if I can't get the song over with a guitar or a piano, it's not done. I should be able to sit down and sell the song to you with just a guitar and my voice. And if I can't, then there's no reason to make the record. [Laughs]

Do you think in terms of production and record-making while writing the song, or does that come later?
No, not till it's done. Maybe a little. It's usually an afterthought, where you finish it, and then there's a million ways to approach it. You think, "Wow, now what kind of record am I going to make?" And that's a whole other area. Starting to make records.

When you play a song for the band, do you have a clear idea of what you want it to sound like?
Yeah. More and more I do. Sometimes too clear, I think, for their liking. You don't want them to feel like hired hands.

It's a little bit of a problem if I've done a demo, and I've completely worked out every note of the record. It's not what they want to hear, because they want to contribute what they feel as well. So you have to strike a happy medium. And really every time, I can have the idea, but, say, what Mike [Campbell] is going to bring to it is going to be a little more than what I did. That's the beauty of having a band. Because they really have a way of taking what you had in your mind and making it even greater. That's a really good band.

Is it always clear where the harmonies are going to go?
No, not always. It's just hit and miss. Howie [Epstein] used to have a mike on the floor, which is really unusual, at tracking dates, because there is so much leakage and everything. But he'd have a mike turned on really low, and a lot of times he'd just try harmony things while we were tracking the song. Usually they're during playbacks, while we're doing the overdubs, I'll sing along with it, and I'll think, "This would be good here." But very rarely do I have the harmonies before we do it.

Howie's harmonies with your voice was a great sound.
He was a great, great singer. Just a *fantastic* harmony singer. I miss him. Tragic story. [Pause] It's just a tragic story. I always think of people who have dope problems as people who have a lot of pain to kill. I kind of feel that I couldn't really get a handle on where his pain was coming from. But he was clearly a person in a lot of pain.

Howie was such a loner. His life was always isolated. He was very gregarious and nice, and the sweetest guy you'd ever meet. But his life, his social life, was in another area. He always seemed *very* remote. He didn't have much family; his mom and dad had died, and he had one brother who he sort of saw and one brother who he never saw. I think we were his family. The Heartbreakers is kind of the family unit for all of us. Because, since we were kids, this has been the hearth. The Heartbreakers. And I don't think any of us had much family outside of the group. We always questioned, did we do enough for him? Did we help him? And I think we did. We tried so hard to pull him away from that. It's such a strong drug, such an evil drug. I mean, it just took *years* to kill him. It's kind of like in that last year, we kind of knew it was going to kill him. You just had to look at him to know it was going to kill him. We were all very prepared for it.

You were?
Yeah. We knew he was going to die. We kicked him out of the group. That was the last thing we could do to tell him to wake up. It got to be where we felt we were enabling him. All we were doing was keeping a steady stream of money coming in for him to live that life. And we thought that maybe if he lost the group, he'd have to get his shit together. And we got him to go to rehab. But he just wouldn't stick with it. Then, of course, you know heroin makes you a fabulous liar. So it was kind of hopeless. But I do miss him, and I loved him, and we all did. He was a great musician.

It's hard to believe there was such pain in his life, because he belonged to one of the world's greatest rock bands.
Yeah. That's something you really have to do. You have to say, "Hey, life is great. I mean, we're really lucky boys. Look how great things are." Because you don't see it that way day to day. You get kind of caught up in life. You need somebody in your life to remind you. I have [my wife]

Dana to tap me on my shoulder, and say, "Hey, this problem really isn't that great. Take a look around. Things are really great." I don't think he had that person that cared about him in that way. I think there were people who said they did, but I don't think they really did. Maybe I'm wrong, but you need that so much. You need somebody.

It's such an unusual life we've been through. And such an *extraordinary* one, in so many ways. But you're still a person. Success is never going to make your life simple. It's everything that it's cracked up to be, but it's not going to simplify the fact that you're a human being trying to live on the planet with other people [Laughs] and you want to be happy. It's not going to do that. You have to do that.

It reminds me of your great line from "Crawling Back To You": "Most things that I worry about/Never happen anyway..."
[Laughs] Yeah, I like that line. Well, worry is just thinking about something that hasn't happened yet. That's what some wise person said. [Laughs] I think it was Deepak Chopra. Thinking about something that hasn't happened. But I still do it all the time.

Do you?
Yeah. It's human nature. We all worry.

There are those who think that when you are a successful rock star, like you, that there are no worries. That's it's just perpetual paradise.
[Laughs] Right. There are people who think if you are a rock and roll star you just run up onstage, and have an arena full of people love you, and then you go off and party and do it again. That's just not the truth. There's a lot involved with what we do. We work really hard at what we do. It's more than a full-time job.

Is it?
Yeah. I'm only, at this point in my life, getting a little time off. [Laughs] I'm having to learn how to live life when there's *nothing* going on. I go completely besides myself. Like "What are we going to do?" Dana says, "We're just going to relax. We're just going to relax." I'm used to, at 4:00, we go to sound check. [Laughs]

You've been on a constant schedule of writing, recording, touring, doing promo, and doing it again. It just keeps going for years.
And Heartbreakers has become a big business over the years. There's a big business to keep an eye on. There's publishing, and merchandising, and you name it. It just goes on and on. If I let it, it can consume me. There's just so much stuff to deal with.

You get involved with all that stuff?
Oh, yeah, yeah.

Because we think you have managers, and business managers, to deal with that stuff for you, so you can stay creative and think about music.
Yeah, and then you don't have any money one day. [Laughs] I am very involved—always have been—in our management, and how the group's presented. And really every aspect of it. I do have a business manager, and a longtime relationship with Tony [Dimitriades] and Mary [Klauzer], our managers, that does allow me to step away and be creative. But you've always got to step back in, too, and take a look at what's going on, and say, "This is how I want it to be done." They call me a control freak.

Do they?
Tony does. He says, "You're just a complete control freak." But it's not really being a control freak. I just want us to be presented in the way I want to. If we're Kentucky Fried Chicken, I'm the Colonel on the bucket. It it's being done in my name, I really want to see that it's being done the way I want it done. But I can't always do that. It's bigger than me. But I do try to keep an eye on the business. That's a lot of what I'm doing this year: just catching up on running the Heartbreaker empire. [Laughs]

The website, that's a whole other thing. Like this interview, I wanted to do it just to have a chance to speak to everyone. Say, "Look, here's where we're at, and here's what's going on." Because you don't really get a chance to. And they probably have a lot of questions.

I'm particularly excited about the idea of websites. I think there's *so* much you can do that hasn't been tapped yet. It's such a perfect way of delivering music, and really giving things to the hardcore fans, giving them extra things that they might be interested in more than the casual fan. And that's a business, as well. You have your store, and your merchandise, and your records. But I think it can actually be an artistic enterprise. But what the problem with it is that it takes so much time to get all that together, and if you're playing as many dates as we do, and in the studio as much as we do, and somebody says, "Hey, how about the website?" you just get a groan of "Uh-huh. It's not time to deal with the website." But that's something that I want to work on this year. I want to work on it a little bit, and try to bring it up to speed.

For my birthday, Dana asked me what I wanted for my birthday. I told her I wanted to go to the record store, and be allowed to stay there as long as I can. Because when I go to the record store, everyone usually wants to leave before me. But I said, "On my birthday, I want to be able to shop for as long as I want." So I went there, and I stayed for two and half hours. And I just bought a huge amount of records. They had to get me a box.

You buy new music and old music both?
Yeah. I buy anything that strikes my fancy. That's one of the nice things, the nicest thing, [Laughs] really, about being wealthy in a way, is to do that. Because that's *such* a luxury. Because I grew up pretty poor. I used to go to the dumpster and get bottles out to cash them in, any way I could, to buy an album. And now I can afford it. And I think it's a good thing, because you're putting money back into the industry. I think it's a good way to support the industry, and it's so much fun. So I love to do that.

I've always had the feeling that free records don't sound as good as the ones you buy. Because you're not rooting for them. [Laughs] If you *bought* it, you really want it to be good. So you're sitting down and really rooting for this thing. Whereas if somebody sends it to you, or gives it to you, which is something that happens in the music business, I don't really like to get them that way. I'd rather buy them. I often say, especially with my friends, "No, I'm going to the store so I can buy it."

Are there any new bands or artists you like?
Not incredibly new. I like the White Stripes. I think they're good and they're really starting to hit their stride. I like a lot of different kinds of music. I listen to all kinds.

Do you listen to jazz?
Just the classic stuff. I don't really listen to any new jazz. I buy a lot of old albums. I love the older stuff. I think that's where my heart is. I'm still working my way back. [Laughs] You know I go further and further back trying to find stuff I missed, or stuff I always wanted to hear but never really got the chance to. There's *so* much music.

You know I'm doing a series of radio shows now for the XM satellite channel. It's going to be *Tom Petty's Buried Treasures*. It's going to be hour-long shows of music I put together by whoever. I've got eight shows completed already. Mostly old music.

With an eye to turn people on to stuff, especially younger people, who might not have heard this stuff. And it's a lot of fun.

XM radio is pretty cool, because you can get a whole show of great songs.
I love it. It sounds terrific, too. If you're going to have that many choices, you might as well have them all. [Laughs] You know? I drove all the way out into the desert on this trip we took, and we were in the car for four hours or so, and I was completely entertained all along without ever putting in a CD. Just by going through the channels and listening to stuff. Yeah, I think it's terrific. I think radio needs to see something exciting come along. I think it's exciting.

One of the things that *The Last DJ* touched on is that record companies don't take artists and nurture and develop them like they once did. So that every year there seems to be a bunch of new artists, but none of them stay around very long.
Yeah. I think it reflects the culture we're in. We're in a culture of short attention spans. There's a lot more media than there used to be. There's a lot more specific areas to go for music. Like you don't just turn on the radio and hear everything. You go to a specific place for different kinds of music.

And that's so expensive, to nurture a group. It's really expensive. With us, for at least a year before we had any record out, the record company completely supported us. They paid our rent, bought our food. We lived as employees. We were just taken under their wing, and given a studio to work in, and we developed, and learned our craft. And they stuck with us. Though we were kind of unusual in that our first record became a hit. And we continued to have hits. So, when you're in that situation, they *really* nurture you.

But I also know people the [record company] didn't just drop, though they didn't have a hit. Because it isn't always about having a huge hit record. If you're an artist, you're going to go through periods when sometimes you're doing stuff that's completely valid, but maybe not commercial. I think that is kind of vanishing, where they want success or they don't want you at all. Maybe it's easier to bring along the next new thing than to take a chance on somebody coming back with something again.

But I think it hurts in the end. Because I don't think the artist develops a relationship with the audience. I always felt we had an audience that kind of knew us. And that's how I felt about the artists I admired. I felt I knew them, and that I was taking the ride with them. Though I think maybe now it's a bit more quick-fix than that. The result is that you see these artists who are maybe really successful *record* artists, but they can't sell 3,000 tickets. Because the audience doesn't really know them, or trust them, to that extent. So good things still come along. And I think the audience is really happy with it. And maybe some day it will turn around to where the record companies will see the value in development. But I don't really know. It's beyond me now.

You now have such an enormous repertoire of songs. Even if you chose only hits, that's still too many songs to play in one show.

Inevitably, after every show, there's someone who's upset that you didn't play this or that. But you're going to be there forever if you play everything. Plus, we want to keep ourselves interested. So I kind of try to rotate as much as I can in the show, and at the same time I want the show to be good every night. And I want it to have a pace.

Because everybody doesn't travel from Detroit to Cleveland to see the next show. [Laughs] But the fifty people who did are, like, "Hey! This is the same thing I saw last night." Well, yeah it is, because a lot of these people didn't get to see the show the night before.

How do you keep yourself interested in doing the same songs each night? Do you change the arrangements?
Yeah, they vary tour to tour a little bit in how you play them. We have, fortunately, such a large catalogue of popular songs that we can actually rotate them year to year, or tour to tour. The next tour I do I'm thinking of doing a completely different set of music. That I think would still be popular songs, but maybe the second rung, so that they're not so overplayed. But that's way down the line. Tours. I don't know how many I can do.

And you'll have another new album by that time, right?
Yeah, that's the idea.

Speaking of second-rung songs, I wish you would do "Two Gunslingers," which is a great song. I love that line "I'm taking control of my life now."
[Laughs] We've done that song occasionally. On rare occasions. I used to do it alone. I used to just go out and do it on guitar. It was fun to do.

Another great one is "All The Wrong Reasons," also from the *Into The Great Wide Open* album. It's got great lyrics, and a beautiful melody.
Benmont [Tench, the keyboardist] likes that song. [Laughs] He brought that up recently, that that would be a good one to play.

Would you consider playing it?
Yeah. I'd play anything, really. I don't mind. You can do a whole show of hits, and people really love it. But you do strive to fit other things in there, as well. I don't think you'd want to do a show where there are no hits. I think people would be disappointed. I'm from this school of wanting to please the audience. [Laughs] And I know there are people that don't really see that as an artistic endeavor. But I do. It's worth doing. [Laughs] But you do have to be very careful. You want to offer them new things, too, and you want to challenge them a little bit, too. I think you always want to give them something that has a little bit of a challenge for the audience. And then by the time you get to the end of the show, they feel as if they've been somewhere. You know? We've been somewhere at the end of this music event. We've heard a *lot* of music, and we've heard a lot of different kinds of music, and different

textures. And we've been somewhere. And then, by the end, we can all party and hear the big hits [Laughs] or whatever.

But getting the program for a show down is really important. And the pacing of a show is very important. I'm talking about arena shows. I guess in a bar you can do whatever you want. In an arena, where you're playing to a really large crowd, and they're some distance away from you, there's an *art* to it. Of how do you that, and how you make it work. And we're really good at it. We're one of the best at it.

Are there any songs you will never perform?
I don't think so.

You told me once you didn't want to play "You Got Lucky" again.
You know what, though? We did that, and I really enjoyed it. I was surprised. See, you just don't know. Sometimes we'll go back to a song and I'll go, "That's a good one." [Laughs] Sometimes you've got to go away from them for a while. But nothing just leaps to mind that I don't want to play. "Breakdown" I don't want to play very often. I think because, early in our career we played it *so* much, I think I relate it to being twenty-five. It doesn't feel like a song I would sing now. But never say never. That's one we don't play very much. Hardly ever.

It's such a great song.
Yeah, it is. It's a great little record. When I hear it on the radio, I really like it.

You said earlier that you can't make a good record without a good song. But can you take a good song and not make a good record out of it?
Make a bad record out of a good song? Yeah, that could happen. I could see how you can do that. Well, the good thing about the studio is that you can fix anything. As opposed to life, where you can't. I think I like the studio so much, because just about anything can be fixed. You can find a way to make it work. If you're patient. I think I'm much better at making records than I used to be. I don't know if I'm *better*, but I know it's easier to make a record than it used to be. I'm *much* better at the whole thing, at the craft of putting one together.

Because it used to be that we didn't really know how it was done, and we were just kind of hoping. And fumbling through the dark. And, fortunately, some good stuff got made. Now I think, as record producers, we're much sharper than we used to be. We can do it much quicker than we used to, and it's more fun that way. Because it's not so much fun to labor over a song for months and months in a studio.

It can get tedious.
Yeah. "Refugee" was a good one hundred takes. It went on for days, weeks, months. You know, of coming back to it. It was a really hard record to get. I think if that song came along now, and we wanted to make the record, we'd make it really quickly, it would take us a day or two. But back then it took us a long time. I think we're just better record-makers now. We know more about what not to do. What to leave out. We know as a group the *minute* something wrong happens. "*Wrong!* Don't do it!"

We'll usually run through something. Before we're going to do many takes. Maybe the first take we do, or the second, we'll go in and listen to it. And then everybody will make their notes. Like, "This ain't working." Or, "This bit *is* working. Let's concentrate more on this." Or maybe there's not enough space. Maybe you should not play as much, or you should play more, or *whatever.* Or the tempo should change. But that's a good thing to do before you spend an hour playing the song, and you're all beat on it.

You seem to be in great shape. Do you regularly work out?
Yeah, I'm fifty-three now, and I have to work out a lot. I'll work out five or six times a week. Because it's so physical. The show is physical. And the traveling, [Laughs] and everything. I always say, "Teenagers would drop in my wake." [Laughs] Sometimes life really starts to go fast. And you really run. It's not unusual for us on a day on the road to wake up in one town, fly to the next town, do the sound check and the show, and then get back in the jet, and fly to the next town. So, by the time you go to bed, you're in the third city that day. I defy many people to do it. [Laughs] It really takes a lot out of you. That's one of the things I always laugh about when people think, "Oh, your job is just jumping up onstage and playing." Try doing 150 plane rides in three months.

What kind of workouts do you do?
I box, mostly. I box a heavy bag, and lift weights, and various other things. I have to be a little more diligent with it now than I used to.

Does staying in shape physically help the songwriting, too?
I think it helps everything. To stay mobile and physically fit helps everything. It helps your state of mind. Nobody wants a big fat Tom Petty out there. [Laughs]

I've heard you don't like to talk about the *Echo* album, because it was such a dark period for you. But that's a great album. It really holds up.
You know, that was my position for a long time. I didn't listen to *Echo*. That was one of the worst periods of my life. When I made that record. I was going through a divorce, and really life had just gone to hell. [Laughs] I was having a really hard time. Living alone. Rick Rubin [the producer] swears I wasn't there on that record. Yeah. So that's the best Tom Petty record that Tom Petty wasn't at. [Laughs]

I didn't play it for many years, and then we were driving into town one day, and it came on in the car, because Dana had been playing it, and I started to turn it off, and she said, "No, listen to this." And I did, I listened to it, and I really enjoyed it. It was so much fun, because I had *no* idea what was coming next. It was one of those records during which I had shut down *so* much that I didn't even remember some of the songs.

They came on and I said, "What's this?" I've never done that before. [Laughs]

But then again, there's other things like that. Rick Rubin came by the other day and gave me this boxed set of Johnny Cash. And there's a duet on there of me and Cash singing a Merle Haggard song called "The Running Kind." And it was a really good take, and I have no memory, at *all*, of us doing that. I can't remember it. I guess so much happened in that period, that I don't remember doing it. [Laughs] That's a nice surprise when you hear things like that.

But we did so much recording between *Wildflowers* and the end of *Echo*. There was a lot of recording done, with different projects like the Johnny Cash stuff. I still think that's the best Heartbreakers record. *Johnny Cash Unchained*. It's the best playing we ever did. I *love* that record. And I'm so proud that we did it, and did it so well. And now I guess there's more stuff on the boxed set that's come out. There's nine or ten tracks we did that didn't come out. There was one night in the studio when Carl Perkins was there. And we were recording with Johnny Cash and Carl Perkins. And we had the *best* time. It was just a million laughs, till your ribs hurt. We were just *so* in awe of these guys, Carl Perkins and Johnny Cash, and I felt so great when I was reading the liner notes, and Johnny wrote, "That was one of the greatest nights of my life." And that made me feel so good, because it was really one of mine, too. And I didn't know John felt that way about it.

What a voice he had.
What a *man*.

Was he healthy during that period?
Yeah, he was pretty healthy.

He would get sick at times. He would get very tired. But he was so determined. I know there would be times when he would just stop for an hour, and take a nap. He'd stop for an hour, and then come right back and hit it again. He was determined. Of course, he worked right to the end of his life and left such a great store of music. Just that thing Rick brought me was five CDs of unreleased music. You listen to it, and it's great.

So that was inspiring. That really inspired me to hear that boxed set. 'Cause I kind of struggle in the world with the fact that I'm getting older, [Laughs] and what do I have to offer? If I'm going to keep doing this, I want to make sure I have something to offer. So that kind of inspired me—look at *this* guy. He went much longer and really was relevant all the way out.

You've made great music both during times of great happiness and dark times. You made *Echo* during a dark time, and it's a great album.
Well, I'm glad you think so. It was a dark, dark time and I think some of that is reflected in the music.

I love the song "Counting On You" from *Echo*. It has kind of an R&B chorus, with that line "There's a rumor going round..." It's a great record.
Yeah, "Counting On You." See, that was another one that I forgot about. Why didn't they put that out as a single? That was such a good single. I don't understand why they didn't release that. Why you would release "Room At The Top" as the single, instead?

Well, "Room At The Top" is beautiful, but not a typical single.
It's *de-press-ing*! It's a depressing song. That's one thing that record companies do that kind of weirds me out in this day and age: They don't *listen* much beyond the first track. I kind of feel if I put "Counting On You" as the first track, that would have been the single.

They decide what is going to be the single. And you can go in and say, "No, you're wrong, this is going to be the single." But then you're dealing with a bunch of people who are going, "If this doesn't hit, it's not *my* fault. I told you." [Laughs] So you're kind of damned if you do and damned if you don't. So you try to get behind what they want to do. But I think that record had a lot of good songs. When I heard it recently, I just thought there were a lot of good songs that just didn't see the light of day.

The song "Echo" itself is beautiful. It has a gorgeous melody.
Long song. But it was a good song. But, again, it's not the most upbeat thing in the world.

You thought "Room At The Top" was a depressing song?
Yeah, I thought it was depressing. I thought it was a very lonely, removed song.

It's a nice opener for the album.
Yeah, it made sense to start the record that way. A lot of stuff that we've done, the nicest thing is that you can go back to it and it will hold up. I would be really disappointed if I went back and felt this was crap. And I don't really have that feeling about much of it. The one that annoys me the most is *Hard Promises*. Because I think it's mixed shitty. I would love to go back and mix that record.

But, of all your albums, there's not one somebody could point to and say that its mostly filler. All of your records are packed with strong songs.
You're going to have your songs that stand out more than others. But I think they all serve their purpose. And there's always someone who's going to like a song you didn't dare dream they would.

If your fans wonder what you're going to be doing now, since you're not touring, what is the answer? You're programming the XM shows and working on songs for a new album?
Yeah, I'm almost done with the radio thing now. I think I'm going to do ten. And then we'll see how the show goes.

And my plan now is to start writing and recording. I don't know if we will get a record out this year. I think it will probably be next year. Then I think there will be another side project of putting out a live record. We did a live record in '84 and I never thought it was the great live album that this band should put out. And we've recorded *so* much stuff on the road. Really almost every show we've done on the road for years has been recorded.

It's the project now of Robert Scovill, our sound engineer on the road. He's sorting through these mountains of tapes. And he's going to bring me what he thinks are the best takes of a *lot* of different songs. So that's kind of another project we have going, to get this live album recorded and out at some point. If it went really quick, maybe it would be out this year. But I don't know yet, because I haven't heard it.

When we did twenty nights at the Fillmore, all that was recorded. And we played 120 different songs over the twenty nights. So it could be an exciting thing. But it's just such a *huge* project that, if I was going to get too deep into it, I would never get anything done. So I've got Robert helping me, and whenever he gets it down to twenty or thirty tracks that's when I'll get involved. He's going to give me choices of each song, and a list of songs, and then I think we can get it down to a two-CD album. I think it could be really good.

There's also talk of bringing out *Greatest Hits, Part II.* With maybe a new song on that. These are all things I don't know if they'll happen this year or the next.

Basically, I'm just trying to get The Heartbreakers' house in order. There's been a lot of projects that we'd like to do, but we just never had the time. So we're going to take the time this year. And it's going to be my job to oversee it all. The live album is one thing that has been there and has been neglected for years, because no one wants to take on all that work. And I think that we should make a new record. It's time. And that's always a long process of getting the material and then getting the record done.

To come up with that material, do you have to seclude yourself and get away from everything?

You kind of never stop writing, in a way. I kind of always think about it. I always have the guitar in my hand, and I always think about it. But when I know I'm going to make a record, I kind of dedicate a period of time to it, and sit down and really dedicate myself to coming up with some music that I like, and which is worthy of recording. And that can be a lot of trial and error.

Over the last ten years, I've been writing a lot more than I use. The hardest part of it is that I don't think that I ever write a really bad song. But I write what I call my "A stuff" and my "B stuff." And sometimes the "B stuff" can be really deceiving. You want all "As." So usually there's a lot of stuff written, and it will be demoed up, in most cases.

The Heartbreakers have a clubhouse, with offices, and a stage where we can play. So for a long time we went there every day and played, with no agenda. Just jammed and played three or four hours a day. And it was all recorded. So one of the engineers has brought me several CDs of stuff they mixed down from that. And it's *really* good, some of it. The band would start to play, and I would improvise, and we'd see what we got. There's probably ten or twelve of those things that I would like to put out. But I don't want to put it out as a serious project. I just want to put them out to whoever is interested. [Laughs] So that's another thing.

For quite a while there, between tours, we were going there and playing. We did *The Tonight Show* about four times last year, and we'd used it to rehearse. And then it got to where we said, "Let's just come in every day and play for three or four hours, just to keep our hand in." And it's also a way of kind of exploring thing. Sometimes there would be ten minute jams on things, and then we'd sit and play it all back. And it was fun. And what I want is for people to hear how ridiculously good the band is.

Most of it starts with me playing through a chord progression once on guitar, and then they fall down on it, and you just can't believe how good they are on it. It's *staggering*. I'd really like people to hear it. I think there's a portion of the audience who would really enjoy that. So I think that's the kind of thing I could release through the website somehow.

This is what I would like to see happen with the website. Where it becomes an outlet for music. And there's another idea about making the website a kind of trading post for bootlegs. Because there are so many hundreds and hundreds of bootlegs. I would kind of like to make them authorized. To make a place where all these bootlegs can be attained. Maybe for a membership, you can have as many as you like. [Laughs] If you're really into that sort of thing. So there's a lot of things that I want to get done with the website that I'm going to try to do this year. Not all of my fans will want bootlegs, but, for those who do, I want to have that musical outlet on the website.

You spoke about the "B songs" and the "A songs." Can you ever rewrite a "B" to make it an "A"?

Sometimes. Sometimes they're modular. Sometimes you'll say, "That song isn't really that great, but it has a really great bridge." [Laughs] Or it had a really great set of words in one verse. Maybe take that set of lyrics and try to make it work elsewhere. So sometimes they're modular. Like we're hunting for a middle eight, and you say, "You know what? There was a really good one in this other song, and if we can make it fit into this rhythm, maybe it will work." Sometimes it does, sometimes it don't.

Does the band have much say into what they consider an "A song" or a "B song"?

The Heartbreakers really have never held back having their say about anything. [Laughs] The phrase that comes up is "It's a rough room." [Laughs] "It's a really tough room." They are not short of opinions. Not an easy place. And that's good. For something to survive that room, it's got to be pretty good. 'Cause they're not shy at all about saying, "I don't like it." Between mainly Ben and Mike and myself, there's a lot of opinion in the room. But it's *good*. It's people who have played together since we were really young, and we know each other really well, and they know if I'm working where I should be.

When you write, you like to write alone mostly?
Yeah, pretty much. For *Full Moon Fever* and *Into The Great Wide Open*, I wrote with Jeff Lynne quite a bit, nose to nose, in the same room. We did a lot of writing that way.

Mike [Campbell] and I have never written that way. It's usually by tapes. He'll do his bits, and send it to me.

On a song like "You Wreck Me," which was based on Mike's music, does he give you a track with no singing, or is there a melody?
No, it's just a track. Almost always.

It's interesting, because that song has series of fast-moving cascading chord changes, and the melody just floats over the top of it.
Yeah, that's the good thing about having two people write a song together. I might see a song completely different than he does. There are times when he sent me something, and I wrote the song, and he *liked* it, and he'd say to me, "You know, I had the chorus where you have the verse. It's completely turned around from the way I had it in my head, but I like this way better."

So he'll send me the chords, the basic track, and I'll write to that, and often write a bridge on my own and change a chord or two. But sometimes I don't change them at all. We have never, ever, sat down and tried to write a song together. But, with Jeff, that's how it worked.

With Mike, have you ever given him a lyric first?
No, I've never done that. But that might be an interesting thing to do. [Laughs]

You said "You Wreck Me" took you years before you got it right.
It took a long time. I knew it was there. [Laughs] It just needed to fall into place, the words. It was called "Mike's Song." [Laughs] It didn't have a title for a long, long time.

And then it was "You Rock Me."
Yeah, it was "You Rock Me" for a while. I knew that wasn't going to float. When it changed to "You Wreck Me," the whole song was right there in front of me.

That's a great example of the way one key word can change an entire song.
It really can. You've got to be careful with every line. It makes all the difference.

And if it ain't there, it's worth waiting for.

You spoke about how The Heartbreakers are a great band, which is certainly no new news to your fans, but one great affirmation of that is when you played with Dylan.
Yeah, we've backed up a lot of the great ones by now.

With Dylan, nowadays in concert he'll often do songs which are so changed they are almost unrecognizable now. Did he do that with you guys or would he play his songs the same each night?
He would do that. He would change them from time to time. Though a lot of nights, he would play them the same way. He wasn't as radical as some people say, but some of the times, he would throw something out that we hadn't *ever* played. And you just had to get it, and get with it.

His way of doing shows is really different than ours. He's going after a different kind of thing. On some nights, it can be *really* spontaneous. I always thought, after those shows, that I played a *lot* of music. I'd always go back to the bus, or my room, and just feel completely drained, and I felt like, "*Wow*, I played a lot of music tonight."

But I think Dylan, he did so much for this band. He really took us that extra mile. He made it a band that maybe it wouldn't have become, in a way. He showed us a whole different side of performing, and gave us a lot of courage that I don't think we'd have had. A lot of courage. Like, "Let's do it. Let's just throw this song down and do it."

Or "Let's change directions suddenly." And he's a genius at that.

We did a lot of rehearsing for that. But a lot of times, the show wasn't anything that we rehearsed. I guess it was kind of like working out. You build in your muscle, and then you use it. But we didn't always do what we rehearsed. You learned a whole bunch of songs, and then, when you got to the show, it was a whole different set of songs.

Nowadays you will see him sometimes, and it can be hard to figure out which song he's playing, because he's changed it so much.

Well, he's a riddle wrapped in an enigma. [Laughs] It's hard to talk about Bob Dylan, 'cause I just don't have the answers. It's his vision. He's got one of the great minds of the twentieth century. One of the true geniuses. There aren't many geniuses.

Are there any other messages for your fans that you want to impart that we didn't get to today?

[Laughs] We have really good fans. They've been really loyal. They're the greatest audiences to play to. If you'd never been to one of our shows, I think you'd be surprised at just how frenzied the thing is. It's really exciting, and the adrenaline is just going. Say I do a show at 9:00, it'll be dawn before I come down from it. It will be several hours after it before I really even make sense. I'll pace. I'll just be pacing around, and not really myself for a few hours. And then it will take me a *long* time to go to sleep, and then the process starts over again in the morning. You spend a day gearing to do it, and then a night getting over it.

Is it tough, the day of a gig? Are you comfortable?

Yeah, I've gotten to where I'm pretty comfortable. I don't really get nervous until about an hour before it. And then I have to be alone. It's everybody out of the dressing room. I need this hour to kind of set my mind, and think about what I'm going to do, and get in that frame of mind. But up to then, I'm pretty okay. I've learned not to let that throw me. [Laughs] I'm not going to spend my day worrying about it.

It's a challenging thing to do day after day. You don't feel like doing it every night. That's another thing people don't think about. Some nights you just don't feel like doing it. But as soon as you hear [the audience], you do. You really count on them. And with a group like us, especially, the more they give you, the more you're going to give back. Our band *thrives* on the audience.

But I don't know if people understand what it's like for us. We've never been a band that hangs out after the show and shakes hands. There are a lot of musicians who want to hang out after a show and be told how wonderful they are, but we've never done that. I leave *immediately*. I leave the second the last chord is played.

Why is that?
Because, honestly, if I met you, or talked to you, I wouldn't hear you. I'd be in another place, nodding, smiling, shaking hands and not really listening to you, which gives you kind of a queasy feeling inside. And too much of that will make you nuts. And also I need to get where I'm going. Because I have another town to get to, and I've got to try to get a little bit of sleep before this thing starts again. So that's really the reason we don't hang around.

And I'm actually kind of a shy person. I'm a very private person [laughs]. To be a rock and roll star is an awkward position to put myself in, my particular personality and temperament. I don't do it that well. As far as being in a room with a *lot* of people in it, I get kind of shy and scared. And I don't know, maybe scared is not the right word. Those meet and greet things, *much* to the record company's aggravation, I just never have been able to do it, or do it very well. I see what other acts go through. The amount of stuff they do. To me, it's just far-out stuff. Just the amount of interviews they do. It's far out to me, how they can do that.

When we were young, when we were kids, and we did a town, we'd do three radio shows, and do the show, and stay, and meet all the DJs and everyone. And you can do that for years, but I can't do it anymore. I haven't done it for many years. I kind of like to save all that energy up to get a really great show. If I spend my day talking, I'm not going to sing well that night. You can burn yourself out. So I just like to stay focused on what we came there to do.

Is it ever hard for you to play the old hits, or can you always find a way to connect with the older material?
You know, when you hear that big roar in the first couple of seconds of it, you connect.

That does it.
Kind of. Because you know they want to hear it so bad. So you pretty much connect. [Laughs] I think. If they hated them, I wouldn't connect. But, you know, "American Girl" is probably not what I would go to play if I was playing. But they're clearly just overjoyed to hear it, that you kind of just swing with it. And it's fun.

Songs like that bring back parts of our lives—
And mine. It does the same for me. It brings back a part of my life.

And that song, and others you wrote back then, are still very powerful songs.
It's really a blessing to have those songs. You can't take that lightly, to have such a great catalogue of songs that you enjoy and that hold up. It's really a blessing.

Where did all the great songs come from? Was it hard work, diligence, luck, or more?
I don't know. One at a time they came. I know this: we really loved doing it. We really loved doing it, and still do. It was never like work. It was like we would have done it anyway. It was a really enjoyable thing. I *loved* doing it.

When you did *Full Moon Fever* solo with Jeff Lynne, did you always know you would return to The Heartbreakers?
Yeah. I never ever thought I was going to leave The Heartbreakers. Maybe they did.

Will you do other solo albums?
Yeah, I think I will. I wouldn't be surprised. I think when I did the solo thing and the Traveling Wilburys, [the band] felt a little uncomfortable. You know, "Is he leaving? What's he doing?" I understand that. But I wasn't going to leave. It did me some good to have a little space. And when I came back to the band, I was really happy to be back. So I think that goes on with all of us. I think that's Mike's trip, you know, with his band.

And I don't think he's going to leave The Heartbreakers. I think everybody just needs a little space from time to time.

But we all recognize and really respect what a good band it is. Whether we're angry with each other, or whatever's going on, we all respect *that*. We're not going to rock that boat. [Laughs] Nobody's going to come to the stage and not try to make it the great wonderful Heartbreakers. [Laughs] You know? It's a pretty happy family, after all.

Author interview with Tom Petty, March 31, 2004, Malibu, California

Chapter Eighteen

Tom, Woody, And The Genius Of Simplicity

> His songs are deceptively simple. Only after they have become part of your life do you realize how great they are. Any damn fool can get complicated. It takes genius to attain simplicity.
>
> Pete Seeger, preface to Woody Guthrie's autobiography, *Bound for Glory*, 1943

Although those words, written by the great Pete Seeger, were about his friend and fellow songwriter, Woody Guthrie, they also apply perfectly to the singular genius of Tom Petty. Tom, like Woody, well understood this fundamental truth at the heart of great songwriting. It's something he's known since he was a kid, entranced by perfect singles by Buddy Holly and others that created an entire universe in under three minutes. He realized from the start that it's easier to write a dense, complex song than to write that pure, essential one: that song which says everything and more with the timeless grace of simplicity.

Tom was not only a vastly gifted, creative artist and beloved popular entertainer, but also a master of simplicity, which, in songwriting and record-making, goes a long way. Though influenced and inspired by Bob Dylan, his brilliant big brother in the Wilburys, Tom's songwriting spirit was really much closer to that of Woody, who wrote "This Land Is Your Land" and other classic songs for the people. These songs celebrated, in the spoken language of the people, America's spirit of hope, inclusion, and expansive, natural splendor. And he did it with melodies so simple and sweet that any kid could learn it—and we all did.

Woody and Pete played and wrote folk songs—the songs of the people. It's that world where Dylan came from, imitating Woody and writing his first real song in honor of his idol, "Song For Woody." Tom played rock and roll, but at his core was also a folk singer. His songs, like those of Woody, are folk songs. Songs for the people, about the people, and relatable to their lives. "The worst thing that can happen is to cut yourself loose from the people," Woody wrote in his notebook, which Pete Seeger found and preserved in his book *Pete Seeger In His Own Words*. "And the best thing is to sort of vaccinate yourself right into the big streams and blood of the people. To feel like you know the best and the worst of folks that you see everywhere, and never to feel weak or lost, or even lonesome anywhere."

Tom did that. His music—especially by the time of *Full Moon Fever*—appealed to all ages. Knowing that children grew up loving his music made him happy, he said, "because kids don't lie." He wrote songs for all people: songs in their language and in their own words. He wrote about where he came from—about the South in many songs—confronting directly the ongoing echoes of the Civil War, which still divide America to this day. In the opening verse of his beautiful, epic reflection of his Southern roots, he lays the truth on the line, referencing the "southern accent" where he comes from.

Throughout the years, Tom reflected Woody's genius of simplicity in his writing. Both were savvy songwriters who knew what it took to make a good song, and that simplicity wasn't random—this was something they both honed and developed as time went on.

Take Dylan's "Like A Rolling Stone," Springsteen's "Thunder Road," or "Strawberry Fields" by Lennon, for example. You hear greatness, but you don't hear simplicity. So many of Tom's songs have a simple elegance and a kind of magic charm: "Free Fallin'," "You Wreck Me," "Room At The Top," "Wildflowers," and many others. You get the sense they were almost immaculately conceived. Other songwriters reached that divine place, such as George Harrison with "Here Comes The Sun" or Dylan's "If Not For You." But for those guys these songs were exceptions. Tom did it over and over.

It wasn't accidental. Tom was always keenly sympathetic to the balance of elements in a song. For example, if a verse was heavy or long, he would compensate by ensuring the chorus was simple. He didn't want his songs to be too heavy. They should be, as he said, "light—but not lightweight." A perfect crystallization of this is in the aforementioned "Down South" from *Highway Companion*. The verses are so complete with beautifully rhymed details—such as his love of dressing like Samuel Clemens (aka Mark Twain, one of his heroes)—that he felt the original chorus was too ponderous and needed simplification. So, Tom freely broke the conventional rule of anchoring the chorus around the title. He instead crafted a poignantly tender chorus around a humble request and promise with words of sweet simplicity—both musically and lyrically—that are essentially Tom: he'll give you all he has, and "a little more" if he can sleep on your floor.

In both his songs and his thoughts, as expressed in our conversations and others, Tom's brilliance is reflected in a kind of folk wisdom. He had the rare ability to understand simple, fundamental concepts about songwriting and music-making that many people never grasp. He could also express brilliance, as he did in songs, with whimsical human stories.

Tom was extremely savvy about the craft of songwriting, knowing what he called all the "songwriter tricks" utilized for dramatic effects—such as key changes. He was careful not to use "tricks" that seemed like obvious contrivances—such as dramatic key changes—and understood that craft only matters when it enriches a song, not for its own sake. "Often musicians tell me, 'Tom, you have *got* to hear my new song. I use this chord you would *never* expect to hear in *any* chord progression!' Well, the *reason* you would never hear that in a chord progression is because it doesn't sound good!"

It's a simple concept, yet one so often missed. Many times over the years, Tom reflected this same idea. "If you are working on a song, and you come up with a chord that seems really unusual, like it doesn't fit there, it's because it doesn't. Take it out!" In other words, you're not writing songs to impress fellow musicians. You're doing it to create "something timeless," as he put it, something that sounds great now, and will only sound better tomorrow. His heart was always filled with love for the 45s he got as a kid—full of great, simple three-minute songs. Though he loved Dylan's expansive epics, Tom was always about making great records. This began with inspired and generously invested songs—designed precisely to be records—with the philosophy of "don't bore us, get to the chorus." This was art, but also entertainment.

To be clear, this is not to say Tom used the same chord progressions that had been used many times before. He didn't. His genius shines most overtly to musicians who learn to play his songs and realize—as I have many times—that he was endlessly ingenious with chords. But chords, as he'd be the first to remind you, can only go so far. The chords only matter as much as they support and enable the melody. Tom was one of the great melodists of our time, forever finding new visceral approaches to tuneful expressions of soul. Melody is as ancient as mankind, and still mysterious; primal, timeless and forever linked to our memories of our lives. To this day, scientists know less about how our minds perceive and remember melody, and why they impact us so deeply, than they do about how to get to Mars and back.

Songwriters, entranced by melody since before they could speak, live inside this mystery. I've asked countless legends if they can answer what makes a melody strong. Most can't. Not because they don't know, but that it's something that is beyond words. Literally. Others answered with a riddle, as did Dave Brubeck, who said, "The secret of a melody is a secret."

Tom, however, though always cognizant of the cosmic aspects of his work, broke it down into simple terms, even starting his answer with a statement of simplicity: "I think it's as simple as, can you hum it in your head? Does it do something to you when you hear it? Is it a friendly thing? Do you want to hear it again? Easily said, though not so easily found." And there in that answer is the essence of the songwriter. That a great melody, as he knew intimately, is not someone one invents. It is something one finds. It's a journey of discovery always, enabled by acquired wisdom over the years. Not so easily found. Yet the most one searches, the most treasures found. He never stopped searching. When I mentioned that many of his songs do everything songs can do, and are only about three minutes, he said, "Yeah, that's the idea. If you can do it." He did it countless times.

This ambition was exemplified in the idea, as expressed by Krishnamurti, that limitation creates possibilities. Within this small, restrictive, ancient song form, he could create whole universes. Rather than be limited by the narrow confines of the thing, he was enlivened by the limitless possibilities. He did it, not by reinventing the form or the vocabulary, but by using these elements in ingenious ways. Though he certainly had inborn musical talent, especially for writing great melodies, he educated himself seriously in songwriting the best way there is—by studying the architecture of other songs, a kind of creative reverse engineering that forever enriched his music.

Just as countless songwriters who rose in his wake learned by studying his songs, he delved into the songs of others. His use of simple, repeating chord changes to underpin a compelling melody was something he learned from Buddy Holly. "He could take the simplest chord structure," Tom said regarding Holly, "where it never really moved, and find these incredible melodies." It's a technique Tom used in his most famous song, "Free Fallin'," which repeats the same three-chord pattern over and over, but with one of his greatest and most memorable melodies. The melody, he emphasized many times, and not the chord progression, is what matters most. Although musicians might be impressed by unusual chord usage, people are moved, as they have been for eons, by melody.

But he was forever brilliant in his usage of fresh chord progressions, but always with simplicity and grace. Like Buddy Holly, he worked with the very limited number of chords available, and yet always created new universes. He had a theory that Buddy Holly's greatness can be attributed to a singular song obsession: "I think Buddy got really hooked on the song 'Love Is Strange' by Mickey & Sylvia… I think it had a *huge* influence on him. Because he wrote every derivation of 'Love Is Strange' that you can write. He turned those chords inside out, around, backwards."

As any musician who has played Tom's songs knows well, he did the same thing as Buddy. He took the elemental chords of blues—and rock and roll—and turned them inside out, backwards, and in every variation he could conceive. The one objective never shifted: It has to sound good.

Every piece had to be in place so all considerations, all signs of craft, would fall away. What remains is only that which is essential.

Like Woody, Tom understood the aim in songs was genuine expression, in authentic language, the way real people really speak. Like Woody, who felt the radio airwaves to be sacred, Tom cared deeply about his songs and how they were heard. Forever he fought to ensure that his work retained a pureness of heart and never seemed false or hackneyed.

Tom's hope and intention, although sometimes misconstrued, was that his most personal, specific statements in song would be received as being about all people, not only himself. Although his producer Rick Rubin disagreed, Tom wrote the lyric "You don't know how it feels to be me" not about himself, but about the human condition. That we all feel that way.

Yet personal truth, as all humans come to learn, can both unite and divide people. Even today—headlong into the twenty-first century, more than 150 years past the American Civil War—the North-South divide in America is more pronounced than ever. Tom believed in laying the truth on the line in his lyrics, though he acknowledged it was a line he walked carefully, like a balancing beam, throughout his career.

Tom wrote "Rebels," as he explained, not as a historian, but as a songwriter. It emerged from an expression of reality, as seen through the eyes of a character. It's a song genuinely reflecting that North-South divide, written in the language as it's spoken. Many critics interpreted it not as a reflection, but a true expression of Tom's core beliefs. That same reaction to his work occurred with the release of *The Last DJ*, an entire song cycle condemning the crassness of modern times, with the music industry at its center. That was but one symbol of cultural change that he used, but it was not intended to be his personal attack on the industry. Of course, it was taken that way, so when Tom waved a Confederate flag onstage during "Rebels," the flame of misunderstanding was fanned. He regretted this, and although he knew the potential risk of alienating the multitude of his Southern fans, he did his best to set the record straight. When a fan threw a Confederate flag onstage during the song, he stopped everything and said, "*Look*, this was to illustrate a character. This is not who we are. Having gone through this, I would prefer it if no one would ever bring a Confederate flag to our shows again, because this isn't who we are."

Who we are, Tom felt, was Americans. Like Woody, he had a genuine reverence for America and its promise. That flame of hope, which has periodically dimmed, still persists in shining, and is woven through his songs—from the first to the last. From his final album, *Hypnotic Eye*, came a sadly revised American dream, "American Dream Plan B." It's not Tom talking in the song. For him, the American dream came true. Beyond true. Yet he knew that most Americans weren't famous rock stars and many could never afford to go to a concert. Like Woody, he never lost touch with the reality of being a real person in America and in the world. He never cut himself off from the bloodstream of the people, and wrote their songs. In one of his final songs, he delivers the new alternate to the old optimistic American dream, painted in the voice of America.

The song he ended his shows with for years—and was the last song he performed live—is an essential, though bittersweet, American anthem. It's about America as a country, the undying American spirit—which reverberates through all his songs—and the eternal yearning for something better in the core of the essential American girl, the one who would never stop thinking, never give up believing that American promise: that something good would be coming, that there was a more to life than just the waiting, and the yearning.

Author article originally published in
American Songwriter *magazine, 2019*

Chapter Nineteen

Tom Petty & The Heartbreakers At The Forum In Los Angeles. October 10, 2014

There were several transcendent moments during Tom Petty & The Heartbreakers' opening-night concert of two at the Forum in Los Angeles on October 10. The first was during what has become Tom's most famous song, "Free Fallin'." It's a song of much vocal range, as Tom leaps to the upper octave for its iconic chorus. And he sang the hell out of it. And the audience was with him, singing along, all united by the love and momentum of a singular song. Rarely, especially since the passing of Pete Seeger, has the power of song been more evident. It's a delicate thing, a song—just words and music combined—though, of course, delivered with enormous power and grace by The Heartbreakers, one of the greatest rock bands of all time. But to witness that—so many thousands of people together, more than the population of most American towns—all bonded in song, was chilling. And beautiful.

It happened again during "U Get Me High," from his most current album, *Hypnotic Eye*. The man simply has a knack for writing great and visceral songs which build and build to ecstatic and singable choruses, and this one does that so powerfully. It showed me that Tom Petty, at sixty-three, many decades beyond that in which many of his peers peaked, is at the top of his game.

He seemed to have a great time. But who wouldn't, playing with musicians of that caliber? A single solo by Benmont Tench—the remarkable keyboardist—or guitar hero Mike Campbell—is enough to make the blood boil. But Tom was also happy to be home, as he joked to the crowd. "Great to be here at the fabulous *Forum*," adding that he first played there in 1980. Expounding, he explained that although his band met up in Gainesville, and formed in 1975, that it was here in Los Angeles they truly came together, and have remained ever since.

"So I'd say we're an LA band," he announced, to a much understandable ovation from the crowd. He then added, "All our friends, family—they're all here tonight. Ex-wives, girlfriends... Everybody I owe money to is backstage."

He then informed the crowd this would be an "industrial strength, extra length" show, and suggested those who needed to should inform their babysitters.

In fact, since the great Stevie Winwood opened with a full set, and Tom didn't start till after nine, he played just over two hours. Not Springsteen or Grateful Dead length. And as with every concert this man gives—due to the sheer and staggering profusion of great songs he has written over these years—including all the hits and all the strong songs that weren't hits—he can't ever do every Tom Petty song you love. He also wants to inject new songs into the mix, and as *Hypnotic Eye* is one of his most popular albums ever, that made a lot of sense.

So we didn't get famous ones like "You Got Lucky," "The Waiting," "You Don't Know How It Feels," "Stop Draggin' My Heart Around" or "Don't Come Around Here No More." But we did get wonderfully burning renditions of ones we didn't expect, like "Yer So Bad," "So You Wanna Be A Rock'N'Roll Star" [the show's opener, written by Roger McGuinn and performed by the Byrds, one of Tom's most favorite bands], as well as a tribute to the recently departed Paul Revere, "Stepping Stone," a song made more famous by The Monkees, but which was first recorded, as Tom reminded us, by Paul Revere & The Raiders, "who made great singles," Tom said. (He knew his stuff.)

He also introduced the new album with its grunge-rock opener, "American Dream Plan B," one of many songs which touch on the dark side of modern America while also allowing Mike Campbell to show why he is so revered. His rhythm part—pure Nirvana grunge—explodes into remarkable, burning leads. Like Keith with Mick, Mike is tuned into Tom's every move, every measure—and is his ideal counterpoint, remarking on the lyrics with great, arch lead lines and powerful rhythm parts. Tom even took several guitar solos himself through the night, walking around the stage while bending notes like one of the two gunslingers in his song of that title, while Campbell took over rhythm guitar duties.

And though I know well many Heartbreakers purists still miss Stan Lynch in the drum chair, there's no missing just how powerful Steve Ferrone is, the engine that keeps this big train moving forward, locked beautifully into Ron Blair's bass lines. Ferrone, Tom announced, is the newest member of the band; this is, remarkably, his twentieth year with the band.

And while all Pettyheads will debate song choice, there's no mistaking that the man presented a wide range of his work—from very early anthems like "American Girl," which closed the show, through songs from solo work such as "I Won't Back Down" to the classic "Rebels" from *Southern Accents* to the wonderful "Mary Jane's Last Dance" and Tom's tribute to open-ended thinking, "Into The Great Wide Open."

And from the new album, we also got Tom's reflection on his own legacy, "Forgotten Man," and on those vampires who still populate Ventura Boulevard and elsewhere, "Shadow People."

The sound at the Forum is so necessarily huge that it does become not unlike a giant airplane roar in a metal hangar, so that although we could sometimes see Benmont playing away on piano, we couldn't always discern it that well. But Mike Campbell's lead and rhythm parts came through with authority and grace, and the vocals throughout were strong and stellar. As Tom has said, getting your vocal part right always matters a lot in this band. It's the reason he got the late great Howie Epstein in on bass when Ron Blair left the band. Howie was a fine bassist, but also a very gifted harmony singer.

Now Tom has his good pal Scott Thurston in the band, who fills in all the parts nobody else can cover—harmonica lines, keyboard pads, guitars electric and acoustic, and especially vocal harmony parts throughout.

When Tom and the boys started out in 1975, it was evident that he had greatness in him. But would it last? Whereas so many of his peers from them faded in many ways, he's only gotten stronger over the years, and at 63 rocks as hard as he ever has. It gives us all hope. And he seemed to be having a great time, and rejoicing in his ability to unite a small town like this with the power of song. Long may he rock.

Author article originally published in American Songwriter, *October 14, 2014*

Chapter Twenty
Hypnotic Eye

Exultant. A masterpiece. Tom rocks through this album with the great Heartbreakers, and does the unthinkable for most songwriters of his age: he's written some of the best songs of his life.

Much more common, as we all know, is for a songwriter to peak in his twenties, and never match the greatness of their first work. Not so Mr. Petty, who started with greatness and has continued to ascend over the decades, while so many of his peers aren't even in the game anymore. It is remarkable at any age to write great songs. But at this age, and after so much success, it's triumphant.

Produced by Tom and Mike Campbell with Ryan Ulyate (who also recorded and mixed), it's an album of much disquiet, of superstition, corruption and evil unchecked, leavened only by the limitless power of love. It's also an album of much beauty and fury. Even in the bluesy songs comes a chorus of exultant tunefulness, reminding us that the man knows how to construct a song. He knows how to speak to our hearts and our minds at the same time. Though even those he loves, it seems, are not always on his side. The result is one of his strongest and most focused collection of exceptional songs.

But you don't have to take my word for it. Listen to "Faultlines," a great essential new song for the uneasy emotional landscape which is Los Angeles, using the constant threat of total disaster—an earthquake—as a symbol for the disquiet of love. Which wouldn't be great, of course, without a killer groove and great tune. It's another gem he wrote with Mike Campbell, who gives Tom tracks to which Tom writes lyrics and a tune. Some of these have been famously passed on, and handed off to other hitmakers, so that both Henley and Hornsby have had hits with

Tom's discards. Wisely, he didn't pass on this one, and instead created one of the best songs ever about this city, and the romances which are born, and sometimes die, here at the most western edge of this continent. As far west as you can go, wrote Jack Kerouac, before you fall into the ocean. And Tom, who lives right on the ocean, having come all the way from Florida, understands this Californian dynamic: when you live forever on top of active faultlines, love, like our city, can falls through the cracks.

It all starts with grunge. The opening song "American Dream Plan B," (the title says it all, time for an alternate plan as that first big one doesn't seem to be working out) is launched by a grungy electric rhythm guitar, as if Tom plugged into a tiny amp, distorting in the rawness of the night. It's a song about endurance, about holding onto the dream against all odds. This isn't Tom Petty narrating, it's an American struggling with the modern American struggle—recognizing one's own weaknesses while resolutely not giving up the fight.

The sound is essential and great. I know well how some fans of The Heartbreakers—purists, sure—will never be happy with Steve Ferrone, and still want old Stan Lynch behind the drums. But there is no denying the great sound of Ferrone's snare slams—except for John Molo and Ringo Starr, there is no drummer who so masters the greatness of the cracking snare backbeat—it falls right between the rhythm guitar bursts, and is eloquent and right. This is Tom Petty raw, and it's great.

The Heartbreakers. They are distinguished for the greatness of their playing. It was good fortune—serendipity maybe—that brought deeply gifted players like Benmont Tench and Mike Campbell into his world even before he jettisoned Florida to make it big in LA. Tench, a child prodigy, could play all of *Sgt. Pepper* on the organ as a kid, and those chops have just grown more soulful and resplendent over the years. And Mike Campbell is simply one of the world's great rock guitarists, a master of burning, eloquent solos always, sometimes on slide, sometimes not—and visceral, raw guitar riffs perfect for fueling a song. Never too much, his choices always resound with purity; he's one of the most tasteful guitarists around. Not to mention the fact that he's a great songwriter whose singular focus on music and groove results in wonderfully powerful, if sadly dark, songs.

Then the tempo shifts and speeds up, that Ferrone snare still the engine driving this train—and we are in "Faultlines." Built around a great and slinky riff by Mr. Campbell, this is the essence of The Heartbreakers: all momentum, forward motion, perfect for this lyric of the ground breaking open physically and spiritually. Then on the chorus, on "I've got a few of my own faultlines running under my life," we get the great sweetness of Heartbreakers harmonies, and the effect of this rawness and sweetness fused is visceral and poignant. It's a familiar sound—Tom's reedy voice enriched by other voices in perfect harmony (being a great harmony singer always mattered as much in The Heartbreakers, Tom said, which is why the late Howie Epstein got the job)—and makes us feel good even in this uneasy panorama where the earth can open up—figuratively and literally—and swallow up your life at any moment. It is that knowledge of foreboding cataclysm which lies at the center of this work.

"Red River," a mysterious and beautifully detailed and lovingly melodic if furious song, invites an especially superstitious woman to meet the singer at the Red River to "look down into your soul," with lyrics that bring to mind Steely Dan's brilliant "Two Against Nature" with its arcane admixture of spooky, black magic ingredients, spelling the length to which a soul will go to protect or inspire one's self. We get a great American blend of the accepted holy and unholy ("she's got a rosary and a rabbit's foot") all of which leads to the same place, the unceasing unfolding of our lives. The true source of peace, not unlike Springsteen's answer, is the river itself, the flow, the force of real life.

"Sins of My Youth" starts with a beautifully arpeggiated minor guitar chord on an electric, the ideal opening to this plaintive ballad of reflection. It's a coming to terms song, a stated understanding that present love means more than all those endless nights of youthful indulgence, sung inside a weary but beautiful tune.

"Power Drunk" is one of his most explicit and forceful songs about the one percent, those in this society that allow their own status to overwhelm any internal moral compass. With classic sinewy Mike Campbell lead lines weaving together the vocal lines, we get Tom telling us of how power corrupts forever.

"U Get Me High" is a great love song using this play on herbal fun to apply instead to love, replete with a resplendent Petty melody. Though the title might seem lightweight in print, when Tom sings it, it goes straight to the heart, and the meaning isn't just clear, it is overt. That there is only one place to look for a real high, something that will last and be there for strength when needed.

"How am I gonna tell her I love her/When words don't mean a thing?" (from "Full Grown Boy"). Well, one way is writing a song. It's the reason songwriters become songwriters. Without music, these words just don't mean as much. Put a great groove and heartrending melody in there, and it suddenly means a lot. As Jackson Browne said, songwriting is a forgiving medium. Not forgiving the songwriter for not writing more lucid words, but forgiving of what is not stated. Music fills in the gaps. Something about the momentum and grace of music and rhythm combined adds a whole level of meaning to lines that, in conversation, might seem nonsensical. When he sings, in "Full Grown Boy," "the full moon seems to know me," we are right with him. Even if we are with him in different ways, according to what the full moon means to us. It's the beauty of song.

"Burnt Out Town" is a half-time shuffle punctuated by perky harmonica exhortations, leading Tom to narrate with spoken words at first, answering a woman who asks him why he looks so down. The answer is this burnt out town—but this town seems to extend to all of America more than his adopted Angeleno home.

As always, these dark tales are illuminated by wonderful musical moments, such as the drum and harmonica breaks here, which separate us musically and remind us, regardless of everyday American reality, of the redemption inherent in music.

It all comes to a close with "Shadow People," which starts with solo piano and leads the listener to believe we are going to close this one, as he does others, with a piano ballad. But then the grungy and slinky guitar riffs and rhythms enter, and we are on still shaky ground, ready to break open. It brings to mind the famous vampires on Ventura he sang about back in the day in a previous incarnation, in which the city is peopled at night by dark and sinister souls. Now those shadow people are out in the open, in the light of day, darkening everything they touch with infectious fear and foreboding. It's about people who have internalized the shadows cynically used to scare them, so that they isolate themselves ominously—even in big cities—with a kind of fear that destroys all it can't understand.

It ends with an elegy, just Tom solo with an acoustic guitar, after The Heartbreakers have gone home, with this last rather ambiguous vision of the end, the shadowless sun, straight overheard. Or is it the beginning? It's a beautiful and portentous ending to one of his greatest works.

Author article originally published in American Songwriter *magazine, 2014*

Chapter Twenty-One

The Beatles On *The Ed Sullivan Show*

The last time I interviewed Tom was in 2014. I wrote several pieces for the website of the Grammys in honor of the fiftieth anniversary of The Beatles' famous first appearance on American TV, on The Ed Sullivan Show *on February 9, 1964. I interviewed several artists about the impact this had on their lives for little individual pieces, and was encouraged to invite Tom to do one. I didn't know if he'd want to, but it was The Beatles after all, and a momentous occasion. Fifty years! Tom's world was rocked forever that night. Still, I did not know if he would want to do this. But I called Mary Klauzer, who—unlike most other managers, as well as most of the humans I know—always delivers a clear and decisive answer. She called back quite quickly, as she has at other especially exultant moments in my life, with good news. Tom said yes.*

We did it over the phone. As always, it was heartwarming to hear that distinctively friendly voice. I thanked him for doing this.

He said, warmly, "I did it because it was you." I'll always remember that.

For the version published on the website, I removed my questions to put it all into Tom's words, as was the template for this series. But for this book I went back to the restored interview with the questions still intact, to match the conversational spirit of this book.

It's well known what a profound impact The Beatles made on your life. Can you remember how seeing them this first time struck you?

TP: Yeah, *that* I can remember. I was thirteen, and already somewhat of a music fan. This was the great moment in my life, really, that changed *everything*. I had been a fan up to that point. But this was the thing that made me want to play music. Because you *saw* that it could be done. There could be a self-contained unit that wrote, recorded, and sang songs. And it looked like they were having an *awful* lot of fun doing it.

Did your whole family watch?
Not really. I watched it with my little brother. My mom and dad were there, but they weren't interested in it. They laughed at it and left the room. But my brother and me, both of us, we just *flipped out*. We thought it was the greatest thing ever.

I was only six then, but I remember it perfectly, too. It was electrifying. Unlike anything we'd seen before and way better. People who weren't alive then don't know the context of that time, so soon after JFK's assassination. It gave us a reason to be happy again.
Yes. It's very hard for people to understand how monolithic it was, looking at it today. But it was absolutely *earthshaking*. These weren't days when you had rock and roll on television very frequently at all. And [The Beatles] were so ready for it. They're so professional, and they have their act so down. Their presentation is beyond compare. It's *amazing*, when you watch it now, how aware they are of where the cameras are, and what to do. And their songs were just fantastic, and so original. They were the right people at the right time at the right spot with the right songs.

America was never quite the same after that.
Yeah, absolutely. Culturally, it changed everything in America, and probably the world. The influence on every part of our lives was huge, from social issues to fashion issues to music issues. From that point on, The Beatles were the North Star for me and my generation. And we're *very* blessed to have had them.

I know that vision of a band, which they presented, as opposed to a solo performer—really spoke to you and shaped your dreams.
Yes. Very much so. Because, before The Beatles, there were a lot of singers, like Elvis. But it was really great to see a real *band*. I had seen bands around town before, but I never saw one that really did *everything*,

that was a vocal group and an instrumental and songwriting group. I also got the idea of writing songs from then. Writing songs had never occurred to me before them. I knew that they wrote their songs. I had the little single "I Want To Hold Your Hand," with "I Saw Her Standing There" as the B-side. Before I saw them, with that great photo of them on the front in the gray collarless jackets. "Lennon/McCartney" was prominent under each title, so I knew that they wrote the songs. It made it all seem possible suddenly. And I said, "Hey, this can be done. You just need four guys who can play their instruments. And, if we do this, we can have a great time."

Really, within weeks of that show, you began to hear the sounds of garage bands on the weekends leaking through the neighborhood—of kids out in the garage playing. And it became my mission to find an electric guitar, and to meet friends who could play with me. And that happened rather organically. So many people were doing it.

It's interesting that you saw in them the ultimate of what a band can be, and you created your career and your band based on that template: Great musicians who are also friends and cool people, writing your own songs, making great singles and records, and dynamic rock and roll shows. Even their great harmony singing, which, as you said, was always important in The Heartbreakers.

Yes. You've got to sing your part right in The Heartbreakers. Back then, though, I don't think I really knew what harmony was. I didn't know how they did it. But I loved the sound their voices made. I would learn these things from trial-and-error situations with my friends playing. We eventually figured out how to make that sound, and what a harmony was.

Back then, everyone didn't have a guitar. Not like now, where anyplace you go, there's a guitar. It was a different world then. Fender sold themselves to CBS that year because the demand [for] guitars just overwhelmed them.

If you talk to any musician my age, I think we'd all tell you—especially the American ones—that night had a profound effect on the rest of [our] lives. It did have a great profound effect on my life, and I thank them for that. I still think The Beatles [made] the best music ever, and I'm sure I'll go to my grave thinking the same thing.

There will never be another moment like it, I don't think, in music. I don't think you could have another moment like that, because of the innocence of the audience. That innocence doesn't exist anymore. It was just a really great time to be alive, to be a teenager, and to experience that.

It should be celebrated, and I'm glad there's so much attention being given to it. I think that everyone in America with an electric guitar should all hit an open *E* chord at eight o'clock on February 9. I'm gonna do it.

Author interview with Tom Petty, 2014

Chapter Twenty-Two

Tom Petty & The Heartbreakers At The Hollywood Bowl

I wrote this review of his final show not knowing, of course, it would be his last. Given that, my closing sentences seem now especially poignant: "Long live Tom Petty & The Heartbreakers. Long live rock and roll."

It felt more like a party than a concert. The very last leg of what Tom called a "*really* long tour," that started back in April, it delivered a Petty even more exultant that usual. Delightfully gregarious hosting this big party, he seemed happier than he's ever been in concert, beaming with infectious joy from the first chord onward. Sounding positively giddy when talking to the crowd, especially when extolling the greatness of The Heartbreakers and sharing unprecedented tales of his great fortune at meeting them all.

Hearing the ecstatic tone of his speaking voice, one nearby audience member wondered aloud, "Is Tom Petty *drunk*?"

To which came the immediate answer: "Drunk on *rock and roll, dude*!"

Indeed. Tom and the band's connection with the original juice of rock and roll remains so vital and pure that all of these shows have transcended spectacle to become inspirational celebrations of rock and roll itself. Unlike other famous bands who transformed into little more than summer jukeboxes, churning out hits with little more soul then Karaoke singers, The Heartbreakers never allowed their rock and roll flag to fade. With unparalleled musicians such as Mike Campbell on guitar and Benmont Tench on keyboards, two of the greatest players to ever empower an American band, each show is a joyful and electric journey directly into the still beating heart of rock and roll.

Add to that band the monumental Steve Ferrone on drums, original Heartbreaker Ron Blair on bass, Scott Thurston on a multitude of instruments (harmonica, keyboard, guitars and more), and for the first tour ever, added harmony vocalists, the Webb Sisters, singing and dancing up a storm, and you have a rock and roll show unlike any other, as incendiary and also delicately dynamic as Tom's songs themselves, and every bit as real. Which is what it all comes down to. This is the real deal. Tom learned long ago this stuff can't be faked, not the songwriting, not the musicianship, not the shows. If it is fake, the audience knows. And they also know what is real. Which is why this man and this band remain beloved through four decades of making music.

As his devoted fans know well, Tom replaced original drummer Stan Lynch back in 1994, not because Tom found his drumming inadequate. He didn't. But simply because they didn't get along. (When I asked him if he and Stan fought about the music, Tom laughed and said, "No, we fought about everything!")

So to preserve his own sanity and preserve the passion, Tom replaced Stan, which was not easy for him. The man who got the job was Steve Ferrone, who had previously drummed for everyone from Johnny Cash through Clapton, Slash and Scritti Politti. He was the ideal choice. A man of great joy and calm, his groove is so precise and yet funky at the same time that the rhythmic foundation of each song is remarkable, soulfully solid and also unbound and electric. Of his drumming on the supercharged "You Wreck Me," Tom said he was astounded. "He does stuff," Tom said, "that drum machines can't do!" That is for sure.

Also bassist Ron Blair, an original member of the band who left long ago to start a bikini store in LA and was replaced by the late great Howie Epstein, is back in the fold, and powerfully so. His simple but elegant bass lines were deeply in the pocket with Ferrone all night, providing a tremendously sturdy rhythmic bed on which Mike and Benmont could soar. Even Tom took many guitar solos, always smiling, and never trying to dazzle as much as add more musical kindling to this great blazing rock and roll fire.

Mike Campbell's playing is always exceptional, and this night was no exception. He plays flawlessly amazing solos and parts on each song, and with an ease and flair that seems to delight Tom. So many times when Mike was soaring on a solo, Tom looked transported. As Tom said when introducing the band, Mike is simply one of the greatest guitar heroes of any American rock band ever. That this wasn't mere hyperbole was evidenced by the vigor and grace of his playing all night long.

Benmont Tench also astounded and amazed both Tom and the audience all night with his immaculately rich keyboard parts and solos. When he took an organ solo early in the show, for example, it had all the singular command and unique elegance of a Hendrix guitar solo. He's also the calm in the frenzy of this hurricane, holding down the fort with great harmonic grace and power as furious solos were being swapped all around him.

But as already has been proved countless times, great musicians alone do not ensure great concerts or records. It all starts with the songs. But precisely because Mr. Petty's passion for the art and craft of songwriting has been so pure and expansive over these forty years, the timeless force of his songs is unbound, and fuels the rocket of this band to something positively supersonic.

After all, even Dylan rarely had a band of this greatness, with the exceptions of The Band, of course, and his own 1986 tour playing with Tom & The Heartbreakers. Dylan recognized during that tour what we all understand. It doesn't get better. Not only are The Heartbreakers all remarkable musicians, they all share the same element with Tom that holds the thing together: genuine passion. When they play, you can tell it feels as good to them as to us. This isn't phony. It's the real deal. (In fact, so overwhelmed was Dylan by the sheer power and focus of Petty & The Heartbreakers, as he related in his beautiful book *Chronicles* [which Tom said resonated with him like a beautiful epic poem], that he found himself with an intense lack of confidence and capacity to connect with the power that he once knew.)

In this age of corporate rock, when so much is contrived as a spectacle for mass consumption, building something this immense on the power of purity, of real rock and roll fire, is tremendously rare and vitally necessary. Petty genuinely loves music. The passion that ignites all his songs and which explodes with unchained dynamism, is authentic.

"Other people who do what I do," he told me once, "do other stuff, like go to Hawaii or play golf. *This* is what I love to do best."

That love has resulted in a remarkable bounty of great songs which has been incrementally expanding for four full decades now. And though Tom's been every bit as artistically expansive and ambitious in his songwriting over these decades as famous pals, he's also surpassed nearly all of them as a remarkable hitmaker. He's got so many he has to leave many of them out. Which is a good problem. Countless beloved classics such as "You Got Lucky," "Stop Draggin' My Heart Around," "Don't Do Me Like That," "The Waiting" and others were left unperformed on this night.

But with such a profusion of solid, inspired songwriting that was performed, those songs weren't missed. And as his fans know well, Tom's got a profusion of songs that were never charting hits but are every bit as brilliant and powerfully constructed as the singles.

(Examples of this abound, such as "Insider," the visceral duet with Stevie Nicks that Tom first intended for her to sing solo before reconsidering and giving her "Stop Draggin' My Heart Around." Also "Two Gunslingers," one of the funniest serious songs he's ever written, "Southern Accents," which resounds with such intimate beauty that it stands as his "Let It Be," and "The Best Of Everything," produced by Robbie Robertson for the *King of Comedy* soundtrack.)

On this tour, however, Tom is performing several of those rarely performed gems. He started the show with the first song he ever recorded on his first album, "Rockin' Around With You," which led into a glorious eighteen-song set that concluded with one of his first monster hits, "American Girl."

Perhaps most moving of these non-hits was the poignant "Crawling Back To You," from *Wildflowers*, presented in a mini-set of songs from that album which also included a stridently expansive rendition of "It's Good To Be King" and a gentle acoustic "Wildflowers." Set in Los Angeles, "Crawling" contains one of Tom's most intimate human admissions in a song in its final verse, which he told me was entirely true to his nature – most things that he worries about "never happen anyway".

Though many still cling to the myth that as great as Petty might be, he still stands forever in the shadow of famous friends like Bob Dylan and George Harrison, it just isn't so. Over these four decades, in which Tom emerged from the start with powerful songs, he's consistently evolved and expanded his musical palette, expression and execution, creating a miraculous bounty of real songwriting greatness. Unlike so many of his peers who also started strong and then peaked back when MTV was still in vogue, he never stopped learning and growing. Never did he abandon the essential Americana rock and roll fire of The Heartbreakers for long, even when stepping out alone to other musical parts of town.

(When Dave Stewart and Tom used drum machines and synths in 1985 to create the tracks that became "Don't Come Around Here No More," for example, achieving a fresh and brilliant soundscape even without The Heartbreakers, Tom still managed to bring in the band for the big double-time rave-up ending. On this night the band played the whole song, easily making it their own, with the great Mr. Ferrone echoing and expanding the famous drum pattern.)

In 1989, as is famously known, Petty took a break from the band completely to make his first solo album, *Full Moon Fever.* Produced by Jeff Lynne, who Tom called "the best producer I have ever worked with," it was a departure from the band that liberated his artistic spirit, and resulted in one of the most pure, heartfelt and inspired albums of our time, *Full Moon Fever.* With a chain of classics that includes his most famous song ever, "Free Fallin'," it was an instant landmark of rock.

Which is not to say the industry, or his label, supported what they considered an audacious breach of rock and roll ethics, a singer leaving his band to go solo. The first time he brought in the finished album to his label, they listened and were markedly unimpressed.

"Sorry, Tom," they said, "we don't hear a single." They refused to release it.

Keep in mind this is the album with "Free Fallin'," which became his biggest hit ever, a song so famous it's become a modern standard. But that wasn't all. The album had not one but *five* hits in all: "A Face In The Crowd," "Runnin' Down A Dream," "I Won't Back Down," and "Yer So Bad." It's a great lesson for all songwriters and musicians. Tom knew what he had. The songwriter knows. But often it takes a while for the industry to catch up.

The songwriter also knows the full greatness of his songs, separate from any reviews or sales figures. "You Wreck Me," another famous non-hit as beloved as any of his hit singles, is the quintessential example of this. So universally embraced that it's been elevated to the penultimate encore song of the night, preceding "American Girl." Written with Mike Campbell, "You Wreck Me" is a perfect lesson in direct rock and roll simplicity. As Tom explained in our book *Conversations With Tom Petty*, it's a song which took a full year to complete. The title which kept insisting itself, he knew, simply wasn't quite right. This shows both his persistence, and also how one word in a song—which is such a short form that each word is monumental—makes all the difference. The original title was "You Rock Me," which never felt right to him. So he kept at it, for a full year, until that one word could be replaced and the song was complete as "You Wreck Me."

"Once I got there," he said, "to that title, I knew I had it. But sometimes it takes a long time even to get one word."

It's that degree of dedication, which applies also to the production of his albums and his live shows, that explains the multi-decade phenomenon which is Tom Petty. The guy first got plugged into rock and roll as a kid seeing The Beatles on TV and meeting Elvis, and never has he disengaged since. Forty years on and he's as great as ever, if not greater. On behalf of rock and roll itself, let's hope this is not, as Tom has suggested, the final tour.

Long live Tom Petty & The Heartbreakers. Long live rock and roll.

Set list

Rockin' Around (With You)
Mary Jane's Last Dance
You Don't Know How It Feels
Forgotten Man
I Won't Back Down
Free Fallin'
Walls
Don't Come Around Here No More
It's Good To Be King
Crawling Back To You
Wildflowers
Learning To Fly
Yer So Bad
I Should Have Known It
Refugee
Runnin' Down A Dream
Encore:
You Wreck Me
American Girl

September 25, 2017, concert review by author, originally published in American Songwriter *magazine, October 3, 2017*

Chapter Twenty-Three

Purity & Passion

If the old proverb "God loves the happy man" is true, there's no question that Tom Petty is divinely beloved. He's a happy man for a number of reasons, as I learned while interviewing him in a succession of Saturday afternoons through interviews connected and preserved in our book. Petty is happily married to the ebullient Dana Petty, happy being the father of three children and happily making new music (as well as playing old favorites on the road with The Heartbreakers, one of the greatest rock and roll bands of all time). The new music was made differently than in the past: It's a solo album called *Highway Companion* and is the product of only three musicians—Tom (who plays guitar, keyboards and, remarkably, drums on the album), Jeff Lynne (who was a Traveling Wilbury with Petty, and also the producer of the magical *Full Moon Fever* album) and Heartbreaker Mike Campbell (who plays fluid slide guitar throughout the album).

Petty proudly played the album for me during one of these joyful Saturdays, at very loud volume (because "I'm partially deaf," he said with a smile) in his home studio in Malibu, California. It's a great album, matching and maybe even surpassing the level of Petty's previous work. "I think it might be the best thing I've ever done," he said, later asking me to change the sentence to read in the book, "I think it might be one of the best things I've ever done." It starts with the slinky funk of "Turn This Car Around" and proceeds through a string of strong songs, including "Down South," a masterful return to Petty's past in Florida, and "Square One," which is tenderly painted by two acoustic guitars and is one of the most sweetly haunting songs Petty has written in years.

The original impetus for the book was to talk in depth and length about Petty's music. I had interviewed Tom several times in the past, and have found him to be one of the warmest and most likeable of music's superstars. We both soon realized that the book should contain more, however. As Tom wrote in the foreword to the book, "As the interviews progressed, it became clear that to understand the music one would have to have knowledge of my life and how it has unfolded." His is an extraordinary life in music, which created the timeless blueprint for some of the most memorable songs of the past thirty years.

It's a life that took shape in Gainesville, Florida. Tom was one of two sons to a loving mother and an abusive, somewhat crazy father. "My dad was pretty wild," Tom said. "He used to always be going to get his car out of a ditch somewhere. [Laughs] I thought it was *completely* normal to run your car into a ditch... Now I realize, *wow*. And he was quite a gambler... and my mother hated it. It was quite a turbulent household, really. Very turbulent." Asked why his father was hitting ditches all the time, he answered, "He was quite a drinker... just as wild as the wind, really."

His father used to take him hunting and on fishing trips, both activities that Tom despised. "I never liked it," Tom remembered. "My dad was a *hard* man, hard to be around... He wanted me to be a lot more macho than I was. I was this real sort of tender, emotional kid. More inclined to the arts... I didn't want to be trapped in a boat with him all day." About hunting, Tom said, "It was *awful*. It was sitting in fields, just fucking cold, to shoot a bird... I remember birds stuffed in bags, and cleaning the birds, picking all the feathers off. It was *gross*. I hated it."

Petty's father would often perform feats to prove just how macho he was to his tender son. "One day this small alligator came up by the boat," Tom said, "and I actually saw my dad take his forefinger and his thumb, and punch the eyes in on the alligator. To show me that he could knock the alligator out... and the gator rolled over in the water. He was just *nuts*. But he wasn't afraid of anything. I once saw my dad grab a rattlesnake by the tail, swing it round his head, and pop his neck. That's pretty wild, you know? So I was kind of scared of him."

Ironically, when Tom showed interest in playing music, his father bought him his first instrument of choice, a Kay electric guitar. Tom took two lessons, but they were too formal for him, and he preferred to learn from friends. "I met a kid in the neighborhood, who actually knew how to play," Tom said, "and [h]e showed me chords, and we sat and played guitar. And… you learn really quickly that way. The first key I learned was *C*, so you had to have *F*, and *F* is a tough one. I remember playing 'Wooly Bully' on guitar. It was the first one I mastered, and I was on my way. And from there it just went on."

He started writing his own songs as soon as he learned how to play. His first was called "Baby, I'm Leaving," which Tom described as a "12-bar blues kind of thing. It was in *C*," he said. Both parents were impressed and slightly incredulous about his ability to write his own music. "[My father] was really proud of it," Tom said. "When he would have a friend over, he'd say, 'Bring your guitar out and play a song for this guy.' [My mother] was amazed that I could do it. Just *amazed*. She'd say, 'I can't understand how you can do it if you didn't have any lessons, and you don't know how to write music. How do you do it?' And I said, 'I don't know, I just learned it from other kids.'"

He yearned from the start to make his living playing music, but he didn't have any idea of a pathway that would lead to such a life. That is, until he saw The Beatles. "The minute I saw The Beatles on *The Ed Sullivan Show*… *there* was the way out. *There* was the way to do it. You get your friends and you're a self-contained unit. And you make the music. And it looked like so much fun… *this* really spoke to me. I had been a big fan of Elvis, but I really saw in The Beatles that here's something I could do… It wasn't long before there were groups springing up in garages all over the place."

Tom was soon in one of those groups, which he organized with Gainesville friends. He knew a kid named Dennis Lee, who played drums. They both had long hair, which was revolutionary at the time, and they bonded. Tom went over to his house one day with guitar in hand, and the two jammed. But it was a pretty girl who crystallized his desire to form a band. "Her name was Cindy Crawford," Tom said. "Go figure." She was in charge of dances in the school and had a DJ set to play records, but she needed a band to play in the intermission. He said, "Sure, my band can do it." And so he quickly went to see his friend Richie Henson, with whom he often played guitar, and told him they were forming a band. Henson got Robert Crawford, another guitarist, and they enlisted Dennis Lee to play the drums. "We got together one afternoon in my front room and played," Tom remembers fondly. "It was the biggest rush in my life, the minute it all happened."

They learned four songs, all instrumentals, including "House Of The Rising Sun" and "Walk Don't Run." They all wore blue shirts and jeans, Tom said, "so we looked like a band." They were such a hit that they were invited to play at during the next intermission, and they repeated the same four songs. At the end of the night, as they were packing up their instruments and amps, an "older kid" came up to them and asked, "Do you guys ever play fraternity parties?" Tom answered, "No, we've never played anywhere but here." The guy said he could get them some bookings. This was a Friday night, and the following Saturday Tom and the group were in Dennis Lee's garage, trying to learn more songs. "And it never stopped from that moment," he said. They called the band The Sundowners.

It was the beginning of Tom's attaining his dream. The guy came through with some gigs, including one at the local Moose Club, where a battle of the bands was held. The winner got a contract for the whole summer to play every Friday night. The Sundowners won. They were paid one hundred bucks a gig. Tom was only fourteen—couldn't drive a car yet—so he depended on parents to ferry them to gigs. As his own mother was dubious about his ability to write songs, she too was quizzical about his ability to earn money from playing music. "My mom was like, 'Where did you get this money?' and I told her I got it for the show. She said, '*Really*, where did you get this money? If you took this money, you're gonna have to own up to it.' I said, 'I swear to God, Mom, they paid me this for playing.' She didn't believe me. So she called the Moose Club, and the guy said, 'Yeah, they get the door, and that's what they made.'"

By the end of the summer, Tom remembered, he'd made about $200, all of which he put into the band, buying a better amp. Then his father surprised him again by buying him a Gibson bass. Up to this point, The Sundowners had three guitars and drums. With his new instrument, Tom became the bass player, teaching himself how to play with a little help from his friends.

Tom and the other Sundowners rehearsed avidly, and the practice paid off; soon gigs became abundant. "We worked constantly," Tom said. "Gainesville had so many opportunities to play... There was a fraternity row where they had parties every Friday and Saturday... and they had socials that you could play in the afternoon. It would be only an hour gig. So, if we were really lucky, we'd have a social in the afternoon and then we'd do the show that night and maybe a dance... We were working guys. We were obsessed with it. *Completely*."

While he was in The Sundowners, Tom was asked to fill in as a bassist with an established band comprising of older kids, The Epics. They liked him so much that they urged him to join the band as bassist and singer, and he accepted. "It was kind of mind-blowing [to join The Epics]... They worked all up and down Florida... That's when we first started to go on overnight gigs. You'd go and stay in a motel room. And these guys were... *crazy*. [Laughs] They were *really* into girls, and really into bringing them back to the room... That's where I kind of grew up, in The Epics, watching these guys. They were... just completely bonko, wild, partying, drunk... But they had a *really* good drummer. The guy just played the most *solid* beat... I loved playing with him."

But despite the high level of the rhythm section, The Epics became more interested in partying and less inclined to work on their music, which dismayed Tom. They added another guitarist, Tom Leadon, with whom Tom became close friends, and in time the two Toms left The Epics to form a new band. That band was Mudcrutch. They put an ad up in Lipham's Music store, which was the musical center of activity in Gainesville. A drummer named Randall Marsh responded to the ad, and Tom and Tom went out to his place. Petty told Randall it was a shame that they didn't have a rhythm guitarist, and Randall said, "My roommate plays guitar." And in came Mike Campbell, carrying a Japanese guitar.

"He kicked off 'Johnny B. Goode'," Tom recalled, "and when the song ended, we said, 'You're in the band, man.' He had to be in the band. And he didn't necessarily even want to be in the band... Somehow we convinced him to stay in the band. And that became the Mudcrutch that people know... Mudcrutch got to be *very* popular in Gainesville. That band really worked."

It was also at Lipham's Music store, a few years earlier, that Tom met keyboardist-extraordinaire Benmont Tench, who was only 13 at the time. Benmont came into the store, sat down at the Farfisa organ, and proceeded to play all of *Sgt. Pepper*, adjusting the stops to get various sounds. Everybody there was astounded at the kid's virtuosity. "But I never saw him again," said Tom, "until, God, about 1970, and my roommate came in the door one night with this guy, and he was all bearded and had really long hair... Slowly I realized it was Benmont. It was like, 'You're the kid!' And he said, 'Yeah, I have a band in New Orleans…' I said, 'We have a gig tomorrow night, do you want to play with us?' He said, 'All I have is my Farfisa organ.' I said, 'Okay, you're in.'" Ben made it to the show with organ in tow, and winningly played five sets with the band, all with no previous rehearsal. Tom knew Benmont was ideal for the band.

At this time, Petty was committed to getting the band a recording deal. And he knew that he would never get this deal if they were simply playing covers of Rolling Stones and Dylan songs. So he began bringing in his original songs to the band. He'd written a song called "Up in Mississippi" ("You have to be pretty far south to go up to Mississippi," he said), which they recorded and made into a 45. The record received a lot of airplay on Gainesville radio stations "'cause we bribed our friends into calling the request line." It led to more gigs, and Mudcrutch became one of Gainesville's foremost bands. The band thoroughly reveled in the recording of the song, a love that lasts to this day. "We fell in love with it," Tom said. "Totally. We just fell in love with the whole idea of being in the studio and hearing it come back on those great big speakers. And it sounded so *good*. But it was all the dough we had to pay for one session."

I asked him what it was like to hear his song on the radio. He answered, "Oh man, it was such a *gas*. *Such* a gas." The band began presenting their own festivals in a field behind the shack where Randall and Mike lived. (Tom still lived at home, but used it just as a place to crash.) Tom and the boys reckoned that if they put up some posters and got some other bands on the bill, they could have a successful rock event. And it worked. Several thousand people flocked to the show.

Following the first festival, some local promoters proposed the idea of doing another one, for which they enlisted many bands. It was also a massive success. The cops showed up, but knew if they attempted to shut down the show the crowd might become a mob and riot. Afterwards, Mike and Randall were told they were being evicted. Figuring at that point that they had nothing to lose, they held a third festival, which also was an immense success. "That was the key to our success," said Tom. "We became really famous around town, and when we played a lot of people came. Before that, we used to play at Dub's. We would play there six nights a week. Five sets a night. Got a hundred bucks a piece a week."

The Dub's gig did more for them than generate money. It also taught them how to be a band. But at Dub's, the crowd wanted covers, and

Tom yearned to play his own songs. So, to get around this problem, he would say, "Here's one by Santana," and play an original.

Tom and the band increasingly felt they were on a merry-go-round, playing all the same places over and again. "So that's when California came into the picture," he said. "We were constantly just trying to keep enough gigs to pay the rent, and keep working. But we could see it wasn't going anywhere. How big can you get in Gainesville? We had certainly hit the top of the ladder there. We were probably even then the most famous band in Gainesville... I *still* meet people who tell me they saw Mudcrutch... But we knew we had to break out of there."

So, along with their girlfriends, the members of Mudcrutch piled into a van, and headed west to California. It was a momentous trip for Tom, who had never been west of the Mississippi. He delighted in simple pleasures along the way, such as the sighting of real cacti. The first day that they arrived in Hollywood, the group—led by Tom—began dropping in on record companies with their tape. Tom said he felt that it didn't matter if he got rejected; he only needed one company to say yes.

"The only addresses we had," he said, "we'd written down from record ads in *Rolling Stone*. And I was trying to find some more, so I went into... Ben Frank's diner on Sunset, and I went to a phone booth to look up record companies. And on the floor of the phone booth there was a piece of paper... and it's a list of twenty record companies, with their phone numbers and addresses... I kind of went, 'Shit—there's a lot of people doing this.' But I swear to God it was there." On that very first day, the band "hit paydirt" at MGM, where they were invited to record a single. The next day London Records also expressed interest in the band, wanting to sign them right away.

Following that, Capitol Records also got on the Mudcrutch bandwagon: "[They] wanted to book demo time in their studio. We were so silly and indignant that we didn't want to do a demo, and we didn't know there was a difference between record companies. We were really green. We just felt that if they put out records, that was fine with us. We didn't know there'd be any difference between Shelter Records or Capitol Records. They all put out records nationally, or internationally. That's all we were interested in.

"We stayed for a few more days, and on the last day we were here, we went by Shelter Records, and gave the tape to this girl named

Andrea Starr… She opened the door, and she thought we were cute, she told me later. She took the tape to Simon Miller Mundy, who was their A&R guy. We went home [to Florida] and sold everything we owned, and got ready to come to California. And literally, in a rehearsal, the phone rang and I answered it, and it was Denny Cordell. I thought he was calling about a car we had for sale. And he said, 'I really want to sign your group. I think you guys are really great. I think you guys are like the next Rolling Stones.' I was like, 'What is this?' But we knew who Denny Cordell was. We knew he had done 'A Whiter Shade Of Pale' and the Joe Cocker stuff. We knew that he was a real guy we were talking to on the phone. But I had to say, 'Well, I'm really sorry, but we already promised London Records we would sign with them.' And he said, 'I'll tell you what. If you're going to drive out here, I've got a studio in Tulsa, Oklahoma. And that's going to be not far out of your way. Why don't you stop in Tulsa, and meet with me, and then you can see if you like us.'"

Tom and the band took Cordell up on his offer, and drove to Tulsa, where Leon Russell had a studio. Once there, they met Cordell in the middle of a windstorm on the street. He brought them to Shelter's studio, which was built in a church. "It was called the Church Studio," Tom recalled. "It was a really nice studio. [Cordell] said, 'So spend the night, and tomorrow we'll go in and do a session. And we'll see how you like it.' And we were like, 'Wow, we get to do a session in a studio! Hell, yeah, we'll spend the night.'… We spent the next day recording, and he went, 'That's it. I'm sold. I want to sign your band.' And we liked him a lot, much better than the guy at London, who was an executive type. So we said, 'Okay, we'll go with you.'"

Mudcrutch recorded an album, with the song "Depot Street" released as a single. But it failed to fly, and the band split up. Tom was offered a solo deal from Shelter Records. He cut some tracks with a phenomenal lineup of musicians, including Al Kooper, "Duck" Dunn, and Jim Gordon, but didn't relish the idea of being a solo artist, preferring the camaraderie of a band. At the same time, Benmont organized a group to record his own songs, and invited Tom to play harmonica. The band consisted of Mike Campbell on guitar, Ron Blair on bass, Stan Lynch on drums, Randall Marsh also on drums, Jeff Jourard on guitar, and Benmont on keys. "And it instantly hit me," Tom said, "that man, you know, this is home. This is where I should be. And I quickly did my pitch about talking them into going in with me." Tom wanted Lynch, Blair, Campbell, and Tench to be in his own group, and convinced them to join by saying he already had a record deal. They accepted, and The Heartbreakers were born.

Skip ahead several years to the present. Tom Petty & The Heartbreakers are one of America's most beloved and enduring rock and roll bands. Inducted into the Rock and Roll Hall of Fame in 2002, they have released countless classic albums (such as *Damn The Torpedoes* and *Southern Accents* in addition to Tom's great solo albums, such as *Full Moon Fever* and *Wildflowers*) and have amassed a wealth of hit songs, including "Refugee," "American Girl," "The Waiting," "Don't Come Around Here No More," "I Won't Back Down," "You Don't Know How It Feels," "Mary Jane's Last Dance," and more. They are also one of the greatest touring bands to ever hit the concert stage. They have so many hits, it would be easy for them to become a nostalgia act, but Tom is careful to remain presently and vitally connected to his work, and "not to become a jukebox," imbuing his work with a timelessness of energy, purity, and passion.

"We've got a lot of material," he explained. "We're not stuck with the same fifteen songs. It's a big temptation sometimes just to play the really huge songs, because the crowd loves it, and if you let them have their way, they'll demand that. It's important to give them something in a show that they didn't expect. And to take them somewhere that they didn't really plan on going...

"Sometimes I feel like I don't want to play 'American Girl' anymore. We've been playing it for thirty years. But then maybe you'll get two hours into the show, and the place is frenzied, and the vibe is so great, and the first couple chords of that song come on, and there's such a rush of adrenaline throughout the building, that the next thing you know, you're really digging playing 'American Girl.' And I'll feel, I can't believe I'm digging this again, but I am.

"It's important to us that we don't turn into an Oldies act. We don't want to turn into that great nostalgia machine. We've seen many of the people who we came up with turn into that. I think you always have to have something new. That's what keeps us going."

He is optimistic about the potential of rock and roll to endure, despite the encroachment of other genres. "I think rock and roll is going to go the way of blues and jazz. It's not the predominant music anymore. But

I think we can keep going on as long as we're honest. The music makes you feel young. It's a good way to stay in touch with that feeling. I think we can do it for a long time as long as we remain honest in what we're doing, and we don't try to be something we're not. Our audience is a rock and roll audience. It hasn't turned into one of these passive, sit-in-the-seat kind of audience. And I'm so grateful for that. But maybe the reason for that is that we never tried to pander to a young crowd. We never tried to pretend we were something we weren't, and so they always took us at face value. We're not trying to be teen idols. We had our days of doing that, and we're trying to grow up with the music. We tried to grow up, and as time went by, the music had to grow with us."

Asked if there are new places to explore in his music, he answered, "I think there will always be new places to go, musically. And I think that's true because I've got a unit that can go anywhere I want to point them. The frustrating part for me is having songs for them to play. If you ever hear this band warm up, it's scary! They play so effortlessly and so unbridled, and so great. But I get frustrated because I want to harness that, and get it into a song, and it's hard to keep supplying them with material that will showcase that… It's hard to write a great blues or a great rock and roll song. Because there's a purity there you can't fake. Try writing 'Long Tall Sally.' It isn't easy. It's a difficult thing to write because it has to be done with a certain spontaneity. It's not something you can overwork. So those kind of things just aren't handed to you every day. It has to just burst out of your heart. Those aren't things you can plan. You can't say, 'I'm gonna sit down today and write "Long Tall Sally".' It's got to boil inside of you and then burst out. They're hard songs to write.

"It's a constant education," he continued. "As you get older, you get more perspective on your body of work. I can see things that I'm better at than other things. So I'm trying to find the things that I'm good at and improve on. Rather than go all over the map and try everything. Though I'm still looking. I'm still searching. I try to be optimistic… The thing now is to keep refining, keep growing, keep finding things in us that we didn't know about ourselves. I think as long as we enjoy doing it, we'll keep doing it."

Author article originally published in
American Songwriter *magazine, November 2005*

Chapter Twenty-Four

In Memoriam: The Life And Times Of Tom Petty

It was four days since Tom died, and I was both in some shock and surrounded by sorrow. Like the death of loved ones, this was hard to accept, and I channeled my sorrow, broken heart, and grief into this reflection on his life. It is, perhaps, "too much and not enough," a quote from Dylan about one of his songs that goes on forever and still seems to him deficient. Words alone couldn't express the fullness of what I was feeling, or what any of us felt then. That's why God invented song, and songwriters to write them.

"I don't want to be one of those people who are miserable even when they're successful," he said in our first interview, back in 1994. "That's not the way I want my life to go."

He learned early on that none of it mattered, the music, the band, the success, if he was unhappy. Gradually, and with the real love of his beloved wife Dana, he succeeded in creating a life of calm and joy even while spinning in the very heart of a rock and roll hurricane for four decades. Though the life and times of Tom Petty were never simple or without challenges, he was never derailed, and he came up with ways of making it all work. "I'm not sure if people know," he once said, "but those crowds at my shows—they're downright *frenzied*."

But his authentic connection with the muse, and with the electric current of rock and roll, empowered him over those years to transcend the frenzy. He knew as long as he stayed plugged into that source, and never took it for granted or tried to fake it, that he could not only maintain but prosper. Asked for the secret of his onstage joy, that infectious spark which has been igniting reverent rock and roll fires for decades, he said it was all about truth. Faking it, in rock and roll, is simply not an option. Not for Tom Petty & The Heartbreakers, anyway.

"The secret, really," he said, "the most important thing, is: *Have a good time*. Don't take it too seriously. You've got to take it seriously enough that it happens. But don't let anything throw you. You can't be thrown by something breaking, or this or that. You've got to remember that they all came to see *you*, they *like* you [Laughs] and all they want to do is see you and hear you play some songs."

"If you keep it on that level, and be sure you're enjoying it," Tom continued, "then that will carry and they'll enjoy it… If I go up there and really enjoy myself, it's going to travel, and [the audience] is going to pick it up in the furthest regions of the room… So I always try to enjoy it. And the audience sustains me. That is the truth."

The truth. It's where his journey began and ends. And the truth was that there was nothing Tom Petty loved more than music. Since he was a kid growing up in Gainesville, Florida, it was everything for him: his joy, his passion, his solace, his escape, his dream come true. And he never wavered from that love. "A lot of my friends," he said, "they love to go to Hawaii or play golf or something. This is what I love to do."

That love for all aspects of his work, from the songwriting through the record-making to live performances and touring, sustained him over the decades, and never was removed from his work. Not once did he allow himself to become disengaged for long. Plugged directly into the original juice of rock and which flowed through Elvis into The Beatles, the Byrds, the Stones, and the other bands that electrified his youth, Tom never abandoned that authentic passion. His music was based on that simple, visceral equation of electric guitars, bass, drums and keys united in song, always playing together in a deep pocket as only a solid unit can. Even in the studio, he knew the key to capturing the essence of rock and roll was when the band played together. Sure, he could overdub parts and add a lot afterwards. But it all started with the band playing it live, just as The Beatles always did, creating an energy that cannot be created in any other way.

Even among legendary songwriters, his extraordinary instinct for writing songs which appealed to a vast swath of humanity was exceptional. His popularity expanded incrementally over the years, and by the time of "Free Fallin'" and other hits from *Full Moon Fever*, he crossed over all demographics to appeal to everyone from young kids to old timers in a way few rock artists have done since The Beatles. Back when music acts were divided up into those with youth appeal who went on MTV, and those on VH1 who skewed older, Tom & The Heartbreakers were on both.

"Demographics," however, was a word Tom hated and refused to use. To him, that kind of thinking—how best to divide an audience for maximum marketing potential—was antithetical to the spirit of rock and roll. His goal was never to direct material to any one segment of the populace. It was the exact opposite, and audacious as it might seem, he wanted to write songs all people of all ages could love. Few things made him happier than knowing that his music appealed to kids. "I get a lot of letters from little children," he said. "And I really like that, because little kids don't lie."

More than anything, he was never phony. He knew rock and roll was about real musicians playing together, and whether live or in the studio, and recognized that the energy of live performance was the fuel for his rocket ship. To the very end, his final show of his final tour, September 25, 2017, he remained dynamically and directly connected to the source. After having completed a "really long tour," as he put it, that started in April of this year, he seemed happier than I've ever seen him. He was home again, in his element, at the historic Hollywood Bowl on the same stage where his beloved Beatles performed, and at the immense helm of a cherished band of world-class musicians. All was right with the world. Though word circulated that this could be his final tour, Tom looked so happy and sounded so strong that no one believed for a second he was ready to stop. Never did the idea occur that this was to be his last show ever.

Still it doesn't seem possible. Tom was such a force of nature, and such a positive one, that the thought of a world without him simply seems wrong. How is it possible that Bob Dylan is still alive and kicking, while Tom—his little brother in the Wilburys—is already gone? To quote Bob, it's the sign of a world gone wrong.

He made it seem easy. All of it: writing songs, making records, giving concerts. Because Tom was real, always invested completely in the art and science of authenticity, and because his songs sparkled with a charming and direct simplicity (hence their almost universal appeal), many made the false leap that it was all effortless for him. That was the exact impression he intended to make, as rock and roll, in terms of songwriting, production and live-performance, must never seem labored. It's about spontaneous passion, not calculations contrived to deceive. There was nothing at all deceptive or false about anything Tom did; not in the musicianship of the band, the level of the songwriting, or the production of his albums. None of that could be faked. That is real magic. Unlike the illusory magic of magicians, writing and recording a classic song is no trick. It's authentic magic, impervious to time.

When a great one came through him, such as the haunting "Southern Accents," which he wrote at about 4:00 a.m. on the piano in his home studio, it thrilled him. "It was one of the best songs I ever wrote," he said. "It just *appeared.* I did it all real fast on the piano. I taped it on a cassette deck. I *loved* the bridge. The bridge was what made it for me, when I found that. I hit those chords. Sometimes you have a lot of tries for a bridge. I actually hit those chords on my first pass… It's what makes you keep doing this. You get something like that… I don't remember a lot of them, but I remember just playing that cassette over and over, and I stayed up all night. I couldn't possibly go to sleep. I was so excited. I wanted to play it for somebody."

That great bridge revolves around a dream vision of his mother, similar to "Let It Be," another elegiac piano ballad. When asked if he ever heard it referred to as his "Let It Be," Tom said, "No, but that's a pretty good analogy for that one."

But although "Southern Accents" came through him, as did "Wildflowers," those were exceptions. Still people would hear a song which seemed to spill directly from Tom's rock and roll heart into his songbook—such as "Free Fallin'," or "You Don't Know How It Feels"—and conclude it just arrived, with no coaxing from its creator. In fact, Tom worked hard on every aspect of his work. As he explained, it takes a whole lot of effort to make the thing appear effortless. After Tom worked on it long enough that the work doesn't show, the whole thing zips by in about three minutes, creating the sense that he doesn't write these songs, they simply arrive.

In truth, he wrote his songs in any and every way there was. Some remained unfinished for a long time, such as "Mary Jane's Last Dance," for which he wrote a chorus a full year after writing the verses.

Sometimes he'd finish all but one tiny part of a song. A perfect example is the classic "You Wreck Me," which grew, as have many of his great songs, from seeds planted by Mike Campbell. Mike's way was to give Tom a cassette tape containing many tracks of music, to which Tom would write a song.

Tom was both quite crafty when it came to ingenious songwriting and construction, but also had a lot of respect, as well as patience, for this dynamic of discovery. "You Wreck Me" took almost a whole year to complete. Sensing that the title would be three syllables, he had "You Rock Me" for many months, which fit metrically, but never felt right to him. When he finally arrived at "wreck," he knew he'd gotten there, a new instant classic that only took a year to finish. It's powerful proof of the pure patience and endurance required to do what he did.

It was on the occasion of the 1994 release of *Wildflowers*, his second solo album, that our first interview happened. Still living in his Encino home then with his first wife Jane and his two daughters, he was brimming with joy about *Wildflowers*. That record, with brilliantly intimate songs like the title cut, "You Wreck Me," and "Crawling Back To You," reflected a songwriter at the very peak of his powers. Unlike so many greats who peaked decades earlier, here came Tom after the early triumphs, after the remarkable and joyous reinvention of *Full Moon Fever*, with a new album overflowing with every kind of song under the sun—from gentle acoustic ballads to pure electric rock and roll—each completely invested with the heart and soul of the songwriter.

In fact, even since *Full Moon Fever*, with its bounty of greatness, including his most famous song ever, "Free Fallin'," it seemed that Tom's connection with the rock and roll muse had only intensified over the years. Hearing those songs—the playful lyrics, the beautifully infectious melodies, the warm and rich textures, the impassioned vocals, the resplendent harmonies—was hearing a songwriter in love with the art and craft of songwriting itself. That brutal judgmental part of himself seemed to have been jettisoned so that he could get out of the way to plug directly into the source in a way few songwriters have ever done with such consistent purity.

Asked if those songs emerged more from leading them or following, he said, "More like just letting them happen. Getting out of the way."

Letting on that I was a fellow musician and that I was stunned by the organic, unforced and joyful nature of his new songs, all of which shone as evidence of a songwriter in love with songwriting, his eyes sparkled with happy concord that the full meaning and moment of his journey was understood, and our conversation instantly deepened.

Like Lou Reed, who said that if you tell journalists of the true mystic dimensions of songwriting they will ridicule you, Tom was reticent to shine much light into the mystery with most journalists. But musicians to musicians always open up, sharing a common language, and Tom was happy from the very start to discuss this thing about which he had gained so much wisdom and expertise over the years with someone who understood what it all meant.

It created a bond of trust and mutual admiration that extended over many subsequent interviews for different magazines—and one for a United Airlines inflight audio entertainment show—and ultimately led to the great honor for me to collaborate with him on a full book of conversations with him. Doing the book required me to spend more than a year of Saturdays with Tom, discussing in depth all facets of his life and career.

Working on the book with him was truly joyful. By 2004, when the work commenced, he'd gotten remarried to his beloved Dana, and moved into his sprawling Malibu mansion just off the Pacific Coast Highway. It's there, in his little recording studio, where we met mostly, though on a few occasions we'd meet instead at his other Malibu house, a charming little cottage right on the ocean where Dana painted and kept her art supplies. ("This is where we rough it," Tom said of their hide-away. "We even make our own beds here!")

As he kept rock and roll hours his entire life, our meetings never commenced prior to noon, soon after his wake-up time. He'd arrive sometimes sleepily, but never in a bad mood. Always ready to work, and with a happy spirit that buoyed my own, he not only made doing the book easy, he made it fun.

Usually we'd meet in his home recording studio, where he used a conga drum as a table for the little bottles of cold Coca-Cola we always drank. Always attired in something cozy and often whimsical—big colorful cardigan sweaters, funny knit caps, big fur-lined boots—he always devoted ample time and thought to answering my endless questions. He loved that I would show up, as he wrote in the intro, "ridiculously prepared, to the extent of knowing how to play the songs himself." This was true, as knowing the song from the inside out, and understanding its ingenious architecture, is the only way to truly discuss the totality of a song with its songwriter.

He appreciated the singular focus on songwriting and the creative process maintained in our previous interviews, which led us to the concept of doing an entire book of conversations that would focus entirely on his songs and his songwriting, as opposed to a biography about his life.

That was the original idea. But almost immediately after doing a couple conversations, it became evident to both of us that all his songs were about his life, and his entire life was built on song. And so what started as a book about art, creativity and music became a book about being an artist in the world, and all it entails.

At the same time, we did focus intensely on each and every song and record he'd created up to that moment, including discards later used in his boxed set. After a session in which several songs were named about which he had little memory, he suggested that from now on we plan in advance the ten or so songs we intend to discuss. He was a pro, that way, and took everything he did seriously. For the rest of our time working on the book, he'd spend a week doing homework prior to each interview, listening to and reflecting on his past songs and records.

His comprehensive answers and memories about all these records—even quite obscure ones—astounded many readers and reviewers who simply couldn't fathom that Tom Petty—a rocker who had famously championed weed in several songs—possessed a memory so sharp as to recall every song and every record he'd ever made. He found that funny.

In addition to shining light into the origins of all his songs, he also divulged the truth, as he knew it, about his personal origins. All sorts of rumors abounded about his history, including the notorious assertion that the Pettys moved to Florida because Tom's paternal grandfather, Pulpwood Petty, killed a guy in Georgia.

Tom confirmed that this was the story his father told him, though not till later in life. "My grandmother was a full-blooded Cherokee Indian," he said. "My grandfather was a white guy. [She] was a cook in a logging camp. He worked there. They made [the timber] into pulpwood. He married my grandmother, which was not popular, to mix the races."

Fearing they could be in danger, his grandparents attempted to flee with a horse and wagon in the middle of the night. Suddenly stopped on the road by several guys, "some kind of violent situation came down about him being with an Indian. And somebody got insulted, and my grandfather ended up killing a guy."

Had that murder never occurred, the history of American rock and roll as we know it would have been written differently.

Growing up in Gainesville, Florida, wasn't easy for this tender, slender, sensitive and musical boy. His father could be wildly unhinged, a man who was forever driving his car into ditches. An insurance man who loved to fish and hunt, he had no love for Tom's long hair, grown out then in 1965 to emulate The Beatles. But he did appreciate and even encourage Tom's musical proclivities, buying him his first guitar, a Stella, when Tom was 12. Often when his dad would have a friend over, he'd tell Tom to come out and play a song.

Frequently, though, his father would force him to come along on the boat for fishing, or on a hunt to shoot quail or some other easy target. Tom hated every second of it. "It was kind of mandatory for a while that I went with him," Tom said. "But I never liked it. My dad was a *hard* man. Hard to be around. He was really hard on me. He wanted me to be a lot more macho than I was. I was this real sort of tender, emotional kid. More inclined to the arts than *shooting* something."

His father's behavior always could surprise and even scare Tom. Most notably the time they were out fishing, and a large gator came right up to the boat.

"I actually saw my dad take his forefinger and thumb," Tom said with awe, "and punch the eyes in on the alligator. To show me that he could knock the alligator out." Even while saying it, he seemed to disbelieve it himself, and echoed it as if to convince himself. "Took his *thumb and forefinger, pushed* the alligator's eyes in, and the gator rolled over in the water."

"He was *nuts*," Tom said of his dad. "But he wasn't afraid of anything. I once saw my dad grab a rattlesnake by the tail, swing it round his head, and pop his neck. That's pretty wild shit, you know? So I was kind of scared of him."

His father's attitude towards him mirrored how he was treated by most of the town. In Gainesville, Tom couldn't get hired anywhere with his long hair except for one job. Gravedigging. "Actually," he said, "there wasn't that much gravedigging. Mostly it was mowing the lawn."

Since he was a kid, he had an uncanny knack for memorizing nursery rhymes perfectly, a skill which extended to songs as soon as he started collecting 45s. Like a musical sponge, he'd absorb every record he could get, with an early love of rockabilly. It was an education that served him well. At twelve he started playing guitar, and with only two lessons took to it naturally. Almost as soon as he could play and learn new chords, he started writing his own songs. Songwriting, like playing guitar, came instinctively to him, and he loved it. His first was called "Baby I'm Leaving," and had four chords: *C*, *F*, *G* and *A* minor. A crafty songwriter from the start, he was especially proud of that *A* minor.

As soon as he started writing songs he never stopped. Being in a band was all that mattered, a vision galvanized the first time he saw The Beatles on *The Ed Sullivan Show*. From that day forward, he was a changed man.

"Once we saw [The Beatles]," Tom said, "we were never the same. There was nobody else with a self-contained band like them. The only bands I had seen were at the teen rec center, and they played surf music... [Pop stars] were not self-contained units then. I've never even dreamed of that. To me, I would have loved to have been a rock and roll star. But I just didn't understand how you got to be a rock and roll star. How did you suddenly have a mohair suit and orchestra?

"But the minute I saw The Beatles—and it's true of thousands of guys—*there* was the way out. *There* was the way to do it. You get your friends and you're a self-contained unit and you make the music. And it looked like so much fun."

He never looked back. His first band was The Sundowners, formed on the spot when a pretty girl whose name was Cindy Crawford (not that one) asked him if he had a band for the school dance. "Yes, I do," he lied, and then went off to assemble one. They rehearsed in his living room: three guitars all plugged into one Silvertone amp, a sax and drums. They learned four instrumentals. The first time they played together, Tom said, was "the biggest rush of my life."

Their first performance was such a triumph that they repeated their set of the same four songs later in the night. Afterwards, a guy said he could get them gigs at fraternity parties if they learned new songs. Tom leapt at the chance, and playing in bands was his life and his love from that moment on. With The Sundowners gigging often, he started making more money than he did at the graveyard. Other local bands, such as

The Epics, noticed him and invited him to fill in for their bassist, eventually convincing him to leave The Sundowners to join their band. He did.

That band gradually morphed into the band Mudcrutch. It was then that two future Heartbreakers came into his world, both remarkable virtuoso musicians from the start, guitarist Mike Campbell and keyboardist Benmont Tench.

Campbell, who Tom said was as great then as he is today, was so much greater than anyone Tom had ever heard he knew Mike had to be in his own band.

Benmont, who is three years younger than Tom, was still just a kid when they first met years earlier. But he was no normal kid; he was a musical prodigy, a fact made exceedingly evident when he sat down at the organ at the local music store and played all of *Sgt. Pepper.* Years later Tom realized that same amazing kid was a teenager now, and enlisted him for his band.

Mudcrutch became quite popular in Gainesville, playing bigger and bigger shows until the day came to follow their dream, and go to LA to get a record deal. So naïve was Tom about how the business worked, he came to town with a list of record companies, went to Ben Frank's diner on the Sunset Strip, and started calling them to announce his arrival. No one told him it wasn't done this way. Remarkably it worked, and he got offered a record deal.

More than once music execs told him they liked him, but persuaded him to drop the band idea. They told him they saw him as a solo artist, and offered substantial bucks if he'd drop his band. He refused. Unlike the traditional music business method of walking over your friends to get to the top, Tom Petty was always loyal, and always dedicated to his band. The first album came out in 1977. Consecutive masterpieces followed, and decades of hits and amazing songs. Forty years later, on September 25, 2017, they performed their final show at the Hollywood Bowl at the top of their game. Tom went out at the very height of his powers.

Working on the book with him almost every week for more than a year, I came to feel his emotions powerfully as he related chapters of his life both happy and dark. The happy chapters came across with infectious joy, exactly like that which he projects onstage performing with the band.

But his sorrow was also palpable, and several dark chapters of his life came with a heavy, foreboding darkness that was impossible to ignore. The darkest of all and most difficult for him to was the story of Howie Epstein, the bassist he heard in Del Shannon's band and brought to The Heartbreakers when Rob Blair left. Tom loved Howie for his bass playing, but said there were a lot of great bassists. The thing that really won Howie the job, Tom said, was his singing. He could always perfectly nail the harmony parts. "And when you're a Heartbreaker," Tom said, "you need to sing your harmonies perfectly."

But Howie's heroin addiction gradually overcame his life, and he started messing up, missing recording sessions, and not even showing up for the photo shoot for *Echo*. Tom loved Howie and gave him many chances to mend his ways, but to no avail, and Tom had no choice but to fire him. Tom never saw him alive again. Soon after that, Howie's dog Dingo died, and the next day Howie overdosed and died.

Tom told the Howie story slowly; it was clear it was really hard for him to talk about it. The darkness was in the room, like a giant boulder weighing down on him. Yet he persisted, and told me all the sad details. He got the news of Howie's death from Dana. It crushed him. "Even though we had all seen it coming," he said, "it's still really hard to believe when it happens."

Afterwards Tom was especially drained and down. It took a lot out of him. That night he did something he never did before. He called me up. In his soft drawl, he said, "Hey, would ya mind doing me a favor? I was doing some thinking about our Howie talk today, and it just seemed *way* too dark and sad. Would you mind terribly throwing that all out so we can start over?"

That said so much about Tom, about what a genuinely kind guy he was, and also such a loyal friend. It hurt him that the only portrait of Howie he painted was this dark, desolate one, which left out all the good parts. It mattered so much that he wanted to start over completely, which is exactly what we did. The second time around, which is the part used in the book, began and ended with happier memories of Howie.

Looking back at that section now, the saddest part is Tom's experience of watching Howie performing with the band on TV, and describing the surreal sorrow of seeing his friend still so alive, still in the pocket, yet knowing somehow he's gone. It's exactly the same way so many of us, those whose lives have been forever enriched and illuminated by his songs, feel today about Tom. It simply seems impossible that someone so vital, so fundamental to our lives, so evidently alive in every way, could truly be gone.

"I still can't believe he's gone," Tom said of Howie. "I saw a rerun the other night of [when we did] *Saturday Night Live*. And there he was, and he looked so vibrant and healthy, the way I remember him most. And he was just the sweetest person. I never heard anything but positive statements from him. He was never negative. And he always looked for the good in things. And it's weird, because he hasn't become like a photograph to me. He's still 3-D to me."

But just as substantial as was his sorrow when relating dark chapters was the sense of joy he radiated when detailing happy ones. Except for the story of falling in love with Dana, no chapter was related with more pure joy than his time with the Wilburys. It was a time and a project unlike any other in his life, based purely on the love of songwriting, making music and being in a band. It wasn't about commercial success or creating a hit (though they created several). It was about the joy of making music with friends. Friends who happened to be five of world's greatest living musicians, each of whom had made a significant impact on the arc of popular song.

It all started, as is famously known, as a lark dreamed up by George Harrison of forming a dream band of his favorite friends and musicians. He enlisted Tom, Jeff Lynne, and Bob Dylan first, all of whom immediately accepted. To entice their ultimate dream singer, Roy Orbison, to join the band, they got a limo to Anaheim, where Roy was performing, headed straight to his dressing room in Anaheim to invite him in-person. Hearing Roy say, "Sure, sure, I'll do it. I'll be in your band," was one of the most exultant moments of his life. "We were just high as kites [on that ride home]," he said. "A natural high. Like, 'Roy Orbison's in *our band*!'"

Making the Wilburys records was pure fun. Recording the first album at Dave Stewart's home studio in Encino, the five Wilburys would meet every morning, each with an acoustic guitar, and write a new song then and there. Everyone would toss in lines. Endearing songs of great charm quickly emerged, each of which would be recorded that very day, following a great meal prepared by their chef. It was the very rare instance of five legendary artists making music entirely for the joy of it. And that joy, like the passion projected by The Heartbreakers in every show, is genuine and infectious, and injected directly into those Wilburys tracks. If ever you feel like connecting with the ecstatic joy Tom felt making that music with those friends, it's preserved there forever.

Learning to fly, as Tom wrote, isn't easy. Though becoming a rock star as famous as The Beatles was always his aim, adjusting to fame and becoming an icon was not something he took to naturally. Always grateful for his vast network of fans around the world who sustained his career with fervent loyalty and love for over forty years, he was nonetheless reasonably cautious about getting too close to those who become dangerously fanatical. In 1987, a woman who claimed to love him set fire to his Encino home. To save his wife, daughters and housekeeper, he had them all immediately leap into the swimming pool.

That came only seven years after Lennon was shot dead by a fan. But it was the attack on George Harrison's life that darkly haunted him forever. He never got past it. He and George were more than friends, Tom always said. They were brothers. And George of all people was, as the world knows, one of the most spiritual, peaceful and beautifully centered souls around. So for him to be attacked in his own home, as he was on December 30, 1999, was a brutality far too horrific for Tom to digest, and forever darkened his outlook.

"George was attacked *much* more brutally, *much* more viciously, than they let on," Tom said. "They didn't want people to know the extent of it. But it was way worse than people knew."

Although he worried about his safety, Tom also wanted to live as normal a life as possible. Though often accompanied by his pal and driver, Bugs, he refused the advice of those who insisted he enlist a bodyguard because, as he said, "I don't want to walk around with a big gorilla."

Still at times there was a sense that Tom felt somewhat trapped by his celebrity. He described fame to me once as being similar to "going to a party with your psychiatrist." By which he meant that everyone would scrutinize his every move, his every word, and rarely just let him be.

He also told me a few rather scary stories about being in public when veritable mob-scenes erupted around him, triggered by some guy spotting him and announcing to the world, "Oh, my God, it's *Tom Fucking Petty*!" These near-riots would both shake his car and rattle his soul, leading him to conclude that staying home behind his big walls was the safest thing to do. True to his nature, which was genuinely humble and grateful, he phoned me the night after telling me that and other horror stories of crazed fans, with a gentle suggestion. "Hey, you *know*," he said, "I was *thinking*, maybe we should just cut out all that stuff out that we talked about today. Nobody really wants to hear Tom Petty complaining about how hard it is to be a rock star."

In recent years, however, he showed up at many public events, including his pal Jeff Lynne's Hollywood Walk of Fame star ceremony, at which he spoke. Following that, he generously signed autographs for every fan who asked for one. Among the vast legion of Hollywood autograph collectors, he was adored. Said one about him, "That dude never said no! I love Tom Petty."

Though he could get dark, he had a good sense of humor about himself. Often he'd refer to himself laughingly as "Tom Petty," underscoring the surreality of being an icon. In the movie *Waterworld* he played himself—Tom Petty—but far into a very watery dystopian future. When Tom first met those who had been the early idols of his own existence—such as Harrison and Dylan—he learned to dampen his own tendency to deify them. It's the reason he's not only a beloved artist but also, like George, a famous friend. Those who loved him knew a warmth and loyalty that was the essence of the man. He was, above all, real. And for that reason, even those that became rock gods before him became best pals with Tom Petty.

This included even the guy Tom considered the cagiest and most mysterious of all. Bob Dylan. George Harrison and Dylan had become good friends and co-writers years earlier, and both warmly welcomed Tom into their fold. Tom said he realized, both from getting to know Dylan and also reading his book *Chronicles* (which Tom loved, and said was like a great epic poem), that even Bob was human, and like him, needed people in his life who knew that.

"I saw a lot of people running circles around Bob and being afraid of him," Tom said. "I always found that if I asked Bob a direct question, I would get a direct answer. So maybe our friendship wasn't that difficult, because I made up my mind that I would treat him like anybody else, though I was certainly in awe of his talent. But people are just people."

The single aspect of Dylan that most impressed Tom was his essential honesty, and lack of pretension about himself. "One of the nicest things about Bob," Tom said, "is that he's an honest guy. Really, really honest. Not someone who would ever lie. Not someone who would blow his own horn… He has insecurities like everyone else has. When you're that famous, people just don't give you that benefit of the doubt. They kind of just assume that you understand how great you're supposed to be. But the truth is, you're only a human. And you still go through everything that humans go through."

But being human isn't always easy, and many times Tom projected a perpetual yearning to transcend his own daily discontent. He touched on this most poignantly in his beautiful song from *Wildflowers*, "Crawling Back To You," a rarely performed ballad that he included in his final tour.

As those who knew him knew, Dana was his saving grace. She arrived like an angel in his life at a time he so needed one, and helped him turn his car around forever. They met at one of his shows in Texas, described by Tom as love at first sight. "I never believed that was true before," he said. "But it was."

Soon after that first meeting, long before they got to know each other, he dreamed of her face. It was a vision which surprised him, because he knew what it meant. It was a dark time in his life, having recently left his family to move into the Chicken Shack, a little cabin off of Sunset Boulevard. It's there he wrote "Angel Dream," a song of love and redemption which he said she inspired "word for word."

Dana's love, both for the man and his music, went a long way in giving Tom that peace for which he yearned. When they first started spending time, he let her know that he never listened to his own music. She told him that was a problem because she loved those records and played them a lot. He said, "That's fine. Just don't play them anytime I'm around." He tried to explain that it was impossible for him to hear them without painful analysis of every aspect, especially all the imperfections.

She wouldn't have it. In time she gently eased his resistance, and helped him appreciate the true and positive impact of his music in the lives of so many. It was an awareness that initially threw him, so entrenched was he in his thinking. But after listening to his classic albums with Dana, a weight was lifted from his soul. "I must say I'm pleasantly surprised by it," he said. "I hear [the music] and go, 'God, that wasn't a waste of time. We really did do something that is pretty good.'"

Sure, "pretty good" is a serious understatement for what he did. But it speaks to her profound impact on his life and spirit. Not only did she give him a more expansively generous estimation of his own work, she kept reminding him every day, in gentle ways, of the true magnitude of the blessings in his life.

"She reminds me," he said, "that I shouldn't take for granted what's happened to me, the life I live... My life is no easier than most people's lives... Success doesn't solve all your problems... So it's good to have someone who can bring you around and remind you that we're okay, we love each other, and everyone's healthy, and the bills are paid. So why are you upset?"

Her daily impact on him, forever brightening his spirit anytime she was near, was touching to witness up close. While working on the book, she frequently appeared with a warm smile and maybe some smoothies—or delicious home-made chili she'd just cooked up—and his aspect would be instantly eased, and that sparkle would return to his eyes. It was true love.

A world without Tom Petty in it. It's not something that we, his fans forever, are prepared for in any way. But the music remains. He left us behind a bounty of songs and records so timeless, true and inspirational that they will enrich our lives forever. He gave us way more than anyone has any right to expect. Had he written only one song at the level of "Free Fallin'" or "Insider" or "Southern Accents," he'd be an artist we'd revere forever. But he did so much more. He devoted nearly forty solid years to writing and recording the purest, truest rock and roll he could coax out of his soul. And not once did he let us down.

He found great joy and took genuine pride in writing songs. Asked how long that heady glow of satisfaction from writing a great one lasted, he said, "It can last for years." Being a songwriter in the world, he knew, was an important job, and he felt lucky that he had a natural instinct for it, and the ongoing capacity for being a constant receiver over the years. To enunciate one's world-view in a way both poetic and musical, as he put it, was a great and rare blessing. "It's a gift," he said. "It's not something you learn, or get out of a manual. It's just a gift."

Few gifts ever made him happier. He loved the way a song could suddenly come alive after never existing. And though it was something he rarely expressed, it also gave him solace and some measure of joy to know that his music would live on beyond him.

"It always feels good to finish an album," he said, "because I've done it long enough to know these things are gonna be around a lot longer than me. It's something that wasn't there and now it is there. I *love* that about art. You just created something, and now it's here and it could be here longer than you."

Author article originally published in
American Songwriter *magazine, October 6, 2017*

Discography

MUDCRUTCH

Singles

Up In Mississippi Tonight / Cause Is Understood
1973 Red Pepper

Depot Street / Wild Eyes
1975 Shelter Records

Scare Easy
2008 Reprise

Trailer
2016 Reprise

How Much Do You Need (SiriusXM exclusive)
2016

Albums

Mudcrutch
2008 Reprise

Mudcrutch 2
2016 Reprise

TOM PETTY & THE HEARTBREAKERS

US Singles

Breakdown / The Wild One, Forever
1976 Shelter Records / ABC Records

American Girl / Fooled Again (I Don't Like It)
1976 Shelter Records / ABC Records

Breakdown / Fooled Again (I Don't Like It)
1978 Shelter Records / ABC Records

I Need To Know / No Second Thoughts
1978 Shelter Records / ABC Records

Listen To Her Heart / I Don't Know What to Say to You
1978 Shelter Records / ABC Records

Don't Do Me Like That / Casa Dega
1979 Backstreet / MCA Records

Refugee / It's Rainin' Again
1979 Backstreet / MCA Records

Here Comes My Girl / Louisiana Rain
1980 Backstreet / MCA Records

The Waiting / Nightwatchman
1981 Backstreet / MCA Records

A Woman In Love (It's Not Me) / Gator On The Lawn
1981 Backstreet / MCA Records

You Got Lucky / Between Two Worlds
1982 Backstreet / MCA Records

Change Of Heart / Heartbreakers Beach Party
1983 Backstreet / MCA Records

Make It Better (Forget About Me) / Make It Better (Forget About Me) (instrumental mix)
1985 MCA Records

Don't Come Around Here No More / Trailer
1985 MCA Records

Rebels / Southern Accents
1985 MCA Records

Needles And Pins (live with Stevie Nicks) / Spike (live)
1986 MCA Records

Jammin' Me / Make That Connection
1987 MCA Records

All Mixed Up / Let Me Up (I've Had Enough)
1987 MCA Records

Learning To Fly / Too Good To Be True
1991 MCA Records

Into The Great Wide Open / Makin' Some Noise
1991 MCA Records

King's Highway / All Or Nothin'
1991 MCA Records

Peace In LA / Peace In LA (Peace Mix)
1992 MCA Records

Mary Jane's Last Dance / The Waiting
1993 MCA Records

Walls (Circus) / Walls (No. 3)
1996 Warner Bros.

Free Girl Now (MP3 promotion & radio only—no retail single)
1999 Warner Bros.

Swingin' (Radio only—no retail single)
1999 Warner Bros.

Room At The Top (Radio only—no retail single)
1999 Warner Bros.

Surrender (Radio only—no retail single)
2000 Warner Bros.

The Last DJ (Radio only—no retail single)
2002 Warner Bros.

Good Enough
2010 Reprise

I Should Have Known It
2010 Reprise

First Flash Of Freedom
2010 Reprise

Don't Pull Me Over
2010 Reprise

American Dream Plan B
2014 Reprise

U Get Me High
2014 Reprise

Keep A Little Soul
2018 Reprise

You And Me
2018 Reprise

Gainesville
2018 Reprise

The Best of Everything
2019 Geffen

For Real
2019 Geffen

Albums

Tom Petty & The Heartbreakers
Rockin' Around (With You) – Breakdown – Hometown Blues – The Wild One, Forever – Anything That's Rock'N'Roll – Strangered In The Night – Fooled Again (I Don't Like It) – Mystery Man – Luna – American Girl
November 9, 1976 Shelter Records

You're Gonna Get It
When The Time Comes – You're Gonna Get It – Hurt – Magnolia – Too Much Ain't Enough – I Need To Know – Listen To Her Heart – No Second Thoughts – Restless – Baby's A Rock'N'Roller
May 2, 1978 Shelter Records / ABC Records

Damn The Torpedoes
Refugee – Here Comes My Girl – Even The Losers – Shadow Of A Doubt (Complex Kid) – Century City – Don't Do Me Like That – You Tell Me – What Are You Doin' In My Life? – Louisiana Rain
October 19, 1979 Backstreet / MCA Records

Hard Promises
The Waiting – A Woman in Love (It's Not Me) – Nightwatchman – Something Big – Kings Road – Letting You Go – A Thing About You – Insider – The Criminal Kind – You Can Still Change Your Mind
May 5, 1981 Backstreet / MCA Records

Long After Dark
A One Story Town – You Got Lucky – Deliver Me – Change Of Heart – Finding Out – We Stand A Chance – Straight Into Darkness – The Same Old You – Between Two Worlds – A Wasted Life
October 1982 Backstreet / MCA Records

Southern Accents
Rebels – It Ain't Nothing To Me – Don't Come Around Here No More – Southern Accents – Make It Better (Forget About Me) – Spike – Dogs On The Run – Mary's New Car – The Best of Everything
March 1, 1985 MCA Records

Let Me Up (I've Had Enough)
Jammin' Me – Runaway Trains – The Damage You've Done – It'll All Work Out – My Life/Your World – Think About Me – All Mixed Up – A Self-Made Man – Ain't Love Strange – How Many More Days – Let Me Up (I've Had Enough)
April 21, 1987 MCA Records

Into The Great Wide Open
Learning To Fly – Kings Highway – Into The Great Wide Open – Two Gunslingers – The Dark Of The Sun – All Or Nothin' – All The Wrong Reasons – Too Good To Be True – Out In The Cold – You And I Will Meet Again – Makin' Some Noise – Built To Last
July 2, 1991 MCA Records

Songs And Music From She's The One
Walls (Circus) – Grew Up Fast – Zero From Outer Space – Climb That Hill – Change The Locks – Angel Dream (No. 4) – Hope You Never – Asshole – Supernatural Radio – California – Hope On Board – Walls (No. 3) – Angel Dream (No. 2) – Hung Up And Overdue – Airport
August 6, 1996 Warner Bros.

Echo
Room At The Top – Counting On You – Free Girl Now – Lonesome Sundown – Swingin' – Accused Of Love – Echo – Won't Last Long – Billy The Kid – I Don't Wanna Fight – This One's For Me – No More – About To Give Out – Rhino Skin – One More Day, One More Night
April 13, 1999 Warner Bros.

The Last DJ
The Last DJ – Money Becomes King – Dreamville – Joe – When A Kid Goes Bad – Like A Diamond – Lost Children – Blue Sunday – You And Me – The Man Who Loves Women – Have Love Will Travel – Can't Stop The Sun
October 8, 2002 Warner Bros.

Mojo
Jefferson Jericho Blues – First Flash Of Freedom – Running Man's Bible – The Trip To Pirate's Cove – Candy – No Reason To Cry – I Should Have Known It – U.S. 41 – Takin' My Time – Let Yourself Go – Don't Pull Me Over – Lover's Touch – High In The Morning – Something Good Coming – Good Enough – Little Girl Blues (iTunes bonus track)
June 15, 2010 Reprise

Hypnotic Eye
American Dream Plan B – Fault Lines – Red River – Full Grown Boy – All You Can Carry – Power Drunk
Forgotten Man – Sins Of My Youth – U Get Me High – Burnt Out Town – Shadow People – Playing Dumb
July 29, 2014 Reprise

Compilation and Live Albums

Pack Up The Plantation, Live!
So You Want To Be A Rock'N'Roll Star – Needles And Pins – The Waiting – Breakdown – American Girl – It Ain't Nothin' To Me – Insider – Rockin' Around (With You) – Refugee – I Need To Know – Southern Accents – Rebels – Don't Bring Me Down – You Got Lucky – Shout – Stories We Could Tell
November 1985 MCA Records

Greatest Hits
American Girl – Breakdown – Anything That's Rock'N'Roll (UK version only) – Listen To Her Heart – I Need To Know – Refugee – Don't Do Me Like That – Even The Losers – Here Comes My Girl – The Waiting – You Got Lucky – Don't Come Around Here No More – I Won't Back Down – Runnin' Down A Dream – Free Fallin' – Learning To Fly – Into The Great Wide Open – Mary Jane's Last Dance – Something In The Air
November 16, 1993 MCA Records

Playback

Disc 1 The Big Jangle
Breakdown – American Girl – Hometown Blues – Anything That's Rock'N'Roll – I Need To Know – Listen To Her Heart – When The Time Comes – Too Much Ain't Enough – No Second Thoughts – Baby's A Rock'N'Roller – Refugee – Here Comes My Girl – Even The Losers – Shadow Of A Doubt (A Complex Kid) – Don't Do Me Like That – The Waiting – A Woman In Love (It's Not Me) – Something Big – A Thing About You – Insider – You Can Still Change Your Mind

Disc 2 Spoiled And Mistreated
You Got Lucky – Change Of Heart – Straight Into Darkness – The Same Old You – Rebels – Don't Come Around Here No More – Southern Accents – Make It Better – The Best Of Everything – So You Want To Be A Rock'N'Roll Star – Don't Bring Me Down – Jammin' Me – It'll All Work Out – Mike's Life, Mike's World – Think About Me – A Self-Made Man

Disc 3 Good Booty
Free Fallin' – I Won't Back Down – Love Is A Long Road – Runnin' Down A Dream – Yer So Bad – Alright For Now – Learning To Fly – Into The Great Wide Open – All Or Nothin' – Out In The Cold – Built To Last – Mary Jane's Last Dance – Christmas All Over Again

Disc 4 The Other Sides
Casa Dega – Heartbreaker's Beach Party – Trailer – Cracking Up (Nick Lowe) – Psychotic Reaction (live) – I'm Tired Joey Boy (live) – Lonely Weekends (live) – Gator On The Lawn – Make That Connection – Down The Line – Peace In LA (Peace Mix) – It's Rainin' Again – Somethin' Else (live) – I Don't Know What To Say To You / King's Highway (live)

Disc 5 Through The Cracks
On The Street – Depot Street – Cry To Me – Don't Do Me Like That – I Can't Fight It – Since You Said You Loved Me – Louisiana Rain – Keepin' Me Alive – Turning Point – Stop Draggin' My Heart Around – The Apartment Song – Big Boss Man – The Image Of Me – Moon Pie – The Damage You've Done

Disc 6 Nobody's Children
Got My Mind Made Up – Ways To Be Wicked – Can't Get Her Out – Waiting For Tonight – Travelin' – Baby, Let's Play House – Wooden Heart – God's Gift To Man – You Get Me High – Come On Down To My House – You Come Through – Up In Mississippi Tonight
November 21, 1995 Warner Bros.

Anthology: Through The Years

Disc 1

Breakdown – American Girl – Hometown Blues – The Wild One, Forever – I Need To Know – Listen To Her Heart – Too Much Ain't Enough – Refugee – Here Comes My Girl – Don't Do Me Like That – Even The Losers – The Waiting – Woman In Love (It's Not Me) – Stop Draggin' My Heart Around (featuring Stevie Nicks) – You Got Lucky – Straight Into Darkness – Change Of Heart

Disc 2

Rebels – Don't Come Around Here No More – The Best of Everything – So You Wanna Be A Rock'N'Roll Star – Jammin' Me – It'll All Work Out – Love Is A Long Road – Free Fallin' – Yer So Bad – I Won't Back Down – Runnin' Down A Dream – Learning To Fly – Into The Great Wide Open – Two Gunslingers – Mary Jane's Last Dance – Waiting For Tonight – Surrender
October 31, 2000 Warner Bros

The Live Anthology

Disc 1

Ladies and Gentlemen... – Nightwatchman – Even The Losers – Here Comes My Girl – A Thing About You – I'm In Love – I'm A Man – Straight Into Darkness – Breakdown – Something In The Air – I Just Want To Make Love To You – Drivin' Down To Georgia – Lost Without You – Refugee

Disc 2

Diddy Wah Diddy – I Want You Back Again – Wildflowers – Friend Of The Devil – A Woman In Love (It's Not Me) – It's Good To Be King – Angel Dream (No. 2) – Learning To Fly – Mary Jane's Last Dance – Mystic Eyes

Disc 3

Jammin' Me – The Wild One, Forever – Green Onions – Louisiana Rain – Melinda – Goldfinger – Surrender – Dreamville – Spike – Any Way You Want It – American Girl

Disc 4

Runnin' Down A Dream – Oh Well – Southern Accents – Crawling Back To You – My Life/Your World – I Won't Back Down – Square One – Have Love Will Travel – Free Fallin' – The Waitin – Good, Good Lovin' – Century City – Alright For Now
November 23, 2009 Warner Bros.

Mojo Tour 2010
King's Highway – You Don't Know How It Feels – I Won't Back Down – Drivin' Down To Georgia – Breakdown – I Should Have Known It – Good Enough – Runnin' Down A Dream
December 14, 2010 self-released

Kiss My Amps (Live) (limited edition vinyl only LP)

Side 1

Takin' My Time – I Should Have Known It – Sweet William – Jefferson Jericho Blues

Side 2

First Flash Of Freedom – Running Man's Bible – Good Enough

November 25, 2011 Rhino

Live 2013

So You Want To Be A Rock'N'Roll Star – (I'm Not Your) Steppin' Stone – Love Is A Long Road – Two Gunslingers – When A Kid Goes Bad – Willin' – The Best Of Everything – Tweeter And The Monkey Man – Baby, Please Don't Go – Rebels – A Woman In Love (It's Not Me)

June 24, 2014 self-released

Kiss My Amps Live Vol. 2

So You Want To Be A Rock'N'Roll Star – A Woman In Love (It's Not Me) (I'm Not Your) Steppin' Stone – Love Is A Long Road – Two Gunslingers – When A Kid Goes Bad – Willin' – The Best Of Everything – Tweeter And The Monkey Man – Rebels – A Woman In Love (It's Not Me)

April 16, 2016 Reprise

Live At Fenway Park 2014

So You Want To Be A Rock'N'Roll Star – Mary Jane's Last Dance – American Dream Plan B – Forgotten Man – A Woman In Love (It's Not Me) – U Get Me High – Shadow People – You Wreck Me – American Girl

2016 Shoreline Gold, LLC

An American Treasure

Disc 1

Rockin' Around (With You) – Anything That's Rock'N'Roll – Listen To Her Heart – Louisiana Rain – Here Comes My Girl – King's Road – Keep A Little Soul – Straight Into Darkness – Don't Treat Me Like A Stranger – Rebels – You're Gonna Get It – Walkin' From The Fire – The Best Of Everything

Disc 2

I Won't Back Down – Two Gunslingers – Crawling Back To You – Wake Up Time – Accused Of Love – Gainesville – You And Me – Like A Diamond – Southern Accents – Insider – Something Good Coming – Have Love Will Travel – Hungry No More

September 28, 2018 Reprise

The Best Of Everything

Free Fallin' – Mary Jane's Last Dance – You Wreck Me – I Won't Back Down – Saving Grace – You Don't Know How It Feels – Don't Do Me Like That – Listen To Her Heart – Breakdown – Walls (Circus) – The Waiting – Don't Come Around Here No More – Southern Accents – Angel Dream (No. 2) –

Dreamville – I Should Have Known It – Refugee – American Girl – The Best Of Everything – Wildflowers – Learning To Fly – Here Comes My Girl – The Last DJ – I Need To Know – Scare Easy – Runnin' Down A Dream – American Dream Plan B – Stop Draggin' My Heart Around – Trailer – Into The Great Wide Open – Room At The Top – Square One – Jammin' Me – Even The Losers – Hungry No More – I Forgive It All – For Real
March 1, 2019 Geffen

TOM PETTY

US Singles

I Won't Back Down / The Apartment Song
1989 MCA Records

Runnin' Down A Dream / Alright For Now
1989 MCA Records

Free Fallin' / Down The Line
1989 MCA Records

A Face In The Crowd / A Mind With A Heart Of Its Own
1989 MCA Records

Yer So Bad / Love Is A Long Road
1989 MCA Records

You Don't Know How It Feels / Girl On LSD
1994 Warner Bros.

It's Good To Be King / Cabin Down Below
1995 Warner Bros.

A Higher Place / Only A Broken Heart (acoustic version)
1995 Warner Bros.

Saving Grace
2006 Warner Bros.

Flirting With Time
2006 Warner Bros.

Big Weekend
2006 Warner Bros.

Somewhere Under Heaven (Non-album single)
2015 Warner Bros.

US Albums

Full Moon Fever
Free Fallin' – I Won't Back Down – Love Is A Long Road – A Face In The Crowd – Runnin' Down A Dream – Feel A Whole Lot Better – Yer So Bad – Depending On You – Apartment Song – Alright For Now – A Mind With A Heart Of Its Own – Zombie Zoo
April 24, 1989 MCA Records

Wildflowers
You Don't Know How It Feels – Time to Move On – You Wreck Me – It's Good To Be King – Only A Broken Heart – Honey Bee – Don't Fade On Me – Hard On Me – Cabin Down Below – To Find A Friend – A Higher Place – House In The Woods – Crawling Back To You – Wake Up Time
November 1, 1994 Warner Bros.

Highway Companion
Saving Grace – Square One – Flirting With Time – Down South – Jack – Turn This Car Around – Big Weekend – Night Driver – Damaged By Love – This Old Town – Ankle Deep – The Golden Rose
July 25, 2006 Warner Bros.

TRAVELING WILBURYS

Albums

Traveling Wilburys, Vol. 1
Handle With Care – Dirty World – Rattled – Last Night – Not Alone Anymore – Congratulations – Heading For The Light – Margarita – Tweeter And The Monkey Man – End Of The Line
October 25, 1988 Warner Bros.

Traveling Wilburys, Vol. 3
She's My Baby (with Gary Moore) – Inside Out – If You Belonged To Me – The Devil's Been Busy – Deadly Sins – Poor House – Where Were You Last Night? – Cool Dry Place – New Blue Moon – You Took My Breath Away – Wilbury Twist
October 19, 1990 Warner Bros.

MUSIC VIDEOS

Refugee (1979)
Here Comes My Girl (1979)
The Waiting (1981)
Woman In Love (It's Not Me) (1981)
Insider (1981)
Letting You Go (1981)
Stop Draggin' My Heart Around (1981)

Change Of Heart (1982)
You Got Lucky (1982)
Don't Come Around Here No More (1985)
Make It Better (Forget About Me) (1985)
So You Want To Be A Rock'N'Roll Star (1986)
Jammin' Me (1987)
Runnin Down A Dream (1989)
I Won't Back Down (1989)
Free Fallin' (1989)
A Face In The Crowd (1990)
Yer So Bad (1990)
Learning To Fly (1991)
Into The Great Wide Open (1991)
Too Good To Be True (1991)
Mary Jane's Last Dance (1993)
You Don't Know How It Feels (1994)
You Wreck Me (1994)
It's Good To Be King (1994)
Walls (Circus) (1996)
Free Girl Now (1999)
Swingin' (1999)
I Need You (from *Concert For George*) (2002)
Saving Grace (2006)
I Should Have Known It (2010)
Jefferson Jericho Blues (2010)
First Flash Of Freedom (2010)
Something Good Coming (2010)
Good Enough (2010)
Mojo (2010)
Don't Pull Me Over (2010)
Spike (2012)
Keep A Little Soul (2018)
You And Me (2018)
Gainesville (2018)
For Real (2019)

Home Videos/DVDs

Pack Up The Plantation, Live!
American Girl – You Got Lucky – It Ain't Nothin' To Me – Don't Do Me Like That – The Waiting – I Need To Know – Don't Come Around Here No More – Spike – Southern Accents – Rebels – Breakdown – Refugee – Little Bit O' Soul – So You Want To Be A Rock'N'Roll Star – Make It Better (Forget About Me) – Route 66
1985 MCA Music VHS

Hard To Handle: Bob Dylan With Tom Petty & The Heartbreakers
In The Garden – Just Like A Woman – Like A Rolling Stone – It's Alright Ma (I'm Only Bleeding) – Girl From The North Country – Lenny Bruce – When The Night Comes Falling – Ballad Of A Thin Man – I'll Remember You – Knockin' On Heaven's Door
1986 Fox Home Entertainment VHS & DVD

A Bunch Of Videos And Some Other Stuff
Jammin' Me – Here Comes My Girl – I Need To Know – The Insider – Don't Comes Around Here No More – The Waiting – You Got Lucky – Breakdown – Even The Losers – I'm Stupid – Refugee – I Won't Back Down – Women In Love (It's Not Me) – American Girl
May 31, 1989 MPI Home Video VHS

Full Moon Fever: The Videos
I Won't Back Down – Runnin' Down A Dream Free Fallin' – A Face In The Crowd – Yer So Bad
June 5, 1990 Universal / MCA VHS

Take The Highway: Live
King's Highway – Too Good To Be True – I Won't Back Down – Free Fallin' – Out In The Cold – Psychotic Reaction – Ben's Boogie – Don't Come Around Here No More – I'm Tired Joey Boy – Into The Great Wide Open – Love Is A Long Road – Refugee – Runnin' Down A Dream – Lonely Weekends – Built To Last – Makin' Some Noise
May 5, 1992 Universal / MCA VHS

Playback
Here Comes My Girl – Refugee – The Waiting – A Woman In Love (It's Not Me) – Insider – You Got Lucky – Change Of Heart – Don't Come Around Here No More – Jammin' Me – I Won't Back Down – Runnin' Down A Dream – Free Fallin' – A Face In The Crowd – Yer So Bad – Learning To Fly – Into The Great Wide Open – Mary Jane's Last Dance
November 14, 1995 Universal / MCA VHS & DVD

High Grass Dogs: Live At The Fillmore
Intro California – Jammin' Me – Runnin' Down A Dream – Swingin' – Breakdown – Listen To Her Heart – You Don't Know How It Feels – Mary Jane's Last Dance – Mona (featuring Bo Diddley) – Lay Down My Old Guitar (Alton Delmore) – Even The Losers – Walls – Angel Dream – Room At The Top – County Farm – You Wreck Me – I Don't Wanna Fight – Free Fallin' – Free Girl Now
November 9, 1999 WEA / Warner Bros. VHS & DVD

Live At The Olympic: The Last DJ And More
The Last DJ – Money Becomes King – Dreamville – Joe – When A Kid Goes Bad – Like A Diamond – Lost Children – Blue Sunday – You And Me – The Man Who Loves Women – Have Love Will Travel – Can't Stop The Sun – Change Of Heart – I Need To Know – Shake Rattle And Roll – Around And

Around – Mary Jane's Last Dance – You Wreck Me – Packaged With a Bonus CD—I'm Crying – Done Somebody Wrong – I Got A Woman – Oh Carol
September 16, 2003 WEA / Warner Bros. DVD

Soundstage: Tom Petty
Baby Please Don't Go – Crawling Back To You – Handle With Care – I Won't Back Down – I'm Cryin' – Angel Dream – Melinda – Born In Chicago – Red Rooster – Carol – Refugee – Love Is A Long Road – Black Leather Woman – I Done Somebody Wrong – I Got A Woman – Thirteen Days – Wake Up Time – Rollin' In My Sweet Baby's Arms – Lost Children – Two Men Talking – You Wreck Me
January 11, 2005 Koch Entertainment DVD

Tom Petty: In Concert
Baby Please Don't Go 2. Crawlin Back To You 3. Handle With Care 4. I Won't Back Down 5. I'm Cryin' 6. Angel Dream 7. Melinda 8. Born In Chicago 9. Red Rooster 10. Carol 11. Refugee 12. Love Is A Long Road 13. You Don't Know How It Feels 14. Black Leather Woman 15. Done Somebody Wrong 16. I Got a Woman 17. Thirteen Days 18. Wake Up Time 19. Rollin' In My Baby's Arms 20. Lost Children 21. Two Men Talking 22. You Wreck Me
October 29, 2007 ILC Entertainment

Tom Petty and the Heartbreakers – Runnin' Down A Dream – A Film By Peter Bogdanovich

Disc 1
Gainesville 2006 – Elvis – What's In A Name – Mike Benmont – B.Y.O.F (Build Your Own Festival) – Fast Forward – Deals – A Broken Bond – Ron & Stan – Tom Petty and the Heartbreakers – Third – Fuel – Howie – Poet

Disc 2
Bob Dylan – Strange Coincidences – Scott – The Bottom Line – Steve – John – Round Trip – Rock & Roll Heaven – Runnin' Down A Dream (End credits)

Disc 3 (30th Anniversary Concert)
Listen To Her Heart – Mary Jane's Last Dance – I Won't Back Down – Free Fallin' – Saving Grace – I'm A Man – Oh Well – Handle With Care – Stop Draggin' My Heart Around (with Stevie Nicks) – I Need To Know (with Stevie Nicks) – It's Good To Be King – Down South – Southern Accents – Insider (with Stevie Nicks) – Learning To Fly – Don't Come Around Here No More – Runnin' Down A Dream – You Wreck Me – Mystic Eyes – American Girl

Disc 4 (Bonus Soundtrack CD)
Breakdown – Anything That's Rock and Roll – Fooled Again (I Don't Like It) – American Girl – Shadow Of A Doubt (A Complex Kid) – Stories We Could Tell – Keeping Me Alive – Honey Bee – Lost Highway
November 23, 2007 Rhino

Classic Albums: Damn The Torpedoes
24 Carat Rocker – Third Albums – Refugee – Even the Losers – Here Comes My Girl – Shadow of a Doubt – Century City – Louisiana Rain – Don't Do Me Like That
August 3, 2010 Eagle Rock Ent

About The Author

Paul Zollo is a singer-songwriter, author, photographer, and music writer. Since 1987, he's dedicated himself to interviewing the world's greatest songwriters as editor of *SongTalk*, the journal of the National Academy of Songwriters. His book *Songwriters On Songwriting* is a collection of those interviews (featuring his first interview with Tom Petty, as well as ones with Bob Dylan, Paul Simon, Leonard Cohen, Carole King, Frank Zappa, Randy Newman, and others) and has been called "the songwriter's bible." Its sequel, *More Songwriters On Songwriting*, was published in 2016. He's also the author of *Hollywood Remembered: An Oral History Of Its Golden Age*, *The Beginning Songwriter's Answer Book*, *The Schirmer Rhyming Dictionary*, and *Zappa On Zappa*. Born in Chicago, he graduated from Boston University and has contributed to many magazines, including *Sing Out!*, *Billboard*, *Variety*, and *Musician*, contributed CD liner notes for artists including Paul Simon, Laura Nyro, and Dan Fogelberg, and written for the annual Grammy Awards program. As a songwriter, he's written songs with many artists, including Darryl Purpose ("Orange Raincoat," "When Buddha Smiled At The Elephant," the entire *Still The Birds* album), Severin Browne ("Angelyne"), Dan Bern ("Midnight In Nebraska"), the late Steve Allen ("Blue Stars"), Bob Malone, Neil Rosengarden, Stephen Kalinich, Jeff Gold, James Coberly Smith, and Steve Schalchlin. He released one self-titled album with his band The Ghosters and two solo albums, *Universal Cure* and *Orange Avenue* (which features "Being In This World," a duet with Art Garfunkel). His photographs have been published in many magazines, newspapers, and books, including this one, and have been displayed in Los Angeles and Costa Mesa. His photos of Tom Petty and others are represented by Morrison Hotel Galleries in New York, Los Angeles, and Maui.